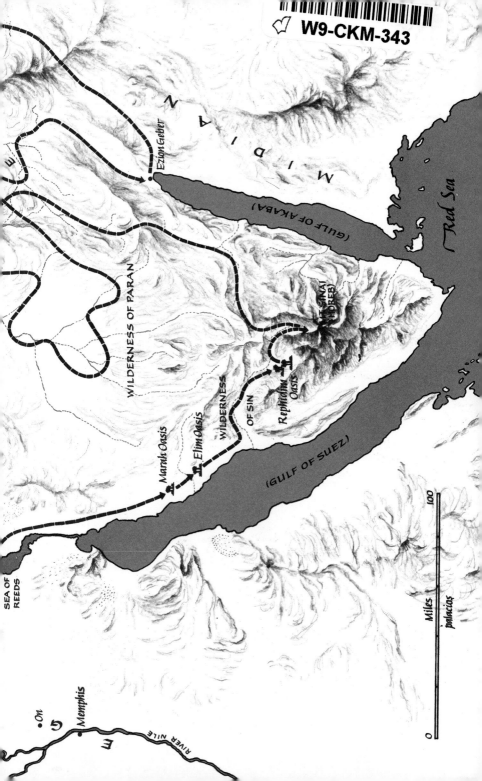

W9-CKM-343

The Book You Always Meant to Read
The Old Testament

Margueritte Harmon Bro

The Book You Always Meant to Read

The Old Testament

Doubleday & Company, Inc., Garden City, New York   1974

Library of Congress Cataloging in Publication Data

Bro, Margueritte Harmon, 1894–
    The book you always meant to read: the Old Testament.

    1. Bible. O. T.—History of Biblical events   I. Title.
BS1197.B76   221.9′5
ISBN 0-385-05667-2
Library of Congress Catalog Card Number 72–92193

Scripture quotations are from the *Revised Standard Version of the Bible,* copyrighted 1946 and 1952 by the Division of Christian Education, National Council of Churches, and used by permission.

The endpaper maps and those in the text were designed and executed by Rafe Palacios and are used with his permission. In addition, the map appearing on page 161 is from *Asimov's Guide to the Bible, Vol. I, The Old Testament.* Copyright © 1968 by Isaac Asimov, and used with the permission of the publisher, Doubleday & Company, Inc., and Mr. Palacios.

To
Joseph Henry Jenkins
Lois Stapley Jenkins

who serve their church and their community in Cable, Wisconsin—kindling light in our darkness, causing our inner deserts to bloom, enlarging the place of our tent, sustaining our strength with their song, staying our minds in peace, offering us renewed covenant, and leading us when they can into paths of practical righteousness.

Introduction

There are at least two ways to read the Old Testament: in the past tense or in the present tense. Read in the past tense, the centuries from which the religious heritage of the Western world derives begin to come alive, particularly the nineteenth to the second centuries B.C. Shifting political dominance in the lands bordering the Mediterranean, the rise and fall of empires in the Tigris-Euphrates and Nile valleys—spreading out into areas in northern Africa, southern Europe and western Asia—all become the scene of absorbing action. And the people caught in the action are not only empire makers; they are the progenitors of our linguistic development, the parents of our culture, the founders of our law, definitely the instigators of our religious cults and customs. We begin to care about their vicissitudes and marvel at their insights. But however expansive the effect of reading the Old Testament in the past tense, the ancients remain the ancients while we are the moderns.

Reading the Old Testament in the present tense is a more disturbing, even disruptive, experience. We start with a feeling of identification. After all, what was all that different about the Hebrews leaving Egypt for the sake of religious liberty and our own great-grandparents leaving England and other restrictive parts of Europe? The Canaanites seemed no fiercer to the advancing Hebrews than the Indians to the American colonists; and neither Hebrews nor colonials paid any attention to the fact that the land they pre-empted belonged to already established land-needy groups.

In the pages of this library of thirty-nine slender books bound

together and called the Old Testament, or the Scriptures, we see
our own mirrored countenance—some of us in high places playing fast and loose with the public good; some well-heeled entre-
preneurs forcing up prices by taking advantage of the common
people's need for food and raiment; unorganized sectors of labor
struggling to escape virtual enslavement. None of the double-dealing in ancient Palestine seems remote. We move among here-and-
now people as we listen to the scornful voice of Jeremiah, the
vituperation of Isaiah, the pleading of Hosea. We know why
Amos visioned the Lord with a plumb line in his hand. Sometimes we would like to shake off this present-tense feeling and
get the ancients back into their own context.

Finally we read in double focus. Past and present run together.
Life repeats itself but old truths take on new splendor because
they have proved themselves. A fulcrum of past experience sup-
ports our own ventures of faith. In our dark hours an incan-
descence from a light that did not fail our forefathers beats down
on our shadowed path. And we move ahead.

Unwittingly it was my mother who set me to writing this running account of the Old Testament story. When she started col-
lege in 1889 my grandmother put her foot down on Mother's
taking Greek. She was not going to have a bluestocking for a
daughter, the only girl among five tall brothers. So my mother, a
born woman's-libber and a determined little body, added to the
usual French, German and plenty of Latin, four years of Hebrew
alongside the young men studying for the ministry. When she was
graduated she had an invitation from President Harper of the new
University of Chicago to become an assistant in his Hebrew department. Instead, she married one of the ministerial students and
when I came along, started telling me Bible stories well before my
second birthday. She was the thorough type, who did not skip or
skimp even on the measurements of the tabernacle, who did not
intend to get in Eli's fix of being unable to regulate the conduct
of her own offspring, who justified the action of Elisha with the
she-bears, and insisted that Jezebel got her just deserts when
Jehu threw her off the second-story porch. And she always had a
ready text for her pronouncements. When I got too critical, which

I must admit included questions about the omnipotent wisdom of the Almighty, she sent me to my father's study to question him for a change. This I enjoyed; he had rows of history books, including Josephus; and *he* knew Greek. So this book was a long time in gestation. I went to school for twenty-one years and absorbed a background of more or less related biblical studies, from Egyptian history to collating original Greek manuscripts, a procedure which does not make a scholar but does promote the inclination to work a Bible story into almost any kind of public or private discourse.

But the test for the practicality, even the viability, of the stories and teaching reported in the Bible was six years of living in China, well before the Second World War. Try to tell the practical Confucius-oriented old-line Chinese anything new about highhanded rulers, or the ground-down faces of the poor, or about benevolent seers, or ancient poets with masterful figures of speech. If the Bible is to make its place one finds one has to have something more than words to share. Comes a day, though, for the appropriate story from the dignified book with the black leather cover. A time for the twenty-third psalm, or the fortieth or fifty-fifth chapter of Isaiah. (With the Beatitudes coming up.) One shares only what is really one's own. Also a day comes when one holds a sick Chinese baby all night while a Western-trained doctor says, gently, that the child cannot live but his mother says firmly, "The child of the Shunammite woman came to life." And so did hers! The book with the black leather cover was not just another book.

In China our own children played antiphonal choirs singing at the gates of Jerusalem. "Who shall ascend the hill of the Lord? And who shall stand in his holy place? He who has clean hands and a pure heart." Especially, at times, the clean hands. Probably it was inevitable that I would finally get to Jerusalem and walk through those same gates. And spend several months at the American School for Oriental Research asking questions of the real scholars—notably Marvin H. Pope, Herbert G. May, and John Marks, traipsing to the excavations where archaeologists prove that the ancient cities were for real, climbing up the face of a cliff into Cave Four and Cave Eleven where some of the Dead

Sea Scrolls were found, getting tossed across the chasm into the cave of Adullam where David hid, joggling in a Land-Rover through rocky hills and across fertile plains where the people of the Lord—just as the prophets promised—are reclaiming the land. Openhearted land, however desolate, which responds alike to Moslems, Jews, and Christians. Then there were the special days when Haig Mekhalian walked me around the Sea of Galilee, which he had known from childhood—acres of spring flowers (the "lilies of the field"), a warm light rain, friendly farmers—retelling Bible incidents and highlighting the meaning behind the words. I began to really want to know the Scriptures.

Mostly, we follow the cult practices of our faith and absorb secondhand instruction from sermons, without realizing how sketchy is our knowledge of our scriptures. Jewish fathers get all starry-eyed at a son's bar mitzvah as they hand the sacred scroll to their scion and instruct him to follow its precepts; but chances are that the boy never saw his father crack the book at home. And Christian parents with proud smiles and carnations in their lapels go to see their offspring confirmed and receive a nice new Bible to guide their lives; then they go home and put the book in a good safe place so that the son or daughter can always keep it. Good as new, too. Well—we lose. What do we lose? We almost have to read in order to find out.

Young or old, a Bible reader needs a modern version with ample notes. My own preference is the Oxford Annotated Bible, revised standard version, published by Oxford University Press. The notes are superb; they make it difficult not to understand. The other indispensable book is The Interpreter's One Volume Commentary on the Bible, published by Abingdon. Here each book of the Bible is expounded, almost verse by verse; and special articles are added on geographical and historical settings, the making of the literature, variations in translations, decisions regarding the canon, plus an excellent section of maps; and much more besides. Third, probably Harper's Bible Dictionary. To add helpful books one really has to browse. Both Jewish and Christian scholars have learned the art of writing to be read with zest.

No one finishes a manuscript without having many helpful (and often long-suffering) friends to thank. I hope my parents are look-

ing over their pink clouds. This book was begun, so far as actual
writing is concerned, under the stimulating prodding of the Walter
Hovings, who also acquainted me with the excellent library of the
American Bible Society, where translations into almost every
known language are housed, as well as rare editions. Wainwright
House, Rye, New York, and especially John Hewitt, offered quiet
hospitality. My youngest son, Andrew, who has an ear for redun-
dancies, cheerfully cut sections to ribbons, thank goodness. The
"Buber Girls," addicted to theology and argument, aided and
abetted, and to the stimulating discussions led by Rabbi Frank
Rosenthal we all owe appreciation. Good friends Ruth Wolf,
Dianne Moss, Elva Iid and Kathleen Spears faithfully typed reams
of pages and raised good questions. Finally, there are my editors,
Alex Liepa and Maud Savage, supportively patient and resourceful.
Thank you, all!

> Let us know, let us press on to know the Lord;
>   his going forth is sure as the dawn;
> he will come to us as the showers,
>   as the spring rains that water the earth.

The Book You Always Meant to Read
The Old Testament

Genesis

Beginnings

Genesis—the book of beginnings: the beginning of the universe, the beginnings of life on earth; the beginning of God's dealing with man and of man's conscious response to God, of his responsibility for his fellow man, of his choices which led to disobedience, sin, estrangement and punishment; of great adventures in faith, and the first covenant between God and man. Also the beginning of the trek of the Hebrew people from place to place.

Genesis is also a book of history but the early history leaned heavily on legends which were told, sung, danced and ritualized as they passed from father to son, elaborated in the process. Along the way someone wrote down some of the best-known tales, someone else incorporated certain early records; then another writer in another locality did the same until eventually—with Genesis it took several hundred years—a final editor gathered up all the accounts and wove them into one document, not too much bothered by a few discrepancies and inconsistencies. One thing to note about biblical history is that it was seldom recorded in order to present exact factual information, even when figures and dates were given. Rather, its purpose was to show God's direction of human affairs, Hebrew affairs in particular.

Other cultures than the Hebrew have other accounts of beginnings. In many times and places other peoples have searched for the ground of their being and felt that God had revealed himself to them. In their earliest records groups have universally claimed their own special relationship to God; the mightiest God of whom they could conceive was their God, peculiarly their own. So with the Hebrews, who called their God Yahweh, a name later corrupted in English to Jehovah. Yahweh was a tribal God, later a national God. As time went on and experience broadened, someone would occasionally glimpse him as universal. To be God *at* all he would have to be God *for* all. But this was a far-out thought and generations came and went with the conviction that the Hebrew people were protected and directed by a Hebrew God.

Amazingly the Hebrew people sensed their God as one and indivisible, beyond representation in wood or stone. If in times of stress he seemed unhearing, or if their neighbors appeared to out-prosper them under the aegis of a different god, then they might borrow a god or two to augment Yahweh but only until some towering Hebrew leader recalled them to the knowledge that Yahweh would brook no seconds. They and their God belonged wholly to each other.

Genesis in anything like the form we know it was not the first full scroll produced among the thirty-nine books which make up the library we call the Old Testament. In fact, it was not put together until the last half of the sixth century B.C. at the earliest. The Hebrews knew the book of Exodus much earlier and it was their questions about their own beginnings which prompted the compilation of the material gathered into the book of Genesis. There must have been great rejoicing when it was given circulation in written form. Something tremendous swept into the stream of history with this wide-angled panorama of creation, recorded in wonder, with God's creatures emerging in the order of their dignity, man in God's image coming last.

In the Beginning God Created

The idea that the universe just happened has never seemed tenable to most people. The human heart seems to claim a creator. With God all things began, and even today the mind can scarcely stretch itself wider or higher than the Hebrew perception of the mystery of beginnings.

Ours is the generation which heard the first verses of Genesis read from a spacecraft miles above the earth by an envoy returning from man's first trip to the moon! Reading Genesis, we ponder: way back yonder, when God was evoking night and day, calling forth the firmament and making man in his own image, was the moon trip already a conceptual possibility?

In the beginning God created the heavens and the earth. The earth was without form and void, and darkness was upon the face of the deep; and the Spirit of God was moving over the face of the waters. And God said, "Let there be light"; and there was light. And God saw that the light was good; and God separated the light from the darkness. God called the light Day, and the darkness he called Night. And there was evening and there was morning, one day. . . . And God saw everything that he had made, and behold, it was very good. . . . Thus the heavens and the earth were finished, and all the host of them. 1:1–5, 31; 2:1

So God created man in his own image, in the image of God he created him; male and female he created them. 1:27

The Adam and Eve of It

The Hebrew story was that the first man and the first woman, called Adam and Eve, lived in an idyllic garden called Eden, where only the fruit of the tree of the knowledge of good and evil was denied them. Eve was tempted by a serpent to eat the forbidden fruit and after eating it she tempted Adam into having a bite. Later, he blamed his wife. They both knew they had disobeyed God and they hid from him. That evening, when "they heard the sound of the Lord God walking in the garden in the cool of the day," they no longer cared or dared to walk with him as they were accustomed to do. But the Lord called them forth, confronted them with their disobedience and in good firm tones sentenced them to hard labor.

Some people read the story as factual; others as myth in the sense of universal human experience as old as the race, deeply buried in the collective unconscious. They point out the two aspects of consciousness, the male and female in each individual. Adam, the male, they take to be predominantly reason; Eve as predominantly feeling. Both were tempted into overindulgence in sensory experience, primarily sex experience for its own sake. And so they lost the original balance of their natures, no longer living in harmony with the whole of creation and its inscrutable

source, called God. There are many other levels of insight into
this story told with such condensed simplicity. Whatever the interpretation, this is a story of human failure to live up to whatever
were felt to be the laws of God. When God looked Adam and
Eve in the eye they knew that he knew they had failed him. They
had had a choice and they had made a weak decision, with results
which had to be faced. The first pair of human beings lost their
openhearted companionship with their Creator.

This first recorded experience of mankind was pure tragedy—
except for one thing. God did not turn his back on his disobedient children. They had taken on themselves a self-con-
sciousness which was a new dimension of mind for them, a dimension of limitless possibilities, so God gave them a new set of terms.
And remained available. The epic of love and redemption was
on its way. Genesis now becomes a book of growth and development, a line drawing of the potential implicit in humankind.

Excalibur!

Then the Lord God said, "Behold, the man has become like one of
us, knowing good and evil; and now, lest he put forth his hand and
take also of the tree of life, and eat, and live forever"— . . . He
drove out the man; and at the east of the garden of Eden he placed
the cherubim, and a flaming sword which turned every way, to
guard the way to the tree of life. 3:22, 24

If God had not put that revolving sword of flame to guard the
tree of life succeeding generations might also have eaten its fruit
of life and lived forever. Could anything be more tragic than end-
less physical life in a world where people could not be trusted to
obey what they felt to be the laws of God!

The new terms meted out to Adam and Eve and all their future
offspring were stiff. From that day on, women were to bear their
children in pain and men would have to work and earn their living
by the sweat of their brow. And so it has remained. To be sure,
God could scarcely have meant that medical science was not to
develop drugs which would ease and safeguard physical childbirth; but remove as much physical pain as we may, the stress of
modern childbearing (and child rearing) still entails inescapable
suffering. And God could hardly have meant that man was to in-

vent no labor-saving devices. But implement the work of his hands with technological devices as he may, the feeding and clothing of the earth's population remains *work*. God was really saying to his children, "Look, you arrogant, self-indulgent human beings, who thought you could disobey my fundamental laws with impunity—meaning without punishment and meaning *you*—now grow up the hard way."

And his terms still stand. The achievements of our forebears have to be constantly compounded by more work, and a new birth is still a painful process, as any individual knows who faces the job of becoming a mature person on his own in a co-operative society where he can never be on his own! The double responsibility and double hazard.

Back to that flaming sword. It is the way with the world's great swords, too mighty for common mortals to handle, that they can be wielded only by a man who is pure in heart, without self-interest, free of hate, malice, even of recrimination. Much later in the Bible record such a one appears and wins back the lost immortality. And offers it to others. But only on terribly stiff terms. Including God's first penalty: labor and suffering.

Rest

In the early part of the story of creation there is an amazing statement. Amazing, that is, when we think of the whole sweep of the Creator's activity, during those long-ago "days" when he was exerting his creative energy on the far reaches of the universe.

Thus the heavens and the earth were finished, all the host of them. And on the seventh day God finished his work which he had done, and he rested on the seventh day from all his work which he had done. So God blessed the seventh day and hallowed it, because on it God rested from all his work which he had done in creation. 2:1–3

God rested—why? Was he not the eternal self-renewing source of energy in all its manifest forms? Besides, there were still tasks ahead; he still had to shepherd his people day and night, millenniums on end. Why did he feel so strongly about a day of rest that he later issued an order: "Six days you shall work, but on the seventh day you shall rest. . . ."

Back in the ninth century B.C., when the early versions of this record of beginnings were first being put down, men and women already had extremely busy lives, what with having to adjust to the speedy ways of their cities, watching out for chariots on the main streets and trains of donkeys pushing them against doorways. They had fashions to follow and economic trends to keep up with, political upheavals to accommodate to. Some of them also gave time to temple service and to various kinds of good works. God must have foreseen from the beginning how pushed people would become. Should there not be exceptions to this seventh day of rest in times of crisis when the chariot needed washing, the field needed cutting, the inventory checking, the overdue report editing? The constant stress of sundial and calendar! Couldn't God set a better example by keeping at his job and driving through?

It seems as if he sensed that the only way he could get a word in edgewise with his children—back in a primitive day, of course —was to issue an absolute decree: they must have a sabbath, a day of rest, one day in seven. He had his reasons. When he rested he taught the trees to acquiesce to the stilled sap of winter; he taught the fields to lie fallow for a season; he taught the animals to find a hidden place where they could lie quiet for a time; he taught the pulsing hearts in all his living creatures to rest for a moment between beats. He taught the silence. He made himself felt through dreams and an inner knowing, impossible to interpret in constant action. Anyway, God rested. Even God. And he cautioned his children to rest. One day in seven.

Moment of Opportunity

Stories we know as Bible history—hero tales, romances, tragedies, factual records, allegory, and a few thrillers—could never have lived for generations, told around a campfire, rehearsed under the stars, unless they had some spellbinding quality and made a point which mattered to the hearers. One of the earliest melodramas was a murder mystery with a moral.

In this first murder story there are three leading characters: a pair of brothers called Cain and Abel, and God. In the background, like a Greek chorus, are "the people" among whom Cain later lived. The story calls Cain and Abel the sons of Adam and

Eve. It takes a bit of imagination to think of the first man and woman, who must have lived centuries before Neanderthal man, having offspring who lived to reach the relatively advanced stage in which they tilled the soil. But the recorders of early history had imagination and they were not plagued by archaeologists and their ilk.

So here were the brothers: Cain, "a tiller of the ground," and Abel, "a keeper of sheep," at the yearly harvest festival, when the best of their produce was offered in sacrifice. One theory about sacrifice was that the fire and smoke of the offering would catch the attention of God, who would then look closely at their needs and in appreciation of their devotion send blessings. Cain's offering was of fruit; Abel's "the firstlings of the flock and of their fat portions." God approved Abel's offering, but "for Cain and his offering he had no regard." Why he scorned Cain's offering we are not told. Perhaps Cain decided he could get by with offering something less than his best and then sell his top produce at a smart profit! Because of the fat on Abel's meat his fire naturally burned higher than Cain's, and had a more tantalizing odor, so that more people gathered around. Or maybe it was just that Abel was sacrificing with joy in his heart, while Cain's dour looks showed that he begrudged his gift. Cain himself must have known the reason God scorned his sacrifice because he became very angry "and his countenance fell."

> The Lord said to Cain, "Why are you angry, and why has your countenance fallen? If you do well, will you not be accepted? And if you do not do well, sin is couching at the door; its desire is for you, but you must master it." 4:6–7

Looking at himself was the one thing Cain did not intend to do and when he refused, he lost his chance to bring his jealousy to heel. He could speak no word of authority to the couching beast at his door.

Modern sociologists point out that Cain and Abel symbolize the clash in cultures between agriculturists and roaming herdsmen, but the ancient storyteller thought in terms of story with movement and moral, the moral being the necessity for a man to master his own passions. Cain muffed his chance for reinstatement with

God when he refused to look within himself for the cause of his anger. Now he had to look outside himself for someone to blame for God's disapproval. There was his brother whose gift had shown him up. Plainly the solution was to get rid of Abel. He may have been the first to scheme up the device of eliminating a better product. He invited Abel to take a hike in the fields with him.

The Second Big Question

A modern scriptwriter might prolong the next scene (the Bible tells the whole story in sixteen short verses), depicting Abel striding along lightheartedly, taking it for granted that Cain felt as approved by God as he did, and remarking that the annual sacrifice was really a great occasion. But Cain was not in a jovial mood and some place in their walk he killed Abel. Whatever he intended to do next is not told. Maybe go back home and act as surprised as the next one when Abel was found dead. But God stopped him with a question: Where is your brother Abel? This is the second big question God ever asked man. The first question he had put to Adam: Where are *you?* Now he asked: Where is your *brother?* Cain did not like the question. He said shortly, "Am I my brother's keeper?"

This question he hurled back at God has disturbed the mind of mankind from that day on. How can one individual be accountable for another? Slowly God has got the answer through to us: we become responsible by using our imagination, our holy imagination. Some call it walking in the other fellow's shoes, and the other fellow may not even have shoes. Or feet. But it took centuries before God could even talk to man in terms of a golden rule. Instead, the record has him answering Cain in the pictorial phrases which marked the literary genius of the Hebrews.

And the Lord said, "What have you done? The voice of your brother's blood is crying to me from the ground . . . which has opened its mouth to receive your brother's blood from your hand." 4:10–11

God's decree was that Cain should become "a fugitive and a wanderer on the earth." No wonder Cain cried out, "My punishment is greater than I can bear." No one wanted Cain around.

No one. And God would not let him be killed. The people of his community, under threat of sevenfold vengeance, were ordered to let him live. Even though Cain was responsible for his own actions, the clan had to become caretakers of the weakest among them; they had to learn to live with the murderer. They found there was no solitary suffering, nor any way for the innocent to escape the burden of the guilty. Inevitably the weight of the bundle of life had to be shared.

The Book of the Generations

After the murder of Abel the record picks up a long genealogy in which the ages of Adam's descendants are carefully set down. This kind of detail was important to some of the later editors who put together the final version of Genesis. Most modern readers discount the astounding life-span here recorded as primitive hyperbole or a miscalculation of the calendar. But it is notable that in the biblical account the life-span diminishes epoch by epoch. Between the early population and the time of Abraham it dropped from the tall figures of Methuselah, who is said to have lived 969 years, to a mere couple of centuries or so. The idea was that increasing sin decreased life expectancy. A well-known proverb had it: "The fear of the Lord prolongs life, but the years of the wicked will be short," as if the anxieties behind our sins might actually shorten our days.

More interesting in the genealogical records than mere longevity —although that in itself is a kind of geriatric challenge—is the occasional descriptive phrase which characterizes a man by his achievements. Enoch son of Cain had a city named for him; half a dozen generations later Jabal "was the father of all those who dwell in tents and have cattle"; Jubal "was the father of all those who play the lyre and pipe"; Tubal-cain "was the forger of all instruments of bronze and iron"; Enoch "walked with God; and he was not, for God took him."

(It sets one to wondering how to characterize the members of one's own family in a phrase. Uncle Jack, the compulsive giver of presents; Aunt Minnie, the loving giver of gifts; Uncle Pete, who ran himself to death for good causes; second cousin Jerry, the father of all those who tinker with plumbing; Brother Dick, who

lived to wash his car. Then the nobler ones. And the real skunks.
And ourselves. What about our own one-phrase record?)

A New Start, World Scale

Years passed with their cargo of human lives, men and women
striving for what they wanted for themselves, experimenting with
all varieties of power. Evil grew and spread "and the earth was
filled with violence." The record of the way God dealt with this
decadent situation by sending a flood is a retelling of a much
older, Babylonian account known as the Gilgamesh epic, found
on one of a series of tablets, deciphered in 1872, known to have
been a part of a royal collection made for an Assyrian king in the
seventh century B.C. However, the story itself is plainly much
older and recalls a universal flood sent by the gods, one of whom
saves the hero of the epic by ordering him to build an ark in which
he and his family, the skilled artisans and the needed animals can
be secure. Several of the details of the older recording are repeated
in the story of Noah. Apparently a racial memory persisted of a
time when the known world—probably the country between the
Tigris and Euphrates rivers—was all but flooded out of existence.
There were, of course, no Hebrews at that time, but a later
Hebrew historian thought his way into the meaning of the event.

> The Lord saw that the wickedness of man was great in the earth,
> and that every imagination of the thoughts of his heart was only
> evil continually. And the Lord was sorry that he had made man on
> the earth, and it grieved him to his heart. 6:5–6

Indeed, God was so disappointed that he decided it would be
better to blot out his creation, man, beast, everything. He would
flood them off the face of the earth. But there was one good man!
How could he drown a world in which one good man stood surety
for a possible future? The man's name was Noah. With one
"righteous man, blameless in his generation," God concluded
maybe he could start over. So he gave Noah explicit instructions
for building an ark that could ride out a deluge. He told him to
round up his sons, their wives and families and also two of every
kind of animal, bird, and creeping thing, along with food for all of
them. The story says nothing about the way his neighbors must

have laughed. A flood? To destroy the earth with all its cities and villages, its palaces and huts, its multitudinous people? But Noah probably realized that men who listen to God often appear foolish to their neighbors.

When Noah and his family and all the creatures God had designated went into the ark, "all the fountains of the great deep burst forth, and the windows of the heavens were opened. And rain fell upon the earth forty days and forty nights . . . and the waters increased, and bore up the ark, and it rose high above the earth . . . and the ark floated on the face of the waters. . . . And the waters prevailed upon the earth a hundred and fifty days." For all practical purposes, the earth was returned to its primordial state.

But the story predicates a God of long runs and ultimate purposes. That little cache of people there in the ark atop a flooded world were God's investments in mankind. "And God made a wind blow over the earth, and the waters subsided . . . and the waters receded from the earth continually," and finally a dove released by Noah came back with a freshly plucked olive leaf—sign of returning vegetation. God was pleased with the fresh new world. He let Noah and his entourage leave the ark. And Noah, in wonder, built an altar and worshiped God. That first altar on the face of the redeemed earth stirred God to a pledge for the future:

"While the earth remains, seedtime and harvest, cold and heat, summer and winter, day and night, shall not cease." 8:22

As a sign of his promise God set a rainbow in the sky, a covenant of mercy overarching justice, of faithfulness outspanning man's deserts. No matter how people fail, it writes across the heavens, God can always start over if he has one truly righteous man. This is the eternal hope in a society afraid to believe that the action of one individual can matter.

After the flood Noah lived three hundred and fifty years. All the days of Noah were nine hundred and fifty years; and he died. 9:28–29

The historian then inserts a chapter of genealogy beginning with the sons of Noah; "and from these the nations spread abroad on the earth after the flood."

Building Our Ziggurats

"Now the whole earth had one language. . . ." Could any state be more idyllic! All people everywhere able to understand each other. But then one group in the plain of the Tigris-Euphrates basin decided to outdo all their neighbors and make a name for themselves by building a seven-story tower (no doubt one of the stepped pyramidal temples known as ziggurats), "with its top in the heavens," reminiscent of the mountains from which their Sumerian ancestors had come.

However, before their tower was finished "the Lord came down to see the city and the tower, which the sons of men had built." One might think he would be stirred to hope by the fact that everyone spoke the same language. But he saw that the builders were really flaunting their overwhelming superiority. No people could build a good world in that mood. ". . . and this is only the beginning of what they will do," observed God, "and nothing that they propose to do will now be impossible for them." In other words, increasing success would only compound their arrogance. In spite of their common language they had no sense of mutuality. So God simply confused the builders' tongues. Let them wrestle with a mess of vocabularies. Whereupon the in-group had to climb down from their ziggurat and struggle to make themselves understood.

(Personally, most of us build our ziggurats half-consciously. Our sense of superiority marks even our common speech: Britannia rules the waves; Deutschland über Alles; America, God's country; not to mention wop, chink, bohunk, kike, nigger. And other labels: the Establishment, the jaded generation, hippies, pigs, finks. We have forgotten the sign language of the heart.)

Father Abraham

A stancher patriarch than Abraham never walked the hot desert sands, trekked more determinedly on camelback, or risked more for his faith. Nevertheless, if he lived today doing the deeds he did then, he would land in a penitentiary. First of all, he was a polygamist, marrying such subsidiary wives as he wished and fathering children by servant girls. Second, he sent one of his secondary wives and his son Ishmael off into the wilderness to starve or make it on their own if they could. Third, he was a double-dealer: down in Egypt he passed his beautiful wife Sarai off as his sister so that no man would kill him in order to take her, and when Pharaoh did add her to his harem he used the connection to gain favor and build up his herds and flocks. Fourth, he fought at the drop of a kaffiyeh if he felt his territorial rights threatened, even taking on five kings at one time, and he highhandedly carried off loot, including women and children. He even laughed at God.

But—and this is the big thing, the thing that earned him his fame, honor, and multitudinous descendants—he did listen to God when he heard him speak. He obeyed such leadings as he took in; hence he developed enormous faith and faithfulness. Born a nomad, he became a patriarch worthy of generations of veneration, which shows that a man has to be judged on his merits as a dedicated human being in the context of his own times. It was through faithfulness to the value priorities he had that God used Abraham. And hence raised Hebrew society above itself. Odd about God—he keeps on using the individuals at hand. (It poses a question as to how the choices look now, when men absorb themselves fighting wars with napalm and defoliating the countryside, polluting the rivers, the seas and the air; making garbage dumps where parks could be, effecting an imbalance in nature with insecticides; short-cutting devotional states with psychedelics; starving the poor, cheating the rich of their birthright of brotherhood—but the list becomes depressing. Fortunately God always seems to have at hand a few dedicated souls, old and young.)

Emigrant Extraordinary

Modern history is alight with the names of famous emigrants who felt an urge to leave the place of their forefathers to go forth into a new environment, a new way of life. Ancient history was no different: Terah, father of Abraham, was such a man. He lived in "Ur of the Chaldeans," a major city on the Euphrates south of Babylonia. We think of Abraham as a nomad because he shepherded his flocks and herds on long treks but if he came from Ur within a century or two of the year 1900 B.C., he knew a well-developed culture which included distinguished architecture, tools of copper, tin, and bronze, not to mention flint, bone, ivory; gold and silver ornaments; extensive medicines for every disease which had a name. For warfare he knew chariots, bows and arrows, and spears. He was certainly acquainted with an elaborate system of taxation, even of import-export duties. And he lived under a fairly well-developed legal code. The long ascendancy of Sumeria was giving way to the expansion of the Babylonian kingdom, which may have been one reason Terah decided to take his son, then called Abram, his son's wife Sarai, and his grandson Lot and move out. It proved a momentous decision.

On their way to Canaan they paused for some years at a place called Haran and there Terah died when only a couple hundred years old. Afterward Abram evidently had a period of postfuneral soul-searching, as often happens. What next? He was only seventy-five years old, with the best of his life ahead of him. Finally he felt the Lord himself was directing him to push on to Canaan, where he would found a nation. "So Abram went, as the Lord had told him." Just like that. It could have been this disposition to wait for the word of the Lord and then act on it that made it possible for the Lord to work through him.

Claiming an Inheritance

Abram pushed on toward the Negeb, bordering the Sinai Peninsula, erecting altars wherever he had a fruitful conversation with the Lord. When famine came he went into Egypt, passed off his wife as his sister, profited by her place in Pharaoh's harem, had his duplicity exposed, accepted apologies and presents from Pharaoh and returned to the Negeb, taking his family and his nephew Lot with him. "Now Abram was very rich in cattle, in silver, and in gold." Finally arriving at a place near Bethel where he had formerly built an altar to the Lord, he realized that the land would not support all their combined flocks, herds and tents so he made a generous offer: let Lot take his choice of a locality in which to settle and he himself would take whatever remained. Lot chose the rich Jordan valley and "Abram dwelt in the land of Canaan." Then it was that God said to him:

"Lift up your eyes, and look from the place where you are, north-ward and southward and eastward and westward; for all the land

which you see I will give to you and to your descendants for ever."
13:14–15

Even God couldn't give him larger holdings than he had the vision to take in.

Renewed Promises

The Lord, reminding Abram that he was to father a nation, brought him outside his tent and said: "Look toward heaven, and number the stars, if you are able to number them." Then he said to him, "So shall your descendants be." He even changed Abram's name to Abraham, which in Hebrew was a shift from "exalted father" to "father of a multitude." And Sarai's name was changed to Sarah, meaning "princess."

Promises were all very well but when Abraham was ninety-nine years old he still had no children. He was forging a clan as best he could, circumcising the males of his tribe, whether born into his household or bought from foreigners, he was caring for dependents, but he was not producing descendants. Moreover, Sarah was ninety, which did seem a shade late for conception. So what did Abraham do when God again renewed his promise about fathering a nation? He "fell on his face and laughed." It just doesn't happen to centenarians.

It was three strangers, perhaps disguised "angels," who delivered God's promise about Abraham's fathering a nation. When Sarah, standing at the door of her tent, heard their words she also laughed. The Lord did not like her derision. He asked her, "Is anything too hard for the Lord?" a question mankind has pondered for centuries. In the spring Sarah bore a child! He was named Isaac, meaning "he laughs." In ritual fashion he was circumcised on the eighth day, and on the day he was weaned his father made "a great feast."

God's Dark Face

There are mean characters in the Bible: wicked men and wicked women. There are also saintly characters: good men and good women. But the confusing characters are the good people who suddenly act in most despicable ways. And God, at once all-powerful and yet highly dependent on human beings to make himself known, does not always appear to intervene to right a wrong, so profound is his respect for his children's free will.

An unlovely incident prompted by Sarah involved Abraham's older son, Ishmael, whose mother, Hagar, was an Egyptian concubine. Evidently Sarah was jealous of Ishmael's status as the older son and perhaps irked because Hagar held her head too high. So Sarah insisted that Abraham cast out both Hagar and Ishmael. "And the thing was very displeasing to Abraham"—but Sarah as head wife had her rights. God assured Abraham that even if Sarah did insist on her prerogative, Ishmael would also father a nation.

> So Abraham rose early in the morning, and took bread and a skin of water, and gave it to Hagar, putting it on her shoulder, along with the child, and sent her away. And she departed, and wandered in the wilderness of Beersheba. 21:14

Soon food and water were both gone. Hagar found a bush for shade and there she put the child. Not wanting to watch him die, she sat "a good way off, about the distance of a bow shot." Not far enough, though, to keep from hearing the child cry.

> And God heard the voice of the lad; and the angel of God called to Hagar from heaven, and said to her, "What troubles you, Hagar? Fear not; for God has heard the voice of the lad where he is. Arise, lift up the lad, and hold him fast with your hand; for I will make him a great nation." 21:17–18

At this point the recorder makes a cogent comment:

> Then God opened her eyes, and she saw a well of water; and she went, and filled the skin with water, and gave the lad a drink. 21:19

As might be expected, it was after she turned to the Lord that she was able to take in the possibilities of her circumstances. The spring had been there all the time.

> God was with the lad, and he grew up; he lived in the wilderness, and became an expert with the bow. 21:20

The Habit of Obedience

The richer land Lot had chosen lay near the notorious cities of Sodom and Gomorrah. But Lot had not proved a reforming influence and after some time the Lord told Abraham he planned to destroy the cities because of their wickedness. Abraham pleaded that they be saved if as many as ten righteous men could be found. When ten good men could not be found God decreed destruction.

Lot himself was informed of the impending doom by two angels disguised as strangers, or foreigners, who appeared at the gate of Sodom where Lot was sitting among the men of affairs. Acting according to the laws of his own people, Lot immediately rose and offered the strangers hospitality, overcame their remonstrance, took them to his home, and had the customary feast prepared. That night, when the lecherous men of Sodom came to demand release of the strangers for their immoral practices, he further fulfilled the duties due strangers by protecting them even to the point of risking the lives of his daughters. And in obeying the best he knew, Lot found that he had literally entertained angels unawares.

Then it was the angels' turn to prove Lot's benefactor. They ordered him to gather his household and flee to the country because Sodom and Gomorrah were about to be destroyed by God for their wickedness. Lot's prospective sons-in-law simply would not believe Lot's word that it was God who had so spoken. If anything looked permanent it was those cities. Even Lot himself lingered in leaving. But because he was trying to obey, the angels took the family by the hand and led them forth. Then some kind of holocaust, perhaps an erupting volcano, destroyed the cities.

"But Lot's wife behind him looked back, and she became a pillar of salt." Underlying this statement is an ancient tradition documented in other early cultures that it was perilous to look back after any sort of exorcism or escape from danger. At the moment of her backward glance there may have been some catastrophe from volcanic ash which the recorder used to illustrate the fact that backward-looking regret is likely to prove fatal.

Faith Rewarded

All the promises of God which had sustained Abraham were centered in his son Isaac. Through him alone God could make good his promise that Abraham's descendants should be as numerous as the stars. And yet Abraham was suddenly confronted by an inexplicable imperative.

After these things God tested Abraham, and said to him, "Abraham!" And he said, "Here am I." He said, "Take your son, your only son Isaac, whom you love, and go to the land of Moriah, and offer him there as a burnt offering upon one of the mountains of which I shall tell you." 22:1–2

How could Abraham feel that God had ordered this tragic obedience? Had his Canaanite neighbors taunted him? For them human sacrifice was not uncommon; when the tribal gods seemed to withhold their blessing from some crucial endeavor of the clan, the king or the ranking priest might make the final gesture of obeisance by sacrificing a precious son or daughter. Abraham may have decided to demonstrate his devotion to Yahweh on the theory that his God would surely not ask less than the Canaanite gods. Or he may have decided he was putting devotion to his son ahead of devotion to God. For some reason he felt he was being tested. How great his temptation to disavow God's voice we do not know. At any rate, he decided that God had ordered him to sacrifice the very son through whom descendants had been promised.

So Abraham rose early in the morning, saddled his ass, and took two of his young men with him, and his son Isaac; and he cut the wood for the burnt offering, and arose and went to the place of which God had told him. 22:3

He made no explanation to Isaac but traveled three days with the boy and the servants to the spot appointed. To Isaac, if he knew only that he was going with his father to some place of special sacrifice, it may have seemed a fine excursion. Perhaps en route the father told again the story of God's past protection during the days of his wanderings—a recollection intended more to comfort himself than to inspire the boy. At the appointed place Abraham ordered the servants to wait while he and his son went on a bit farther. Isaac carried the wood while Abraham carried the fire and knife. Only then did it strike Isaac as strange that they should be preparing an altar with no sacrificial animal at hand. He asked where the lamb was.

Abraham said, "God will provide himself the lamb for a burnt offering, my son." So they went both of them together. 22:8

Chances are they proceeded in silence. But Abraham did not falter. He built the altar; he laid the wood in order; and then "bound Isaac his son, and laid him on the altar, upon the wood." Then Abraham put forth his hand, and took the knife to slay his son. The boy may have screamed and pleaded in terror but it is also possible that he was quietly compliant, having decided that his father was testing him; confident that his father would never make the fatal thrust. He may have smiled at his father. A man whose faith in God is every day manifest to his son will find his son having faith in *him* beyond the point of reason. Indeed, it may have been as much in answer to the boy's faith as to the father's that the angel of the Lord called to Abraham:

> He said, "Do not lay your hand on the lad or do anything to him; for now I know that you fear God, seeing you have not withheld your son, your only son, from me." 22:12

And there before Abraham's wonder-filled eyes "was a ram, caught in a thicket by his horns." And so, of course, Abraham sacrificed the ram, his son looking on in awe. The recorder's final comment on this astounding example of faith, which held through its primitive testing is this:

> So Abraham called the name of that place The Lord will provide; as it is said to this day, "On the mount of the Lord it shall be provided." 22:14

Custodians of the Faith

It may well have been Sarah's death, at the ripe age of 127 years, which set Abraham to thinking about a wife for Isaac. Where could a woman be found who would be to Isaac what Sarah had been to him? He called his most trusted servant and instructed him to return to Mesopotamia, the general locality of their kindred, taking ten camels bearing choice gifts, and go to the household of Abraham's brother Nahor to inquire about a wife for Isaac.

Upon reaching his destination the servant made the camels kneel down outside the city by the well of water at the time of evening when women go out to draw water, and he prayed that God would direct a young woman to the well whose offer of water to a stranger would be a sign of God's approval of her. And so it was. "Before he had done speaking," his prayer was answered by the arrival of a maiden "very fair to look upon" who filled her jar, drew water for the camels, and offered lodgings in the name of her father, Bethuel, son of Nahor. The servant was talking to Isaac's second cousin Rebekah! He quickly presented her with a gold ring and bracelets and followed her home where the entire household excitedly gathered around to hear about Abraham and his family. There was royal entertainment, after which the servant stated his errand. Both Rebekah's father and mother approved the betrothal, then asked her whether she was willing to go to this far land of Canaan to marry Isaac. Her answer was, "I will go."

The journey may have seemed long to Rebekah. Or she may have been the kind of girl who delighted in new experience, relieved that she did not have to marry one of the more stodgy local yokels. When the caravan finally reached the Negeb, where Isaac was tented, he happened to be meditating in the field and, looking up, he saw the camels coming! The servant made his report and presented Rebekah.

> Then Isaac brought her into the tent, and took Rebekah, and she became his wife; and he loved her. So Isaac was comforted after his mother's death. 24:67

At this point more genealogy is inserted into the record. Abraham married a second time, a woman named Keturah, and lived to be 175 years old. His descendants and the descendants of his son Ishmael are recorded; then the children of Isaac. A story about Isaac's passing his wife off as his sister, much like the story of Abraham and Sarah in Egypt, is inserted; perhaps the same story, confused as to identities through generations of retelling. The family chronicle then continues.

Advancing a Heritage

Isaac's life followed the general pattern of his father's, especially as to livelihood. He moved his flocks and herds around the countryside in times of drought, making sure there were dependable watering places. Customarily springs were encased to

become wells, which were protected by placing a large flat stone
over the top. Even so, wells silted up or, more threateningly, they
might be deliberately filled up by enemies. Then they had to be
redug.

And Isaac dug again the wells of water which had been dug in the
days of Abraham his father; for the Philistines had stopped them
after the death of Abraham . . . And he moved from there and
dug another well. 26:18, 22

In every generation it is the same. One man digs a well. The
water is ample so that the need of his family and neighbors is met
but he dies and the well silts up. What shall the sons then do?
Re-dig the well!

A Bartered Birthright

Isaac was forty when he married Rebekah; sixty when she first
became pregnant, apparently in answer to Isaac's prayer. She gave
birth to twins! They were named Esau and Jacob.

When the boys grew up, Esau was a skilful hunter, a man of the
field, while Jacob was a quiet man, dwelling in tents. Isaac loved
Esau, because he ate of his game, but Rebekah loved Jacob. 25:27–
28

One day when Jacob was boiling a thick meat-and-lentil pottage "Esau came in from the field, and he was famished." He
wanted some of Jacob's soup. There must have been a bit of
brotherly dialogue, such as:
What will you give me for it?
What do you want?
How about your birthright?
Sure, sure.
The recorder was not without a sense of humor. He had Esau
add, "I am about to die; of what use is a birthright to me?" But
Jacob was not playing games; he made the older brother swear
that the birthright should be his, quite contrary to custom. Esau
was a man who wanted what he wanted when he wanted it; also
a man of stout physical appetite. He took the oath, no doubt concentrating more on the pottage than on his brother's freakish talk,

and ate his fill of the good soup with bread "and rose and went his way."

Sometime afterward an inevitable day came when Isaac, grown old, became concerned about his own death and felt the time had arrived for the ceremony of legalizing the birthright, which meant he must officially bless his older son in the presence of witnesses and establish the accepted primogeniture. Isaac ordered preparations made for the ceremony and told Esau to take his bow and arrows and go kill some of the game his father was most fond of, after which he would dine and forthwith bless Esau.

As soon as Esau went out to hunt, his mother—who had overheard the conversation—called Jacob and told him what was going on. She had a plan. Jacob should go kill a couple kids and she would make the kind of stew his father loved, after which she would see to it that he blessed Jacob instead of Esau. Jacob remonstrated; Isaac would have to lay his hands on him in order to bless him and even if the dim-eyed old man could not see, he would know that this smooth-skinned son was definitely not hairy Esau. However, the mother had that all taken care of. She would dress Jacob in Esau's best clothes, which smelled of Esau, and cover his hands and the back of his neck with a bit of kidskin.

So—when Isaac had eaten his wife's stew which he thought was made with Esau's game, he called for Esau to kneel before him. Jacob knelt and Isaac felt his son's head, face and hands. The old man was confused. "The voice is Jacob's voice but the hands are the hands of Esau." Then growing rapturous over the smell of Esau's garments, which carried the scent of field and forest, he gave the blessing which transferred the inheritance to Jacob.

Of course, in due time Esau returned from the field, discovered the ruse, and "he cried out with an exceedingly great and bitter cry." Completely stymied, he decided that after his father's imminent death he would kill his double-dealing brother. But that, too, was told to his mother, and Rebekah decided Jacob had better leave home. Consequently she persuaded Isaac that it would never do for Jacob to marry a Canaanite woman; better he should be sent at once back to her brother Laban to marry one of his own nice cousins. So off Jacob went to Paddan-aram, where his father had gone before him, while Esau added to his two Hittite wives the daughter of Ishmael.

Not a great deal more is recorded about Isaac who was never the colorful figure that his father Abraham and his son Jacob were. However, his life left an impression of faithfulness and dependability. Either he recovered his health and lived a long time after Jacob's departure or his biographer lost track of the time sequence, because his death is reported as occurring years later, after Jacob's return from Paddan-aram with eleven sons.

Jacob Loved Rachel

At the end of Jacob's journey to his mother's country, a wife was waiting for him. It would be interesting if just one of the recorders of early Israelite history had written from a woman's point of view, but in an ancient feudal society women were at best treasured property and always subservient to the father or husband.

The day Jacob arrived must have been the most astounding day of Rachel's life. Beginning like any other day, it ended with a handsome kinsman from afar gazing at her with love in his eyes. We do not know how old she was when Jacob met her; maybe fourteen, fifteen, sixteen. We know she lived in "the land of the people of the east" in the home of her father Laban, an Aramean sheepherder, and was accustomed to taking the sheep to water at a well, the mouth of which was protected by a huge stone. Ordinarily she met other shepherds who removed the stone, but on this day she met instead an enterprising young stranger who removed the stone, watered her sheep, walked over and kissed her and started to weep. Jacob broke the news: he was the son of her father's sister Rebekah gone from her old home with her husband Isaac these many years. Rachel must have been astonished but she was not speechless; "she ran and told her father."

Her father came with alacrity. "Surely you are my bone and my flesh!" said Laban in the poetical idiom of his day. He took the young man to his house and Jacob must have helped handsomely with the farm work, because at the end of a month Uncle Laban offered nephew Jacob wages to stay on. "Tell me, what shall your

wages be?" Jacob had his answer ready. "I will serve you seven
years for your younger daughter Rachel."

But the record mentions another member of Laban's household,
who later complicates the story: "Now Laban had two daughters;
the name of the older was Leah. . . . Leah's eyes were weak, but
Rachel was beautiful and lovely." Laban accepted Jacob's terms;
to acquire a free farm hand for seven years suited him just fine.
"So Jacob served seven years for Rachel, and they seemed to him
but a few days because of the love he had for her."

A seven-year engagement. Rachel, busy with housework and
sheep, had to be grateful just to see Jacob when he came in from
the field to wash up, and maybe to serve him at the table. However, there were festivals and lovely starry nights at the time of
the harvest and at the spring equinox; there were the weddings of
relatives, family gatherings, the arrival and departure of travelers.
When the seven years were up Jacob happily demanded his wife.
Fine, said Laban in effect, and began to prepare for a wedding
feast. After the festivities the veiled bride was presented to Jacob
at the door of his quarters but when daylight came Jacob discovered that his silent bride was the older sister, Leah! It is to be
hoped that Jacob did not blame poor Leah but he did go in a good
huff to her father. "What is this you have done to me?"

Oh, that, said Laban. "It is not so done in our country, to give
the younger before the first-born." Jacob could still have Rachel
but he would have to work another seven years for her. Jacob
had no choice; his marriage to Leah had been consummated.
Months later, when Leah bore a son, she called him Reuben,
"Because the Lord has looked upon my affliction; surely now my
husband will love me." With Jacob, though, it was still Rachel.
And this was also sad because after Rachel and Jacob were finally
married she had no children while Leah had four sons.

Because Jacob loved her, Rachel could not be reconciled to her
childlessness and gave her maid Bilhah to Jacob. With the
peculiar identity of mistress and maid common in her day,
Rachel felt she could at least have a son vicariously. So Bilhah
had two sons for Jacob. Not to be outdone, Leah gave her maid
Zilpah to Jacob and Zilpah had two sons, after which Leah had

two more sons. Ten times Rachel watched and waited while another woman bore a son to her husband.

And then Rachel had a son of her own—Joseph!

Family Maneuvers

In its original Hebrew, the tricks and counter tricks of Jacob and Laban are very amusing, which was the storyteller's intention. Every early culture has its trickster stories, some of them true. A later editor tried to give Jacob some patriarchical dignity, which, of course, he probably acquired as the years went on. After some years Jacob announced he had to go home to his aging father and he would like a division of the profits for his years of work. Laban was disgruntled but custom was custom and Jacob definitely had something coming in the way of divided flocks. Jacob struck an odd bargain with his father-in-law: he would take only the speckled and spotted sheep and the black lambs. Laban, being a born trickster, thought up a clever ruse: the night before the division of the flocks he picked out the speckled and spotted and sent them off to pasture with his own sons "three days' journey."

Upon discovery, Jacob contrived a counter ruse. He took fresh rods of poplar, almond and plane, peeled white streaks, set them up by the troughs where the sheep came to drink and breed ". . . so the flocks brought forth striped, speckled, and spotted." Trick by trick, Jacob grew exceedingly rich until he had "large flocks, maidservants and menservants, and camels and asses." Naturally the more Laban and his sons were outsmarted the more resentful they became. Finally the Lord saw that the situation had become untenable and directed Jacob to leave. So when his father-in-law went off to shear sheep Jacob rounded up his wives, sons, servants, cattle, sheep and camels and took to the hills. Rachel, still angry with her father for the way he had tricked her in her marriage, stole his household gods, which were not only important for family worship but often necessary as witnesses to legal contracts. When Laban returned and found that a big half of his estate had vanished he and his sons set off in hot pursuit. After a week he caught up with his son-in-law, recriminated him for not allowing his beloved father-in-law to send him away with mirth and gifts and "kiss my sons and my daughters farewell" and why did you steal my household gods? Jacob, who knew nothing of Rachel's duplicity, swore to kill anyone in whose luggage the gods should be found. A thorough search was made but Rachel, feigning menstruation, sat on her camel's saddle in which she had hid the gods, and did not rise. Finally a truce was declared and the two men gathered up stones and built a pillar as a perpetual witness of their amnesty. They called the pillar Mizpah, or Watchpost, and Laban said, "The Lord watch between you and me, when we are absent one from the other," a prayer intended more as threat than blessing.

Jacob's way led through Edom, which was the country of his brother Esau. Remembering their past, Jacob expected trouble and prepared a lavish present of cattle, camels, goats and asses, sending them ahead to Esau. Still apprehensive, he then sent his wives, children and servants across the Ford of the Jabbok, hopefully to safety, and stayed behind in the chasm of the deep valley. He was afraid and he had to think out his future. If Esau proved strong as well as angry and would not let the caravan pass, what then? He could not turn back to the pointless life of serving Laban. But if he went ahead what would conditions be like in his father's territory? Had it really been the voice of God directing his return? Was he being led, challenged, or betrayed—which? The record says merely: "Jacob was left alone." Sooner or later it happens to everyone and the experience can scarcely be communicated except to those who also have been left alone.

Peniel

The Ford of the Jabbok is located at the bottom of a steep ravine so deep-shaded that the trees and shrubs are tropical. Bright pink oleanders grow luxuriantly. Little hopping, crawling creatures rustle the ground-vines at one's feet. Birds seem muted and muffled; the trees talk; darkness descends in midafternoon. The night must have seemed incredibly lonely to Jacob until he became accustomed to the sudden eerie breezes followed by a moment's breathless silence. Spirits are supposed to inhabit the stream, powerful mysterious river-gods who can bless or curse a man's life. Such a god is said to be able to change form and appear as man, beast, or ghost, and if he appears to a mortal he has to be dealt with. Jacob knew that if any such encounter occurred he would have to prove himself.

What really happened in the depths of the gorge as Jacob sat pondering is clouded by tradition but this much has come down to us: In the night a figure appeared; "a man wrestled with him until the breaking of the day." Man, angel, or demon? An inner fear or an outer adversary? We only know that when dawn came the struggle was not settled and a spirit was said to vanish when daylight touched the depths of the gorge. Jacob was not one to carry an indecisive battle into the new day, so when his adversary demanded, "Let me go, for the day is breaking," Jacob said, "I will not let you go, unless you bless me."

Apparently this grim decision to hang on until he won his blessing was the turning point in Jacob's life. The adversary realized that Jacob had found his courage for the days ahead; he had found *himself*. So the adversary asked his name and then said, "Your name shall no more be called Jacob, but Israel [He who strives with God], for you have striven with God and with men, and have prevailed." And thus he blessed Jacob.

The testing was over. Now Jacob had really come into his birthright. The days of his trickery and double-dealing were past and Jacob the future patriarch faced forward.

So Jacob called the name of the place Peniel, saying, "For I have seen God face to face, and yet my life is preserved." 32:30

Peniel—the face of God! A wonder of that peculiarly transforming sort when a man knows that he has encountered God and forever after ponders how he lived through the revelation.

Here the recorder of the story inserts a less lofty detail. He says that Jacob's thigh was put out of joint in the struggle with the adversary so that he limped afterward, which is the basis of the fact that Israelites do not eat the sinew of an animal's hip. After all, in every culture—including our own—certain folkways have to be accounted for.

Reconciliation

After Jacob's encounter at Peniel even an antagonistic meeting with Esau would probably not have seemed too overwhelming.

had time only to name her son Ben-oni, "son of my sorrow," before she died. Later, Jacob changed the infant's name to Benjamin,
son of the right hand, indicating power and fortune.

> So Rachel died, and she was buried on the way to Ephrath (that is,
> Bethlehem), and Jacob set up a pillar upon her grave; it is the pillar
> of Rachel's tomb, which is there to this day. Israel journeyed
> on. . . . 35:19–21

From this point on the editors use the name Israel for Jacob.

The love story of Jacob and Rachel had ended. Or had it?
There were still Rachel's sons, Joseph and Benjamin. When
Jacob slept at night under the stars, or came suddenly upon something Rachel treasured, she was at hand. How do we know these
things that are not written into the story? We know them because
it was the genius of the authors of this book of beginnings to depict true-to-life characters.

A Summing Up

The demise of a great man is sometimes recorded very simply,
almost like a census report. The record says simply:

> And Jacob came to his father Isaac at Mamre . . . (that is, Hebron),
> where Abraham and Isaac had sojourned. Now the days of Isaac
> were a hundred and eighty years. And Isaac breathed his last; and
> he died and was gathered to his people, old and full of days; and his
> sons Esau and Jacob buried him. 35:27–29

"Full of days"—the way life is lived out.

Here the recorder inserts another genealogy, giving the book
of beginnings a kind of historical authenticity which, although it
cannot be checked, serves to keep the story within a framework
of fact.

Journey into Egypt

Now the story shifts to a new main character: Joseph. Scholars
point to major elements in the story as closely resembling legends
in other cultures, but when has there not been a time that life repeats itself both in character and incident? Moreover, the rags-to-
riches biography is a favorite in every generation. For the editors
who compiled the history some centuries later the problem was to

account for the fact that the Hebrews had gone to Egypt at all.
Why? The biography of Joseph was an answer.

It seems reasonable to place Joseph and the journey of the
Hebrews to Egypt during the time the Hyksos dominated the
Egyptian court, perhaps around 1600 B.C., give or take a century. The Hyksos were themselves of several cultural strains:
some Semites, including 'Ibarus (Hebrews), some Canaanites,
some Hurrians descended from the warrior influx which swept into
the area around 1710 B.C. bringing a powerful new military
weapon, the horse-drawn chariot. By the time of Joseph the chariot
was in common use.

Joseph was the older of Jacob's two sons by his favorite wife,
Rachel. When he was seventeen and shepherding the flocks with
his older brothers he did not like some of their actions and reported them to their father. Naturally, they did not like *his* action.
Moreover, they were jealous of a handsome coat with sleeves
which their father had given him . . . "they hated him, and could
not speak peaceably to him." Matters were not helped when
Joseph told his brothers about a dream he had:

> ". . . behold, we were binding sheaves in the field, and lo, my sheaf
> arose and stood upright; and behold, your sheaves gathered round it,
> and bowed down to my sheaf." 37:7

Nice going if he wanted to be friends with his older brothers: So
his brothers "hated him yet more for his dreams and for his
words," which did not deter Joseph from telling his second
dream, in which the sun, moon and eleven stars bowed down to
him. This time even his father took note.

One day the brothers went off to pasture the family flocks near
Shechem and after a time Jacob sent Joseph to see how they
were getting on. When they saw their father's pet they were
irritated.

> They said to one another, "Here comes this dreamer. Come now, let
> us kill him and throw him into one of the pits; then we shall say that
> a wild beast has devoured him, and we shall see what will become
> of his dreams." 37:19–20

A rugged way to dispose of troublesome dreams. But Reuben
persuaded the other brothers merely to throw Joseph into a

dried-up well after taking off that despised robe. A caravan of
Ishmaelites came along "with their camels bearing gum, balm,
and myrrh, on their way to carry it down to Egypt." The brothers
sold Joseph for twenty shekels of silver—without the coat. They
then dipped the coat in goat's blood and returned to their father
with apparent proof that his favorite son had been killed by wild
animals. Jacob mourned. Nothing and nobody could comfort him.

A Tabloid Tale

At this point when the story is building up first-rate suspense,
the author detours to tell about another of Jacob's sons, named
Judah, who married a Canaanite woman and had three sons,
the first of whom "was wicked in the sight of the Lord; and the
Lord slew him." Jacob sent the second son to marry the
widow according to custom but the second son would not honor
the dead brother by having children for him, so the Lord, displeased, "slew him also." The widow then had to wait for the
third brother to grow up, but Judah had no notion of risking the
life of his youngest son by marrying him to unlucky Tamar. He
sent her home to her own people.

After some years Judah, now a widower himself, went to visit
in the district where Tamar lived. Having heard of his coming,
Tamar waited at the town gate in order to talk to her father-in-
law about marrying that younger son. Seeing a woman wearing a
veil sitting there, Judah took her to be a prostitute and made her
a proposition, promising a kid if she would let him come to her.
No doubt surprised or even shocked—or was she?—wily Tamar
asked for a pledge that the kid really would be forthcoming.
Judah handed over his staff, cord, and signet. So Tamar acceded
to his wishes. Afterward, before he could redeem his personal
property, Tamar again put on the garments of her widowhood.
Three months later someone reported to Judah that his daughter-
in-law Tamar was pregnant. Scandalized, Judah ordered that she
be brought forth and burned according to custom. But Tamar
sent back the staff, signet and cord to her father-in-law in order to
identify the father of her unborn child. "Then Judah acknowledged them and said, 'She is more righteous than I, inasmuch as I
did not give her to my son Shelah.'" Tamar bore twin sons.

And that was the end of the melodramatic tabloid for the sake of which the author suspended the action of his main story about Joseph at the point where he was on the way to Egypt.

Shall the Righteous Prosper?

Joseph had been resold to a captain of Pharaoh's guard named Potiphar. Meanwhile "The Lord was with Joseph, and he became a successful man." Potiphar realized that everything Joseph did prospered. "So he left all that he had in Joseph's charge; and having him he had no concern for anything but the food which he ate." An idyllic life for any landed aristocrat.

"Now Joseph was handsome and good-looking." Enter, the villainess. Day after day Potiphar's wife tried to seduce her husband's trusted superintendent. Finally, one day when all the menservants happened to be out of the house she made a big play, grabbing him by the coattail. "But he left his garment in her hand, and fled and got out of the house." Outraged, the two-timing wife called the servants, reported that her husband's overseer had attacked her, then told the same story to her husband, who forthwith clapped Joseph into jail, "the place where the king's prisoners were confined." Even in prison, however, ability will out and soon Joseph was running the prison for the delighted warden, who realized that "the Lord was with him; and whatever he did, the Lord made it prosper."

Came a day when both the chief butler and the chief baker of the king's household displeased his majesty and were also consigned to prison. One night each of them had a dream; major dreams; disturbing dreams. In prison there was no one to interpret their dreams except Joseph who happened to be a natural psychologist able to understand the pictorial language of the subconscious. The butler's dream portended his restoration to his former position within three days, and Joseph requested that when he had an opportunity he put in a good word with Pharaoh and get Joseph's unjust sentence lifted. The baker's dream, on the other hand, meant that in three days he would have his head cut off. Events proved Joseph's interpretation correct but the butler forgot to mention Joseph to Pharaoh.

Two years went by and Pharaoh himself had a major dream

his servants that the men would dine with him at noon. Probably the servants were not too surprised, for some of the hardy nomad traders were powerful desert chiefs whom it paid to cultivate. The brothers themselves were overwhelmed at the very idea of dining with Egypt's prime minister. However, they brought their gifts and came to dinner. When Joseph saw his brother Benjamin he managed to greet the boy: "God be gracious to you, my son"; then hastily retired to his own chambers to weep. "Then he washed his face and came out; and, controlling himself, he said, 'Let food be served.'"

The author of the story recounts that meal superbly; Joseph eating alone at his table, as befitted his station; the Egyptian officials at their own table, not deigning to mingle with such foreigners; and the table of the brothers to whom Joseph constantly sent choice portions from his own table—"but Benjamin's portion was five times as much as any of theirs. So they drank and were merry with him."

This time when the brothers prepared to return home Joseph ordered that their sacks be filled with grain and food, the money returned as before, but his own silver cup put in Benjamin's sack. The brothers had not gone far before officers from Joseph's household overtook them, accusing them of having stolen Joseph's divining cup. This was no small accusation. Apparently, along with his ability to interpret dreams, Joseph also had the gift of divination, seeing pictures of future events form in a silver cup of water. This was the cup the brothers were accused of making off with. Affirming their innocence they offered their sacks to be searched, insisting that if the cup was found in any man's sack that man should die and the rest of them would become slaves. The cup was found in Benjamin's sack! Back they all went to the city. Still vehemently protesting, they nevertheless offered themselves as slaves to Joseph. But Joseph decreed that he would keep only the one in whose sack the cup had been found. Judah, frantic for his father, became the brothers' spokesman, describing their father's devotion to this boy, "the child of his old age . . . and his father loves him." The description of his father was too much for Joseph. Ordering all the attendants from the room, he made himself known: "I am your brother, Joseph, whom you sold into Egypt."

Their stricken faces were reaction enough. Quickly he begged them not to be distressed. They wept together.

Family Reunion

But this is not a sad story. It is a success story. Joseph sent the brothers home to gather together their families and belongings and return to Egypt. Pharaoh heard what had happened and largess flowed from his royal hand. Joseph's final admonition showed that the family was genuinely back together again, aware of each other's dispositions and predispositions. "Do not quarrel on the way," said Joseph.

Back home, when the entourage arrived in the family court-yard Jacob could not believe his eyes. But when he heard his sons' story he packed with alacrity and headed for Egypt and his now-famous son Joseph. On the way he paused in Beersheba to offer sacrifices to the God of his father Isaac.

> And God spoke to Israel in visions of the night, and said, "Jacob, Jacob." And he said, "Here am I." Then he said, "I am God, the God of your father; do not be afraid to go down to Egypt; for I will there make of you a great nation. I will go down with you to Egypt, and I will also bring you up again; and Joseph's hand shall close your eyes." 46:2–4

A later editor inserted from some ancient record the names of the members of this huge family, ". . . all the persons of the house of Jacob, that came into Egypt, were seventy."

The reunion of the family was tremendous; Pharaoh promptly ordered them to settle "in the best of the land," which happened to be Goshen, near the delta of the Nile (the site of the Hyksos capital) and made them keepers of his own cattle. Then Joseph brought in his old father, whom Pharaoh also welcomed, inquiring solicitously about Jacob's age, which, Jacob assured him, was only 130 years. After that "Jacob blessed Pharaoh," which must have been touching to the monarch, who recognized the dignity of age, the good fortune of many sons, and an enviable kind of simplicity that accrues to one who has lived near the earth.

For the family of Joseph things got better and better in their adopted land. Also Pharaoh's fortunes improved because as the famine worsened Joseph exchanged the monarch's stored grain for the peasants' horses, flocks, herds and asses, and the next year exchanged more grain for title to their land. In fact, Joseph made Pharaoh a multimillion-shekel fortune in land and livestock.

The Art of Dying Well

Seventeen happy years Jacob spent in Egypt; then, at the age of 147, he felt his time had come to die. One of his last acts was to bless Joseph's two sons, Ephraim and Manasseh, and in performing the ceremony he crossed his hands so that his right hand, which according to custom would assure the rights of primogeniture to the older son, actually rested on the head of the younger son. Nor would the stubborn dying man change; Manasseh's descendants would be great, he said, but Ephraim's "descendants shall become a multitude of nations." Then, in a last outburst of affection toward this generous son of his beloved Rachel, he told Joseph, "Moreover I have given to you rather than to your brothers one mountain slope which I took from the hand of the Amorites with my sword and with my bow." After that the second sight which sometimes comes to the dying took over and Jacob prophesied the future and delineated the character of each of his twelve sons. The author concludes,

> All these are the twelve tribes of Israel; and this is what their father said to them as he blessed them, blessing each with the blessing suitable to him. 49:28

How many dying fathers can do as well? Devoted old autocrat, warrior, patriarch that Jacob had become.

After his father's death Joseph wept in the warm Hebrew way and then had his father's body embalmed in the scientific Egyptian way. The funeral entourage was impressive as they set out for Canaan to bury Jacob in the cave in which Abraham and Sarah, Isaac and Rebekah, and Jacob's first wife, Leah, were buried. On the way they lamented and mourned in the Hebrew manner, then finally buried their father as he had directed.

Ultimate Purpose

Once back in Egypt the brothers became apprehensive and went directly to Joseph to ask forgiveness for their original betrayal. Joseph wept, then made a few remarks which sum up the author's purpose in preserving the history of the Hebrews in Egypt.

> But Joseph said to them, "Fear not, for am I in the place of God? As for you, you meant evil against me; but God meant it for good, to bring it about that many people should be kept alive, as they are today. So do not fear; I will provide for you and your little ones." Thus he reassured them and comforted them. 50:19–21

Joseph lived 110 years—which to the Egyptians was the ideal life-span; the Hebrews felt 120 years the desired length of life. His great-grandchildren were around him when he died and his last message to his remaining brothers was that God would be with them to lead them back "to the land which he swore to Abraham, Isaac, and Jacob."

Thus the book we know as Genesis, or "beginnings," comes to an end; enough text to fill out one entire scroll; enough history to assure its readers that God had indeed led his people from the very beginning; enough insight to relate each succeeding generation to its original forebears, who were presented as individuals given to human frailty, sometimes stooping to treachery, but also as a striving people, aware of their destiny, struggling to embody the trustworthiness they felt their God expected of them.

Sources of Genesis

When we read the Bible for encouragement, comfort, correction, we are not much concerned with the writers of the various books, or with the editors who gave the books their final form. But often, as in the book of Genesis, the editorial background adds considerable understanding and explains some of the duplications, even contradictions; for instance, those two accounts of beginnings which differ as to the order of creation because there were two main traditions of the story stemming from different sections of the country. Chapter 2 presents the older account, having been recorded by someone whom the scholars designate as J (Yahwist) because he called God *Yahweh,* meaning "the Lord." (The use of J for the Y sound was of German derivation.) Second, there was E (Elohist) who used the term *Elohim* for God. Third, the source known as P, standing for the priestly redactors who later re-edited and added to the material.

J

J saw God as thinking and acting in very human fashion, *walking* in the garden, *talking* to Adam and Eve, even having to *hunt* for them. J's stories tend to be humorous and given to puns very pointed in Hebrew. He was curious and philosophical, always asking *why* questions: why must women suffer in childbirth, why does man have to work, why did the deluge come about? He used few adjectives and moved quickly from tale to tale, was intrigued by the meaning of names of people and places, and firm about the fact that from the beginning God demanded righteousness but left men free to make decisions. Apparently J lived around the time of Solomon, tenth century B.C. Although we do not even know his name we are enormously indebted to him and when pulpits ring with gratitude for the faith of our fathers Abraham, Isaac and Jacob we might put in a word of thanks for author J, who conserved so many stories.

E

Apparently E lived about a century after J, in Ephraim, the southern district of the Northern Kingdom. E was especially interested in dreams and visions, and in the details of stories such as Joseph's. He emphasized ritual and liked to exhort.

P

Finally there was P, which stands for Priestly. P can best be thought of as chairman of the committee of priestly scholars who lived during, or immediately after, the Exile, when the Hebrews were in Babylonia, in the sixth century B.C. Evidently about that time there was a concerted movement to gather up, edit, and put into solid permanent form the traditions and scattered manuscripts available. To P, genealogy was important as was the support of Hebrew institutions such as the temple in Jerusalem. The Jews always had to struggle heroically to maintain their identity, especially off in Babylon and as a people recently returned to their homeland. So P stressed the covenants God had made with Israel's notable ancestors and argued for strict observance of Mosaic law administered by an orthodox priesthood. P also editorialized, not so much by intruding long commentaries as by slanting the stories to carry a priestly point of view (the way many newspaper editors now effect public opinion).

D

Later there was D, standing for the Deuteronomic editors who revived and revised the laws of Moses and edited or wrote (or some of both) the book of Deuteronomy, probably in the latter half of the seventh century B.C., when the reforms of King Josiah offered a hospitable climate. He (they) also added comments to some of the other books.

With the writers and editors in mind we begin to read the Bible through double lenses, noting both the original stories in the context of their own times and also the problems and points of view of the times in which the final editors lived. The Almighty no doubt takes in both points of view simultaneously and also notes the effect of the record on the conduct of our generation.

Thus Saith the Lord

If so many men of old wrote, revised and edited the word of God, how then can the scriptures be the true unadulterated word of the Lord? There are at least two possible answers. God can be thought of as the all-powerful source who furnished the right word not only in the original languages but through every translation. Or he can be conceptualized as creating human beings with inquiring minds animated by curiosity and quickened by devotion but left free to make choices as to the experiences they felt significant and the words they used. Either way, God no doubt had concepts too big for men's minds at a given stage of growth. With long-range vision he could afford to be patient and wait for his children to catch onto some of his larger ideas. He may even have had to exercise his celestial sense of humor at the sight of writers who thought they were giving the final word. And when considering readers who think they have the final interpretation. His word may be plainer to future generations than it was to the people of Moses' day, or ours. Further revelation will probably come as we live up to what we now understand.

Exodus

A Time of Movement

Since definite dates cannot be given for either Joseph or Moses, it is impossible to say how much time the Hebrews spent in Egypt, but at least two centuries may be a sound guess. The first definite mention of a group of people called *Hibaru,* or a closely related term which may signify the Hebrews, is in the Amarna letters, found in 1887 at Tell-el-Amarna, once the capital city of Pharaoh Akhenaton (Amenhotep IV, d. 1359 B.C.). These letters, some 350 in number, were diplomatic correspondence written in Babylonian cuneiform on clay tablets mostly by city kings of Syria and Palestine reporting on the conditions of their vassalage in the fifteenth and fourteenth centuries. All the Hebrews had not gone to Egypt, of course, and some who remained in Palestine were evidently among the restless peoples reported as threatening the stability of the Egyptian Empire.

These were years of economic as well as political expansion for Egypt. On the African continent trade was brisk with Kush, Nubia and the Sudan, in northern Africa. Hieroglyphic records mention "ships laden with ivory, ebony, and every other beautiful product of the land in addition to the yield of the harvest." Ships from the Somali coast also came "heavily laden with the wonders of Punt—plants, heaps of myrrh, live myrrh trees, ivory, gold, costly woods, incense, eye cosmetics, apes, monkeys, greyhounds, leopard skins, slaves." From Syria and Palestine came soldiers and their upkeep, male and female slaves for building and mining; horses and chariots, great herds of cattle, sheep, goats, elephants and bear, incense, oil, wine, honey, ivory and desirable metals, gold, copper, lead, manufactured vessels, and conifers from Lebanon. Egyptian and Syrian trading vessels cruised the coast of the Mediterranean to Asia Minor and the land of the Hittites, westward to Cyprus and the islands of the Aegean Sea, sometimes as far as Greece. As a medium of exchange rings of gold or sacks of gold dust were commonly used.

Ties of trade were further augmented by the Egyptian custom of carrying off the sons and daughters of conquered kings, leaving the kings themselves on their thrones to administer their states according to Egypt's direction while the younger members of their families were being brought up in the Pharaoh's palace, where, although hostages, they were thoroughly schooled in science, particularly astronomy, in which the Egyptians excelled, and in Egyptian literature and general culture. Then when the king of their native country died they were returned to rule, properly indoctrinated. Often there was also advantageous intermarriage. And not to be ignored was the interchange of language.

But Egyptian dominance was constantly threatened; troops stationed in tribute countries were often unpaid by Egypt and hence turned to plunder. Excavations in Palestinian cities of the Late Bronze Age (1500–1200 B.C., named for the dominance of bronze as a useful metal before the common use of iron) disclose an increasing impoverishment of the native population. Egypt was almost continuously at war. The Phoenicians, an energetic seafaring people, had come—probably from Crete—to settle on the fertile plains of Palestine. There was much movement of population in the whole Mediterranean area. The Hebrew exodus from Egypt was not an exceptional emigration.

Book of Exodus

The book of Exodus is a superb mixture of traditions, legal formulas, hero tales, extrasensory experiences, history and theology. The authors J, E, and P all had a hand in compiling, emending and editing this conglomerate report of the trek of the Hebrew people from Egypt to that thin strip of land along the eastern Mediterranean coast which became known as Palestine. Their purpose was to show what kind of God directed the Hebrew people and called them to account; what kind of people he was willing to make his own, and by means of what experiences and regulations they maintained their solidarity.

A Man for the Hour

More space is devoted to the story of Moses than to any character in the Old Testament. Beginning in the second chapter of Exodus his biography continues through the books of Leviticus, Numbers and Deuteronomy. And yet the central character in this long story is never really Moses, but God. Moses was directed, empowered, punished, restored, companioned by God; no other. Moses also had bred into him the highest qualifications for leadership. As the adopted son of Pharaoh he was well educated; he knew the ruling class intimately and yet was sensitive to the problems of his own people; he was determined, dependable, not afraid of risk, open to inspiration. For conducting an emigration of an entire cultural group, the times had bred a man God could use.

Hard Times

Now there arose a new king over Egypt, who did not know Joseph. And he said to his people, "Behold, the people of Israel are too many and too mighty for us. Come, let us deal shrewdly with them, lest they multiply, and, if war befall us, they join our enemies and fight against us and escape from the land." Therefore they set taskmasters over them to afflict them with heavy burdens; and they built for Pharaoh store cities. 1:8–11

The current Pharaoh was probably Ramesses II (c. 1290 B.C.), who became so concerned about the possibility of losing his Asiatic empire that he moved his new capital to Thebes, which happened to be in the prosperous fertile section of the Nile Delta where the Hebrews had originally settled and continued to prosper. Hence they became increasingly important to him.

Customarily, government buildings were constructed by slaves and through *corvée,* an obligatory service required of certain types of citizens. Pharaoh began to demand more labor of the semi-naturalized Hebrews, then harder labor, then impossible labor. And still the Hebrews flourished. So Pharaoh took extreme measures and ordered the midwives of the area, who were Egyptians, to kill all Hebrew male infants—which the midwives, being humane and neighborly, did not do. The Hebrews went on thriving, so Pharaoh issued an edict that all Hebrew male infants were to be cast into the Nile. The ensuing months were horrible for pregnant Hebrew women, who had to stifle even their wishes for sons and live in dread of their own birth pangs.

In one Hebrew family whose most notable ancestor had been Joseph's brother Levi, a Hebrew mother had a baby boy whom she cradled in a waterproof basket and took down to the river where the reeds were tall, leaving his sister to watch him. One day a group of young ladies of the court, including the royal princess, came to the river to bathe. What happened next is known to multiplied millions, because Moses is an interfaith hero of Jews, Moslems and Christians. And besides, the story of a humbly born hero found by a highborn protector and reared in splendor to become the deliverer of his people is one of the basic hero tales of mankind, a collective myth which dramatizes itself constantly in the form of dreams and reveries as well as in history; boy from log cabin, up from slavery, all the incredible difficulties of the human condition through which a deprived child cannot live—or an oppressed people, or a beleaguered state—but does.

The princess had a whimsey for adopting this unsuspecting infant. He was reared in the palace as one of Pharaoh's sons and received a thorough and probably grueling education, for the Egyptian rulers were not weak or ignorant men. He also learned the ways of the court, heard the discussions of those who were making world history, and realized the position of his people.

The first report of Moses' public life is one of three occasions when he all but ruined his career and certainly defeated his own purposes through anger. One day when he came upon an Egyptian overseer beating a Hebrew workman, he killed the Egyptian and quickly buried him in the sand. But his act had been seen, was reported, and he had to flee the country. When next heard of, he was in Midian, across the Gulf of Aqabah.

This self-banishment was God's opportunity—perhaps his plan —to temper Moses' temper. It could be that God had hoped to use Moses earlier while he still had influence in high places but he had to wait for Moses to get himself in hand. (It could also be that the Lord has plans for some of the rest of us but our lack of discipline holds him back.)

Upon arriving in Midian Moses sat down by a well. Wells were prominent in the lives of his forefathers; so were girls who came to draw water for their flocks. This time it was the seven daughters of the priest of Midian who were helped by Moses. Gallantry came with the clan. Their father Reuel (who is also variously called Hobab or Jethro) invited Moses to his home and in due time gave him his daughter Zipporah for his wife.

A Calling

While Moses was in Midian, the ruler of Egypt died but the bondage of the Israelites became ever more painfully burdensome. Definitely, Moses wanted to do something about the situation.

> Now Moses was keeping the flock of his father-in-law, Jethro. . . . And the angel of the Lord appeared to him in a flame of fire out of the midst of a bush; and he looked, and lo, the bush was burning, yet it was not consumed. . . . God called to him out of the bush, "Moses, Moses!" And he said, "Here am I." Then he said, "Do not come near; put off your shoes from your feet, for the place on which you are standing is holy ground." And he said, "I am the God of your father, the God of Abraham, the God of Isaac, and the God of Jacob." And Moses hid his face, for he was afraid to look at God. 3:1–2, 4–6

God, speaking from a bush? Later historians of Moses' life must have asked themselves what kind of bush could have appeared to Moses to be in flames. There was fraxinella, colloquially called the gas plant because in hot weather its flowers exhale vapor which is spontaneously combustible. There are also phosphorescent plants. And an optical illusion is possible. But debate, even proof, is pointless, because Moses saw a flame which to him represented the spirit of the Most High and he knew that the place where he stood was holy. The God of his fathers was, incredibly, speaking to *him!* The divine mysterium, fearful, reassuring, transforming.

God explained his intention to deliver the Hebrew people from their present oppression and bring them "to a good and broad land, a land flowing with milk and honey. . . . Come, I will send you to Pharaoh that you may bring forth my people . . ."

Who? Me? Who am I? We all ask the same questions.

"But I will be with you," God promised. Then he gave Moses a "sign," an assurance, that when he had brought the Hebrews forth he should again serve God on that very mountain. This "sign" is one of the most authentic elements in the story. There sometimes comes to an individual facing tremendous difficulty—a battle, a deed of courage, a surgical operation, an impossible expedition—a moment when he knows that his undertaking will be successful. Perhaps the knowledgeable unconscious, which spans so much more time than the immediate instant, "sees" the outcome; at least the outcome is inwardly affirmed. This is a widespread human experience, always authoritative to the individual; but it does not always happen when hoped for, even though the undertaking may eventuate in success. When Moses received that peculiar inner assurance he knew this trip of his was about to transpire.

But he still did not see how to proceed. The Hebrews, suffering although they might be, would want to know where this order to leave Egypt came from. From some foreign ruler? From a god? "God said to Moses . . . 'Say this to the people of Israel, "I AM has sent me to you."'" I AM—that Hebrew verb of being, written without vowels—can be translated in nine different forms and tenses but they all add up to "The One Who Is." And how could God, who is undefinable, be better defined? If the human heart cannot respond to I AM, then we cannot know.

The next scene is an interlude of magic. God turning a rod into a snake in order to impress Moses and then showing Moses how to effect the same trick in order to impress Pharaoh. Later editors might call this episode hypnotic influence or an interpolation by a later hand. The record simply states that the rod was turned into a serpent, the serpent back into a rod, that Moses' hand was made leprous, then instantly made clean. The point of the incident was that God made Moses feel his support. Nevertheless, Moses still felt shaky. "Oh, my Lord, I am not eloquent . . . I am slow of speech and tongue. . . . Oh, my Lord, send, I pray, some other person." Such an agonized human cry!

But God had had enough of this self-doubt. Would he—God!— be sending Moses on an errand he could not perform? Moses could take his brother Aaron, who was eloquent. So Moses accepted the commission, went back to Jethro for his blessing, took his wife, his sons and the rod of God and headed for Egypt. According to his historian he was then eighty years old, which is just the right age to have learned a few things about life and to set forth on a great adventure for God. Obviously he must have kept himself in good health so that the Lord had something to use.

Up from Slavery

Once back in Egypt, Moses and Aaron between them persuaded the Hebrew people that "the Lord had visited the people of Israel and that he had seen their affliction," which was naturally a tremendous inspiration—to be remembered by God!—and "they bowed their heads and worshiped."

Then began the tug of war with Pharaoh. He laid even heavier burdens on them, until they were required to supply their own straw for brick making without reducing their production. When things reached a deadlock, the Hebrews unable to produce more bricks and Pharaoh unwilling to lighten their load, Moses himself became completely frustrated: "Why didst thou ever send me?"

God knew why! He had sent Moses to bring forth the Hebrew people!

And at this exciting impasse, editor P, living some centuries later, inserted into the record as documentary evidence the genealogy of "the heads of their fathers' houses." Then the narrative takes over again.

When persuasion failed with Pharaoh, Moses and Aaron performed their rod-to-serpent miracle but Pharaoh called his own magicians and they did the same trick, which was embarrassing, except that Aaron's rod finally swallowed up their rods. So then God made a major move; he instructed Aaron to strike the waters of the river Nile and turn the river into blood so that the fish would die. Exactly what happened to redden and foul the water has also long been debated. Algae sometimes turn Egyptian waters to a brownish red; red deposits also wash down from the Abyssinian lakes; but explanations are less important than the fact that the most threatening act of God could not change Pharaoh's mind. Plague followed plague. The fish in the Nile having been killed by the contaminated water, hundreds of thousands of frogs appeared and hopped even into ovens and kneading bowls. After the frogs came plagues of gnats and flies, followed by an epidemic of cattle pests and of boils. Then storms: ". . . thunder and hail, and fire ran down to the earth. . . . Only in the land of Goshen, where the people of Israel were, there was no hail." Finally Pharaoh had enough of these national calamities; he would let the Hebrew people go. But when the hail ceased he changed his mind.

Then came the plague of locusts, blown in by an east wind, and when Pharaoh appeared to relent, blown out again by a west wind. The ninth plague was "darkness over the land of Egypt, a darkness to be felt," a devastating experience because the khamsin, or hot wind from the desert, can carry so much sand and dust that breathing becomes difficult. Each time a plague lifted, Pharaoh changed his mind about letting these still useful Hebrews leave Egypt. So the Lord had a final show of strength for this stubborn Pharaoh who believed that his property rights in those Hebrews were paramount over their human right of self-determination. He declared that if Pharaoh did not relent, then on a designated night he himself, the Lord, would pass over Egypt dealing out death. The Hebrews must mark their own dwellings by sprinkling the blood of a sacrificed lamb on their doorposts so that the Lord would pass by. Then they should roast the meat and eat it with unleavened bread and bitter herbs, but they must eat with their robes tucked up under their belts, ready to march forth. Also their sandals must be on their feet instead of waiting by the door, and their staffs must be in hand so that they could start quickly once Pharaoh gave permission. Alert anticipation, preparedness, and faith—the ingredients for a great migration. "This day shall be for you a memorial day, and you shall keep it as a feast to the Lord; throughout your generations you shall observe it as an ordinance forever."

Through the years, traditions of still earlier Hebrew festivals became incorporated into the Passover meal, including the feast of unleavened bread, originally a feast of the barley harvest; and the dedication of the first-born to God, an ancient act of devotion to insure fertility. The place of eating the Passover meal also shifted from the home to the temple in Jerusalem as long as the temple stood. But the primary commemoration remained the Lord's intervention to release the Hebrew people and lead them forth into a future of his planning.

Events moved as the Lord had promised. "At midnight the Lord smote all the first-born in the land of Egypt . . . and there was a great cry in Egypt," so that by dawn the mourning Egyptians "were urgent with the people, to send them out of the land in haste." The Hebrews went forth so quickly that the dough for their bread was not yet risen. Along with their unleavened bread they also carried a quantity of Egyptian "jewelry of silver and of gold, and clothing" which they had asked of their neighbors according to the Lord's direction. How provident to start on a long uncertain trek with plenty of good negotiable gold and silver; it must have comforted them for the unleavened bread. They went empowered by the memory of that terrific night when the Lord had proved himself the arbiter of circumstance for the ordering of his purposes. An event had occurred in history so mighty in its binding power of the people to each other and to God that the occasion called Passover has been faithfully celebrated for more than three thousand years.

A Troubled Way

The first major roadblock met by this conglomerate group of émigrés was a large body of water called in Hebrew "the Sea of Reeds," perhaps a shallow arm of the Gulf of Suez. Just when such an expanse of water should have barred their continuing flight, and at the very time when the pursuing Egyptians were rapidly approaching, an east wind blew the waters back—a phenomenon which occasionally happens to shallow bodies of water—and the Hebrews passed safely to the farther shore. Then when the Egyptians in their heavy chariots drove onto the still-wet seabed, "The waters returned and covered the chariots and the

horsemen and all the host of Pharaoh. . . . Thus the Lord saved
Israel that day from the hand of the Egyptians." Whether the
miracle lay in the disruption of natural law in their behalf or in
the timing of a natural event, the Hebrews knew they had been
led by their God and they were awed into renewed consecration.

An ancient poem is recorded, sung by Moses and the people of
Israel with a refrain sung by Moses' sister and the women dancing
to the accompaniment of timbrels:

> I will sing to the Lord, for he has triumphed gloriously;
>   the horse and his rider he has thrown into the sea.
> The Lord is my strength and my song,
>   and he has become my salvation;
> this is my God, and I will praise him,
>   my father's God, and I will exalt him.
> The Lord is a man of war;
>   the Lord is his name. . . .
> Thou hast led in thy steadfast love
>   the people whom thou hast redeemed,
> thou hast guided them by thy strength to thy holy abode. 15:1–3, 13

After that great deliverance and celebration, the trek proved
difficult. Where then was the hand of the Lord?

> And the whole congregation of the people of Israel murmured
> against Moses and Aaron . . . "Would that we had died by the hand
> of the Lord in the land of Egypt, when we sat by the fleshpots and
> ate bread to the full; for you have brought us out into this wilder-
> ness to kill this whole assembly with hunger." 15:2–3

The answer was manna and quail. Manna, a sticky substance
exuded by small insects which live on the resinous secretion of
the tamarisk trees; "it was like wafers made with honey." Quails
"came up and covered the camp"; migrating birds which cannot
fly great distances without rest, dropping exhausted to the ground
in the evening. Was the need of the Hebrews apparent to the
mind of God millenniums before the trek, back when both tamarisk trees and quails were in process of evolution? Modern
readers may speak of fortuitous circumstance, but the Hebrews
simply knew that God had provided according to his promise.

They were now nomads, with a new life-style which included

few comforts. At Rephidim, in a desert section, "there was no water for the people to drink." They promptly "found fault with Moses"; it was he who had got them into this situation with his big promises. In answer to their need Moses struck a rock and water gushed forth. Next they had to fight the Amalekites. Led by Joshua but directed by the uplifted hands of Moses as he stood atop a hill, the Israelites prevailed.

A Helpful In-Law

Back in Midian, Moses' father-in-law, Jethro, heard "all that God had done for Moses and for Israel his people" and he decided it was time to go see his son-in-law, taking Moses' wife and two sons with him. After due feasting, Jethro sized up Moses' schedule, judging the people "from morning till evening," listening to all complaints, mapping strategy. So he offered some common-sense advice to his famous son-in-law. Moses had better appoint some deputies who could take care of all routine matters, with only the weightier affairs accruing to him. "If you do this . . . then you will be able to endure." Moses knew good advice when he heard it, which made him as shrewd as Jethro. Then Jethro made a second brilliant move: he went home. Having got his advice across, he did not stay to keep calling attention to the fact that the reformed judiciary was his idea.

The Record: Multiple Entries

The setting for the next section of the book of Exodus is Mount Sinai, probably a volcanic mountain against the base of which the Hebrews encamped. This was the scene of their daily life from the first verse of chapter 19 through the rest of the book of Exodus and the entire book of Leviticus until they broke camp to move on in Numbers 10:11 ff. It is impossible to draw up a consistent time sequence for the sojourn at Sinai, or for that matter for the whole journey through the wilderness, because various recollections are woven together. From chapter 20 on, the account is largely of legislation outlining what the Hebrews had to do in order to continue in acceptable relationship to God. To skim the pages too rapidly (or skip them altogether) is like trying to catch a nation's heartbeat without noting that the heart is conditioned by a body.

Holy, Holy Lord God Almighty

The Lord was felt to dwell uniquely on Mount Sinai. That he was one and was everywhere did not mitigate his being particularly present on the mountaintop. Just as today many people feel an immediacy in his presence in temple or church where a congregation habitually gathers to worship him, so did that early congregation of Israel turn in awe toward the mountaintop. And it was there that Moses received God's first message to his migrating people—a tender reminder of his care.

> You have seen what I did to the Egyptians, and how I bore you on eagles' wings and brought you to myself. Now therefore, if you will obey my voice and keep my covenant, you shall be my own possession among all peoples; for all the earth is mine, and you shall be to me a kingdom of priests and a holy nation. 19:4–6

Returning from the mountaintop to the people, Moses relayed the communication. "And all the people answered together and said, 'All that the Lord has spoken we will do.'" So then the Lord instructed Moses to prepare the people for a further message three days later.

> On the morning of the third day there were thunders and lightnings, and a thick cloud upon the mountain, and a very loud trumpet blast, so that all the people who were in the camp trembled. Then Moses brought the people out of the camp to meet God; and they took their stand at the foot of the mountain. 19:16–17

Moses himself ascended to the mountaintop, which was "wrapped in smoke, because the Lord descended upon it in fire." An awesome scene. When Moses returned he had a set of commandments known to succeeding generations as the Decalogue, or the Ten Commandments: prohibition of other gods, of graven images, of taking the name of the Lord in vain, of labor on the Sabbath; an admonition to honor parents; commandments not to kill, steal, commit adultery, bear false witness, or covet a neighbor's property. Later the commandments were elaborated by a long list of ordinances governing the transactions of daily life, with punishment for infringement. The code, both moral and legal, was reported to the people. Under the influence of the mountain's pyrotechnics and the presence of the Lord, the people were caught up in a holy moment of dedication and vowed to remain law-abiding.

Again God ordered Moses to the top of the mountain, where "the glory of the Lord was like a devouring fire." This time he stayed forty days while God gave him detailed instructions for the construction of a sanctuary in which he, God, might dwell in the midst of his people. First, an ark should be built, boxlike, in modern terms approximately two by two by four feet, made of acacia wood overlaid with pure gold; its lid should form the mercy seat, with cherubim of gold at each end, their wings overshadowing it, and from between the cherubim the Lord himself would speak. There must also be a table overlaid with gold on which "the bread of the Presence" should be set; a lampstand with lamps, all pure gold. This central space where the ark rested should be the holiest place, which only the high priest might enter. Around it must be curtains "of fine twined linen and blue and purple and scarlet stuff," embroidered. Just outside the holiest place an altar of bronze would serve for burnt offerings; then a court where people could come to bring their offerings at the appointed time. Over all a tent must be erected, in modern terms 45 by 45 by 15 feet, made of goats' hair. (Probably of reddened ramskins like the ancient Arabic tent-shrines.)

Aaron as high priest with his sons as assistants must preside dressed in elaborate raiment; Aaron's "breastpiece of judgment" was of "gold, blue and purple and scarlet stuff" set with sardius, topaz, carbuncle, emerald, sapphire, diamond, jacinth, agate, amethyst, beryl, onyx, jasper; and "they shall be set in gold filigree."

In chapter 28 two new factors come to attention, two which figure in several crucial scenes in the Old Testament: Urim and Thummim. They were sacred lots customarily cast by a priest when the judgment of the Lord was sought. No one knows today whether they were flat stones, probably etched with symbols, or pieces made of metal, or carved bone. It seems probable from the context that they operated on the heads-and-tails principle and that when two obverse sides bearing the dominant symbol came

up they signified that the time was propitious to proceed with the
project under consideration, while two reverse symbols signified a
direct prohibition, and one obverse with one reverse symbol meant
the question should be refined and further direction sought. The
lots were not to be used lightly and, as a matter of fact, not every
priest could use them effectively. This first reference to Urim and
Thummim directs that they be worn in the breastplate of judgment which was a part of Aaron's vesture, "and they shall be
upon Aaron's heart, when he goes in before the Lord."

Sacrifices were carefully delineated; also "a fourth of a hin of
wine for a libation"; an altar "to burn incense upon" to be made
of acacia wood overlaid with gold; incense to be made of "sweet
spices, stacte, and onycha, and galbanum, sweet spices with pure
frankincense." All in all, there was work enough for all the
weavers, needlewomen, silver- and goldsmiths, carpenters and
other fine craftsmen, pharmacists and perfumers for years. The
God who expected to dwell in that temple was not only holy but
he set incredibly high standards of workmanship, decreeing ac-
couterments so beautiful that no craftsman could resist making
them, and ceremonies so elaborate that both priests and people
would have to put their hearts into their worship in order to fulfill
its demands. Then he ordered a census taken, with every man
"twenty years old and upward" giving an offering, thus underwriting the entire project.

> And the Lord said to Moses, "Say to the people of Israel, 'You
> shall keep my sabbaths, for this is a sign between me and you
> throughout your generations, that you may know that I, the Lord,
> sanctify you. . . . . Six days shall work be done, but the seventh day is
> a sabbath of solemn rest, holy to the Lord; whoever does any work
> on the sabbath day shall be put to death.' " 31:12–13, 15

He did not list exceptions.

> And he gave to Moses, when he had made an end of speaking with
> him upon Mount Sinai, the two tables of the testimony, tables of
> stone, written with the finger of God. 31:18

Test and Failure

Moses may have expected the people to be waiting eagerly for
his return from the mountain with the Lord's set of directions.

They were not. Early in his stay on the mountain they had complained to Aaron that no one knew what might have become of Moses up there in the clouds with Yahweh. They wanted gods they could see. "Up, make us gods, who shall go before us. . . ." Perhaps Aaron was tired of being number two man. He took the leadership upon himself, called for all the gold ornaments, melted them down and fashioned a golden calf such as people in neighboring nations worshiped. It seemed natural to nomadic people of that era and area to have a god objectified in an image which in some unexplained way known only to gods, was connected with the fertility of herds and flocks. The figure of the bull stood in their minds for prosperity, fecundity, good fortune.

Pointing to the impressive golden calf which gleamed in the morning sunshine, Aaron said, "These are your gods, O Israel, who brought you up out of the land of Egypt." The people prepared a feast with hilarious celebration.

When Moses came down from the mountain he was joined by Joshua, who had been waiting on a lower slope, and then proceeded to the scene of revelry. When they took in what was going on, "Moses' anger burned hot." He threw down the tables of stone he had brought from the mountain and "broke them at the foot of the mountain." Then he had the golden calf melted down, ground to powder and scattered upon the water which the people were forced to drink. The plague followed shortly.

Surveying the sorry scene, Moses stood at the gate of the camp and said, "Who is on the Lord's side?" The sons of Levi answered and Moses sent them into the crowd to slay all unrepentant apostates, "and there fell of the people that day about three thousand men." It was a sad, altogether human tragedy for people who intended to be true to their calling but lacked the final stamina. Infinitely sad for Moses too, but he returned to God and pleaded with him to forgive his people's sins; "if not, blot me, I pray thee, out of the book which thou hast written." Plainly Moses cared about his people's welfare, and his demonstrating his feeling may have been his best way of interpreting God to them.

As proof of the restoration of the people to favor, the Lord again called Moses to the mountain where he rewrote his message on two tablets of stone.

When Moses came down from Mount Sinai, with the two tables of the testimony in his hand . . . Moses did not know that the skin of his face shone because he had been talking with God. 34:29

The book of Exodus closes with a detailed description of the building and furnishing of the tabernacle. "Thus did Moses; according to all that the Lord commanded him, so he did." The very fact that he could carry out so difficult an assignment must have given him a sense of renewed adequacy for the remainder of the journey.

Day by day Moses went to the tent of meeting to consult with the Lord.

And when all the people saw the pillar of cloud standing at the door of the tent, all the people would rise up and worship. . . . Thus the Lord used to speak to Moses face to face, as a man speaks to his friend. 33:10–11

From then on the cloud covered the tent when the Lord was present in the holy place, but "whenever the cloud was taken up from over the tabernacle, the people of Israel would go onward."

Leviticus

When we want help and encouragement, something to live by in a religious sense, we are not inclined to hunt up a codification of civil and military law, or the parliamentary procedures of ecclesiastical bodies. Not even if we have an ancestor who signed the Magna Charta. On the other hand, if we want to understand the life of a given cultural group at a certain time in its history, an appraisal of the laws under which the group lived is enlightening. Thus the book of Leviticus is not so much a source of spiritual inspiration as a reflection of Hebrew life as conditioned by Hebrew law at the time of Moses. Actually the laws cover a longer period than the lifetime of Moses, when they were said to have been promulgated, because the compilers of the book, editing in Babylon in the last half of the sixth century B.C., credited to Moses certain agricultural laws, among others, which would have been inappropriate in Moses' period. Apparently they felt that if a law was old and still operating it must have stemmed from the great lawgiver. Anyone who wants to understand the Hebrew people as they grew into nationhood can profitably plow through Leviticus. The terrain may be rough at times but it is not without interest, even glimpses of beauty.

As would be expected, Hebrew law was influenced by the basic laws of the great empires of which the Hebrew people were often a part. It was not so much a matter of borrowing as of dealing with the same problems. The common law upon which ancient codes were based was derived from common experience. Most significant behind Hebrew law was the Code of Hammurabi, greatest king of the first Babylonian Empire (c. 1750 B.C.) who had gathered up the already existing laws and accepted procedures of a widespread area and restated them, adding penalties. This expanded code established regulations for all classes of society, including farmers, merchants, sailors, builders, day laborers, inn-keepers, government agents, judges, prisoners; both slaves and free men. The law even determined the pay of physicians and veterinarians with penalties for overcharge. Moses had precedent for the scope of his laws. In 1902 a fragment of a stele inscribed with 247 of Hammurabi's laws was discovered at Susa, ancient capital of Elam, at the head of the Persian Gulf, where it had been brought as a trophy from the city of Sippar, near Bagdad, on the Euphrates. Moses must have known of this Babylonian code when he was an intimate at the court of Pharaoh. He must have been familiar with the heavy penalties it exacted—an eye for an eye, broken bone for broken bone.

There was, however, one important difference between the two lawgivers, Hammurabi and Moses. Although Hammurabi was a religious man who dedicated his code to righteousness and en-lightenment under the over-all beneficence of Marduk, chief god of Babylonia, he felt himself to be the instigator of the laws; they were definitely the king's pronouncements. Moses, on the other hand, considered Israel's laws to be direct commands from Yah-weh, while he himself was merely the intermediary through whom they were transmitted.

The Voice of God

"Thus saith the Lord." Sometimes Yahweh was reported to speak in a thunderous voice from the mountaintop, the meaning clear only to the ear of Moses. Sometimes he spoke in the still small voice of inner judgment, made plain to Moses as he sat in his tent. Sometimes, through the concerted judgment of the elders as they waited for the Lord's instruction. However the law was disclosed, the Hebrew people knew it was God who was making his will known.

Alongside laws and their penalties, the Lord also prescribed sacrifices and offerings as a means of restoring the lawbreaker to wholeness. Acknowledgment of sin and ensuing sacrifice acted as a religious gyroscope to maintain equilibrium so that the people could not fail beyond redemption. Any people which succumbs to its failures and is ridden by guilt loses its forward motion. The Hebrews moved forward.

Acts of Devotion

The first seven chapters of Leviticus deal with the offerings to be made by persons who had broken a law. The offerings were designed to cost something so that the lawbreaker was undeniably involved in his act of restitution. First he identified with his sacrificial animal by laying his hands on its head before turning it over to the priest for killing. Rituals varied with the nature of the offering, whether animals, birds, cereals, oils, frankincense, unleavened cakes, first fruits, or salt. No offerings of honey or leavened bread were allowed, because they could ferment. And definitely, "All fat is the Lord's."

There were various categories of offerings: A peace offering could be made along with a covenant meal; which meant that the main portion of the animal was roasted and fed to the people. In the mystical fashion of shared food, the meat thus became a bond. A sin offering followed a man's repentance for a taboo which he or a member of his family had unknowingly broken, thus shattering the perfect relationship of the people to their God and leaving the whole community less than it had been before the unintended defection of one member. A guilt offering was required from anyone who had knowingly sinned against man or God. For instance, a man who "has found what was lost and lied about it" was required to "restore it in full, and shall add a fifth to it," after which his guilt offering was acceptable. People-to-people relationships were under God's constant scrutiny. "The Lord said to Moses, 'If any one sins and commits a breach of faith against the Lord by deceiving his neighbor . . .'"; thus even though a sin appeared to implicate only another human being, the broken bond was with the Lord.

The Priests

Special commands to priests emphasized their set-apartness. Detailed directions were given to Aaron, the high priest, and to his sons. Priests were definitely dedicated to the service of the altar, which symbolized God's perpetual covenant. "Fire shall be kept burning upon the altar continually; it shall not go out." Priests were decreed holy by means of their office, and since they ate their portion of the offerings in the holy place they were considered in a state of ritual purity so that anyone who touched them "caught holiness" and since holiness was thus transferable the one who contracted it needed to cleanse himself in order not to pass on to another an undeserved blessing with dire consequences. Holiness could be scoured off a bronze vessel but an earthware pot had to be broken because, being porous, it could hold the infection of holiness. All phases of the priestly life were likewise carefully coded and summarized.

> This is the law of the burnt offering, of the cereal offering, of the sin offering, of the guilt offering, of the consecration, and of the peace offerings, which the Lord commanded Moses on Mount Sinai, on the day that he commanded the people of Israel to bring their offerings to the Lord, in the wilderness of Sinai. 7:37–38

Chapters 8 through 10 deal with the consecration of priests to their office. Since it was they who judged, corrected, disciplined, and encouraged the people it was necessary for them to have their ritual procedures carefully detailed. As in other early cultures uprightness leaned hard on ritual and every detail of a given ritual had meaning. Even numbers carried individual significance, especially the number seven, which recurs frequently.

Customarily when the whole congregation assembled for worship Aaron made atonement for himself and his sons, then for the people, "and the glory of the Lord appeared to all the people. And fire came forth from before the Lord and consumed the burnt offering and the fat upon the altar; and when all the people saw it, they shouted, and fell on their faces."

All penalties were rigid. When Aaron's sons Nadab and Abihu overplayed their roles "and offered unholy fire before the Lord" —possibly feeding the fire too much fat too fast—they themselves caught fire and were burned to death. Their brothers were ordered to carry their bodies out of the camp and the Lord allowed no mourning for them since they had defied his rigid rules.

Diet and Health

The third section of Leviticus, chapters 11 to 15, deals with the distinction between clean and unclean; in other words with sanitation, disease and health; and also with rules for restoration so that an individual made unclean by disease could go through a given ceremony and be accounted clean again. The responsibility for the health of the people fell upon the priests for at least three good reasons: they spoke with divine authority, they were the educated sector of society, and by profession they were dedicated to the good of the people. Dietary laws came first. Animal food: "Whatever parts the hoof and is cloven-footed and chews the cud . . . you may eat." Certain other animals, such as the camel, rock badger, hare and swine, should not be eaten. "Everything in the water that has fins and scales" was edible. A fascinating list of birds could not be eaten. Even the winged insects, "the swarming things," had their register of the unclean. Why? Some creatures may have carried parasites; some may have been highly useful and if killed without restriction might have disappeared. Perhaps a primitive people knew more than we think about ecological balance; and even about the needs of the human body in that climate.

Taboos were decreed regarding a woman's menstrual period and regulations for the delivery of babies, but when scheduled sacrifices were demanded allowance was made for practicalities. "And if she cannot afford a lamb," a lesser offering was acceptable. Stringent rules covered the treatment of various diseases, including the itch. Some of the prescribed procedures sound strange, even superstitious, in our day, but strict regulations seem to have been necessary for the well-being of this nation on trek.

A Day of Atonement

Chapter 16, which makes up the fourth section of the book, outlines the ceremony for the Day of Atonement. Perhaps no chapter in the Pentateuch more plainly defines the position of God in the midst of his people. He was considered *there,* all-knowing, invincibly just, undeviatingly demanding, and approachable only by means of elaborate ritual. Once a year, a day was set apart for

making amends for corporate shortcomings. A day of expiation.
For the ritual of atonement Aaron as high priest was instructed to
go into the holy place "within the wall," later called the holy of
holies, where the ark of the covenant was housed, and within the
ark the Decalogue, on tablets of stone. Above the ark was the
cloud of incense which shrouded the living presence of God. Aaron
must first make a sin offering for himself. Let no one, not even the
high priest, imagine himself to be without sin.

The Scapegoat

When it came to the general sin offering which would cleanse
and re-establish the whole people, two goats were necessary.
Lots were cast to determine which goat would be presented to the
Lord in sacrifice and which would bear the people's sins far, far
from them. Aaron first slaughtered the sacrificial goat, then put
his hands on the live goat to "confess over him all the iniquities
of the people of Israel . . . and send him away into the wilderness by the hand of a man who is in readiness," to Azael, a desert
demon or pervading evil spirit whose place of abode was said to
be the rough boulder-filled terrain where no man dwelt. After the
ceremony of the scapegoat the people felt reinstated in God's
good graces. Their sins were taken away. They had their new
start, their clean page.

> "And this shall be an everlasting statute for you, that atonement may
> be made for the people of Israel once in the year because of all their
> sins." And Moses did as the Lord commanded him. 16:34

And so it is to this day for practicing Jews. To be sure, the
sacrificial animals have disappeared, the scapegoat no longer
plays his part, the priests have given way to rabbis who perform
less-elaborate rituals, but the people still pray the earnest prayers
of atonement. So strong is the binding power of a ritual hundreds
of years old that no matter how attenuated the modern ritual
has become, Jews who never get to temple any other day of the
year turn up on the Day of Atonement—in just about the same
way that Easter Christians go to church. Whether Jew or Christian,
the personal involvement can be slight or emotionally devastating
for once-a-year participants. After the annual deference to God

and custom everybody feels good for days, restored to the ancestors, more closely related to those who revere the same religious
symbols, and dedicated—vaguely or acutely—to the purposes of
God.

Laws for a Dedicated People

Laws which apply to the life of Israel as a holy and dedicated
people form the fifth division of the book (chapters 17 to 26). A
strong point is made that sacrifices are to be offered to God
alone, and in the temple. There was no substitute for the gathering of the faithful in one mind and spirit in the place set apart
for the purpose of worship.

Regulations were prolific; a holy people must avoid the ex-
cesses and irregularities of other peoples. If cultic requirements
and ethical obligations seem equally important, it is because the
cult practices helped to guarantee the ethical conduct. In summary,
"You shall be holy; for I the Lord your God am holy."

In chapter 19 a new dimension of psychological perception is
stressed. "You shall not hate your brother in your heart"; the
inward intention becomes also the Lord's concern. ". . . but you
shall love your neighbor as yourself." At first sight this appears to
be a very early statement of the admonition we know as the Golden
Rule but in this case the neighbor was definitely taken to be a
member of the same cult, a fellow clansman. The same verse cau-
tions, "You shall not take vengeance or bear any grudge against
the sons of your own people."

Sometimes to a modern eye, sense and nonsense seem equally
stressed: "You shall not practice augury or witchcraft. . . . You
shall not round off the hair on your temples or mar the edges of
your beard." The poor deserved special protection; a field should
not be reaped to its border and gleanings must be left for the
stranger. Not only the people but the land "shall keep a sabbath
to the Lord," stressing the divine ownership of the land, which
the people tilled in stewardship. No Israelite could sell himself
into slavery but he might buy non-Israelite slaves, since they were
not members of the covenanting group. For crimes considered
weighty, the death penalty was decreed.

The fiftieth year was decreed to be a year of jubilee announced by the blowing of trumpets on the Day of Atonement, a year when everyone went back to his ancestral holdings, when new leases were to be made. There is no record, however, that the year of jubilee was ever made effective in the prescribed terms.

God's Vengeance

In summation of the law the threat of God's vengeance was strong and direful. In the Lord's own words, if the people did not obey "but walk contrary to me, then I will walk contrary to you in fury, and chastise you myself sevenfold for your sins. You shall eat the flesh of your sons. . . . I will lay your cities waste. . . . And I will devastate the land. . . . And you shall perish among the nations." On the contrary, if the people listen and obey, "then I will remember my covenant with Jacob."

Finally the last chapter of the book, an appendix dealing with religious vows, elucidates certain questions which had apparently arisen over such matters as the privilege of an individual once pledged to the Lord's service to buy back his vow. A tithe of land, seeds and animals is reaffirmed, one tenth belonging to the Lord.

These are the commandments which the Lord commanded for the people of Israel on Mount Sinai. 27:34

Numbers

The fourth book of the Pentateuch takes its English name, Numbers, from the numbering of the people while on their journey from Egypt to the Promised Land, but the Hebrew title, The Wilderness, is more apt. However, the wilderness was not a forest, as the English word suggests, but primarily a wasteland, sometimes a desert, sometimes craggy boulder-filled stretches of rough terrain with oases at intervals.

There are three main characters in the story: God, Moses, and the people, with the narrative told in the third person. The same redactors who contributed to the earlier books—primarily J, E, D, and P—edited this book, with the priestly contributors furnishing some three fourths of the material. Since they wrote a long time after the events recorded they unavoidably interpreted incidents in the light of their own experience and emphasized what they felt to be the purposes of God. Discrepancies with known historical fact are relatively unimportant, since the authors were primarily interested in the manner and reasons for God's discipline of his people. They do a great deal more for history than fill in facts; they bring to life real people behind the facts.

The Census

The book opens with a census taken by tribes, meaning the twelve divisions of Israel, named for the sons of Jacob. The report notes that the census was ordered by the Lord; to have numbered the people without a direct order from the Lord would have been a presumption with dire consequences, as David later discovered. Descendants of Levi, being priests, were counted a separate class not subject to military conscription, so the descendants of Joseph's older son, Manasseh, were appointed to substitute for the Levites, while Joseph's tribe was represented by the descendants of his younger son, Ephraim, whom Jacob had specially designated to succeed Joseph. Every male above twenty years was counted and the total came to some 603,550 males, which would indicate a population somewhere around two and a half million. Obviously the terrain could never have supported anything like that number of people but the discrepancy has a logical explanation in that the count was made by numbers of military units and the word signifying a military unit was understood by the later editors to indicate their own kind of military unit made up of a thousand men, while in Moses' day the military unit was much smaller. Thus modern scholars are sometimes able to clarify what appear to be incredible misstatements which non-believers used to quote in order to discredit Holy Writ. The point the writers were making with their statistics was that the Lord had marvelously blessed his people during their hard years in the Wilderness.

In order to take the census the tribes lined up in assigned places on the four sides of the camp square, much like a New England town square. Inside the square stood the tent housing the ark of the covenant, signifying the presence of Yahweh. Each tribe had its standard after the fashion of present-day desert nomads. "The people of Israel shall encamp each by his own standard, with the ensigns of their fathers' houses. . . ." Tradition holds that the colors of the standards corresponded to the twelve precious stones set in the breastplate worn by the high priest. Each tribe also had its emblem. For instance, Judah's emblem was the lion on a sky-blue banner and the tribal stone was the emerald. At the time of the census, marching order was also designated so that the ark of the covenant was at all times securely guarded.

Complaint

When the people of Israel moved on, they often found the going rough. Being human, they complained, which provoked the Lord: should it not be enough that he was leading them? Occasionally "his anger was kindled, and the fire of the Lord burned

among them, and consumed some outlying parts of the camp."
Then the people repented, Moses prayed for their pardon "and
the fire abated." But once forgiven they grumbled again, particularly about the manna, which earlier had seemed a lifesaving gift
from heaven. Such a plaintive homesick complaint:

> Now the rabble that was among them had a strong craving; and
> the people of Israel also wept again, and said, "O that we had meat
> to eat! We remember the fish we ate in Egypt for nothing, the cu-
> cumbers, the melons, the leeks, the onions, and the garlic; but now
> our strength is dried up, and there is nothing at all but this manna to
> look at." 11:4–6

Moses listened to them; no doubt he could have done with a
bit of meat also. He understood the Lord's anger but he also
understood the people's discontent and felt caught between the
two. How was he ever going to carry so heavy a burden as this
dissatisfied throng?

> Moses said to the Lord, "Why hast thou dealt ill with thy servant?
> And why have I not found favor in thy sight, that thou dost lay the
> burden of all this people upon me? Did I conceive all this people?
> Did I bring them forth, that thou shouldst say to me, 'Carry them in
> your bosom, as a nurse carries the sucking child, to the land which
> thou didst swear to give their fathers?' Where am I to get meat
> to give to all this people? . . . I am not able to carry all this people
> alone, the burden is too heavy for me. . . ." 11:11–14

In fact, said Moses, he would rather be killed outright. His discouragement got through to God and God got through to Moses,
animating his creative statesmanship, and together they picked
seventy of the elders to share the leadership.

As for meat, said the Lord in effect, you are going to have all
the meat you can eat, not just for one day or ten but for a whole
month. Moses was shocked; were they going to kill all their cattle
and sheep? Wait and see, said God. The promise was enough for
the elders, and their spirits lifted so that they began to prophesy
and had a revival meeting right there in the public square. Even
two of the men who had stayed home, Eldad and Medad, caught
the spirit and also prophesied. Joshua, assistant leader, rushed to
Moses to have their prophesying stopped because they had not

been appointed or anointed. Moses was unruffled. "Would that all the Lord's people were prophets, that the Lord would put his spirit into them."

The delivery of the meat is a retelling of the miracle of the quail—thousands of quail migrating over the region, falling exhausted by their flight. A miracle of time and place and the long arm of God. Perhaps it would have happened just the same if the people had not complained, and that fact may have dawned on the minds of later editors, making them ashamed to doubt God's provisioning for the long-range needs of his children. The quail came and the people overate; "and the Lord smote the people with a very great plague." Plague was always considered to be sent by God. Many persons died. The assemblage may have profited by some of the funerals of overeaters and complainers.

In the family of Moses a feud broke out. Miriam and Aaron did not care for the Cushite wife Moses had married in the Wilderness; some wives of famous men are very demanding. They grumbled to their brother, "Has the Lord indeed spoken only through Moses? Has he not spoken through us also?" The Lord heard them; he knew their temperaments. "Now the man Moses was very meek, more than all men that were on the face of the earth." Meek, meaning forbearing, humbly patient. It is understandable that it should be so, for he lived so close to God that he felt his own inadequacies. The Lord called the three to the tent of meeting and himself came down in a pillar of cloud and made a few remarks. To ordinary prophets, he said, he made himself known through visions and dreams. "Not so with my servant Moses . . . With him I speak mouth to mouth, clearly . . . and he beholds the form of the Lord. Why then were you not afraid to speak against my servant Moses?" Why, indeed! The transcendent mystery of God's communication with Moses hung over the people of Israel, and over their history through the centuries. As the cloud lifted, the wrath of God was seen to have left its impression. Miriam was leprous, unclean. "And Moses cried to the Lord, 'Heal her, O God, I beseech thee.'" She was ostracized from the camp for seven days and then restored. One wonders if thinking over her own presumption as she lay awake those seven nights may not have aided the healing.

Appraisal of the Promised Land

A time came when it seemed an astute idea for the Israelites, approaching Canaan, to send men ahead to spy out the land, and the Lord so ordered; a leader from each tribe should infiltrate to find out what both territory and people were like, whether the cities were fortified, what the resistance was likely to be. And to bring back samples of the land's products. So the spies went forth and after forty days brought back specimens of Canaanite produce: fresh pomegranates and figs, and a bunch of grapes so heavy that it had to be carried on a pole by two men. Nevertheless the majority report was pessimistic. They described the heavily fortified cities, the land "that devours its inhabitants"; the fabulously tall people descended from Anak, whose clan of giants founded Hebron. ". . . and we seemed to ourselves like grasshoppers, and so we seemed to them." Caleb, however, made an optimistic minority report, supported by Joshua, who was all for the attack. The listening people, completely cowed, reacted negatively. If most of the spies felt like grasshoppers before the native inhabitants they already felt like ants and they had no verve for combat. Turning to Moses and Aaron they complained bitterly. "Why does the Lord bring us into this land, to fall by the sword? . . . would it not be better for us to go back to Egypt?"

Acting on their own recalcitrant suggestion, they promptly chose a captain to lead them back to Egypt. Watching them, Moses, Aaron, Caleb and Joshua rent their clothes, insisting that the land was not only "exceedingly good, . . . a land which flows with milk and honey," but quite conquerable, since the Lord was on their side. The people's answer was preparation to stone their leaders, and there were enough of them to guarantee a successful coup. "Then the glory of the Lord appeared at the tent of meeting to all the people of Israel" and the Lord told Moses he was through with this people. He would just strike them with a pestilence and be done with them; he could create a better and mightier nation through Moses and his coterie.

Moses was not pleased with the Lord's threat, nor with his encomium. These were his people; they needed a sense of their own worth to offset their disparagement of themselves. He chided the

Lord. Did the Almighty want the Israelites to return and tell the Egyptians that their Lord had delivered them from Pharaoh only to kill them in the wilderness?

"And now, I pray thee, let the power of the Lord be great as thou hast promised, saying, 'The Lord is slow to anger, and abounding in steadfast love, forgiving iniquity and transgression. . . .' Pardon the iniquity of this people, I pray thee, according to the greatness of thy steadfast love. . . ." 14:17–19

The Lord listened to Moses and relented. He understood his man Moses and Moses understood his own position; inescapably a leader must covenant with his people as well as with his God. Having relented, God then decreed that while he would not eliminate the whole people, not one of the complainers should enter the Promised Land. Only Caleb, "because he has a different spirit and has followed me fully." The others over twenty years of age, except for Joshua, should wander in the Wilderness for forty years and then die without entering the Promised Land and Israel would have a new populace.

Some of the hardier souls, ashamed of their doubt, felt that the Lord might reconsider further if they pushed on into Canaan immediately and showed their mettle. Moses cautioned them that so speedy an advance was ill advised but they struck off anyway without either their leaders or the ark. The result was a thorough defeat.

Challenge of Authority

By that time nerves were frayed and rebellion continued, led by three men, Dathan, Abiram, and a younger relative of Moses, Korah. Moses challenged their accusations of mismanagement and brought the matter before the Lord, who again showed his glory to all the congregation assembled for the occasion: Let the three dissenters stand at the door of their dwellings, said Moses, where they would see the decision of the Lord.

And as he finished speaking all these words, the ground under them split asunder; and the earth opened its mouth and swallowed them up, with their households. . . . So they and all that belonged to them went down alive into Sheol; and the earth closed over them, and they perished from the midst of the assembly. 16:31–33

That kind of response from on high might be expected to quell any dissent but some still challenged Aaron's authority as high priest. In reply, Moses ordered one man from each of the twelve tribes to bring him a rod, meaning a leafless branch or stick, along with a rod chosen by Aaron; all were deposited "before the Lord in the tent of the testimony." The next morning it was found that Aaron's rod had "sprouted and put forth buds, and produced blossoms, and it bore ripe almonds." He was definitely the Lord's choice.

Periodically the encampment moved on, the ark covered by its cloud leading the way. There were calamities. The country was arid; the people cried out for water. The Lord ordered Moses and Aaron to speak to a rock and tell it to produce water sufficient for the needs of both the people and their animals. Whether Moses doubted the power of their unaided word or whether he was angered by constant demands, he struck the rock twice with his rod. Water gushed forth. (Modern expeditions in that general area have found that weathered limestone when given a heavy blow by a sharp instrument will sometimes split open apertures from which a stream of water may flow.) The Lord was not pleased with that blow; he had ordered Moses merely to command the water. For Moses' disobedience he was sentenced only to gaze on the Promised Land; he could not himself enter it. Evidently there is a terrible inexorableness about God's leading. If a man aspires to be led of God in order to lead the people, the price in discipline is enormous.

The Onward March

The trek continued but the Edomites refused permission for the Israelites to pass through their country even though Moses offered every guarantee. For that inhospitable refusal the Israelites never forgave them, and future prophets never tired of calling down God's wrath on Edom. Trials multiplied. Both Miriam and Aaron died. The Canaanites attacked from the south but were defeated. Again the people complained of their hardships and were promptly bitten by serpents. The Lord ordered Moses to make a bronze serpent and raise it high; to gaze upon it would cure the dying. When the Hebrews asked passage through the territory of Sihon they were again refused but fought, won, and settled there. When attacked by King Og of Bashan they won again and took over that territory also. At last, east of Jordan and close to Jericho, they reached the border of the country they had come to occupy.

An Ass and an Angel

Early chroniclers were not without humor, and tradition bequeathed them some amusing incidents. One such story related how Balak, the Moabite king, hired a professional prophet named Balaam to curse the invaders. A well-aimed curse was a work of some skill and was expected to bring results. Balaam, first exercising his power of divination, concluded that the God of the Hebrews was a winning god and instead of curses he called down blessings on the approaching Israelites. Later the princes of Moab attempted to bribe him and Balaam, riding on an ass, followed them a short distance but suddenly an incorporeal angel of the Lord blocked his way. Not seeing the angel, Balaam goaded his ass but the ass, gifted with the second sight ascribed to animals, refused to move forward and instead pushed Balaam against a wall so he would not tread on the angel. Balaam, angry, struck the ass, who was promptly given the power of speech to reproach his master. Then the eyes of Balaam were opened to see the angel "standing in the way, with his drawn sword in his hand; and he bowed his head, and fell on his face." We can hear an ancient preacher asking his audience how many among them were as smart as an ass in sensing the presence of an angel.

Defection

Once arrived at the border of their Promised Land, the Israelites might be expected to stand in awe before their Lord, who had led them through so many difficulties. Instead, they were captivated by the sophisticated life of the Canaanites and many of them transferred their allegiance to the Canaanite deity, Baal of Peor. They also "began to play the harlot with the daughters of Moab." Thousands came down with the plague. Finally, when a grandson of Aaron, also a priest, saw an Israelite man bring a Midianite woman into his very household under the eye of Moses and the people, he took up a spear and killed both the man and the woman. That was the end of hobnobbing with heathen neighbors. And the plague was stayed.

Final Days of Moses

After detailed directions were given for Israel's life in the land of Canaan, the Lord told Moses to ascend Mount Nebo and gaze on the sweep of the Promised Land which he could not enter. At this point Moses would logically be expected to pass the command to his successor, Joshua, and die. But editor P (working, we remember, much later) had at hand further documents which purported to be the very words of Moses. These he deferred for another scroll and saved the final acts of Moses' life for the end of the book of Moses' teaching, Deuteronomy.

Law and Cult

All the way through the book of Numbers there are treatises on Mosaic law and cultic practices. Compiler P never hesitated to halt his historical narrative in order to insert a collection of regulations. No contingency was left uncovered; there was a "right" way to take care of almost every situation. Procedures were laid down for the support of the Levites as a priestly class. A cleansing ritual was decreed for an individual who had touched the dead; keeping the Sabbath was underscored; the people were commanded to wear tassels on their garments to remind them of the commandments. Any woman apprehended as an adulteress, or even suspected by her husband, must go through trial by ordeal, drinking water into which the priest had washed a written curse along with dust from the floor; if she was innocent the drink was supposed to be harmless; if guilty, severe illness should follow. (Maybe wayward women took special care to keep their floors clean.) In our day of constitutional rights such an ordeal seems a stiff requirement for an unproved accusation. However, with acceptance of the laws—all the laws literally interpreted—came the sense of dedicated community. Bitter the trials, high the penalties, but enormous the elation at being led by the Lord. It was this awareness of living under the imperial aegis of the Most High which gave the community its cohesiveness and tenacity.

Prayers

Throughout the book of Numbers there appear ancient prayers and bits of poetry which had come down through the genera-tions. Whenever the ark set out on a new stage of its journey, Moses prayed:

> "Arise, O Lord, and let thy enemies be scattered; and let them that hate thee flee before thee." And when it rested, he said "Return, O Lord, to the ten thousand thousands of Israel." 10:35–36

Then the beautiful benediction pronounced by Moses:

> The Lord bless you and keep you:
> The Lord make his face to shine upon you, and be gracious to you:
> The Lord lift up his countenance upon you, and give you peace.
> 6:24–26

And an ancient song of the well sung when water seemed miracu-lously provided:

> "Spring up, O well!—Sing to it!—
> the well which the princes dug,
> which the nobles of the people delved,
> with the scepter and with their staves." 21:17–18

This book of Numbers best proves its historicity by the very primitiveness of some of its poetry, prohibitions, and legends. The Israelites had a long memory; their God had a long arm; and their years in the Wilderness had a long-reaching effect on their reli-gious culture.

Deuteronomy

The book of Deuteronomy, meaning "second law," came by its name because it was presumed to be a restatement of the laws which had accrued to the Hebrews from the time of the Egyptian sojourn to their encampment on the plains of Moab preparatory to a final attack on Canaan, their Promised Land. In other words, a second recounting of the law said to have been laid down by Moses. Some of the material, however, would surely have seemed irrelevant to Moses, for in his day there could scarcely have been such strong emphasis on the centrality of Jerusalem as the one true center of worship, since Jerusalem had not yet been captured. Nor would he have been likely to formulate prohibitions against sacrifice in high places, or against star worship, necromancy and child sacrifice, since they were not problems for the Hebrews in the eleventh century B.C. But they were important when the book was brought together, in the seventh century B.C.

The material the editors were able to gather together was conglomerate: genealogies, records from a variety of sources, the usual tales, songs and poems, plus known current law. It never occurred to the authors to cross-reference dates with codes, or to compare accepted customs with social origins, or to construct some kind of maps for routes traveled. That kind of scholarship came later. It was the period covered and the centrality of Moses which gave Deuteronomy its place among the books of the law. In style it fits better with the ensuing half dozen historical books, Joshua, Judges, Samuel and Kings. The book is composed of three addresses by Moses, and his spirit does indeed characterize the whole work.

What is known about the first appearance of Deuteronomy is told in the second book of Kings. While Josiah was king of Judah it was reported to him that in the process of renovating the temple a book of laws promulgated by Moses had been found. This was stirring news. The time was propitious for the book's turning up, because Josiah was acutely aware that the worship of Yahweh had become badly corrupted during previous reigns and that reform was overdue. Later scholars surmise that the Deuteronomic scroll may have been compiled fifty or more years earlier by priests loyal to Hebrew traditions but that they had had to secrete it until a time when it could safely be exposed. At any rate, as soon as the book turned up the king read it and was overwhelmed. Plainly many of the laws of Moses were not being honored.

Then Josiah had a second thought: was this scroll genuine? After all, only about half the laws here listed were contained in the Exodus collection. He appointed a committee on the book's authenticity and instructed them to consult the prophetess Huldah, one of the three prophetesses mentioned in the Old Testament. She assured the interrogators that the book was indeed authoritative. So Josiah proceeded to put its decrees into practice, underscoring its main point that the laws were not just historical landmarks but that they also applied to the people currently hearing them. Since that was the case, the king decreed, let the laws be carried out in the present tense.

Moses, the Spokesman

Nothing could have authenticated a reform movement like finding it based on the instructions of Moses, the great lawgiver, the authority whom the people knew and revered. In this newly discovered scroll Moses again stood forth before his people, austere but benevolent, a man whose courage and ability had organized and directed the trek of a nation; the uncompromising proponent of the Covenant. This man who had once spoken with God now spoke again for God. In relaying the law to a new generation the book also renewed assurance that God's mercy was immeasurable but that his people dare not trifle with his ordinances.

These three discourses still stand among the most powerful orations in all literature. Today we read them in the past tense because many of the laws are archaic, but their intent and spirit are very much of the present tense, while they reflect a stalwart sense of justice on the part of those who formulated and passed them on as the ethical basis of Hebrew religion.

Land

The first discourse, following a five-verse introduction which sets up the place and occasion, consists of chapters 1:6 to 4:40. Moses was reminding his people that the first of God's promises was of land of their own.

> "Behold, I have set the land before you; go in and take possession of the land which the Lord swore to your fathers, . . . to give to them and to their descendants after them!" 1:8

The lure of land has motivated people as far back as records go. Land for grazing, land for farming, land for homes; land to be owned and handed down. It seems as if man has to have rootage in the earth, his own bit of earth, his own people's earth. Still— one man alone, or even one family alone, however fertile their ground, lives in a desert of loneliness; two families on their own ground are an oasis; but a group of land-owning families becomes a productive community. Moses knew this. He also knew that no one, not even God, could actually give land to a people. Land had to be claimed and used, its products shared. So the next thing Moses pointed out was the way to live on the land successfully.

Justice

If the people wanted the help and privileges of a community, then they had to carry organized responsibilities. And the chief responsibility, said Moses, was justice for all.

> "You shall not be partial in judgment; you shall hear the small and the great alike; you shall not be afraid of the face of man, for the judgment is God's." 1:17

Easier to preach than practice—"you shall not be afraid of the face of man"; not even your own face if it gets photographed among the innovative who lead in reform. Just don't be afraid, said Moses, "for the judgment is God's." Then for the comfort of his listeners he added a further sustaining word based on the authority of his own experience, "and the case that is too hard for you, you shall bring to me, and I will hear it." What more could a community ask than a judge whom everyone knew to be incorruptible?

How Personal Is History

For some people history is an abstraction, a series of actions taken by "somebody" out there. Others make history personal by subscribing to the actions and principles of their forebears and furthering the same ends. Moses attempted to identify the people with their past by rehearsing the travail of their travel, the blood bath of their battles, the struggle of their leaders to provide food, the discipline demanded by sacrifice, always inspiriting them toward their objective, which was living in the Promised Land. As the people listened to his rehearsal they grew taller and their doubt gave way to valor. "O Lord God," said Moses, "thou hast only begun to show thy servant thy mighty hand. . . ." This was what the people needed as they faced warlike neighbors more advanced in weaponry, farming and organization than themselves, assurance that the arm of the Lord was not shortened. And the same assurance was needed again in Josiah's day: God's people must move ahead by supporting the statutes.

> "Keep them and do them; for that will be your wisdom and your understanding in the sight of the peoples, who, when they hear all these statutes, will say, "Surely this great nation is a wise and understanding people!" 4:6

Choice of Distinguishing Marks

Back in Moses' day Israel had met up with an enemy named Og, king of Bashan, who is known to posterity for two things; he lost a battle and with it his country and he had an enormous bed. "Behold, the bedstead of iron . . . nine cubits was its length, and four cubits its breadth." The original king-size bed, seven by fifteen feet. Og belonged to that strain of huge men who once occupied that part of the country, men of whom Goliath was probably a descendant. It gives one pause, this whole matter of going down in history distinguished for the size of one's bed—or one's coin collection, or one's low-number car license, or one's jewelry, golf trophies, or even one's library. They do seem puny alongside the bequests of Moses, all of them intangible. The record does not name a *thing* that Moses owned at the end of his long journey.

> "Only take heed, and keep your soul diligently, lest you forget the things which your eyes have seen . . . make them known to your children and your children's children." 4:9

Passing on an Inheritance

Of course one cannot pass on an experience one has not had, but if one has had a truly transforming experience then it is difficult to keep still about it! Moses had seen what respect for the law was able to make of his people and he passed on both the respect and the useful statutes. (How would he feel today?) And whose laws would sound more archaic—some of his to us or some of ours to him? He at least knew where to turn for direction.

> ". . . you will seek the Lord your God, and you will find him, if you search after him with all your heart and with all your soul. . . . know therefore this day, and lay it to your heart, that the Lord is God in heaven above and on the earth beneath; there is no other. Therefore you shall keep his statutes . . . that it may go well with you, and with your children after you." 4:29, 39–40

Here a bit of social geography is inserted into the record. Three cities are mentioned as ports of refuge for murderers who had killed someone unintentionally; perhaps run someone down with a chariot, or let an arrow fly off-target. Fleeing to a city of refuge was the Mosaic equivalent of demanding fair trial instead of mob retaliation.

Second Address

In the second address, chapters 5 through 28, a wide range of laws and regulations covers both the civil and penal codes. Seventy-eight statutes and ordinances to which they must adhere. Included is a table of twelve curses on particular sins, the curses to be pronounced by the Levites with the people responding a hearty amen. (Now for what dozen current sins would a modern congregation draw up a set of good sound curses?)

If Moses offered this long, unorganized collection of laws and advisements as one discourse he must have had a captive audi-

ence and a contingent of scribes taking notes. Whatever he said,
though, the people were bound to pay attention for a practical
reason: penalties for broken laws were often meted swiftly and
with savage justice, so it behooved a man to know the law. And
Moses had the knack of making the law seem personal: This
means you. Personal in his own time, personal in Josiah's time,
and worth cogitating on today.

Present-tense Covenant

> "Not with our fathers did the Lord make this covenant, but with us,
> who are all of us here alive this day." 5:3

Like telling us that it is we ourselves who issued the Emancipa-
tion Proclamation with all its inherent promises. Most important
was the restatement of the Great Commandment which Moses
conceived as the nucleus of corporate life. The "Shema," as the
Jews came to call his admonition, meaning *to hear:*

> "Hear, O Israel: the Lord our God is one Lord; and you shall love
> the Lord your God with all your heart, and with all your soul, and
> with all your might. And these words which I command you this
> day shall be upon your heart; and you shall teach them diligently to
> your children, and shall talk of them when you sit in your house,
> and when you walk by the way, and when you lie down, and when
> you rise. And you shall bind them as a sign upon your hand, and
> they shall be as frontlets between your eyes. And you shall write
> them on the doorposts of your house and on your gates." 6:4–9

All this the congregation took literally, so for generations the
commandment was worn across the forehead and fastened on the
doorposts. And so do some orthodox Jews continue to this day.

So great a God, Moses continued, cannot be trifled with, no
quibbling or watering down of his pronouncements, "that it may
go well with you." Let the people keep their eyes focused ahead,
for the Lord has promised to see that they overcome obstacles,
"For you are a people holy to the Lord your God. . . . he will
love you, bless you, and multiply you." Then, against the misery
of Hebrew life in Egypt, he pictorialized the future:

> "For the Lord your God is bringing you into a good land, a land of
> brooks of water, of fountains and springs, flowing forth in valleys

and hills, a land of wheat and barley, of vines and fig trees and pomegranates, a land of olive trees and honey, a land in which you will eat bread without scarcity, in which you will lack nothing, a land whose stones are iron, and out of whose hills you can dig copper. And you shall eat and be full, and you shall bless the Lord your God for the good land he has given you." 8:7–10

However, he went on, Israel must remember that the good life is a gift of God's love, not an earned increment. "Know therefore, that the Lord your God is not giving you this good land to possess because of your righteousness; for you are a stubborn people"—which he documented from their past history. God had once let them know what hunger was, "that he might make you know that man does not live by bread alone, but that man lives by everything that proceeds out of the mouth of the Lord." He used a graphic phrase: "Circumcise therefore the foreskin of your heart." Ritual purification could not take the place of the cleansed heart, and personal dedication must always be a contemporaneous covenant.

Religion with Authority

Nevertheless to the writers of the book of Deuteronomy, and reputedly on Moses' own authority, the cult was policeman of the faith. Follow the authorized practices and be rewarded by further direction; take a liberty and expect a reversal of blessings.

Sacrifice and offerings must be centralized in Jerusalem except when distance was so great that animals were better slaughtered on location. All priests must be adequately supported, not only the descendants of Aaron, who officiated in Jerusalem, but also the Levites who performed their duties in outlying areas. Let the people beware of wonder-workers whose prophecies might come true but who enticed worshipers into allegiance to other gods than Yahweh. Moreover, if a city succumbed to a false prophet, let the whole city be destroyed.

Religious feasts and festivals were fixed; Passover, with its unleavened bread, must be celebrated at the central sanctuary; the Feast of Weeks, a harvest festival, entailed a freewill offering "which you shall give as the Lord your God blesses you"; the seven-day Feast of Booths and the autumn thanksgiving festival had their own routines.

Judges and officers must be appointed for all towns; "you shall not show partiality; and you shall not take a bribe." Cases too difficult for a local judge should be adjudicated by a Levitical high tribunal. If a king is chosen, he must be an Israelite who does "not multiply horses for himself; nor wives, nor silver and gold." And lest he forget these admonishments, the king had better copy this part of the law himself!

In listing prohibitions, the Deuteronomists certainly did not follow any topical organization. Murder, manslaughter, theft deserved severe punishment, but a man could not be punished on the testimony of only one witness. Booty was permitted when a non-Palestinian city was taken, but a rebellious Palestinian city must be totally destroyed. No exchange of masculine and feminine garments by the two sexes; no mixing of seed in a vineyard; necessity of a parapet around a roof to prevent falls. Penalties for half a dozen varieties of sexual misconduct. Military hygiene was detailed. Prohibition of Israelites as cult prostitutes; regulations for interest on loans to foreigners but no interest on loans to fellow Israelites; vows must be lived up to; in passing through a neighbor's field, fruit and grain might be eaten as needed but nothing carried away; lashing must be limited to forty strokes administered before a court; an ox should not be muzzled when treading out the grain; mills and millstones must not be taken in pledge; kidnaping was punishable by death; parents should not be punished for the crimes of their offspring, nor children for parents' crimes; justice for the weak, and the rights of the poor must be protected.

Miscellaneous laws covered treatment of beautiful women taken in battle, the routine life of lepers, the inheritance of the first-born even when the father would rather honor the son of a preferred wife, preservation of fruit trees in spite of siege, rites of purification for the city nearest the place where an unsolved murder occurred, treatment of a worthless son accused by his parents: stoning. (That really should teach a son to take care of his parents.) "When a man is newly married, he shall not go out with the army or be charged with any business; he shall be free at home one year, to be happy with his wife whom he has taken." The law of levirate marriage was outlined: the living brother's obligation to marry the widow of a dead brother and raise up children for him. Fear was prohibited! The sight of armies with superior equipment must not overwhelm an Israelite, for his wars are holy.

Final Promises

The third address is covered in chapters 29 and 30. Again Moses summoned all the people:

> "You stand this day all of you before the Lord your God; the heads of your tribes, your elders, and your officers, all the men of Israel, your little ones, your wives, and the sojourner who is in your camp . . . that you may enter into the sworn covenant of the Lord your God, which the Lord your God makes with you this day; that he may establish you this day as his people, and that he may be your God, as he promised you. . . . Nor is it with you only that I make this sworn covenant, but with him who is not here with us this day. . . ." 29:10–14

Thus was posterity included and inculcated with knowledge of the calamities which will come their way also if the people of future generations forget their past and the responsibilities laid upon them. Then comes one of the great pronouncements of the Old Testament:

> "For this commandment which I command you this day is not too hard for you, neither is it far off. It is not in heaven, that you should say, 'Who will go up for us to heaven, and bring it to us, that we may hear it and do it?' Neither is it beyond the sea, that you should say, 'Who will go over the sea for us, and bring it to us, that we may hear it and do it?' But the word is very near you; it is in your mouth and in your heart, so that you can do it. . . . I call heaven and earth to witness against you this day, that I have set before you life and death, blessing and curse; therefore choose life, that you and your descendants may live, loving the Lord your God, obeying his voice, and cleaving to him." 30:11–14, 19–20

There stood Moses three thousand years before the birth of psychology making known the inwardness of the knowledge of the self and the support which is ever available to those who seek. The never-ending search, the ever-answering response. An astounding insight, and perhaps no part of it more so than the phrase "For this commandment which I command you this day is not too hard for you." For his people—men, women and children in families—"the word is very near you . . . in your heart, so that you can do it."

The Everlasting Arms

The account then turns to Moses' own life, and the remainder of the book, chapters 31 through 34, tells of his last days, a story which must obviously have been added after his death. Moses reminded his people that he must now leave them before they enter their Promised Land. Summoning Joshua, he charged him.

> "Be strong and of good courage: for you shall go with this people into the land which the Lord has sworn to their fathers to give them. . . . It is the Lord who goes before you; he will be with you, he will not fail you or forsake you; do not fear or be dismayed." 31: 7–8

Who could speak with such assurance? Moses. Because he knew the Lord of whom he spoke. And the Lord knew him. At the tent of meeting, the Lord appeared again in a pillar of cloud and told Moses, gently we hope, with his tenderest compassion and most intimate assurance, "Behold, you are about to sleep with your fathers." Then, looking down the years, Moses foresaw the "many evils and troubles" which would assail his people. The Lord commissioned Joshua, and suggested that Moses commit the laws to writing and order the Levites to place the text next to the ark of the covenant. Finally, turning again to his people, Moses "spoke the words of this song," a hymn addressed to heaven and earth, proclaiming the majesty of God, the Rock whose ways are justice. A long song whose theme was that "the Lord's portion is his people," followed by a reminder that the Lord's word was "no trifle for you, but it is your life."

At last, following the Lord's direction, Moses ascended Mount Nebo opposite Jericho and viewed the land of Canaan. There he blessed the children of Israel, a particular blessing on each tribe. His final assurance was:

> The eternal God is your dwelling place,
>   and underneath are the everlasting arms. 33:27

According to the record, Moses was a hundred and twenty years old when he died but the length of his days was not the greatest of life's gifts to him; rather, that "his eye was not dimmed, nor his natural forces abated." As long as he lived, *he lived*.

So Moses the servant of the Lord died there in the Land of Moab, according to the word of the Lord, and he buried him in the valley in the land of Moab opposite Beth-peor; but no man knows the place of his burial to this day. . . . And Joshua the son of Nun was full of the spirit of wisdom, for Moses had laid his hands upon him; so the people of Israel obeyed him, and he did as the Lord had commanded Moses. And there has not arisen a prophet since in Israel like Moses, whom the Lord knew face to face. . . . 34:5–6, 9–10

Joshua

The book of Joshua needs to be read in a stouthearted mood, for as a tale of ruthless conquest on the part of a people seeking land it stands alongside the harsher tales of encroachment on occupied territory. To be sure, there were no bombs, no defoliation by powerful chemicals, not even any death-dealing aircraft, but there was a barbarous use of slings and swords, with whole cities set afire and all the population, including women and children, put to the sword. Quite in the manner of their day. If the Israelites ever felt any need to explain their highhanded taking over of territory their justification lay in their need for land, good land, not a rocky stretch of almost untillable wasteland. Just as early American settlers some three thousand years later felt exonerated of guilt in taking land from the Indians because they needed it and were, in their own eyes, God's chosen people, so the Israelites moved with courage under the sustaining hand of God. We are the skeptical readers of history; they were the assured participants. Then as now, in the midst of sanguinary warfare heroic leaders arose, men of dedicated lives. Then as now, success in battle was credited to the Lord with all due honor.

Date

Unfortunately, there being no cameras or tape recorders at the time, the record was not set down as the battles were fought, which was not far from the year 1200 B.C., when iron weapons were a new invention and the memory was still green of the battle of Kadesh, in Syria, when Ramesses II was stopped short by the Hittites. But father-to-son tales took their rise at the site of battles and some early records were kept, some explanations of certain shrines and ceremonies handed down, and some early poems worked into ensuing rituals. The redactors who finalized this book, probably no earlier than the seventh century B.C., were primarily concerned with making plain once more that it was Yahweh who had directed his people and that his benignity always depended upon the faithfulness of Israel. And historians, like the rest of us, felt identification with their heroes.

The book's twenty-four chapters fall into three main divisions: first, the events following the death of Moses and the invasion of the land; second, the division of territory among the tribes; third, arguments with the Reubenites and associated tribes, two moving addresses by Joshua, followed by his death and burial, and the burial of the bones of Joseph.

The advance of the Israelites against their first enemies and the sack of Jericho are described in the first six chapters. Israelite newcomers must have felt considerable trepidation but the Lord himself offered Joshua assurance.

"No man shall be able to stand before you all the days of your life; as I was with Moses, so I will be with you. . . . Only be strong and very courageous. . . . be not frightened, neither be dismayed; for the Lord your God is with you wherever you go." 1:5, 7, 9

Joshua believed the promise. And so he felt invincible, which is probably the greatest gift of spirit a man can receive; if he has it, he seems to invigorate everyone around him.

Joshua was a strategist who believed in using an intelligence agency ahead of his army. He sent two spies into Jericho. They put up at a hostelry owned by a harlot named Rahab, whose place adjoined the city wall. Evidently the city king of Jericho also had his spies, because he soon received word that a couple of suspicious-looking characters were staying at Rahab's pseudo hotel, and he sent his personal gestapo to nab them. But Rahab already had a plan worked out. Having heard before the Israelite scouts arrived about the highhanded ways of the advancing invaders and their invincible God, she was not about to betray men whose armies would soon occupy her city. Instead, she hid the spies under stalks of flax drying on her roof and told the king's interrogators that the strangers had left at sundown, when the city gates were closed: ". . . pursue them quickly, for you will overtake them." Following her advice, the king's soldiers rode out as far as the Jordan, while Rahab went up to the roof and demanded a promise of the Israelites that when they took the city— as they surely would do, because "the Lord your God is he who is God in heaven above and on earth beneath"—they should save her and all her family. They promised. So "she let them down by a rope through the window" and advised them to hide in the hills for three days.

The scouts made their way back, reported to Joshua, and the next morning the entire "people of Israel" led by the ark started toward Jericho. When they reached the Jordan they found the river swollen from autumn rains, but at the place of crossing the water had ceased to flow at all! It was blocked, probably by a landslide, some eighteen miles upstream. They passed across the riverbed dry-shod, like their ancestors at the Sea of Reeds. Awed by their miraculous good fortune, they paused to collect twelve sizable stones, one for each of the twelve tribes into which they were divided, and erected an altar of remembrance on the spot; and, said the compilers of the book of Joshua some centuries later, those stones "are there to this day."

". . . about forty thousand ready armed for war passed over . . . to the plains of Jericho." Then "the waters of the Jordan returned to their place and overflowed all its banks, as before." The report of the stalled river got around quickly and "all the kings of the Amorites" and "all the kings of the Canaanites" were cowed; "their heart melted, so there was no longer any spirit in them, because of the people of Israel." Which is the best way to win a war, of course, letting brave tales crush any spirit of counter combat.

Ancient Rites

Right there at Gibeah-haaraloth—a name that does not mean a thing to a modern reader except to show that the famous war sites of one century may be forgotten by future generations—the

Lord directed Joshua to have all Hebrew males circumcised, a rite which had been omitted on the long trek through the wilderness. And it was done with flint knives, an apt illustration of the way a cult practice can outweigh common sense, since metal knives were in use by that time. While the entire army waited there in pain, the Passover was celebrated. And from that time on no more manna appeared; Israel "ate of the fruit of the land of Canaan."

The Fall of Jericho

It was there also that Joshua saw an apparition, a man with a drawn sword, who said he came "as commander of the army of the Lord" and ordered Joshua to remove his shoes, "for the place where you stand is holy." With the army's power thus augmented by divine leadership the troops followed instructions: for six days they marched once around the walls of Jericho; first the armed men, then seven priests bearing seven trumpets of rams' horns, then the ark, followed by the people who served the fighting force, while ". . . the trumpets blew continually," but they were not permitted to shout until the seventh day. (The magic number seven appears fourteen times in this chapter.) When that seventh day came they marched around the city seven times, trumpets blowing. By then the bewildered people inside the walls must have been ready to surrender to this strange siege. "And at the seventh time, when the priests had blown the trumpets, Joshua said to the people, 'Shout; for the Lord has given you the city.' . . . the people raised a great shout, and the wall fell down flat, so that the people went up into the city . . . and they took the city." In the archaeological excavations of Jericho, one of the most careful and extensive of modern excavations, it was found that at some period in the city's ancient history the wall had indeed fallen flat all at one time; not quite in the period ascribed to Joshua, but the time sequence of ancient traditions is sometimes inadvertently telescoped.

> And they burned the city with fire, and all within it; only the silver and gold, and the vessels of bronze and of iron, they put into the treasury of the house of the Lord. 6:24

An order then went out that there was to be no personal looting. The whole clan of Rahab's relatives were saved and Joshua closed the incident with a powerful curse on anyone who might ever re-build the city. In those days it was not uncommon for leaders to try to dictate to the future.

Group Responsibility

Encouraged by success, Joshua attempted to take also the city of Ai, in the highlands; a small city, requiring, according to his spies, no more than three thousand armed men. But the Israelite army was routed by the men of Ai. Astounded and knowing that the news of Israel's defeat would embolden the attempts of their enemies, Joshua fell on his face before the ark of the Lord: "Alas, O Lord God, why hast thou brought this people over the Jordan at all, to give us into the hands of the Amorites, to destroy us?"

Because, answered the Lord, someone has sinned. Contrary to his express command, some man among the Israelites had appropriated private loot. The next morning Joshua cast the sacred lots to determine the offending tribe, then family by family he searched out the man. "Achan the son of Carmi" confessed that he had coveted and surreptitiously taken "a beautiful mantle from Shinar, and two hundred shekels of silver, and a bar of gold weighing fifty shekels." In accordance with custom, which held the immediate group responsible for one member's misdeeds, Achan and his whole family, including his animals, were stoned and burned. The next man tempted by loot no doubt thought twice, and it was that long second thought which kept order in the camp.

His army cleansed, Joshua approached Ai again, this time setting an ambush behind the city under cover of night, then by day leading his army straight at the city. As the soldiers inside the city came forth to meet Joshua's approaching troops, the Israelite soldiers in ambush rushed in to the city from the other direction, setting buildings afire and destroying the entire populace—some twelve thousand men and women—all except the king, who was brought to Joshua and hanged. This time the Lord allowed the people to keep the captured cattle.

A Time of Recall

After so great a victory an altar was promptly raised and peace offerings were made while a copy of the law of Moses was again written on stone tablets. Then all the people of Israel stood on opposite sides of the ark before the Levitical priests while the entire law of Moses was read to them. A time of remembrance, soul-searching and complete rededication.

> There was not a word of all that Moses commanded which Joshua did not read before all the assembly of Israel, and the women, and the little ones, and the sojourners who lived among them. 8:35

Unintentional Allies

As news of Joshua's conquests spread, all the kings in the hill country, the lowland, and along the coast got together to stop this Israelite expansion. Only the inhabitants of the nearby city of Gibeon thought up a scheme to save their necks without battle. Bedraggled and appearing to have been on a long forced march, they came to Joshua where he was encamped at Gilgal and announced they had come from a far country to make a treaty of non-aggression. Having heard of the exploits of the Israelites all the way from Egypt to Ai, they reported that their fellow citizens had urged them to take provisions for their long journey and go make peace before Joshua advanced on their country. They then showed their moldy bread, which, they said, had been fresh from the ovens when they started; their burst wineskins, which had been new when they left home; their garments and shoes, worn out on the trip. The story seemed so plainly true that Joshua "did not ask direction from the Lord." According to Deuteronomic law, while the Israelites were directed to kill all the near neighbors they were permitted to make peace with those who came from a far country. Consequently a peace was sworn. A few days later the Israelites found out that Gibeon was only a three-day journey distant. Since the oath of peace could not be broken Joshua forced the Gibeonites to become "hewers of wood and drawers of water," burden bearers for the Israelite army when needed. *Live* hewers of wood and drawers of water, however, with Israel bound to them as an ally.

The news of Joshua's habit of conquest continued to travel ahead of him. The king of Jerusalem "feared greatly," and so he persuaded four other city kings to join forces with him in order to overwhelm the great city of Gibeon, now an Israelite ally, and put fear into Joshua. But Joshua "and all the mighty men of valor," true to their treaty, came to Gibeon's aid and completely routed the five kings. As the attacking armies fled, "the Lord threw down great stones from heaven upon them . . . there were more who died because of the hailstones than the men of Israel killed with the sword." In his victory Joshua sang a song of praise—a poem from an ancient collection known as the Book of Jashar:

> "Sun, stand thou still at Gibeon,
> and thou Moon in the valley of Aijalon." 10:12

The final editors of the book of Joshua, mistaking the poetic figure of speech for fact, reported the occasion as another miracle, when "the sun stayed in the midst of heaven, and did not hasten to go down for about a whole day. There has not been a day like it before or since. . . ." Indeed, the final editors saw the whole conquest as a series of military miracles.

Unremitting Conquest

City after city Joshua conquered; king after king he dispatched; "until he left none remaining." When southern Palestine was subjugated, he turned to the kings of the northern hill country, admonished by the Lord to have no fear.

> And they came out, with all their troops, a great host, in number like the sand that is upon the seashore, with very many horses and chariots. And all these kings joined their forces. . . . So Joshua came suddenly upon them with all his people of war, by the waters of Merom, and fell upon them. And the Lord gave them into the hand of Israel . . . and they smote them, until they left none remaining. And Joshua . . . hamstrung their horses, and burned their chariots with fire. . . . Joshua made war a long time with all those kings. . . . So Joshua took the whole land, according to all that the Lord had spoken to Moses. 11:4-5, 7-9, 18, 23

The list of cities which make up the whole twelfth chapter of the book reads like the index of an atlas of sanguinity; "in all, thirty-one kings" were killed.

Territorial Assignment

The Lord said to Joshua, "You are old and advanced in years, and there remains yet very much land to be possessed." Chapter

13 surveys the lands for a considerable distance around the already conquered portions of Canaan, assigning a designated section to each of the twelve tribes except Levi, to whose male members—since they were priests—were given certain "cities to dwell in, along with their pasture lands." Biblical records can sometimes be tedious reading, and yet without the minutiae of detail the difficulties and practicalities of those years when Israel was becoming a people would never come through to us.

Orderly assignment of land precluded internal dissension among rival tribes. Moses might admonish, "Hear, O Israel, the Lord thy God is one God" but Joshua had to make concrete by means of regulations the fact that Israel's people were also one people. Land was apportioned by lot but some of the designated areas still had to be conquered while others were simply infiltrated. Not all the Canaanites and resident peoples in the acquired areas were exterminated; some remained in their towns, intermarried with the Israelites and augmented the Israelite culture. Occasionally, recalcitrant cities were bypassed because "the Canaanites persisted in dwelling in that land." Some sections required agricultural pioneering. To the tribe of Joseph, Joshua said, "If you are a numerous people, go up to the forest, and there clear ground for yourselves in the land of the Perizzites and the Rephaom, since the hill country of Ephraim is too narrow for you."

When the immediate land had all been apportioned and seven tribes remained unassigned, Joshua sent a scouting group of three men from each tribe to reconnoiter and write down their descriptions of the outlying areas, after which he would draw lots for assignments. The tribe of Judah drew too large a portion, so "the tribe of Simeon obtained an inheritance in the midst of their inheritance." As Moses had promised, Caleb was given a special portion, and "When they had finished distributing the several territories of the land as inheritances, the people of Israel gave an inheritance among them to Joshua the son of Nun." Then came the appointment of cities of refuge, where a manslayer might flee "and explain his case to the elders of that city." To the tribes journeying farthest, Joshua gave a special admonition and to all the people a reminder:

Take good care to observe the commandment and the law which Moses the servant of the Lord commanded you, to love the Lord your God, and to walk in all his ways, and to keep his commandments, and to cleave to him, and to serve him with all your heart and with all your soul. . . . One man of you puts to flight a thousand, since it is the Lord your God who fights for you. . . . And now I am about to go the way of all the earth, and you know in your hearts and souls, all of you, that not one thing has failed of all the good things which the Lord your God promised concerning you. 22:5; 23:10, 14

Not only the Israelites were in a period of transition. The Phoenicians were in a state of flux; the Hittites and Egyptians parried, made peace, and then attacked each other again; Assyria was jockeying for position; related language groups defied outsiders. Not only the great countries warred but city-states with their individual kings, scores of them, settled real and contrived grievances. If conditions had been more stable the Israelites would no doubt have met more formidable opposition to their acquisition of land.

Joshua performed a tremendous service in distributing his people as well as he did. If later recorders were not always literally accurate regarding land distribution they did sense the difficulties and determination of the forward movement we know as the conquest of Canaan. A man of lesser stature than Joshua could scarcely have followed Moses in holding the Israelite people together and maintaining their religious allegiance against the pull of local customs and deities, both as powerful as the enemy's armed forces.

Joshua's Legacy

Finally "Joshua gathered all the tribes of Israel to Shechem," again rehearsed their history and climaxed his recital with a call for personal choice:

. . . choose this day whom you will serve, whether the gods your fathers served in the region beyond the River, or the gods of the Amorites in whose land you dwell; but as for me and my house, we will serve the Lord. . . . And Joshua wrote these words in the book of the law of God; and he took a great stone, and set it up there under the oak in the sanctuary of the Lord. . . . After these things Joshua the son of Nun, the servant of the Lord, died, being a hundred and ten years old. And they buried him in his own inheritance. . . . 24:15, 26, 29–30

At Shechem they also buried the bones of Joseph, which they had brought from Egypt; and buried Eleazar, the son of Aaron. So the towering leaders of the conquest were no longer at hand but their mighty shadows bound the people to compelling memories.

And Israel served the Lord all the days of Joshua, and all the days of the elders who outlived Joshua and had known all the work which the Lord did for Israel. 24:31

Judges

Canaan was settled under the judges. That is, under the direction of tribal leaders called judges, or deliverers, or regulators. One aspect of their leadership was judgeship, rendering final decisions in disputes, but they also directed the course of action to be taken by whatever federation of tribes came under their jurisdiction at a given time. Earlier, on the trek from Egypt, final decisions came from Moses and after him from Joshua. Later, when kings ruled Israel, the royal word was final except for strictly ecclesiastic decisions made by the high priest. Not until Jehoshaphat were courts of justice set up according to the Deuteronomic code with two chief justices, one for ecclesiastical matters, the other for temporal affairs. But during the interim between the conquering of Canaan and the rise of kings, top leadership known as the judges advanced the cause of the loosely confederated tribes, bringing erring groups into alignment with what were felt to be God's purposes. Slowly the whole people went forward.

Some records must have been kept during this period of Israel's expansion, roughly 1200 to 1050 B.C., and it is to them that the compilers of the book of Judges turned, their material augmented by legends, ballads and didactic and cult poems. The process of assembling and editing extended from the late-ninth century B.C. well into the postexilic period when the book was eventually finalized. Naturally it was the unusual achievements, the exceptional or bizarre turns of events, which made the best stories to pass from tribe to tribe and thence to bequeath to posterity. As usual the compilers gave history a definitely theological interpretation, utilizing a literary device to frame each judge. (If puns slip into a modern report it is exactly the trap the early Hebrews doted on.)

> And the people of Israel did what was evil in the sight of the Lord. . . . So the anger of the Lord was kindled against Israel . . . so that they could no longer withstand their enemies. . . . But when the people of Israel cried to the Lord, the Lord raised up a deliverer . . . who delivered them. . . . So the land had rest. . . .
> 2:11, 14; 3:9, 11

Their Problems

Two struggles were unceasing: the skirmish for food and the constant endeavor to maintain religious rectitude and solidarity. The land had to produce crops—mainly wheat, olives, grapes, figs. It had also to support sheep and goats, which furnished meat and milk for cheese, as well as abundant sweet fat from the broadtail sheep. Camel's milk made excellent *leban,* a yogurtlike product from which water could be squeezed to leave a cheesy substance that would keep indefinitely when rolled into balls to be carried in the leather pouches of travelers. (This was no doubt the food which Jael gave Sisera when "she brought him curds in a lordly bowl.")

Faithfulness to religious teaching and ritual had constantly to be inculcated. Sometimes defection from singlehearted devotion to Yahweh was caused by what appeared to be the superior blessings of fertility on the part of the gods of Israel's neighbors; sometimes people drifted into adding certain gods of their prosperous neighbors to their own cult, an especially easy corruption when intermarriage with foreigners was common. Sometimes it was simply a matter of wanting to participate in a popular festival, the way many Jews today lightheartedly take on Christmas, and Christians add Santa Claus to the holy family. The judges constantly brought the people to their senses by destroying whatever enemy seemed to be crippling Israel religiously. Spiritual surgery was quicker than spiritual inoculation.

Their Conquests

The first two chapters review the early conquests and emphasize the fact that not all districts could be taken. "Manasseh did not drive out the inhabitants of Bethshean and its villages"—then other towns are named—"but the Canaanites persisted in dwelling in that land. When Israel grew strong, they put the Canaanites to forced labor, but did not utterly drive them out." However, they tried to conquer and the aura of high adventure is dramatized in the very names of the enemy tribes, the titles of attacking kings, and the honorary designations bestowed on places where remarkable events occurred. Who would not gird on his sword to fight the Perizzites, Hittites, Hivites, Jebusites, Canaanites, Moabites, Sidonites, Amalekites, Ammonites and their ilk? Who could refuse to join in a foray against Cushan-rishathaim, king of Mesopotamia? And go out against nine hundred chariots of iron driven by men from Harosheth-ha-goiim to the river Koshon?

The Weary Land

The first judge was Othniel, a nephew of Caleb, to whom the Lord delivered up the king of Mesopotamia, much to the relief of the beleaguered Israelites. "So the land had rest forty years." Such an empathic description of the tortured terrain over which armies contend! Land which is furrowed by chariot wheels, cut by horses' hooves, soaked with human blood, bereft of customary care, can scarcely be productive land, joining itself to the rhythmic pattern of nature. It cries for surcease from human maltreatment, and the writers of Israel's history, near to the land themselves, utilized this telling phrase to describe the years of peace: "and the land rested."

Left-handed Murder

An early exploit was the extermination of Eglon, king of Moab, whose country had dominated Israel for eighteen years, exacting burdensome tribute. The people of Israel were discouraged enough to forsake their false gods and repent whatever sins they had committed; they cried out for deliverance and got behind a new leader, Ehud, a "left-handed man" who used that fact to effect a ruse. Ehud acquired a short two-edged sword and strapped it to his right thigh under his garments. Usually it was the right hand—the hand of sword and dagger—and the left thigh which were watched with suspicion. Then Ehud personally accompanied Israel's annual

tribute to King Eglon. With obsequious deference Ehud told fat
King Eglon that he had an important message from Israel's God
Yahweh which not even the attendants should hear. So Eglon dismissed his retinue. Then as Eglon rose from his seat Ehud reached
with his left hand for his dagger, thrust it so far into Eglon's body
that the fat closed over both blade and hilt; then left quickly, lock-
ing the doors and bowing his way out to his own waiting attendants.
Eventually Eglon's attendants distrusted the long silence, risked
opening the doors unbidden, "and there lay their lord dead on
the floor." By that time Ehud was well on his way home, where he
recruited his army and returned to Moab, "and they killed at that
time about ten thousand of the Moabites, all strong, able-bodied
men. . . . And the land had rest for eighty years."

Strange Distinction

Judge Shamgar's fragmentary biography is told in twenty-three
English words, his only encomium being that he "killed six hundred of the Philistines with an oxgoad," a sturdy sharp-pointed
stick.

A Woman Judge

Again Israel defected and this time fell under the hand of the
king of Canaan, who had a mighty general named Sisera supported by nine hundred chariots of iron. Since the Israelites had
not yet learned to work with iron they felt helpless. However, they
had a resourceful woman judge who was also a prophetess, named
Deborah. She held court in the hill country of Ephraim under a
tree known as "the palm of Deborah." Deciding the time had come
to deliver Israel from Canaan's domination, she instructed Barak,
commander of the Israelite forces, to take ten thousand men and
advance on Canaan, promising that when General Sisera reached
the river Kishon she would deliver him into Barak's hand. Barak
believed her—almost, but said he would go ahead only if she accompanied the army. Deborah may have felt a mite of scorn for
Barak, because although she promised success she added that the
success would not reflect glory on him because Sisera would be
killed by the hand of a woman. Which is exactly what happened.
When Sisera realized that the Canaanite army was losing to Barak

he fled on foot to a friendly tribe of Kenites and hid in the tent of a woman named Jael. Seeing his exhaustion Jael gave him milk to drink and bade him sleep while she kept watch. He slept comfortably—until she picked up a tent peg and drove it through his temple with a hammer "down into the ground." When Barak in hot pursuit arrived at the tent, there was his man dead but killed by the hand of a woman. Nevertheless it was a time to celebrate. "Then sang Deborah and Barak . . . on that day."

This poem, known as the Song of Deborah, is the oldest fragment of poetry of any length in Hebrew literature, an epic rehearsal of the story of Israel's conquest, including a poignant account of the mother of Sisera waiting in vain for her son's expected triumphal return, bearing gifts for her.

> "From heaven fought the stars,
>   from their courses they fought against Sisera. . . .
>   March on, my soul, with might!" 5:20–21

Gideon

The next time the Israelites "did what was evil in the sight of the Lord," the Lord allowed their Midianite neighbors from the desert to attack their crops until neither people, sheep, oxen nor asses had sufficient food. When the people cried out in desperation an angel of the Lord addressed the farmer Gideon as he was beating out his wheat in a wine press, where the warring Midianites would never suspect grain to be stored. "The Lord is with you, you mighty man of valor."

Gideon could not believe his eyes and ears. Who—what was this apparition? Whose voice was he hearing? However astounded he might be, he knew the words were meant for him. Still, he needed proof: ". . . show me a sign that it is thou who speakest with me." Here he was, the least of his family, belonging to the weakest clan of the tribe of Manasseh, feeling he was called of God. How would he get tangible assurance that he was not having delusions of grandeur? Best he should make a sacrifice! So Gideon prepared a kid, added an offering of wheat, broth and unleavened bread, along with his anxious heart, and went forth to a spot under an oak where he could present his offering to God. When he placed his offering on a rock, a fire sprang forth consuming the offering. Sign enough, and Gideon built an altar on the spot, took courage from God's approval, and that very night destroyed his own father's altar to the great Canaanite god Baal. When morning came, however, there was no enthusiastic acclamation of his leadership in doing away with foreign gods. Instead, people wanted to kill him, fearing he might have alienated friendly fertility spirits. Gideon's father came to his aid, arguing that retribution could be left to Baal himself.

The Midianites and the Amalekites "and the people of the East" gathered for war against the Israelites. Would Gideon respond? ". . . the Spirit of the Lord took possession of Gideon; and he sounded the trumpet," which brought immediate and widespread support. Nevertheless, intrepid Gideon was not so assured but that he needed one more sign from the Lord; something supernatural to show that the Lord was supporting Israel. His answer came in the form of a heavy dew that completely soaked the freshly sheared fleece spread on the ground but did not even dampen the ground beneath. No man, no matter how carefully he measured out water, could accomplish that.

So now Gideon was ready to mount an attack but the Lord pointed out that if he went forth with so large an army and won, the Israelites would think they had triumphed in their own might. This was to be the Lord's own battle. So Gideon was ordered to weed out the fearful from his army, which resulted in sending home twenty-two thousand men, leaving a trim regiment of ten thousand. Still too many. Let the soldiers be tested by drinking from a stream. Those who leaned over to lap the water were eliminated; only three hundred were retained—those who dipped up the water in their hands, lifting it to their mouth while keeping their eyes open for the possible approach of an enemy. With these three hundred picked soldiers Gideon prepared to fight. Each soldier carried a trumpet in one hand and in the other hand a pottery jar in which a lighted torch was hidden. At dawn Gideon sounded his trumpet; each soldier answered with his own trumpet and all shouted "For the Lord and for Gideon," then broke their jars and held aloft their torches. Bedlam reigned in the enemy camp and Israel prevailed. In order to pursue the fleeing troops Gideon rallied the support of the men of Ephraim, his kinsmen, but they were angry at being called in so late, so that it took all his persuasion and flattery to pacify and muster them. With his army thus augmented, Gideon captured the kings of Midian and avenged the deaths of his brothers.

A Farsighted Decision

Expectedly the men of Israel pleaded with Gideon to rule over them, "you and your son and your grandson also." But Gideon replied, "I will not rule over you, and my son will not rule over you; the Lord will rule over you"; and "the land had rest forty years in the days of Gideon."

Return to Struggle

After Gideon's death it was Abimelech, his son by a concubine from Shechem, who persuaded the people of Shechem that he should rule rather than one of the seventy legitimate sons of Gideon. Abimelech's army of "worthless and reckless fellows" went to Gideon's ancestral home and killed sixty-nine of the brothers. Only Jotham, the youngest, escaped. But after three years the people of Shechem rose against Abimelech, in return for which "he took the city, and killed the people that were in it; and he razed the city and sowed it with salt" so that nothing could grow there. Proceeding to the nearby town of Thebez he attacked the tower to which people had fled for safety, but just as he prepared to burn down the door of the tower a woman on the roof "threw an upper millstone upon Abimelech's head, and crushed his skull." Dying, he called for his armor-bearer to thrust a sword through him so that it could not be said he died at a woman's hand.

Instant Help

Two judges, Tola who lived in Ephraim, and Jair who "had thirty sons who rode on thirty asses; and they had thirty cities," are passed over by the historian with no further characterization than the length of their reigns. After them the people sinned again. And this time their grievances were more than they could bear so that any punishment the Lord felt fitting seemed preferable to their present woes. "We have sinned; do to us whatever seems good to thee; only deliver us, we pray thee, this day." Instant help—isn't that what we all pray for?

Jephthah's Sacrifice

Their answer was Jephthah, son of a harlot, ostracized from his father's house, who gathered around him "worthless fellows" who went raiding with him. Nevertheless, Jephthah became "a mighty warrior" and in desperation the elders of Gilead persuaded him to lead them. Since he seemed the best man available. ". . . the Spirit of the Lord came upon Jephthah" and he moved against the Ammonites. To insure his success he made a vow to the Lord that if the Ammonites were delivered into his hand he would sacrifice "whoever comes forth from the doors of my house to meet me, when I return victorious. . . ." When he returned victorious it was his daughter, his only child, who "came out to meet him with timbrels and with dances."

Throughout most of their history the Hebrews countenanced no human sacrifice but there were times when the standards of their neighbors, devout in their own way, challenged the Hebrew spirit of sacrifice. No one, not even Jephthah's daughter, suggested that his vow be rescinded. All the daughter asked was two months alone with her close companions in the mountains to bewail her virginity because for a Hebrew woman to die childless was as pointless as never to have been born. "And it became a custom in Israel that the daughters of Israel went year by year to lament the daughter of Jephthah the Gileadite four days in the year." But the historian did not feel it important to mention her name.

In his six-year reign Jephthah had a round of contention with the Ephraimites and whenever fleeing Ephraimites tried to cross a ford held by Jephthah's men the guards challenged them to pronounce the word *shibboleth*. Gileadites and Ephraimites were related tribes who might look alike but they did not talk alike. Ephraimites could not pronounce the *sh* sound, and slaughter followed mispronunciation. (A precedent for language purists.) Fighting continued "and there fell at that time forty-two thousand of the Ephraimites."

Undistinguished Leadership

Ibzan of Bethlehem was famous only for having thirty sons for whom he brought thirty wives in from other clans and thirty daughters for whom he sought husbands from other clans. Next Elon the Zebulunite judged Israel for ten years and died, leaving the record neither better nor worse than he found it, a typical middle-of-the-roader. After him Abdon had thirty sons and forty grandsons who rode on seventy asses; period. "And the people of Israel again did what was evil in the sight of the Lord," which cost them forty years of laboring for the Philistines.

Samson

Then came Samson. Samson was the local strong man, able to perform wonders of physical prowess. Whenever he needed help in a dilemma he called on the Lord and felt he was answered by an influx of "the Spirit of the Lord." Spiritual quickening often seems to precipitate physical well-being. It was reported that before his conception his mother had been warned by an ethereal figure that her son would become a Nazirite who must never touch wine, or eat anything ritually unclean, or allow a razor to touch his head. Samson gloried in his strength. However, he must have had other, unrecorded qualifications for leadership because "he judged Israel twenty years in the days of the Philistines" but local historians mainly recorded the unusual facts which furnished the table talk of the countryside.

In his young manhood Samson made a trip into the country of the Philistines, Israel's neighbors to the west. Having a higher material culture than the Israelites they attracted their country neighbors. On his way Samson was attacked by a lion and barehanded "tore the lion asunder as one tears a kid." Of course not everyone could even tear a kid asunder barehanded but that was a day when men matched raw strength and skill against the forces of nature. Returning from his trip, Samson saw bees making honey in the lion's carcass, helped himself, and took some home to his parents, perhaps to sweeten his request that they promptly arrange his marriage to a Philistine girl he had met in the city. Which they did.

At the wedding feast Samson remembered the lionful of honey and came up with a riddle, promising festal garments to the thirty Philistine male attendants if they guessed it. The Hebrews doted on riddles and puns and Samson no doubt felt very clever, which he was.

> "Out of the eater came something to eat.
> Out of the strong came something sweet." 14:14

Unable to guess his riddle his Philistine friends threatened his bride so that she maneuvered the answer from her new husband. What bridegroom could have resisted the chance to mention to his bride, nonchalantly, that he had killed a lion barehanded? His friends then "guessed" the answer. When Samson realized he had been tricked he commented:

> "If you had not plowed with my heifer,
> you would not have found out my riddle." 14:18

Angered at his new friends, Samson went to a neighboring Philistine town and killed thirty men, whose festal garments he distributed to the wedding attendants according to his promise. Then he left his wife with her father and returned home. Having already had enough of Samson, the bride's father gave her to another man, without notifying Samson. At harvest time Samson decided to return to his wife and only then found she was married to someone else. In great anger he caught three hundred foxes, tied them "tail to tail, and put a torch between each pair of tails," then turned them loose to burn the entire harvest of grain and olive trees. A mad scene perpetrated by an angry hero against tricky enemies who were no doubt envious of the endowments of this man they wished to consider an Israelite bumpkin.

Stripped of their harvest it was now the Philistines' turn to be angry. They turned on Samson's erstwhile bride and literally "came up and burned her and her father with fire." Samson was aghast. ". . . I swear I will be avenged upon you. . . . And he smote them hip and thigh with great slaughter," after which he escaped and hid himself in the rocky highlands.

So the Philistines raided Judah in search of Samson, which frightened the men of Judah into promising to rout out Samson themselves and deliver him up. When they found him they could not bind him; he would have to be killed. But Samson promised that if they would not kill him he would let himself be bound. Then ". . . the Philistines came shouting to meet him; and the Spirit of the Lord came mightily upon him" so that he broke the ropes easily, picked up the fresh jawbone of an ass "and with it he slew a thousand men."

Delilah

Enter Delilah, for centuries since the heroine-villainess of song and story. Samson loved her with his usual ardor. "And the lords of the Philistines came to her and said to her, 'Entice him, and see wherein his great strength lies, and by what means we may overpower him, that we may bind him to subdue him; and we will each give you eleven hundred pieces of silver.'" For some nights Samson gave her false information so that when she had him variously bound as he slept he was always able to break the bonds. But finally "his soul was vexed to death" at her importunities and he told her he had been a Nazirite from birth and would lose his strength if his head was shaved. Consequently that night as he trustingly slept with his head upon her knees, she had his head shaved, then called for the lords of the Philistines, who brought the promised silver, "seized him and gouged out his eyes, and brought him down to Gaza, and bound him with bronze fetters; and he ground at the mill in the prison." The mighty Samson, blind, chained like an ass to a millstone! A desecration of superb human endowment.

"But the hair of his head began to grow again," a portent which escaped the notice of his captors. At festival time they gathered "to offer a great sacrifice to Dagon their god" and to celebrate the fact that Samson was their slave. Finally they brought him out to make sport for them. Samson sensed the size of the crowd; "on the roof there were about three thousand men and women." A gala occasion. ". . . and Samson said to the lad who held him by the hand, 'Let me feel the pillars on which the house rests, that I may lean against them.'" Then he called on the Lord for strength, leaned his weight on the two pillars, "his right hand on the one and his left hand on the other . . . bowed with all his might," and pulled the house down. "So the dead whom he slew at his death were more than those whom he had slain during his life." A tragedy of misdirected strength.

Need for a King

The remainder of the book of Judges is composed of appendixes which offer additional material gathered from various sources to show that Israel needed a king because only chaos resulted from tribal rivalry. Chapters 17 to 18 are in essence a report of the way the tribe of Dan found a new location. An Ephraimite named Micah stole silver from his mother, repented, returned the money and his mother used part of it to make "a graven image and a molten image" for which "a young man of Bethlehem in Judah" was ultimately hired as priest. One day five able men from the Danites, hunting a place for permanent settlement, lodged in the house of Micah, recognized the accent of the priest from Bethlehem, got his priestly approval of their errand, and promptly took both images and priest along with them. When they found themselves at Laish, a northern city famous for its springs and occupied by a people who were "quiet and unsuspecting, lacking nothing that is in the earth, and possessing wealth," they decided to move in against them. Gathering their forces from the rest of the tribe of Dan, they smote the people of Laish "with the edge of the sword, and burned the city with fire." Then they rebuilt it and named it Dan.

Chapters 19 to 21 form the second appendix, a gory tale of sexual excess, murder, war and reprisal. "A certain Levite" who lived in the hills of Ephraim took a concubine from Bethlehem, but the concubine walked out on him and went home. After a year or so the husband decided to forgive her and go bring her back. On their return journey they stopped for the night at a town of Benjaminites where an old man invited them to his house. While they dined, some "men of the city, base fellows," beat on the door demanding the newly arrived stranger for homosexual exploits. The host refused, offering instead his virgin daughter and the concubine. The men accepted the concubine and "abused her all night until the morning," when she fell down at the door of her host's house. At dawn her husband, ready to continue his journey, came out of the house and found her dead. He put her body on his ass, returned home, took a knife, and "divided her, limb by limb, into twelve pieces," sending the pieces to the various districts of Israel, "from Dan to Beersheba," demanding retribution on the Benjaminites. Some "four hundred thousand men on foot that drew the sword" (an improbable number) came forth to avenge "the wanton crime." The Benjaminites gathered for battle, including "seven hundred picked men who were left-handed; every one could sling a stone at a hair, and not miss." Civil war ensued until most of the male Benjaminites were killed, except for six hundred who fled to the rocky wilderness. In their frustrated rage the rest of the men of Israel swore never to give a daughter to be wife of a Benjaminite.

But eventually there came one of the periodic ingatherings of all the tribes of Israel, when sacrifices and peace offerings were made. Only the tribe of Benjamin was missing. Weeping, the people cried out to the Lord, ". . . why has this come to pass in Israel, that there should be today one tribe lacking in Israel?" Blood relationship *was* stronger than anger and the rest of the family of Israel repented the severing of the Benjaminites. Not able to break their oath but determined to find wives for the disinherited Benjaminites lest the tribe die out, Israel decided to attack the people of Jabesh-gilead, east of the Jordan, on the pretext that they had not attended a former gathering of the clans at Mizpah. All the inhabitants of Jabesh-gilead, young and old, were killed except four hundred virgins, who were presented to the beleaguered Benjaminites. However, still more wives were needed so it was agreed that at the "yearly feast of the Lord at Shiloh," when "the daughters of Shiloh come out to dance in the dances," the rest of the Benjaminite men should be allowed to capture wives. Thus no one would actually be breaking his oath by giving a wife to a Benjaminite but the tribe of Benjamin would be replenished with stolen brides and wholeness restored to Israel.

So the book of Judges closes its record of memorable events associated with the tribal forays and achievements of the loosely confederated Hebrew tribes. The fact that God had led them, meting punishment and reward as earned, may have been more apparent to the historians looking back on the record than to the people living it out. The emerging question was whether or not a king could bring about better government for Israel, and the book closes with the observation: "In those days there was no king in Israel; every man did what was right in his own eyes."

Ruth

A legend of devotion, of famine and flight, of foreign marriages and bereavement in a strange land, of a brave journey home, of staunch friendship and finally a pastoral love story—this is the book of Ruth. Although the events depicted occurred "in the days when the judges ruled," around 1200 B.C., the book appears on internal evidence to have been written between 400 B.C. and 250 B.C. The story is not merely a retelling of an historical incident but a tale with social purpose. The unnamed author presents a point of view opposite to that of Nehemiah and Ezra, who underlined the Deuteronomic law that no descendant of a Moabite could belong to the assembly of the Lord even to the tenth generation—a bitterness derived from Moabite refusal to aid the Hebrews in their trek into Canaan—and insisted that all Hebrew men give up their foreign wives. Into the argument as to what constitutes true loyalty steps the book of Ruth. Because of its spirit of friendship and common sense the book became popular and is still read at the Feast of Weeks, a harvest festival. Modern readers do well to approach the book under the bright light of their own prejudices, since the point of view that we-are-the-people did not fade with the death of Nehemiah or with the birth of the United Nations, and many parents still categorically frown on what are termed "mixed marriages."

The Making of a Tragedy

A man named Elimelech, meaning "God is King," whose home was Bethlehem, meaning "house of bread," found famine threatening starvation, so he took his wife Naomi, meaning "my pleasant one," and his sons Mahlon and Chilion, whose names meant "weakness" and "pining away," and headed for Moab and food. The sons married Moabite women: Orpah, meaning "stiff-necked," and Ruth, meaning "companion." Elimelech died and ten years later the sons also died. The material of tragedy: Naomi widowed and far from her own people, her daughters-in-law dependent on her. But Naomi was not the woman to collapse under misfortune. No doubt having heard from passing caravans that prosperity had returned to her own country, she decided to take her daughters-in-law and go home.

But then she had a second thought. She was very fond of her daughters-in-law; why should they go with her into an uncertain future? "Turn back, my daughters, go your way. . . . I am too old to have a husband." She meant she was too old to remarry and have sons who would someday marry them according to the custom of levirate marriage, which decreed that a living brother was duty bound to marry his dead brother's widow so that she could have children in the dead brother's name. She felt it would be better for the young women to return to their own people, re-marry, and lead normal lives. The three women wept.

Ambassador of Kindness

It scarcely seems likely that Naomi thought of herself as an am-bassador of the Lord in Moab but she must have lived out her devotion to her own God in persuasive fashion, because the younger women insisted upon returning with her to her own peo-ple. But Naomi had her mind made up and Orpah finally de-cided that her mother-in-law was right. ". . . and Orpah kissed her mother-in-law" and went back to her own home. Love must have cast a light on her path.

Loyalty Beyond Duty

Ruth determined to continue the journey with her mother-in-law. Her words are as famous as any woman's in biblical history:

But Ruth said, "Entreat me not to leave you or to return from following you; for where you go I will go, and where you lodge I will lodge; your people shall be my people, and your God my God; where you die I will die, and there will I be buried. May the Lord do so to me and more also if even death parts me from you." And when Naomi saw that she was determined to go with her, she said no more. 1:16–18

Women do have a way of understanding women, and these two women were of one mind in heading straight for Bethlehem. When they finally arrived, the town was astounded. "Is this Naomi?" they said to each other. She answered, "Don't call me Naomi (pleasant), call me Mara (bitter), for the Almighty has dealt very bitterly with me." But he had given her a faithful daughter-in-law.

The Harvest

Naomi did not sit down and pity herself. She looked over her relatives and then appraised the barley harvest. The two widows had themselves to support and at the spring harvest there would be work for almost anyone who wanted to labor daybreak to dark. Naomi remembered that a kinsman of her husband named Boaz was a wealthy man whose harvest was bound to be ample and he would follow the custom, which was also a Mosaic law, of leaving gleanings for the poor.

So Ruth went forth to glean, picking up the stalks of grain left by the reapers. Midday, who should appear in the field—of course—but Boaz himself. A landlord at the time of a bountiful harvest was likely to be an expansive man. He greeted the reapers: "The Lord be with you." Plainly the Lord was with *him*. The reapers answered, "The Lord bless you." Commonly the Lord is expected by poor people to bless the rich, especially if the rich are also good. Boaz spotted the girl, who kept her eager eyes on her gleaning as if her armload of barley meant a lot to her. "Whose maiden is this?" he asked. The head foreman answered that she was the Moabite woman who had come home with Naomi: "She said, 'Pray, let me glean and gather among the sheaves after the reapers.' So she came, and she has continued from early morning until now, without resting even for a moment."

Boaz did not need to be reminded of his manners, especially when his duty was so pleasant. He went over to Ruth and told her to stay right there in his fields; follow his own harvesters. He would see to it that none of the young men bothered her. "And when you are thirsty, go to the vessels and drink what the young men have drawn." Fresh water. That was one thing she had to have if she was going to keep on gleaning under the hot Palestinian sky. Ruth bowed to the ground and expressed her surprise and appreciation that he should be so kind to a foreigner. She did not add, "especially a Moabitess," but she probably thought it.

Boaz assured her that he knew all about the way she had stayed with her mother-in-law and made the long journey home with her. "The Lord recompense you for what you have done, and a full reward be given to you by the Lord, the God of Israel, under whose wings you have come to take refuge!"

At that moment he would probably have been surprised if he had guessed that he himself was one of the rewards the Lord was about to bestow upon her. (But how like the Lord! When Ruth left Moab with her mother-in-law she had seen only a little way ahead but God outran her, as is his way, anticipating her needs.) Ruth thanked Boaz: "You are most gracious to me, my lord, for you have comforted me and spoken kindly to your maidservant. . . ."

When the harvest lunch was spread out, Boaz urged her to help herself to the bread and wine; also to the parched grain. Then when the harvesting began again he told his harvesters to let her glean right up beside them and to drop some of the stalks of barley in her path. Neat for the little girl from Moab. All day Ruth gleaned and then beat out her grain, which amounted to about a bushel. Returning to the city, she delivered the gain, the rest of her lunch, and the news of the day to her mother-in-law. Naomi pondered the report and reminded her that, after all, Boaz was one of their nearest kin. Being a pious woman, Naomi added, "Blessed be he by the Lord, whose kindness has not forsaken the living or the dead!"

Harvest Festival

Day after day Ruth went on gleaning, first barley, then wheat. Naomi was no doubt pleased to see their measures of grain increase; it was more than comforting to have a daughter-in-law like Ruth. Nevertheless, she told Ruth she really ought to have a home, and a husband. And on that point she had an idea. There was Boaz! The lord of the manor, no less. Had he not been more than kind? That very night his men would be winnowing the barley, the climax of the harvest season. Let Ruth bathe and perfume herself, put on her best clothes, and go to the festive threshing bee. At such a celebration her finery would not be conspicuous but on the other hand she would probably not be recognized. Naomi admonished, ". . . do not make yourself known to the man until he has finished eating and drinking." She intended the country cousin from Moab to be something of a surprise for Boaz. The older woman continued, "But when he lies down, observe the place where he lies; then, go and uncover his feet and lie down; and he will tell you what to do."

To Ruth the advice seemed proper enough and she did exactly as she was told. When Boaz had feasted "and his heart was merry," he made himself a bed at the end of a heap of grain. He probably had with him the long woolen robe, or cloak, which men of the Palestinian countryside wore against the cold night air of autumn. Immediately he fell asleep. So she uncovered his feet and lay down close by. At midnight Boaz wakened, startled, asking, "Who are you?" She told him, "I am Ruth, your maidservant; spread your skirt over your maidservant, for you are next of kin" —which was her way of saying there were many frolicking young men who had also feasted and drunk and she wished protection. For a man to spread his cloak over an individual meant sponsorship; he would be taking on responsibility for the one he symbolically covered. Even today the symbol persists in some Russian Orthodox wedding ceremonies.

> And he said, "May you be blessed by the Lord, my daughter; you have made this kindness greater than the first, in that you have not gone after young men, whether poor or rich. And now, my daughter, do not fear, for I will do for you all that you ask, for all my fellow townsmen know that you are a woman of worth." 3:10–11

He was indeed a near kinsman, he went on, but there was one nearer to her husband in relationship. If that man did not claim the privilege of buying her husband's share of the land and looking after her, "then, as the Lord lives, I will do the part of the next of kin for you."

Actually, the writer of the story seems a bit hazy on the rights of levirate marriage, because the Mosaic law never demanded that the next of kin marry a widow who had no offspring; only that a brother of the deceased marry the widow. But since the retelling of the tale came some hundreds of years after the event the author should be forgiven a small discrepancy.

In the morning Boaz rose before dawn, told Ruth to hold out her apron while he poured six measures of barley into it, and bade her go on home while he went to interrogate the next of kin, whose rights outranked his. So Ruth went home happily carrying the barley and told her mother-in-law all that had happened. Naomi could not have been more pleased and insisted that before night Ruth would find herself betrothed.

The Happy Ending

Boaz lost no time. He located the next of kin and invited him to sit down by the city gate, where important business was customarily transacted, with a ceremonial bit of refreshment. The kinsman accepted the invitation. Then comes an important comment from the storyteller: "And he took ten men of the elders of the city, and said, 'Sit down here'; so they sat down." It is from this gathering of ten men that the Jewish custom requiring ten males in order to constitute a working quorum in the synagogue takes its rise. Boaz explained to the ten elders that Naomi was about to sell the land of her dead husband and that it was the privilege of the next of kin to buy it if he wished. The kinsman said he would be glad to redeem the land.

> Then Boaz said, "The day you buy the field from the hand of Naomi, you are also buying Ruth the Moabitess, the widow of the dead, in order to restore the name of the dead to his inheritance." 4:5

This was a different matter. The kinsman said, "Take my right of redemption yourself, for I cannot redeem it."

So Boaz took off his sandal and handed it to his kinsman, who put it on as a sign an agreement had been made; perhaps an ancient way of standing in another's shoes. Boaz informed all the people watching the transaction that he had just bought everything that belonged to Elimelech and his sons, including Ruth the Moabitess. The people wished him well, and hoped that "the woman, who is coming into your house," would build up the house of Israel as Rachel and Leah had done.

THE KINGDOM PERIOD

B.C. The United Kingdom
1020 Saul, King of Israel
1000 David, King of Judah
994 David, King of all Israel
961 Solomon, King of all Israel
922 Civil war and the division of the kingdom

B.C.	Judah, the Southern Kingdom — Kings	Judah — Prophets	Israel, the Northern Kingdom — Kings	Israel — Prophets	Assyrian Empire	Babylonian Empire
922	Rehoboam		Jeroboam I			
915	Abijam					
913	Asa					
901						
900			Nadab			
			Baasha			
			Elah		Asshur-nasir-apal II (883-859)	
			Zimri			
			Omri			
877						
876						
873	Jehoshaphat		Ahab	Elijah		
869					Shalmaneser III (858-824) *Battle of Karkar*	
850	Jehoram (Joram)		Ahaziah			
849			Jehoram			
842	Ahaziah / Athaliah		Jehu	Elisha		
837	Joash (Jehoash)					
815			Jehoahaz		Shamshi-Adad V (823-811)	
801			Jehoash (Joash)		Adad-nirari III (810-783)	
800	Amaziah					
786	Azariah (Uzziah)		Jeroboam II			
783						
772				Amos	Shalmaneser IV (782-773) Asshur-dan III (772-756) Asshur-nirari V (755-745)	
750	Jotham (as regent)					
746			Zechariah			

Date	Judah	Prophets	Israel	Hosea	Assyria / Babylonia
745					Tiglath-pileser III (745-727)
742	Jotham	Isaiah	Shallum / Menahem	Hosea	
738			Pekahiah		
737			Pekah		
735	Ahaz				*Syro-Ephraimite war (734)* / *Tiglath-pileser's invasion (733)*
732			Hoshea		Shalmaneser V (727-722) / Sargon II (722-705)
721			*Fall of Samaria*		
715	Hezekiah	Micah			Sennacherib (705-681)
687	Manasseh				Esarhaddon (680-669) / Asshur-ban-apal (668-630)
642	Amon				Asshur-etililani (629-627) / Sinsharishkun (626-612)
640	Josiah				Nabopolassar (626-604)
621		*Publication of Deuteronomy* / Jeremiah			*Fall of Nineveh* / *Battle of Carchemish (605)* / Nebuchadnezzar (604-561)
609	Jehoahaz / Jehoiakim				Asshur-uballit II (612-609)
598	Jehoiachin	Ezekiel			Amel-Marduk (561-559)
597	Zedekiah				Nergal-shar-usur (559-555)
587	*Fall of Jerusalem, Babylonian Exile*				Labashi-Marduk (555) / Nabu-na'id (555-539)
538	*First Return of the Exiles*				*Cyrus the Great extends the Persian Empire, conquers Babylonia, and permits the Jews to return to Jerusalem.*

The story does not recount whether news of the transaction reached Ruth by way of some curious bystander who had been at the city gate or whether she had to wait nervously for Boaz to come with his own announcement. It says simply:

> So Boaz took Ruth and she became his wife . . . and the Lord gave her conception, and she bore a son. Then the women said to Naomi, "Blessed be the Lord, who has not left you this day without next of kin; and may his name be renowned in Israel! He shall be to you a restorer of life and a nourisher of your old age; for your daughter-in-law who loves you, who is more to you than seven sons, has borne him." 4:13–15

Tender words which have sung themselves into the hearts of generations of grateful mothers-in-law: "your daughter-in-law who loves you." At last Naomi again had a man in the family, a blessing every woman appreciates—a strong masculine shoulder.

The author of this tale called his book "Ruth" but he could have called it "Naomi," because hers was the more powerful story. It is harder to make a new start at fifty, enervated by the loss of husband and sons and living in a foreign land, than to face an unknown future at twenty, when uncertainty is colored by a sense of adventure and hope constantly renews itself.

"Then Naomi took the child and laid him in her bosom, and became his nurse." The gesture of laying the babe in her bosom was an old symbol of adoption. Sometimes a newborn child might be left by a caravan at an oasis and for a woman to lay it on her bosom was to signify her responsibility for it. "And the women of the neighborhood gave him a name, saying, 'A son has been born to Naomi.'"

The most important disclosure of the whole tale, the reason for perpetuating this bit of history, lies in the next sentence: "they named him Obed; he was the father of Jesse, the father of David." David the king! David "the sweet singer of Israel," idol of the nation for generations. Ruth, a Moabite woman, was the great-grandmother of David, the line from which the Messiah should come. Let someone find fault with *that*. Or let them genuflect to this loyal great-grandmother adopted into the house of Israel.

First Samuel

The two books of Samuel, fifty-five chapters, and the two books of Kings, forty-seven chapters, were originally one document without chapters. Together they told the story of the rise of kingship in Israel under the guiding hand of Samuel, its peak administration under Saul, David and Solomon, and the ensuing division of the United Kingdom into the two domains of Israel and Judah with their own rulers. On first reading, the book of First Samuel can be confusing because the story seems to have two points of view: kings were a great idea, just what the people needed, and kings were a calamity. The confusion is due to the fact that there were two strains of tradition, and the final editors who gathered the history together wanted to use both. Today scholars call the two strands the Early Source and the Late Source.

Much of the Early Source reads as if it had been written by someone who knew the scene firsthand—possibly Abiathar who was close to David and saw kingship as ordained by God for the good of the nation. Its presentation is so forthright and logical that some authorities feel its author should be called the father of history instead of the Greek historian Herodotus two centuries later. The first compilation of materials probably occurred during the reign of Josiah, in the late-seventh century B.C., when kingship again seemed a successful form of government.

The Late Source was apparently an assembling of materials after the division of the kingdom when both record keepers and public had a much less affirmative view of kingship. Then the two versions were fitted together by the Deuteronomic editors during the exile of the Jews to Babylon a century later. Considerable data were added: military reports contemporary with the events they described, court records, local traditions, legends, poems and interpretive comment. The interweaving of materials without deletion of contradictions brings the turbulent years of the monarchy to life.

Samuel

The story of Samuel begins appropriately in the temple. His mother Hannah, then childless, was there with her husband and his second wife and children for the yearly festival. As she prayed for a child, Hannah wept so heartbrokenly that Eli, the high priest, accused her of being drunk on festival wine. However, when she explained her grief he joined her in prayer. Right there Hannah promised the Lord that if she bore a son she would dedicate him to the temple service "all the days of his life." Within a year the child was born. When little Samuel was three years old she took him to the temple to live. Her song of thanksgiving is one of the earliest hymns in the Bible.

Samuel seems to have been happy with the temple routine, which included festive occasions and a constant stream of people coming to make sacrifices, for the record states, "Now the boy Samuel continued to grow both in stature and in favor with the Lord and with men." Living in the temple, he could not help knowing that Eli's sons who assisted in the priestly functions were dissolute men, cheating the people and ignoring temple regulations. He grieved for Eli, his surrogate father, and in that anxious state he had his first supernormal experience. Jewish tradition says he was twelve when he first heard the word of the Lord, which is about the age when religious concern and psychic ability become noticeable in a gifted adolescent steeped in religious tradition.

One night, sleeping in his usual place near the ark of God, Samuel thought he heard Eli call, but when he went to him the priest insisted he had not called. The third time, Eli realized the boy must be hearing the voice of the Lord and instructed him to respond, "Speak, Lord, for thy servant hears." The message Samuel received was not a happy one: Eli's household was about to be punished "because his sons were blaspheming God, and he did not restrain them." Apparently in the eyes of the Most Holy it was not enough to bring up sons to follow religious ritual; they had to be pure in action. To an observant adolescent the difference was apparent.

By the time Samuel was grown, the record states, "all Israel from Dan to Beer-sheba knew that Samuel was established as a prophet of the Lord."

Both in war and peace the Israelites were badly handicapped by the superior material culture of their close neighbors, the Philistines, to whom they often had to pay tribute. Moreover, the Philistines prohibited the Israelites from working in iron, and all iron implements and weapons had to be bought from Philistine craftsmen. But the Israelites had one possession which bolstered their self-esteem: the ark wherein their God Yahweh dwelt. On one of their periodic forays when they were being repulsed with great loss they decided to bring forth the ark accompanied by the two priestly sons of Eli. As soon as the ark arrived at the scene of battle "all Israel gave a mighty shout," which threw sudden fear into the Philistines, who began to murmur, "The gods have come into the camp." Still—if they gave way to their fear and Israel won they would be the ones enslaved, so they fought desperately and triumphed. ". . . there fell of Israel thirty thousand foot soldiers. And the ark of God was captured; and the two sons of Eli . . . were slain." When the news was brought to Eli, by then ninety-eight years old, he "fell over backward . . . and his neck was broken and he died. . . . He had judged Israel forty years." A good man, faithful to his duties, but never able to discipline his own children. A predicament not confined to the tenth century B.C.

The Philistines carried the captured ark into the temple of their own god Dagon but the next morning Dagon was found lying on his face before the ark. Replaced on his pedestal, he was found the second morning broken into pieces. Soon afterward an epidemic of tumors broke out among the Philistines, causing "deathly panic throughout the whole city." Concurrently the number of mice in the vicinity multiplied. (The ancients connected epidemics of tumors with mice, which makes us suspect bubonic plague, characterized by tumorous growths caused by bacteria carried by the fleas on rats.) That the terror was sent by Israel's God, who dwelt in the ark, the Philistines had no doubt. The ark must be returned! With it went a guilt offering of five golden tumors and five golden mice, a kind of sympathetic magic which indicated respect for whatever power had caused the mice and tumors to run rampant. Unfortunately some seventy men looked into the ark to see if the Lord's presence was discernible and they immediately died, which caused the awed observers to marvel, "Who is able to stand before the Lord, this holy God?" As soon as the ark was back in its home territory with a freshly consecrated priest, Eleazar, in charge, "all the house of Israel lamented after the Lord," indicating they would like to restore relationship to him.

"Here I Raise My Ebenezer"

Again the Philistines threatened invasion, so that the Israelites importuned Samuel to pray without ceasing in their behalf. As the smoke of the burnt offering rose, the Lord "thundered with a mighty voice," a concurrence of storm and revelation which threw the Philistines into confusion. Quickly the Israelites pursued "and smote them"; then, in token of victory, Samuel set up a stone which he named Ebenezer, meaning "Hitherto the Lord has helped us." The countryside had many such stones, or piles of stones, commemorating God's benevolent intervention in righting difficult circumstances.

Popular Demand for a King

For decades Samuel was busy as an itinerant judge. (Imagine the usefulness today if a member of the Supreme Court could go where the trouble was, set up his high court bench, hear the evidence, and then when necessary draw on his psychic power to pin down guilt.)

> Samuel judged Israel all the days of his life. And he went on a circuit year by year to Bethel, Gilgal, and Mizpah. . . . Then he would come back to Ramah, for his home was there, and there also he administered justice to Israel. And he built there an altar to the Lord. 7:15–17

He even appointed his sons as judges but they did not have their father's character; "they took bribes and perverted justice." This must have doubly troubled Samuel, remembering how he had been the messenger of God's wrath to Eli. Sons are probably a father's severest test—unless it is daughters.

As he went around the country Samuel saw that the people of Israel increasingly wanted a king, a full-panoplied king who would unify the country; a king, "that we may be like all the nations." Since the next section of the story derives from the Late Source after the people of Israel were disillusioned about the usefulness of kings, Samuel is presented as reluctant to acquiesce in choosing a king. He prayed and to his disappointment the Lord told him to give the people what they demanded; "for they have not rejected you, but they have rejected me from being king over them." Being ruled by God alone was too difficult. Easier to have an absolute ruler whose edicts could be followed, dodged, or circumvented.

Samuel was one to obey the Lord but not without some eloquent words of warning to his constituency about the demanding ways of kings with taxes, forced labor, conscription into the army, royal appropriation of the best of the cattle, sheep and asses, an expensive court, and still more taxes. "But the people refused to listen to the voice of Samuel."

The Will of God

Now what was the will of God, really, in the matter of Israel's government? No doubt he did have a will, a perfect will, for his people. An abundant life for mature people was probably his intentional will. But the people of Israel also had wills of their own which even God would not violate, so he had to resort to his circumstantial will, nudging them toward the best way to deal with their situation in the currently entangling circumstances, leaving his ultimate will to be worked out in joint endeavor. Apparently at that moment in history the best which the Lord, even the Lord, could do for them was to use his man Samuel to choose a worthy king.

Anointing of Saul

The unsuspecting candidate for kingship was Saul, "a handsome young man," head and shoulders taller than anyone around him, son of a wealthy Benjaminite, who one day went out into the countryside to look for his father's lost asses. When some distance from home he heard of a seer who might be able to locate the lost asses. But for some reason he did not recognize that the seer was Samuel, judge of Israel.

However, Samuel, forewarned by the Lord, recognized Saul as the future king, invited him to a feast, reassured him that his asses had already been found, treated him as chief guest, and upon parting anointed him king! (Here we are back with the Early Source, when record keepers felt Samuel must have had great pleasure in anointing Israel's first king.) "And you shall reign over the people of the Lord and you will save them from the hand of their enemies round about." Then, to prove that he knew what he was talking about, Samuel gave Saul a clairvoyant preview of the next day's events.

Conversion with Testimony

On the way home Saul met a band of ecstatic prophets "coming down from the high place," playing musical instruments and prophesying with such ardor that he caught their fervor and was "turned into another man." Swept by awe and wonder over the ways of God, he experienced conversion with testimony. "God gave him another heart." His own pentecostal revival. People who had known him said in amazement, "Is Saul also among the prophets?"—a question which became a proverb. As in every generation, those who believed in regeneration in the abstract simply could not believe their own eyes when it happened to an acquaintance.

Choosing a King

The Late Source takes over: Samuel was too canny merely to announce to the public that he had anointed Saul king, so he went through the accepted political procedures. When representatives of the tribes gathered at Mizpah, lots were cast to determine the tribe from which the new king should come; then which family of the chosen tribe, finally which member of the family. The decisive lot fell to Saul of the tribe of Benjamin. (Are you listening, Father Jacob, who loved Benjamin above the others?) "And all the people shouted, 'Long live the king!'" Following the acclamation of

Saul, Samuel admonished him at length as to his rights and duties and "wrote them in a book," emphasizing the fact that it was still the Lord who was supreme ruler.

Saul's first royal venture was a successful foray but instead of applauding him, Samuel made another challenging speech, reviewing his own trustworthy character and the Lord's unfailing leadership, threatening disaster if people or king failed to hearken to the Lord. To prove the Lord's ability to send disaster when he wished, Samuel then prophesied a drenching rain on the wheat harvest—a calamity which seemed incredible since rains never came in the heat of summer. But rain it did, in torrents, with mighty thunder for emphasis; "and all the people greatly feared the Lord and Samuel." The point was made; Saul the king reigned under the omnipotent will of God.

Saul's Embattled Career

Saul's career began and ended in battle. In this age of civilized man it seems ridiculous that one national group should have sought to impose its will by force on another people, but in that day men went to war over trade routes, economic pressure, land hunger, forms of government, and just sheer test of superior might, which is understandable because among primitive people war takes so much less mental effort than peace.

Saul had a valiant son named Jonathan who led a skirmish and defeated an unsuspecting garrison of Philistines. So Saul, fearing Philistine retaliation, blew the trumpet and rallied Israel for immediate all-out war. The Israelite troop movement rallied the Philistines in great numbers that grew in the retelling to thirty thousand chariots with all their supporting troops. At Samuel's bidding Saul was to wait seven days at a given location for the prophet to arrive and make the proper burnt offering before battle. Religious warfare had its protocol. But Samuel was late in arriving and Saul, seeing his men deserting, made the offering himself. In the eyes of the Later Source this was unforgivable; temporal power had superseded religious authority. Because of the desecration Samuel decreed on behalf of God (or at least that was the interpretation of the Late Source) that Saul's house should not continue the succession.

In the heat of the ensuing battle Saul commanded the army to fast until victory was won but Jonathan, unaware of the decree and exhausted from fighting, ate some wild honey, quickly restoring his strength. By night Saul's harried hungry soldiers were faint and when the battle was won they "flew upon the spoil," slaying the sheep and oxen and eating them "with the blood," which was a ritual sin. Appalled, Saul built an altar, his first, and sacrificed. Then he inquired of God by Urim and Thummim whether the army should pursue the Philistines. The device failed to work; the Lord made no response. Who had sinned? The lot fell on Jonathan who admitted having broken the fast through ignorance of the order. Saul decreed his death. But "the people ransomed Jonathan," believing he was largely responsible for their victory, and determined that "there shall not one hair of his head fall to the ground; for he has wrought with God this day." A popular and beloved prince.

"There was hard fighting against the Philistines all the days of Saul." Sometimes Samuel seemed more bloodthirsty than Saul, for instance in urging the utter extermination of the Amalekites from king to livestock in the name of the Lord. When Saul completely overwhelmed the Amalekites but spared King Agag and let the people bring back the best of the spoil to sacrifice and feast on, Samuel was angry and reproached Saul with a searching question: "Has the Lord as great delight in burnt offerings and sacrifices, as in obeying the voice of the Lord?" Then he called King Agag before him.

And Agag came to him cheerfully. . . . And Samuel hewed Agag in pieces before the Lord in Gilgal. . . . And Samuel did not see Saul again until the day of his death, but Samuel grieved over Saul. And the Lord repented that he had made Saul king over Israel. 15:32–33, 35

Choosing of David

Samuel's grief over Saul made the Lord impatient. Why should he keep grieving, the Lord asked, when he himself had already picked a new king to succeed Saul, a son of Jesse of Bethlehem? Samuel must go to Bethlehem to make sacrifice and invite Jesse and his sons to the sacrificial feast. Proceeding as directed, Samuel looked over the sons of this prosperous farmer Jesse and thought he knew which one the Lord had surely chosen for the future king.

> But the Lord said to Samuel, "Do not look on his appearance or the height of his stature . . . for the Lord sees not as man sees; man looks on the outward appearance, but the Lord looks on the heart." 16:7

It was the youngest son, David, fetched in from the sheep pasture, upon whom the Lord's approval rested. "Now he was ruddy, and had beautiful eyes, and was handsome." Samuel anointed him with oil, "and the Spirit of the Lord came mightily upon David from that day forward."

Evidently the news of the anointing was not spread abroad; certainly it did not reach the king in his palace (if the word palace can be used for Saul's fortified dwelling place). Nevertheless Saul was distraught, apprehensive, edgy. But then military life is seldom conducive to repose and Saul had begun to be tormented mentally. A member of his court suggested that the music of the lyre might soothe him, and another suggested "a son of Jesse the Bethlehemite, who is skilful in playing, a man of valor, a man of war, prudent in speech, and a man of good presence; and the Lord is with him." So Saul sent for David, who promptly enlisted in his service. "And Saul loved him greatly, and he became his armorbearer."

David and Goliath

Now here we are in another tangle of tradition. There is a second, and different, story of David's introduction to Saul. On this occasion the Philistines were arrayed in battle on one side of the valley with the army of Israel on the opposite hillside. Daily a champion named Goliath, about ten feet tall and fully decked out in bronze armor and helmet, came forth to challenge Israel. A shepherd boy named David, who happened to be visiting his brothers at the front, accepted Goliath's challenge in behalf of Israel, refused King Saul's loan of his royal armor, took up the slingshot with which he had protected his father's flocks from predatory animals, found himself five smooth stones, then paused to answer the giant's taunts with a fine ethical oration composed like an ode

at the moment of battle, ending with a statement of purpose ". . .
that all this assembly may know that the Lord saves not with sword
and spear; for the battle is the Lord's and he will give you into our
hand." Then he picked up his slingshot, inserted the stone, aimed
at the giant's forehead, and let go. The giant fell dead. "So David
prevailed over the Philistine with a sling and a stone," after which
he cut off his adversary's head. Shouting, the Israelites pursued the
Philistines.

Folklore has many stories of giants killed by modest adversaries
who represent the righteous cause, and the stories continue to
appeal to the imagination because they represent real-life happenings: Goliaths *are* killed by Davids. The regard David's contemporaries had for him may have been magnified by his later
biographers but some of the records they drew on were contemporary with David's life. It is the persuasive quality of the life
of the hero which breeds longevity into the report.

After the slingshot episode the historian returns to the place of
David at court and in battle. And to the comradeship of David
and Jonathan, whose friendship has been proverbial for three
millenniums. More than once David owed his life to Jonathan who
came to realize that his apprehensive father was jealous of David.
Small wonder, for everything that David did succeeded. "And this
was good in the eyes of the people." Twice Saul in anger tried to
pin David to the wall with a spear. Eventually Jonathan and
David had to invent signals, such as Jonathan's shooting an arrow
according to prearranged plan to indicate the state of the king's
wrath. That wrath depended to considerable degree on David's
latest successes, for whenever the Israelite soldiers returned from
battle "the women came out of all the cities of Israel, singing and
dancing. . . . And the women sang . . . as they made merry,
'Saul has slain his thousands, And David his ten thousands.'" A
jolly way to flatter the king. Through all their anxieties, "the soul
of Jonathan was knit to the soul of David, and Jonathan loved him
as his own soul."

Michal

The meager biography of Michal is the material for tragic
drama. Under pretext of gratitude for service rendered, Saul of-

fered David his elder daughter, Merab, in marriage and then with-drew the offer. However, Saul's second daughter, Michal, had fallen in love with David and evidently let her father know. David may also have let Michal know she was his preference. Ostensibly Saul approved this marriage but in a mood of simulated mirth he added the provision that David must bring in a hundred foreskins of Philistines, figuring that should be task enough to cost David his life, since a man who both killed and mutilated would be prime target for the enemy's ire. But David complied with the king's obscene request, brought back two hundred Philistine foreskins and claimed the king's daughter.

One day Michal discovered that her father's summons to David to come to the palace was actually a plan to kill him. Skillfully she managed David's escape out a window, then made an effigy with a pillow of goats' hair for a head and put it in David's bed for the servants to mistake for a sleeping form. Next she sent word to the king that David was ill. Angered, Saul sent servants to bring David to him bed and all, whereupon the ruse was discovered and Saul turned his anger against Michal.

Later, when David was an outlaw, Saul gave Michal to another man, named Phaltiel, and still later, when David himself became king, he sent for her to be returned to the palace. His general, Abner, went after her. "But her husband went with her, weeping after her all the way. . . ." What was the right of a subject compared to the right of a king? From then on, there seems to have been no compatibility between David and Michal; she may have preferred the loyal affection of Phaltiel to the royal affection of David. On a day of great festivity, when the ark was finally brought into Jerusalem, Michal watched the procession of ecstatic dancers and musicians from the palace window and felt chagrined at David's uninhibited dancing. Where he thought he was demonstrating exuberant joy, she felt he was making a fool of himself and later told him so. Angry words were exchanged between the woman born to a king's household and the king born in a farmhouse, the old conflict between patrician pride of birth and plebeian pride of power. David would have no more of her, reminding her that, after all, he was the Lord's choice over her father. "And Michal the daughter of Saul had no child to the day of her death."

A House Divided Against Itself

On one occasion when David escaped death by Saul's order he
fled to Samuel at Ramah. Hearing of his location, Saul sent envoys to take him but they ran into a band of ecstatics with Samuel
at their head prophesying in their usual contagious fashion, and
"the Spirit of God came upon the messengers of Saul, and they
also prophesied." A second and third delegation of messengers
met the same happy fate, which so exasperated Saul that he went
after David himself only to find that "the Spirit of God came upon
him also" and he joined the ecstatics.

The days and ways of the court grew increasingly difficult for
Jonathan who was constantly on the alert for David's safety. Extremely difficult also for David. Once when he fled to Nob he had
to ask bread from Ahimelech, the priest who guarded the ark; the
only bread available was the bread of the Presence, holy before
the Lord, but in his desperate situation David felt justified in
appropriating it. Unfortunately that same day one of Saul's garrison arrived and the weaponless David also had to ask the priest
for a sword. The only sword available was the great sword of
Goliath kept as a trophy; armed with it, David continued his flight.
On another occasion he had to pretend madness before the king of
a non-Israelite city. From there he fled to the cave of Adullam, an
extensive cave of winding passages said to stretch from its opening
south of Bethlehem all the way to Hebron. Through the centuries
many a desperado has hidden there because it can be entered only
by jumping across a chasm. Word of David's hide-out got around,

> . . . and when his brothers and all his father's house heard it, they
> went down there to him. And every one who was in distress, and
> every one who was in debt, and every one who was discontented,
> gathered to him; and he became captain over them. And there were
> with him about four hundred men. 22:1–2

When Saul first became king his assignment from the Lord had
been the destruction of the enemies of Israel, but no nation can be
about its main business while also engaged in inside power struggles, and certainly no one can wreck a country faster than an ego-
centric head of state. Saul concentrated on hunting down David,

including his own son Jonathan in his ire. Hearing that David had
been with the priest Ahimelech, Saul sent for the priest and accused him of aiding the enemy. Ahimelech questioned bravely,
"And who among all your servants is so faithful as David . . . ?"
a fact which he documented to the king. The king's answer was to
order his guard to kill the priest. When the guard refused, the king
ordered the informer to kill the priest.

> . . . And Doeg the Edomite turned and fell upon the priests, and he
> killed on that day eighty-five persons who wore the linen ephod.
> And Nob, the city of the priests, he put to the sword; both men
> and women, children and sucklings. . . . 22:18–19

Only one escaped; Abiathar, who fled to warn David and stayed
on beside him. (And very possibly wrote David's first biography.)

When a report came to David that the Philistines were fighting
against the city of Keilah, a few miles south of Adullam, "robbing
the threshing floors," he consulted the Lord, received approval,
attacked the Philistines and saved the city. But Saul heard of the
slaughter and went after David, so that David had to flee to "the
hill country. . . . And David was afraid. . . ." But Jonathan came
to him, assuring him that his father would never kill him and that
David would indeed one day be king. "And the two of them made
a covenant before the Lord."

A Scatological Ruse

Then comes a ribald incident which probably caused raucous
laughter around many later campfires. In pursuit of David, Saul
traveled among the sheepfolds and one morning felt the urge to
defecate and went into a cave. However, David and his men were
already hiding deep within that same cave. Seeing Saul was about
to enter, some of David's men reminded him of the Lord's promise
to deliver his enemies into his hands. David's answer was to
"stealthily cut off the skirt of Saul's robe"—a cloak which Saul
wore against the morning chill. Unaware of what had happened,
Saul went out again and David acknowledged to his companions
that he was ashamed that he had done such a thing "to my lord,
the Lord's anointed." So he followed after Saul, calling his name

and bowing to the earth in obeisance. "Why do you listen to the words of men who say, 'Behold, David seeks your hurt?'"—and he held up the skirt of Saul's robe. Undoubtedly Saul grabbed at his de-tailed coat—and then capitulated. "He said to David, 'You are more righteous than I; for you have repaid me good, whereas I have repaid you evil.'" There was a reconciliation—for what it was worth.

A Famous Brigand Wins a Wife

Peace with Saul was not enduring. David again had to take to the hills and this time he seems to have become a sort of Robin Hood captain of outlaws. There was always the problem of food. His men had to eat and when he heard that a rich herdsman of Carmel was shearing his thousands of sheep and goats followed by an annual feast, David sent ten young men to ask for provisions, reminding the wealthy squire that the outlaw band had not molested the shepherds while they were in their territory. "Now the name of the man was Nabal, and the name of his wife Abigail. The woman was of good understanding and beautiful, but the man was churlish and ill-behaved. . . ." And it was a churlish answer Nabal made to David's men who reported it to David who, in turn, reacted promptly. "Every man gird on his sword."

But one of Nabal's shearers, dismayed, had already gone to Abigail to remind her that David's men had indeed been very good to them when they were out on the range, "a wall to us both by night and by day." Abigail's reply was to prepare five sheep, two hundred loaves, two skins of wine, with plenty of parched grain, raisins and figs, load them onto asses and take them herself to David, accompanied by servants. Fortunately she reached him before he hit the warpath. Her speech was most disarming, her attitude deferential, and her gifts ample. She ended her presentation with the hope that "the life of my lord shall be bound in the bundle of the living in the care of the Lord your God. . . . And when the Lord has dealt well with my lord, then remember your handmaid." Remember her he did.

Abigail went home, found her husband too drunk to hear her report, so waited until he had sobered up the next morning. When he heard of David's enmity ". . . his heart died within him, and he became as a stone." Ten days later he died. And the short of it

was that when David "sent and wooed Abigail . . . Abigail made
haste and rose and mounted on an ass, and her five maidens attended her; she went after the messengers of David, and became
his wife."

Abigail is one of the few women of the Old Testament who comes
through life-size. She had gumption, feminine finesse and common sense. In the course of his long career David had other wives
and many concubines but none seems to have impressed his biographer—and David?—as favorably as Abigail.

David Again Spares Saul's Life

With three thousand men Saul went into the wilderness of Ziph,
west of the Dead Sea, to hunt David, not knowing that David had
spies out and knew more of his whereabouts than he knew of
David's. One dark night David sleuthed his way right into Saul's
encampment where he found Saul and Abner, the commander of
his army, asleep. Saul had "his spear stuck in the ground at his
head; and Abner and the army lay around him." Perhaps they
had eaten and drunk too well, neither the first nor the last
time for an overconfident army. One of David's men took the situation to be a gift straight from the Lord and promptly offered to
dispatch Saul, but David felt that Saul was still officially the Lord's
anointed and the Lord should take care of the manner of his death.
So, still acting Robin Hood, David only took Saul's spear and jar
of water and left. With a sense of humor as well as a flair for the
dramatic, he withdrew across a narrow valley to his own moun-
tainside and called out to Saul's encampment demanding to know
what kind of commanding general forgot to post a watch around
the sleeping king. " 'As the Lord lives, you deserve to die. . . .
And now see where the king's spear is, and the jar of water that
was at his head.' "

"Saul recognized David's voice, and said, 'Is this your voice, my
son David?' " It is, said David, and why had the king of Israel
come out to seek his life " 'like one who hunts a partridge in the
mountains' "? Saul repented again—and probably genuinely for
the moment. " 'Blessed be you, my son David! You will do many
things and will succeed in them.' " Peace again, of a sort. "So
David went his way, and Saul returned to his place."

David Hides with the Enemy

Saul's on-again off-again policy, the out-picturing of his mercurial nature, posed a problem for David, as unstable people have always posed a problem. David decided it was only a matter of time and mood until the king would find a way to kill him, so he escaped to Philistine country taking his six hundred men with him and pledging himself to Achish, king of Gath, asking a country town for his dwelling place. Achish gave him Ziklag and "David dwelt in the country of the Philistines . . . a year and four months," making raids against various outside districts, killing ruthlessly, and bringing back a great deal of spoil.

David had to bide his time until he could move powerfully against Saul and that time seemed to have come when "the Philistines gathered their forces for war, to fight against Israel." When Saul advanced to meet the Philistines and saw the size of the army "he was afraid, and his heart trembled greatly," and probably would have trembled more if he had known that David was fighting with the enemy.

The Medium of Endor

To whom could Saul turn for advice? Samuel had died and his invaluable counsel was no longer available. Some time previous, perhaps because he did not know how to separate wanton witchcraft from reliable clairvoyance, Saul had banished all mediums and wizards. So now who could tell him where his future lay? "And when Saul inquired of the Lord, the Lord did not answer him, either by dreams, or by Urim, or by prophets." He was under too much stress himself to pray with confidence. What he needed, he felt, was a trustworthy go-between, an intercessor, someone with insight.

In spite of his own edict he told his servants to go find him a medium and they finally reported back that there was a mediumistic woman at Endor. So Saul disguised himself, took two attendants, and went to see her by night. Not recognizing him, the woman upbraided this man who dared to come to her, reminding him that mediumship was forbidden. She could not help having her gift, she said, but she could desist from using it for hire. However, Saul "swore to her by the Lord" that no punishment should come to her and asked that she put him in contact with Samuel. So she went into trance and brought forth a discernible impression of Samuel and then, horrified, recognized Saul.

Samuel's message, after he had complained about being disturbed, was that the Lord was about to carry out the sentence he had decreed and would soon deliver the kingdom to David ". . . and tomorrow you and your sons shall be with me; the Lord will give the army of Israel also into the hand of the Philistines." Saul, already worn out from anxiety and fasting, fell to the ground. The medium, coming out of her trance, recognized his terror, recovered her sense of hospitality, quickly prepared hot food and persuaded Saul to eat.

David's Low Hour

Back in the Philistine camp preparing for battle, Achish, king of Gath, expressed his faith in David by appointing him his bodyguard for life, but once they had joined the main army of the Philistines, other officers objected heartily to David's exalted position, insisting that he be dropped from the top ranks. At the height of battle what was to keep him from delivering the Philistines to Israel? Reluctantly Achish acquiesced and David had no recourse but to return to his own town of Ziklag.

There tragedy awaited. The Amalekites had taken advantage of the situation to raid the Negeb and Ziklag, burning the city and carrying off the women and children. David's two wives were among the missing. David and his aides "wept, until they had no more strength to weep." This was his low hour. Even his own men turned against him, having also lost their families, and "the people spoke of stoning him, because all the people were bitter in soul. . . ."

"But David strengthened himself in the Lord his God." Right there, of course, lay his great strength. To prove that the Lord was at hand he called on Abiathar the priest to bring out the ephod, or priest's apron, in the pockets of which presumably were the Urim and Thummim, for determining the word of the Lord. The answer to David's questions about the advisability of pursuing the Amalekites was to overtake them and rescue his people. So David and his small army did exactly that, having left two hundred men behind to guard the baggage. After fighting for twenty-four hours they

rescued all their people, flocks, and herds and brought them with
the loot back to Ziklag. Immediately upon returning, David made
a new decree, which persisted in the manuals of warfare.

". . . For as his share is who goes down into the battle, so shall his
share be who stays by the baggage; they shall share alike." And from
that day forward he made it a statute and an ordinance for Israel to
this day. 30:24–25

Saul Faces the Philistines for the Last Time

Most soldiers do not know when they are going into combat for
the last time; most persons are not aware when they are returning
to the old home for the last time, or reading the morning paper
for the last time. Only a few have that definite sense of transition
which enables them to say, "Tomorrow I die." The usefulness of
such foreknowledge depends upon the way one approaches death.
Having heard from a trustworthy medium that the day of his death
in battle had come, Saul did not retire from combat to side-step his
fate. "And the Philistines overtook Saul and his sons. . . . The
battle pressed hard upon Saul . . . and he was badly wounded by
the archers."

The story of Saul's death comes from the Early Source. After
being severely wounded, he begged his armor-bearer to thrust him
through before the enemy could do so, but the armor-bearer was
afraid to kill a king. "Therefore Saul took his own sword, and fell
upon it," and the armor-bearer did the same. "Thus Saul died,
and his three sons, and his armor-bearer, and all his men, on the
same day together." And the battle turned into a rout for the
Israelites. The next day, when Saul's body was found, his head
was cut off by the Philistines and the good news was carried
throughout the Philistine countryside.

But when the inhabitants of Jabesh-gilead heard what the Philistines had done to Saul, all the valiant men arose, and went all night,
and took the body of Saul and the bodies of his sons from the wall
of Bethshan; and they came to Jabesh and burnt them there. 31:
11–12

Later their bones were buried "under the tamarisk tree," and a
seven-day fast was declared.

Second Samuel

The Second Book of Samuel continues the story of David with a feeling of firsthand reporting that few of the historical books achieve. Most of the material comes from the Early Source, whose recorder was plainly someone who believed that David had outstanding traits of leadership including kingship, generalship, and guardianship of Israel's religious heritage. David's occasional defections are not deleted from the record but the point is made that his constant intention was to honor and obey the Lord.

Grief

The messenger who brought David the news of the death of Saul and Jonathan claimed to have killed Saul to put him out of his misery after he was wounded. David's reply was not a reward but an order to slay the messenger for having killed the Lord's anointed. Then he broke into an elegy, some of the phrases of which have become proverbial:

> . . . How are the mighty fallen!
> Tell it not in Gath. . . .
> I am distressed for you, my brother Jonathan;
> very pleasant have you been to me;
>   your love to me was wonderful,
>   passing the love of women.

Anyone coming out of deep grief finds it difficult to pick up the pattern of his days and David had the sense not to jump into activity before he asked direction of the Lord and listened for the answer. He was told to move to Hebron, that southern city of Judah where Abraham, Isaac and Jacob were buried. There the men of Judah anointed him king, and he showed his kingly stature by sending his blessing, which probably included gifts, to Jabesh-gilead, whose citizens had buried Saul.

War! Continuing War!

There was small time for lamentation over Saul's death. Abner, Saul's general, had made Saul's son Ishbosheth king of the northern tribes of Israel. David's top general was his own nephew Joab. Representatives of both factions proceeded to Gibeon, where they met at the town's pool. Abner suggested that instead of their armies fighting, twelve men from each side should settle the rivalry, tournament fashion; both teams were so successful that they killed each other. Major fighting ensued, in the course of which Abner killed Joab's brother Asahel, who was said to be "swift of foot as a wild gazelle." A bloody feud ensued. "There was a long war between the house of Saul and the house of David; and David grew stronger and stronger, while the house of Saul became weaker and weaker." Eventually General Abner himself defected to David, promising to bring the loyalty of Israel with him. With David's approval he was on his way back north to fulfill his promise when General Joab returned from a raid, "bringing much spoil," and was horrified to hear that David had accepted Abner on such friendly terms. Highhanded Joab, without consulting David, ordered Abner brought back and himself killed him, which evened the score for his slain brother Asahel and removed the threat of another skillful general in King David's forces.

David was angry. Now how was he to bring all Israel into one fold under his kingship? Setting a bitter curse on Joab and all his house, he declared himself innocent, attended Abner's funeral as chief mourner and wept so convincingly that "all the people wept," and as a final tribute to Abner he refused food all day. "And all the people took notice of it, and it pleased them; as everything that the king did pleased all the people."

When Ishbosheth, Saul's son, heard that Abner was dead, "his courage failed" and he became easy prey to two brigands who murdered him while he slept and took his head to David.

But David had respect for kingship, believing it ordained by God. Saul had been the Lord's anointed and his son belonged to his succession; no one had the right to murder a king of Israel, no matter whether Ishbosheth's death benefited David or not. He ordered the murderers of Saul's son killed.

Public Opinion Crowns a King

Being without a ruler, the northern tribes remembered that Samuel had prophesied that David would someday be king of all Israel.

> Then all the tribes of Israel came to David at Hebron and said, Behold, we are your bone and flesh. In times past, when Saul was king over us, it was you that led out and brought in Israel . . . and they anointed David king over Israel . . . and he reigned over all Israel and Judah thirty-three years. 5:1–3, 5

Capture of Jerusalem

David's first official act was to attempt to capture Jerusalem from the Jebusites. Located on a small plateau of Palestine's central limestone ridge, Jerusalem was an old city. It is referred to in the Tell-el-Amarna letters written in the fourteenth century and also mentioned in an Egyptian record of 1900 B.C. David took the supposedly impregnable city by leading his men up a water shaft while the unsuspecting populace slept. Now for the first time a united country had a national capital, "the stronghold of Zion, that is, the city of David." A well-fortified city, commanding all the countryside round about. "And David became greater and greater, for the Lord, the God of hosts, was with him."

Sanctity of the Ark

Since nothing succeeds like success, David's fame spread abroad and Hiram, king of Tyre, sent his skilled workmen with cedarwood from the forests of Lebanon to help build him a fitting palace. This prestige was too much for the Philistines, who felt it high time that this enterprising king of all Israel be stopped in his tracks. But David had a genius for moving swiftly and he led his army against the Philistines so adroitly that they were routed and left their idols at the scene of battle.

Now was the time, David decided, to bring the ark to Jerusalem and make the city the religious center of national life as well as the political capital. "And they carried the ark of God upon a new cart," with the sons of Abinadab to guard the ark while David and the royal retinue "were making merry before the Lord . . . with songs and lyres and harps and tambourines and castanets and cymbals." It was a scene of high jubilation until it was suddenly marred by catastrophe. The oxen drawing the ark stumbled, and one of the priests put out his hand to steady it "and God smote him . . . and he died there beside the ark of God." David was angry. The man had made a normal —and indeed respectful—gesture. David ordered the ark kept right there in the house of a local Gittite, where it stayed for three months before he again had the courage to order it moved. When it was again on trek David's spirits rose and he "danced before the Lord with all his might" and led the sacrifices, and this time the ark came safely into Jerusalem.

Was it fitting that the king should have a house of fine cedar while the ark dwelt in a tent? David decided to build a proper temple. But the word of the Lord came to Nathan, a prophet, explaining that the building of the temple would fall to one of David's sons. David pondered the message. Then he went apart and prayed a moving prayer filled with wonder at the omnipotence of God. His people might consider him a great and successful king but before the Lord he felt insignificant. "Who am I, O Lord God, and what is my house, that thou hast brought me thus far?" Reading the prayer today we feel humility matching courage. His sense of the Lord's direction and his passion for Israel's well-being kept him moving forward. "And David won a name for himself . . . and David administered justice and equity. . . ."

Enduring Friendship

David continued to miss Jonathan. In most people's lives there are friends whose loss never diminishes. "Is there still any one left of the house of Saul, that I may show him kindness for Jonathan's sake?" There was Jonathan's crippled son, Mephibosheth. The king called him and his household to Jerusalem, made provision for their needs, and insisted that Mephibosheth himself eat always at the king's table. The young man's gratitude grew into love and later when the king had to flee from Jerusalem to save his life Mephibosheth grieved openly and upon David's return was completely indifferent to the king's gifts to him. It was David's safety he cared about. In fact, when it came to dividing his share of the spoil with the chief steward his only comment was, "O let him take it all, since my lord the king has come safely home." Two generations of reciprocating friendship! A king needs dependable friends, as much for the sustenance of his soul as for their practical counsel, but in that matter we are all kings.

Friendship Rebuffed

When the king of the Ammonites died David sent a message of condolence to the new king, Hanun, but the new king looked suspiciously at the proffered friendship. What was David maneuvering for? Hanun's princes persuaded him that David's comforters were really spies, so the authorities grabbed the messengers "and shaved off half the beard of each, and cut off their garments in the middle, at their hips, and sent them away." That was insult enough to get David into his armor again. The new war spread until it included the Syrians "who were beyond the Euphrates." The enemy was finally badly defeated and sued for peace.

Weakness in Strength

How can a man who is strong, generous, astute, devoted to his Lord's purposes, also be weak and selfish? Presumably it happens because self-discipline comes slowly and on occasion the lack of it trips up the noblest. The time of David's public success, when he was secure upon his throne and winning battles on all sides, became the moment of his private ignominy.

It was "the spring of the year, the time when kings go forth to battle" but David, well advised, was sitting this one out, allowing his general Joab to carry on the campaign. At home in his palace David went one day to his roof garden and across the housetops saw a beautiful woman, who thought herself unobserved, taking a bath. (Maybe a sunbath?) David's artistic appreciation of beauty in music, poetry and architecture also inclined him toward beautiful women, or so we gather. David sent for her. Israel's historians almost never tell a story from the point of view of the woman involved and we have no way of knowing whether this young woman, Bathsheba, was angry at the king's summons or flattered; whether she was devoted to her husband Uriah off at the front or indifferent to his reputation. David seduced Bathsheba and then ordered her husband sent into a dangerous position in battle where he would certainly be killed. As soon as her period of mourning was over David then sent again for her and made her his wife. Treacherous and immoral conduct by any standards—but a king having instant authority of life and death over his subjects must deal also with the temptations of raw power.

This fundamental lapse from rectitude was an act God could not overlook. He called out his prophet Nathan. All through Hebrew history the prophet was the corrective for moral digressions on the part of the people, no less for the ruler than the ruled. Under civil law the king had the final verdict, while the high priest upheld ecclesiastical law. Both had their accepted mores, the customs befitting their positions. But the prophet was never bound by custom. He had only one guideline: a holy God's expectation of righteous conduct on the part of his people. This was the covenant between Israel and Israel's Lord. No one, not even God, could promise that the prophet's message would be heeded; certainly not that the prophet himself would always be honored even though the calling was honored. But the prophets set a standard for constant reform that has continued to this day.

David's biographer tells little about Nathan but plainly he had standing in Jerusalem or he could not so readily have got the ear of the king. He did not open his interview with a tirade on sexual morality or lead off with biting remarks on the king's responsibility for the ethics of Israel. He told the king a parable, an interesting story, about a rich man who "had very many flocks and herds" and a poor man who had "one little ewe lamb." When a traveler came to the rich man and custom demanded a feast, the rich man killed the poor man's one lamb. What did the king think of such an act? Being a man of innate fairness, David thought the rich man deserved death. Then the prophet said, "You are the man." With many wives and concubines David had ordered a loyal soldier killed in order to steal his wife. Therefore, said the prophet, since David had used the sword so unfairly, "the sword shall never depart from your house."

At first David's marriage to Bathsheba was ill-omened. When her baby came it fell ill and David fasted and prayed "and lay all night upon the ground," grieving. But after the child died he picked up his normal life, remarking resignedly, "Can I bring him back again? I shall go to him, but he will not return to me." Later Bathsheba had another son, Solomon. "And the Lord loved him."

Family Tragedies

All was not peace in David's enormous family; concubines as well as wives had children among whom enmities arose. Amnon, the oldest son, fell in love with his beautiful half-sister Tamar who was full sister to David's second son Absalom. By a ruse Amnon seduced Tamar who was broken-hearted and afterward dwelt, "a desolate woman, in her brother Absalom's house." David was very angry with Amnon, and Absalom more so. But Absalom bided his time, then after two years gave a feast at Hebron where the royal sheep were being sheared and invited all his brothers. There he had Amnon murdered, a catastrophe which struck terror into the hearts of all the king's sons. David was so deeply shocked that Absalom fled the country "and David mourned for his son day after day." How many generations of fathers have shared David's heartache! Finally, through pressure from Joab, Absalom was allowed to return to Jerusalem but for two years he did not come to his father's court.

A Son's Treachery

"Now in all Israel there was no one so much to be praised for
his beauty as Absalom," whose luxuriant hair was his special
pride. But his heart was not as fair as his looks and he used
every occasion to promote the idea that he would make a better
king than his father until he finally worked up enough of an
insurrection to get himself crowned king at Hebron, where his
father had been crowned, and then enough of an army to move
against his father. David fled Jerusalem for the sake of the
people of the city, which otherwise would have been under siege;
also for the advantage he would have fighting in the open country,
which he knew from his early years of fighting Saul. As his
loyal forces left the city "all the country wept aloud." The priests
wanted to take the ark with the army but David commanded
that it remain in Jerusalem as a witness of his intention to
return; and also, no doubt, as protection for the city since the
Lord was particularly available in his ark.

"But David went up the ascent of the Mount of Olives, weeping
as he went, barefoot and with his head covered . . . ," the
people following in tears. One of his counselors, Hushai, was
sent back to the city ostensibly to defect to Absalom but actually
in order to spy out affairs and send word back through the
sons of David's loyal priests, Zadok and Abiathar, as to what
Absalom's next move might be.

Back in Jerusalem Ahithophel, one of the most canny of
David's former counselors who had already defected to Absalom,
offered a plan of immediate attack on David which would probably have caught the fleeing king at a great disadvantage and
won the battle for Absalom. On the point of accepting his
advice, Absalom asked Hushai for his approval, never dreaming
that Hushai had been planted in his council by David. Hushai
quickly proffered a substitute play which allowed David time
to reach the open country, where he could fight to advantage.
Unfortunately for Absalom he accepted Hushai's plan and as
soon as the council adjourned Hushai sent the priests' sons to
inform David. On their way the two men had adventures of

their own and had to be hidden in a well until their way was safe. Ahithophel, whose astute plans for Absalom were ignored, went home and "set his house in order, and hanged himself."

In the meantime David with his entourage on forced march found their needs supplied all the way by loyal subjects until the king was able to reassemble his army in three great divisions. He intended to lead a frontal attack on Absalom's army himself but his men interposed, for "you are worth ten thousand of us." His final charge to his generals was a father's charge, "Deal gently for my sake with the young man Absalom."

The battle was fought in the forest of Ephraim. "And the men of Israel were defeated there by the servants of David . . . and the forest devoured more people that day than the sword." One whom the forest defeated was Absalom.

Riding on a mule under the branches of a great oak, Absalom's head with its famous hair was caught on a branch "and he was left hanging between heaven and earth, while the mule that was under him went on." Joab, hearing of the accident, killed him with darts through the heart. The king's safety and throne were more to Joab than the royal father's admonition to be gentle with his son. Fighting was promptly halted and runners took the news to David, whose anguished cry has echoed in many a war-torn heart:

And the king was deeply moved . . . and wept . . . "O my son Absalom, my son, my son Absalom! Would I had died instead of you, O Absalom, my son, my son." 18:33

When the king returned to Jerusalem his continuing grief dismayed the people who had, after all, fought at great cost in his behalf, so that Joab finally had to persuade David to take up his customary tasks and relieve the anxiety of his subjects. But David still resented Joab's killing of Absalom and made one of his relatives, Amasa, commander of his army in Joab's place. Slowly the men of Judah who had followed Absalom rallied again to David and he was re-established on his throne. But not without further bloodshed. With smart military duplicity Joab managed to kill Amasa and put down an insurrection of Israelites.

Lex Talonis

In David's day the ancient law of "an eye for an eye" and the injunction under the law to return evil for evil in due measure was still the accepted cultural pattern, effective because of its religious sanction. Moreover, calamities of nature were considered to have a moral cause. Pestilence also meant that some sort of sin had been committed by the people. If the sin could be singled out and atoned for, the calamity ought to subside. With this presupposition it was only logical that when famine struck the land for three successive years David should turn to the Lord to ascertain the cause. The answer—whether by an inner word, or the explanation of a prophet, or the priestly use of Urim and Thummim—was that bloodguilt still marked the house of Saul, who had once betrayed the Gibeonites, so David called the Gibeonites together and asked what expiation he could make for Saul. Still blaming Saul, they asked, ". . . let seven of his sons be given to us, so that we may hang them up before the Lord at Gibeon." Two sons and five grandsons of Saul were found and slain.

A tender note marks the story when the daughter of one of Saul's faithful concubines went into mourning for the slain grandsons and kept day and night vigil near their bodies, which had been left hanging in the open, in order to protect them from birds and beasts. David, when he heard of her devotion, was much moved and had the bones of Saul and Jonathan and "the bones of those who were hanged" all properly buried in the tomb of Saul's father. "And after that God heeded supplications for the land."

A long poem, said to be the work of David, is inserted into the record:

The Lord is my rock, and my fortress, and my deliverer. . . .
He reached from on high, he took me,
    he drew me out of many waters. . . .
The Lord rewarded me according to my righteousness . . .
    and from his statutes I did not turn aside. . . .
The Spirit of the Lord speaks by me,
    his word is upon my tongue. . . .

When one rules justly over men
   ruling in the fear of God,
he dawns on them like the morning light,
   like the sun shining forth upon a cloudless morning,
   like rain that makes grass to sprout from the earth. 22:1, 17, 21, 23;
   23:2–4

This is the vivid imagery of a pastoral-agricultural people who knew firsthand both the benign and the terrifying aspects of nature. One of the most perceptive couplets, alive with psychological implications, is the observation:

> He made my feet like hinds' feet,
>   and set me secure on the heights. 22:34

The hind climbs the steeps with back feet tracking in the exact footsteps of its front feet so that there is no slipping and uncertainty; even so, the man whose innermost purposes track with his actions finds his way securely.

The Names of the Mighty

A wonderful touch to this narrative comes from the hand of the historian: "These are the names of the mighty men whom David had." Then he characterizes certain of the powerful men of war who through the years had often attempted the seemingly impossible, persevered, and finally succeeded. Short dramatic plots and homely touches even include a report on the weather, which, as anyone of any age knows, can be a salient factor in victory or defeat. One pertinent characterization: Benaiah, "a valiant man of Kabzeel . . . slew a lion in a pit on a day when snow had fallen." Among the mighty, sadly, is "Uriah the Hittite," the valorous husband of Bathsheba, whom David had betrayed.

Tucked in among the short characterizations is an incident about David at the cave of Adullam when the cave was being used as a stronghold against the valleyful of Philistines. "And David said longingly, 'O that someone would give me water to drink from the well of Bethlehem which is by the gates!'" How many dry-mouthed soldiers have known that overwhelming thirst for good water which becomes at times almost hallucinatory. "Three mighty men" of the company made a highly dangerous sortie at night right through the enemy lines to the well at Bethlehem and brought back the water. Awed, David would not drink it but poured it out as a libation to the Lord. "Shall I drink of the blood of the men who went at the risk of their lives?" Only men who have dared high deeds together in war or peace know the binding power of mutual respect and affection, sharpened by the uncertainty of the next moment.

David decided to number the people of Israel, incited, according to the text, by the Lord. But the same story told in First Chronicles credits Satan with inciting David to take the census and this interpretation seems the more logical because as soon as the census was completed "David's heart smote him"; he was overcome with guilt. The commonly accepted notion, not confined to the Hebrews, was that only God should know the exact composition of a group. Having done this brash act, what could David do to make amends? He feared God's wrath against his people.

The choices of punishment were three years of famine, three months of pursuit by foes, or three days of pestilence. David left the choice to the Lord, who sent pestilence which killed seventy thousand persons. But just as an avenging angel stretched forth his hand toward Jerusalem, the Lord halted him. The place of the vision was "the threshing floor of Araunah the Jebusite" and there the Lord ordered David, through the bidding of Gad the prophet, to build an altar on that very threshing floor. Araunah would have given David the land and the wood and oxen for a burnt offering but David insisted on buying the threshing floor for fifty shekels of silver. There he built the altar, made sacrifice, "and the plague was averted from Israel."

First Kings

The Books of Kings

The two books of Kings, originally one, are the best-known sources for the history of the Hebrew people from the tenth century to approximately the middle of the sixth century B.C. Again there is no hint as to author. Somebody or some group with a scholarly flair for digging out source material assembled the Book of the Acts of Solomon, the official Chronicles of the Kings of Judah and Israel, the temple records, the conclusion of the Early Source of Samuel and the most dependable oral traditions, and from them put together a coherent document which would save the facts for posterity. Apparently the work was first edited toward the end of Josiah's reign (690 B.C.) but later a second editor brought the story to approximately 550 B.C., while the people of Judah were still in exile in Babylonia, and also added comments to the first compilation. The editors' final pronouncement on the worthiness of each king was made on the basis of his commitment to the commands of the Lord.

David's Last Days

The book opens as David's life comes to an end. Even a king, when he grows old, finds his energy waning and David felt cold even when warmly dressed. The remedy offered him is not commonly used today: a beautiful maiden, Abishag, was brought in to nurse him in the old-fashioned manner of sleeping with him, not as a sexual venture but for the reciprocity of vital forces, the theory being that during sleep the younger individual offered strength and absorbed wisdom. A homely touch, this incident depicting the universality of physical diminishment in the poignancy of approaching death. If Abishag had written the story we might know a further dimension of this amazing king's personality, for he must have had sleepless hours when he told her about his former achievements with more insight than he wanted to express in daytime, appraising his life as it passed before the dimming eyes of his memory.

The Succession

Who would succeed David? He was expected to name his own successor, which brought the question of primogeniture to the fore. Would his eldest son, Adonijah, claim the throne as was the custom in most countries or did David intend to designate a different heir? Adonijah was "a very handsome man," and persuasive! Joab, again ranking general, and Abiathar, high priest, approved him to the point of helping him gather an impressive contingent of horsemen and chariots. On the other hand, David's preferred priest, Zadok, and the prophet Nathan, along with Benaiah, commander of the foreign mercenaries, and several of David's "mighty men," hoped for Solomon. Since David himself gave no public indication of his choice, perhaps wanting to hold onto his scepter a while longer, Adonijah got restive waiting, as has many an older son while pretending not to wish his father would hurry up and die. Finally Adonijah gave a feast complete with proper sacrifice and invited all his brothers except Solomon, and most of the royal household except those whose support of Solomon naturally irked him. He probably figured that before the feast was over his guests—some of them in their cups—would hail him king.

But the prophet Nathan was not about to sit out the feast nursing the slight bestowed on him by Prince Adonijah. Instead, he coached Bathsheba to go to David solicitously to ask why Adonijah was acting as if he were already king when David had promised her that their son Solomon should reign. Then while Bathsheba was in the king's apartment Nathan would happen in to call on the king and would support her request. The plan was carried out. "Now the king was very old" but not too infirm to express his royal determination once Adonijah's feast made a public word imperative. Mustering his kingly oath, David affirmed that Solomon should indeed succeed to the throne and promptly ordered Nathan, Zadok, Benaiah and other notables to form a procession with Solomon on David's own mule. Let the trumpets be blown and the people call out, "Long live King Solomon." Then, said David, evidently enjoying his role as master of ceremonies on his deathbed, let Zadok anoint Solomon king. And so it was done! When Solomon appeared on the street riding his father's royal mule, "all the people went up after him, playing on pipes, and rejoicing with great joy, so that the earth was split by their noise."

The furor disrupted Adonijah's feast and canny General Joab sensed what had happened. "Then all the guests of Adonijah trembled, and rose, and each went his own way." Adonijah fled to the tent where the ark was kept "and caught hold of the horns of the altar," thereby claiming its protection. Solomon sent word that his older brother was safe so long as he proved himself a loyal subject.

"When David's time to die drew near," he sent for Solomon and charged him, "Be strong, and show yourself a man, and keep the charge of the Lord your God." Then he added a few final instructions, not the noblest of his life, reminding Solomon that it was Joab who had murdered the commanders of the forces of Judah and Israel and had remained unpunished for reasons of political expediency. ". . . do not let his head go down to Sheol in peace." Also Shimei, who had cursed him when he was fleeing from Absalom, had best be killed. But those who had been loyal should be treated accordingly. Having settled these scores, "David slept with his fathers." And Solomon's throne was firmly, although not instantly, established. The story of the United Kingdom—Israel in the north and Judah in the south—moves on, but the shining shadow of David lay over the land throughout the brilliant reign of his son and on down the corridor of Hebrew history.

After the royal funeral Adonijah made the mistake of asking

his brother, King Solomon, for Abishag, the last and perhaps tenderest woman in David's life. Granting his request would have seemed to many tantamount to acknowledging his right to succeed his father, and Solomon was not one to spend his reign playing games with his half brother, so he ordered Adonijah eliminated—permanently. He also ordered Abiathar, the priest, confined to his home town of Anathoth (later made famous as the birthplace of the prophet Jeremiah). General Joab took in the trend of events and fled to the horns of the altar, affirming he would rather die right there than be pursued all his life. He may have thought he was putting Solomon on the spot and that because of his fame as a general the new king would have to give him freedom of movement but the new king took his preference literally, justifying his execution on the grounds that Joab had killed "two men more righteous and better than himself." Shimei was commanded to stay in Jerusalem; no side trips. Three years later he left the city to round up a couple of slaves and was promptly ordered slain. Benaiah, who had executed all three orders, took Joab's place as head of the armed forces and Zadok became priest.

Solomon, the Wise King

When Solomon had thus ensured his throne and let the country know what kind of ruler he intended to be, he turned his mind to a canny political marriage with the daughter of Egypt's pharaoh, an alliance which brought him much prestige but eventually cost him a great deal of wealth and helped to make him careless of his commitment to worship only Yahweh.

Early in his reign "Solomon loved the Lord" and took care to conduct lavish sacrifices at Gibeon, "the great high place." While there, he had a dream in which God offered to grant him his heart's desire and Solomon asked earnestly for "an understanding mind to govern thy people, that I may discern between good and evil." Pleased with his request, the Lord promised that riches and honor should also be his beyond any other king and, if he continued to walk in the Lord's way, long life besides. Waking, Solomon realized the transforming power of his dream and immediately ordered a peace offering and a feast. That dream may have been his clearest revelation of himself to his people and of the Lord to him.

Court Case

Solomon was soon to prove the wisdom thus granted him in a court case. Two women claimed to be the mother of the same baby, the first insisting that the second had substituted her own, dead child for the first woman's living baby. The king called for a sword, prepared to divide the child. "Then the woman whose son was alive said to the king, because her heart yearned for her son, 'Oh, my lord, give her the living child, and by no means slay it.'" Solomon promptly ordered the child given to the rightful mother. "And all Israel heard of the judgment . . . and they stood in awe of the king, because they perceived that the wisdom of God was in him, to render justice."

Administration

Along with his sense of justice Solomon had a flair for sound fiscal administration. He appointed twelve capable officers, roughly representing the twelve tribes, to provide food for the royal household, one month each in rotation. Since he ruled over "all the kingdoms from the Euphrates . . . to the border of Egypt"—the largest domain Israel ever encompassed—his officers had to provide a sizable number of oxen, cattle, sheep, harts, gazelles, roebucks and fatted fowl, not to mention the fine flour and meal needed each day. Enough to feed three to four thousand households.

Solomon was deemed as rich as he was wise, the theory being that riches are a proof of canny judgment and since Solomon had wisdom, riches would surely follow, which they did. Another aspect of his wisdom was his literary genius. He had three thousand proverbs to his credit. He was also a naturalist of note, who "spoke also of beasts, and of birds, and of reptiles, and of fish." His reputation for knowledge quickly spread abroad, as did the fame of his harem. "He had seven hundred wives, princesses, and three hundred concubines . . ." and fifteen hundred sons.

Building the Temple

Up north at Tyre, King Hiram, who had had great regard for David, sent envoys to the court at Jerusalem proffering friendship and Solomon immediately asked for help in accomplishing his father's dream, the building of a temple for the ark of the Lord.

The record details the assembling of material for the temple and its construction. Cypress and cedar timbers were sent by raft, in return for which Solomon sent Hiram each year 135,000 bushels of wheat and a million gallons of the best olive oil. Israel's exports were largely produced by the 30,000 men in Solomon's levy of forced labor augmented by 70,000 burden bearers, 80,000 hewers of stone in the hill country, and 3,300 officers over the work. "At the king's command, they quarried out great, costly stones" for use in the temple. (After the fall of the temple, in A.D. 68, some of them were retrieved and reused. For size, exactitude and beauty they remain the admiration of archaeologists.)

Solomon's temple was not large by modern standards—about 30 by 90 feet, 45 feet in height, divided into an entrance hall, a sixty-foot nave, and the holy of holies, which was a thirty-foot cube. Around the temple were "side chambers." Inner walls were intricately carved with gourds, open flowers, pomegranates, delicate designs, while the walls of the holy of holies were inlaid with pure gold, as was the altar, beside which cherubim of olivewood covered with gold stood wing to wing fifteen feet tall.

The pictorial phrases of the sixth and seventh chapters of this book of First Kings reflect both the devotion and the workmanship which went into building the temple. Pillars of cast bronze, panels carved with lions, oxen, cherubim, a "golden table for the bread of the Presence . . . lampstands of pure gold . . . flowers . . . lamps . . . tongs . . . cups, snuffers, basins . . . and . . . sockets of gold, for the doors . . . of the most holy place." Then the molten sea supported by twelve bronze oxen—literally a tank containing 12,000 gallons of water for the priests to wash in. (They could have swum in it since its rim was about ten feet above the pavement, and the younger priests may have done so, since priests probably had their hilarious moments in that day as well as in ours. On the other hand, taboos were powerful regulators of conduct.)

Devotion Beyond Duty

Far up on the capitals of the pillars, hidden by the slant of the roof, where no eye but the Lord's could see, was intricate carving of lilywork, an extra devotion executed in fidelity to perfection which is the honor due God himself. Workmen in Solomon's day, as in the Middle Ages, believed wholeheartedly in the reality of this strange and glorious Power-Which-Is, who animates his creation and leans near to bless and lead his children. So believing, even though oppressed, they could put heart into their work.

Of Palaces and Potentates

Solomon was seven years in building the temple; then thirteen in building the royal complex and administrative units: the House of the Forest of Lebanon, longer than the temple; the Hall of Pillars; the Hall of the Throne, also called the Hall of Judgment; "his own house where he was to dwell"; another palace for the pharaoh's daughter (What was she like, really? Proud as an Egyptian king's daughter was reputed? Homesick for the sunny banks of the Nile?). Solomon also built "the Millo," apparently an earthwork or a protective wall south of the temple area; no one knows exactly what the Millo was. At the same time, Solomon began constructing fortified cities in other parts of the country, with stables for his horses, which were a mark of the increasing prosperity of Israel, for previous kings had ridden upon mules while the common people rode asses. Material culture leaped forward as Israel augmented its labor force with skilled artisans from abroad.

Dedication of the Temple

Chapter 8 details a noble description of the participation of the king, dignitaries, elders of Israel, priests, and common people in the jubilant experience of dedicating the temple.

And they brought up the ark of the Lord, the tent of meeting, and all the holy vessels. . . . sacrificing so many sheep and oxen that they could not be counted. . . . Then the priests brought the ark of the covenant of the Lord to its place, in the inner sanctuary of the house, in the most holy place, underneath the wings of the cherubim. . . . There was nothing in the ark except the two tables of stone which Moses put there at Horeb, where the Lord made a covenant with the people of Israel, when they came out of the land of Egypt. And when the priests came out of the holy place, a cloud filled the house of the Lord, so that the priests could not stand to minister . . . for the glory of the Lord filled the house of the Lord. 8:4–6, 9–10

An experience of radiant Presence recaptured only occasionally, when a community truly worships.

Solomon's Prayer

The king addressed the people as they stood before him. Rehearsing their history as a people led by their God, he reminded them how his father, David, had wanted to build this temple but had been restrained by the Lord. Then, lifting his hands toward heaven, he addressed the Lord, marveling at his faithfulness. "Behold, heaven and the highest heaven cannot contain thee; how much less this house which I have built!" (*I* have built? There was some help, O King, from the slaves and forced laborers, the hewers of stone and bearers of burdens.) Beseeching God to hearken to the supplications of all who turned toward the temple when they prayed, he named the calamities for which the people would probably need forgiveness, since only sin could produce catastrophe: defeat by their enemies, drought and famine, pestilence, invasions of locusts and caterpillars, being led into captivity ". . . then hear thou in heaven . . . their prayer . . . and maintain their cause . . . and grant them compassion. . . ." Turning again to the people, he admonished them, "Let your heart therefore be wholly true to the Lord our God," an exhortation which each hearer understood in terms of his own secret sins. Finally the assembly came down from the spiritual heights and partook of food for their physical sustenance in happy fellowship. Then came a week of sacrifice and feasting— did anyone ever hear of climaxing a great religious experience with a fast?—after which the people blessed the king "and went to their homes joyful and glad of heart."

The Queen of Sheba

As Solomon's fame increased so did his activities; he felt supported by his own achievements. Control over the land of Edom gave him iron and refineries; the store cities protected his grain and chariots; the foreigners within the boundaries of his ever-enlarging kingdom increased his forced levy, leaving the citizens of Israel free to be commandeered as soldiers, charioteers and officials. No draft boards were needed, he merely spoke the word. For the first time, Israel had a fleet which sailed all the way to Ophir (probably modern Yemen) to bring back gold, sandalwood, and coveted luxuries.

One astonished individual who heard of Solomon's splendor was the queen of Sheba, a woman of acumen and great wealth. She journeyed to Solomon's capital with retinue, "camels bearing spices, and very much gold, and precious stones," for the purpose of testing Solomon's wisdom. He must have given her the full treatment (the details of which are outlined in the Koran), for she was overwhelmed:

> And when the queen of Sheba had seen all the wisdom of Solomon, the house that he had built, the food of his table, the seating of his officials, and the attendance of his servants, their clothing, his cupbearers, and his burnt offerings which he offered at the house of the Lord, there was no more spirit in her. 10:4–5

Overcome, she blessed the king, gave him a final round of gifts, accepted his overwhelming largess, "and went back to her own land." Folklore affirms marriage between these two opulent rulers, from whose union, however temporary, rose the royal house of Ethiopia, which still bears as its insigne the lion of Judah.

The recorder of Solomon's wonders cannot resist adding a few extra grandeurs to his credit. Gold poured in "from the traffic of the merchants, and from all the kings of Arabia and from the governors of the land," so "King Solomon made two hundred large shields of beaten gold," three hundred smaller shields, "a great ivory throne" overlaid with gold, the like of which "was

never made in any kingdom." From Tarshish (to which Jonah
would later flee) came "gold, silver, ivory, apes, and peacocks."
Everyone brought, sent, and delivered gifts at the palace door.
"And the king made silver as common in Jerusalem as stone."
The really remarkable aspect of the record is that it was prob-
ably not exaggerated.

Alas! Women!

Solomon had too much. Abundance can be boring. What was
left to wish for? He even had cool calm judgment in managing
the kingdom's affairs and never had to eat his heart out in
anxiety. Then, at the height of his splendor, he drifted into
excess. "Now King Solomon loved many foreign women," in
spite of the fact that the Lord had forbidden such intermarriage
lest the women maneuver him into legitimatizing foreign gods
for their sake. Says the record, ". . . his wives turned away his
heart." He "went after Ashtoreth the goddess of the Sidonians";
after all, she had apparently done great things for King Hiram; and
"Milcom the abomination of the Ammonites." He built a high
place for Chemosh, god of Moab, and rebuilt the altar to Molech,
in whose honor children were passed through fire for purifying
when not actually sacrificed by burning. "And so he did for
all his foreign wives. . . ." Was it the largess fancied by the
senile or an expression of kindness toward his faithful foreign
females, to whom their traditional gods meant as much as Yahweh
meant to him? Or was he hoping somehow to be on acceptable
terms with all the gods as he approached the great unknown
beyond death? In his biographer's eyes he lost the last test,
fidelity in old age. "And the Lord was angry with Solomon."

Enemies sprang up. There was Hadad, of the royal house of
Edom, who had fled to Egypt after his country was conquered
by David; now he wanted to return home. There was Rezon,
originally leader of a band of marauders but later king of Damascus; and currently also in Egypt was Jeroboam, an able former
official of Solomon's labor force who had been designated by
the prophet Ahijah as one who would someday wrest the ten
tribes of the north from Solomon and became their king. All
three harassed him so that his last days were far from peaceful.
We can almost hear the historians sigh as they appended the

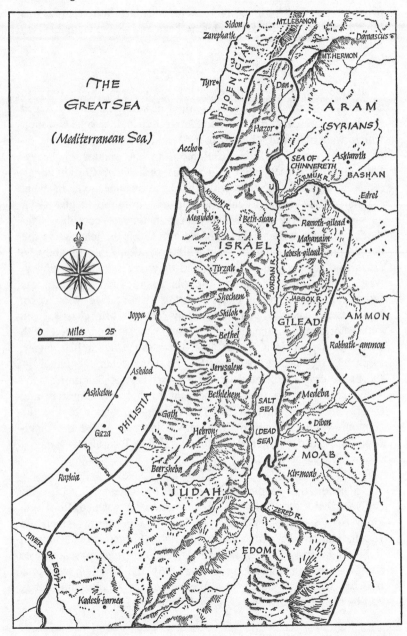

usual obituary: "And Solomon slept with his fathers, and was buried in the city of David his father; and Rehoboam his son reigned in his stead."

The Succession

"Rehoboam went to Shechem, for all Israel had come to Shechem to make him king," but when news of the event reached Jeroboam in Egypt, he returned, interested in the same question which was bothering the people: Would Rehoboam be an improvement over his father, Solomon, in the matter of heavy-handed taxes, forced labor and palace profligacy? Certain dignitaries went to Rehoboam with the head-on question: in what manner did he intend to rule? Rehoboam promised to give them an answer in three days, which gave him time to consult his father's older counselors. They advised him to lift the load, serve the people, and thus maintain their willing loyalty. Unfortunately he also turned to the younger group and they advised a tough policy, which better fitted his mood. So his answer was "whereas my father laid upon you a heavy yoke, I will add to your yoke. My father chastised you with whips, but I will chastise you with scorpions"—indicating the stinging whips encrusted with sharp points of iron which tore the flesh. Astounded, angry, resentful, the people responded, "To your tents, O Israel"— the battle cry. Arrogant Rehoboam—was he not Solomon's son? —felt secure in his rule until he sent forth his taskmasters and the Cabinet-level chief of the Department of Labor to get the economy going full speed. The forced laborers killed the dignitary. Astounded, frightened, Rehoboam fled to Jerusalem.

The Divided Kingdom

Up north, the people of Israel, the equivalent of ten of the twelve tribal states Solomon had ruled over, crowned Jeroboam king. Now the country was split into two divisions, Israel and Judah, just as the prophetic threat had affirmed would happen if Solomon strayed after false gods. Scarcely eighty years since Saul was first crowned king, and already the kingdom was torn by civil war. Rehoboam would have fought Israel immediately had he not been restrained by a word from the Lord.

Up north, Jeroboam built up the city of Shechem to serve as his capital and pondered his religious position. What would his subjects do when the Passover came? Traditionally they offered their sacrifice at the temple in Jerusalem, but that most holy city was now enemy territory. Would there be a Passover exodus? To forestall such defection to Rehoboam, Jeroboam ordered two calves made of gold and set one up in Bethel and the other in Dan. "Behold your gods, O Israel, who brought you up out of the land of Egypt." Symbols of fecundity, gods they see and approach. Doubters could tell themselves that the golden bulls were merely the outward expression of the invisible God of Israel; the steeds upon which Yahweh rode, just as he formerly traveled in the ark. The more simple-minded, the people who customarily followed orders, would accept them along with the altars Jeroboam built on the high places, complete with a priest-hood and customary sacrifices followed by the customary feasts.

A Prophet's Tragedy

While Jeroboam was standing by an altar on a high place ready to sacrifice to one of the golden calves, a "man of God," un-named, came out of Judah to reprimand him. Prophet, seer, or man of God, all three terms are used to indicate the fearless men who called on wrongdoers—whether ruler or ruled—to change their ways, and who also saw and described coming events. This man of God foretold a future king named Josiah, who would one day sacrifice on that very altar the very priests who were at that moment burning incense. In the meantime, said the man of God, the altar would be torn down and the ashes scattered. Angered, Jeroboam ordered the prophet arrested, but the land with which he pointed to the prophet was instantly paralyzed. Immediately, and fearfully, bystanders tore down the altar and scattered the ashes, proving the veracity of the man of God. The king entreated the man of God to restore his hand, the man of God prayed, the hand was restored. So then Jeroboam invited the man of God to come home with him and receive a reward but the man of God replied that he would not accompany the king for half his kingdom, nor would he eat or drink or return by the route he had come, for thus he had been instructed by the Lord. The man of God headed south.

In Bethel an old prophet heard of the episode, called for his ass, and rode out after the man of God, inviting him to dinner. The man of God explained his instructions not to eat, or drink, or return by the way he had come, but the old prophet assured him, falsely, that he had had a later message from God that the man of God was to come with him. So the man of God went. As they ate, the genuine word of God came to the old prophet and he recriminated the man of God for having listened to his invitation instead of sticking to his own revelation. A delicate question: when should an individual stand by a commission which he feels came to him from the Lord and when defer to the opinion of someone supposedly wiser? Repentant, the old prophet quickly put the man of God on his own ass and sent him on his way. But before the man of God had gone far he was killed by a lion. Shortly afterward some men traveling the same road came upon the lion and the ass standing by the dead body and reported the tragedy. Hastily the old prophet came out to the spot and ordered the dead man of God buried in his own grave. Mourning, he then instructed his sons that when he died he was to be buried in the same grave, reiterating that the prophecy made by the man of God regarding the tearing down of the high places of Samaria would one day come to pass.

The reference to Samaria in the story dates its writing, since Israel was not called Samaria until after the Exile. The editors added the further word that Jeroboam did not cease appointing priests not of the Levite line to officiate at the false altars (a breech of cultic regulation in their day) and that it was for this reason that his house was destroyed "from the face of the earth."

Doomed Hours of Jeroboam

Jeroboam's son fell ill and the king sent his wife, disguised but bearing gifts, to the prophet Ahijah, who had originally encouraged Jeroboam to take over the throne but was now bitterly disappointed in him. Ahijah, aged, nearly blind, had been forewarned by the Lord as to who was coming and been given a message for her. So when the queen arrived he called her by name, repeated the Lord's reproach for Jeroboam's apostasy, warned that his line would disappear, and added that any of Jeroboam's family who died in the city would be eaten by dogs, while anyone dying in the open country would be devoured by birds of prey—"for the Lord has spoken it." The sick son, he said, would die as she returned to the city and he would be the only one of Jeroboam's kin to be properly buried. Even Israel itself would one day be uprooted and its people scattered beyond the Euphrates as retribution for Jeroboam's having set up false altars. Exactly so did events come to pass, commented the editors, writing some three hundred years after the event.

Constant War

In Judah, Rehoboam also "did what was evil in the sight of the Lord," allowing the people to reconstitute the high places with their altars and introducing male prostitutes. Egypt's current pharaoh, Shishak, first ruler of the twelfth dynasty—a fragment of whose stele has been found at the excavations of Megiddo—invaded Judah and carried off the treasures of both temple and palace, so Rehoboam died in disgrace. His son Nebat—grandson of Solomon, but who ever heard of Nebat?—had a short, unprofitable reign and left the kingdom to his son Asa, who at least inherited his grandfather's longevity, for he reigned forty-one years. Asa earned the approval of his biographers by removing the male prostitutes and idols, although he did not destroy all the shrines, for the practical reason that centralized worship in Jerusalem was not always easy for people living in the country who wanted nearby places of worship. While still young, Asa performed one courageous act in removing his mother, or it may have been his grandmother, from her position as head of the royal harem, because "she had an abominable image made for Asherah," a goddess popular in that entire region (mentioned forty times in the Old Testament). Asa himself brought his votive offerings into the temple, underwriting his pledge of reformation. Nevertheless he was plagued by continuing war.

In Israel, Baasha, who killed Nadab and followed him as king, also killed all the house of Jeroboam and insisted on fighting Judah. He tried to stop Asa's expansion by building up the city of Ramah only five miles north of Jerusalem but Asa outwitted him by persuading Ben-hadad, king of Syria, to break his pact with Israel and go to war against Baasha. With a canny eye on the gifts of gold and silver Asa had sent him, the Syrian king acceded and was victorious. Then it was Asa's happy task to have Ramah torn down and the stones and timber used for strengthening the fortifications of Geba—probably a scribe's error for Gibeah, once Saul's capital. "Asa was wholly true to the Lord all his days." Wholly true! Then the record adds, "But in his old age he was diseased in his feet." Such human documents, these books of Kings.

In Israel, Baasha's son Elah reigned only two years. One night when he was very drunk the "commander of half his chariots," Zimri, killed him and usurped his throne only to be so badly defeated seven days later by Omri, commander of the army, that he burned himself to death in the blazing palace.

Most of what we know about Omri comes from non-biblical sources which describe Omri as a more astute ruler than he is portrayed in this book of Kings, in which the judgment of his reign is based chiefly on the fact that he allowed worship of both Yahweh and Baal to flourish. Probably his most lasting contribution to Israel was building and fortifying the city of Samaria, hereafter Israel's capital. Set on a 400-foot hill facing north and west, the city commands a wide view of the surrounding countryside, rich in olive orchards. Omri set up caravansaries and bazaars which served the lively trade moving north and south, bringing in goods from the seaports. His dynasty lasted only thirty-four years, through four kingships, but Samaria's economic prominence made Israel known as "the land of Omri" for a century.

Ahab, son of Omri, reigned twenty-two years; apparently an energetic king but heartily berated in the record for the fact that he was married to Jezebel, daughter of the king of Sidon, a queen who remained an ardent supporter of Baal, god of her people. During Ahab's reign Jericho was rebuilt, regardless of the curse put on its rebuilding by Joshua. Ahab also had the presumption to join an alliance of twelve kings headed by King Ben-hadad II of Damascus to check the advance of Assyria—a courageous attempt, for Assyria had the power to make life difficult for the lesser state. Later Ahab split with Syria.

Here Comes Elijah

Out of Gilead Elijah the prophet comes on scene so suddenly as to suggest that the beginning of the story may have been lost. He was certainly the most conspicuous of the psychically gifted individuals whose performances form the basis of Old Testament miracle stories. Since he was different, people hooted at him but since he was so often correct in his prognostications, they consulted him. When he was able to produce physical phenomena they feared him, while at the same time offering enormous inducements for him to work wonders in their behalf. Such was Elijah's plight.

Evidently Elijah had been watching the northern king, Ahab, and his queen, Jezebel, as they erected altars to the Canaanite god Baal and led the people away from the God of Israel. He decided to challenge the whole movement and since Baal was supposed to be the god who controlled the rain he would challenge him at the point of his strength. So he appeared at Ahab's court and made his threat. "As the Lord the God of Israel lives, before whom I stand, there shall be neither dew nor rain these years, except by my word." Big laugh no doubt on the part of the court; laughter tinged with anxiety. Ought not this loudmouthed prophet be put out of the way? Evidently the Lord also thought a little distance would be good, because he ordered Elijah to move east of the Jordan, beyond Ahab's jurisdiction, where the brook Cherith would furnish him water and the ravens would bring him meat and bread. So there Elijah lived until the brook dried up for lack of the rain his pronouncement had withheld.

Then the Lord directed Elijah up the Phoenician coast, naming a town where a widow would feed him. When Elijah located her and asked for water and bread she told him sadly that she had only a handful of meal and very little oil which she was about to make into a last meal for her son and herself. Elijah instructed her to go ahead and bake her small loaf; it would suffice. "For thus says the Lord the God of Israel, 'The jar of meal shall not be spent, and the cruse of oil shall not fail, until the day that the

Lord sends rain upon the earth.'" She probably doubted. Most of us would; we only believe metaphorically in the all-sufficient hand of God. But Elijah seemed to speak with authority—after all, he had just been fed by ravens—"And she went and did as Elijah said." And the meal and oil sufficed as long as needed. However, later the woman's son became ill and died. She turned to Elijah; had she sinned? Elijah's answer was to stretch himself over the dead child's body and give him mouth-to-mouth resuscitation, pleading with the Lord to let the child's soul return. Then, carrying the son to his mother, he said, "See, your son lives."

In the third year of drought the Lord sent Elijah back to Ahab, who had just sent the overseer of his household, Obadiah, off hunting throughout the land for water and grass to save the animals. "Now Obadiah revered the Lord greatly," and he had hid one hundred of the true prophets of the Lord in a cave where he could care for them. When Elijah met him on the road he told Obadiah to go back and tell the king that Elijah had returned. When Elijah himself arrived the king was ready with a greeting: "Is it you, you troubler of Israel?" Elijah did not press the point that Ahab must believe in him if he blamed him for the drought but he rebuked the king as the one who really troubled Israel by breaking the Lord's commands. Then he challenged the king to a combat of gods, a test between Baal and the Lord of Israel. With a scorching sarcasm and an almost diabolic sense of humor, Elijah directed the contest. This is a scene which anybody with an appreciation of primitive drama needs to read directly from the record, so effectively is it delineated.

Elijah directed that four hundred and fifty prophets of Baal and four hundred priests of Baal's consort Asherah, "who eat at Jezebel's table," were to be gathered at Mount Carmel, along with "all Israel." The crowd gathered. As Elijah watched the Baalites prepare for a ritual rain dance, he queried the onlookers, " 'How long will you go limping with two different opinions? If the Lord is God, follow him; but if Baal, then follow him.' And the people did not answer him a word." A tough choice; should they turn their backs on their sovereign and choose the God of the old prophet? He sounded frighteningly sure of his ground.

Elijah ordered up two bulls, of which the prophets of Baal

should choose one, cut it in pieces and lay it on the wood ready for a fire to be lit, but light no fire. He would do the same, one prophet against four hundred fifty. "And you call on the name of your god and I will call on the name of the Lord; and the God who answers by fire, he is God." To which the people agreed, the king anxiously looking on.

So the prophets of Baal prepared their sacrifice, placed it on the wood and began to call on the name of Baal "from morning until noon." No fire. Elijah mocked them. "Cry aloud, for he is a god; either he is musing, or he has gone aside, or he is on a journey, or perhaps he is asleep and must be awakened." Baal's prophets doubled their ardor, slashing themselves "with swords and lances, until the blood gushed out upon them," as was the custom in a religious frenzy. "No one answered, no one heeded." So at midafternoon Elijah took his turn. He repaired the altar of the Lord with twelve stones representing the twelve tribes, laid the wood in order, put the meat offering upon it, and commanded that both offering and wood be drenched with water and the trench around the offering be filled with water. Then he prayed.

"Answer me, O Lord, answer me, that this people may know that thou, O Lord, art God. . . ." Then the fire of the Lord fell, and consumed the burnt offering, and the wood, and the stones, and the dust, and licked up the water that was in the trench. And when all the people saw it, they fell on their faces; and they said, "The Lord, he is God; the Lord, he is God." 18:37–39

Might Versus Mercy

From the vantage of a later-day morality it would be comforting to write that Elijah immediately called together the prophets of Baal and began to instruct them in the way of the Lord, retelling the story of God's care on the long trek through the wilderness, teaching them the songs of David, and inculcating the basic teaching of Israel that an ethical God demanded ethical conduct. Actually he moved with fine military dispatch and had the prophets of Baal killed.

Proof That God Is Very God

All of us look for proof of God in terms we can understand. And often, mercifully or sadly as the case may be, we get a demonstration. Elijah ordered Ahab to break the fast, "for there is a sound of the rushing of rain," a sound no one but Elijah heard, certainly. He sent his servant up the hill to look toward the sea, the direction from which rain usually came; were clouds gathering? Not that could be seen. Seven times the servant climbed the hill until he finally reported ". . . a little cloud like a man's hand." Enough for Elijah. He advised Ahab to mount his chariot and get himself home ahead of the rain. Then excited Elijah ran ahead of the chariot the whole seventeen miles to be on hand when Jezebel got the news. But if he thought he would have part in a triumphal scene he was mistaken. Jezebel's reply to Ahab's report of rain was a message to Elijah that he would be as dead as the prophets of Baal the next day. And Elijah grew afraid! With all that demonstration of the power of the Lord he was afraid of Jezebel and he fled to Beersheba.

How the Lord Answers

Elijah reached the safety of the wilderness, sat down under a tree and decided he was not so much after all. What was his one life against the iniquity of Israel? He was ready to die. He fell asleep under a broom tree and while he slept an angel touched him, an angel with common sense; he should get up and eat something. The food was at hand—"a cake baked on hot stones and a jar of water." Then Elijah traveled on, all the way to Mount Horeb, also called Mount Sinai, where Moses had received the law. There he lived in a cave and "the word of the Lord came to him" telling him to go stand upon the mountain. There he spread out the need of Israel before the Lord, whose answer was a demonstration of power.

> And behold, the Lord passed by, and a great and strong wind rent the mountains, and broke in pieces the rocks . . . but the Lord was not in the wind; and after the wind an earthquake, but the Lord was not in the earthquake; and after the earthquake a fire, but the Lord was not in the fire; and after the fire a still small voice. . . . And the Lord said to him, "Go, return on your way to the wilderness of Damascus. . . ." 19:11–12, 15

So there he was, silenced, strengthened, commissioned and sent back to work.

His orders were to anoint Hazael king over Syria and Jehu king over Israel, and Elisha to be a prophet in his place. The task would not be easy; there would be great slaughter in Israel. "Yet I will leave seven thousand in Israel, all the knees that have not bowed to Baal."

A Two-sided Coin

Here the final editor inserts some history favorable to Ahab. For the most part Ahab seems to have been considered a betrayer of the covenant but in his time of need his subjects came loyally to his support, so he must have had his strong side. His enemy, the king of Syria, rounded up allies—including thirty-two kings, probably rulers of city-states—and moved against Israel, making preposterous demands and bragging of their sure victory. Ahab answered with a proverb to the effect that a man did well not to boast as he put his armor on but as he took it off. The army of Syria and its allies took its position against the city of Samaria but unfortunately the hilarious kings stopped for cocktails which lasted a long time. They were still drinking the next day at noon, when Ahab's smaller but well-organized forces found it relatively easy to slaughter them. The king of Syria escaped, however, and the next spring attacked again, this time with seasoned generals. On this occasion "the people of Israel encamped before them like two little flocks of goats, but the Syrians filled the country." But again the army of Israel won and the Syrian king sued for his life. Ahab spared him and worked out a treaty with him, only to be reprimanded by a prophet who disapproved of his generosity. The prophet's critical attitude made Ahab "resentful and sullen."

A Vengeful Queen

Ahab's vengeful wife Jezebel was a headstrong woman who brooked no refusals. The king coveted the vineyard of his next-door neighbor, Naboth, so that he could enlarge his garden but Naboth did not want to part with his family inheritance and according to custom even a king could not commandeer a man's land. Ahab was "vexed and sullen," refusing food, which irritated Jezebel, who thought the idea of a commoner holding out

on a king ridiculous. "Do you now govern Israel?" If he could not
act like a ruler, she could.

> So she wrote letters in Ahab's name and sealed them with his seal,
> and she sent the letters to the elders and the nobles who dwelt with
> Naboth in his city. And she wrote in the letters, "Proclaim a fast,
> and set Naboth on high among the people; and set two base fellows
> opposite him, and let them bring a charge against him, saying, 'You
> have cursed God and the king.' Then take him out, and stone him
> to death." 21:8-10

Her command was followed and as soon as she heard Naboth
was dead she notified the king to go claim his garden.

Re-enter Elijah

Right then Elijah had one of his clairvoyant visions disclosing
the whole episode, and he heard a pronouncement from the Lord
which he was to transmit to Ahab; in the place where dogs had
licked up the blood of the stoned neighbor, dogs would also lick
up the blood of the king. When Elijah arrived at the palace Ahab
felt the prophet's mighty ire and asked, "Have you found me,
O my enemy?" Elijah delivered the warning, including the further
decree that Jezebel would also be eaten by dogs. The message was
too much for the king. He put on the sackcloth of repentance and
fasted "and went about dejectedly." His remorse must have been
genuine, for the Lord postponed punishment.

"For three years Syria and Israel continued without war," until Jehoshaphat king of Judah came for a visit, at which time the
two kings planned an attack on Syria to reclaim lost territory. In
order to guarantee their success they consulted a group of some
four hundred prophets, who immediately blessed the venture.
However, their approval was so pat that Jehoshaphat suspected
fawning compliance; did not Ahab have a more independent
prophet? He had one, Micaiah, "but I hate him, for he never
prophesies good concerning me." Nevertheless Micaiah was called
and in sarcasm repeated the words of the fawning prophets, but
when pressed he stated his true insight: this was no time to attack
Syria. And for his honesty he was ordered confined to prison
"with scant fare of bread and water" until Ahab returned in

peace. The battle was heavy and Ahab, king of Israel, although disguised, was wounded, dying that evening, "and the blood of the wound flowed into the bottom of the chariot." And when his chariot was washed at a pool "the dogs licked up his blood . . . according to the word of the Lord."

Jehoshaphat returned home and remained a good king, "doing what was right in the sight of the Lord," although he did not stamp out worship on the high places. In Israel, Ahab was succeeded by Ahaziah, who "did what was evil in the sight of the Lord" and provoked the Lord to anger.

Second Kings

Second Kings continues the story of the divided kingdoms, Israel and Judah, as they struggle against outside forces and fight among themselves. The first seventeen chapters report the state of affairs in both countries up to the end of Israel, in 721 B.C., then the decline of Judah to the exile in Babylonia, in 587 B.C. A brief account of a temporary governor in Jerusalem under Babylonia and the improved position of the exiled king of Judah in Babylon bring the record to the mid-sixth century. However, the book is not primarily political history, and certainly not an unbiased account of events, but an appraisal of the moral leadership in the two countries in relation to their commitment to their God and his response in dealing with them.

A Misdirected Question

The opening episode is a royal tragedy. King Ahaziah, of Israel, son of Ahab and Jezebel, fell through the railing of an upstairs porch of his palace in Samaria and was so severely injured that he sent to a temple of Baal to inquire of the psychic priests whether he would recover. Before the messenger could reach the temple of Baal, clairvoyant Elijah tuned in on Ahaziah's anxiety and gave the word that Ahaziah would die. When the pronouncement was told to the king he sent a captain accompanied by fifty soldiers to reason with Elijah but unfortunately when the captain saw the venerable prophet sitting on a hilltop he pulled rank and demanded that Elijah come down. Elijah was not one to countenance disrespect for his profession as a prophet of the Lord and he promptly called down fire from heaven to consume the captain and his fifty men.

Astounded, the king sent a second company on the same errand and since they had the same haughty attitude Elijah called down a second flash of fire. Whether a season of electrical storms with fatal lightning came to his aid is not recorded. Ahaziah certainly could not lose a company a day, so he sent a third contingent in a more respectful mood, and this time the Lord instructed Elijah not to deal with the military at all but to go directly to the king. When Elijah reached the court he propounded a sarcastic question of his own; had the king sent to consult a foreign god because there was no God in Israel? Then he told Ahaziah again that he would die from his injuries, and the king died. The throne passed to his brother, Jehoram.

Elijah's Approaching Death

Perhaps it was the king's death which caused Elijah to ponder the fact that he had reached the end of his own days. No matter how deep one's faith, facing one's own end is an experience of unprecedented awe. However, Elijah apparently had an inner awareness that at the right time and place unseen forces would lift him easily from his worn body. He started for the propitious place, trying all the way to dissuade his faithful, stubborn disciple Elisha from accompanying him. Bands of prophets—religious devotees in training—met them at each stop, asking if Elisha realized that this was the day the Lord was going to take his master. Elisha knew. At the Jordan, Elijah took off his mantle and struck the water so that the river parted, allowing the two men to cross dryshod, with some fifty of the prophets looking on.

A Parting Gift

Finally Elijah paused to ask Elisha what he could do for him at parting, and the answer was Elisha's famous remark, "I pray you, let me inherit a double share of your spirit." A tremendous request. He was asking for what may be the most difficult responsibility known to man: the ability to help mankind mold the future by means of prophetic clairvoyance, an endowment which requires tremendous dedication to the will of God and a bold courage to speak what is perceived. The older prophet wondered if Elisha would sustain such a gift but finally decided that if Elisha was sufficiently developed spiritually to see the manner of his passing then he was adequately prepared to carry a double portion of his gift.

Transcendence

Elijah was now confident and ready for death. Anticipation of the inexplicable—the *mysterium tremendum*—hung like a luminous haze over the expectant moment.

> And as they still went on and talked, behold, a chariot of fire and horses of fire separated the two of them. And Elijah went up by a whirlwind into heaven. And Elisha saw it and he cried, "My father, my father! the chariots of Israel and its horsemen!" And he saw him no more. 2:11–12

After the Miracle

Was there a sudden swirl of desert dust through which the overwrought Elisha thought he saw the supernatural figures? Did Elijah thus shrouded from sight then stumble on behind some rock and, his assignment finished, simply wait out his own end? Or did he actually enter a realm of experience beyond the three-dimensional, a realm into which mortals are only occasionally vouchsafed a glimpse? Persons who have themselves experienced the incommunicable seem most likely to accept the report as given.

What to Do with Doubters

Elated, stunned, Elisha picked up Elijah's mantle, "that had fallen from him," and returned to the river where the curious band of prophets waited. There he rolled up the mantle and struck the water as Elijah had done, calling on the name of the Lord, and again the waters parted! Awestruck, the band of prophets then knew that the power of Elijah had indeed come into Elisha. Nevertheless, being practical men and still in training, they insisted against Elisha's advice on looking all over the valley and mountain for Elijah. Probably Elisha could not have convinced them if he had tried that the prophet was not to be found. So he let them operate on the physical laws they knew. It seems as if advanced souls always have to wait out the comprehension of their mundane brothers.

Fact or Fiction

There are reports of miracles as old as time and as new as to-morrow. Either they are imagined events or they are incredible incidents which operate through laws we are just beginning to understand. It must be admitted that overcredulous followers are often given to overstatement. For instance, the incident in which small boys jeered at tonsured Elisha, calling him a baldhead until he cursed them and brought out of the woods two she-bears which tore up the fifty-two boys! Would a man of God be *that* short-tempered, that overzealous for respect for his profession? Or did befuddled parents who could not discipline their children invent stories about she-bears and the wizardy old man? The historian who reported the story believed the incident as given.

The Moabite Record

Israel's war against Moab is not only recorded in the third chapter of the book of Second Kings but is also attested by a famous inscription known as the Moabite stone inscribed around the time when Jehoram was king of Israel; the largest single literary document yet found outside the Old Testament records. Discovered in 1868 near the Dead Sea, it is now housed in the Louvre. The language of the inscription is closely akin to Hebrew and, while the Moabite record claims a smashing victory for Mesha, king of Moab, the story is in the main the report recorded in Second Kings.

While Jehoram, also Ahab's son, was king of Israel (849–842 B.C.) Mesha, king of Moab, decided to stage a rebellion and end Moab's enormous yearly tribute to Israel: 100,000 lambs and the wool of 100,000 rams. Immediately Israel called on Judah, more or less Israel's vassal, to give support and Judah called on its Edomite ally. Unfortunately at the end of seven days' travel the augmented army found itself at a dry wadi, or river bed, without the water they had counted on for men and beasts. Only in a totally arid country can soldiers know such despair. Informed that Elisha was not far away the three attacking kings went to consult him.

Elisha immediately called for a minstrel whose music would put him into a trance and then proclaimed the Lord's promise that the next day the dry stream bed would be filled with water, even though there would be neither wind nor rain. Moreover, the Moabites would be delivered into Israel's hands.

Sure enough, next morning water did indeed pour down from the heights of Edom "red as blood"—probably colored by the red sandstone of the hills. The advancing Moabites thought the red water must be colored by shed blood and concluded that the attacking kings had fought each other and were thus weakened for conquest by Mesha's army. "Now then, Moab, to the spoil!" But when the Moabite soldiers met the Israelite army, the waiting Israelites completely routed them. In a final desperate effort to stay the army of Israel, Mesha took his stand on the wall of his last fortress and before the horrified eyes of the army of Israel offered his son, the heir apparent, as a burnt offering to Chemosh, Moab's god. Such shocking action panicked Israel, unused to human sacrifice. Surely now Moab's god would punish the armies of Israel, whose attack had caused so dreadful a deed. The three kings forgot the Lord's promise to deliver Moab into their hands and retreated in haste toward home. The inscription on the Moabite stone credits Moab's victory to Chemosh.

A Widow's Full Supply of Oil

One day the widow of one of the sons of the prophets came to Elisha reporting that a creditor was about to seize her two children as slaves. When Elisha asked about her resources and found she had nothing but one jar of oil, he instructed her to borrow her neighbors' pans, bowls, kettles, any kind of vessel, and start pouring her oil into them. From that small supply? Nevertheless she obeyed; what was the sense in consulting a man of God if she did not intend to follow his directions? Borrowing until there was not another vessel to be had, she filled them all! Then Elisha made a practical suggestion. "Go, sell the oil and pay your debts, and you and your sons can live on the rest." Faith and works, an eternal parable.

A Needy Rich Woman

It was a rich woman who provided a room for Elijah whenever

he came to her locality—even as rich women have frequently done for poor preachers from that day to this. Elisha was grateful, for he often came in from a mission tired and road-weary. One day he mentioned to his servant that he wished he could do something for this generous benefactor. The servant said the woman's only lack was a son, so Elisha promised her that she should bear a son the following spring. The son was born on schedule but when he was old enough to follow the reapers into the field he had a sunstroke and died. Wasting no time, the mother went to Elisha for help and Elisha promptly gave the boy mouth-to-mouth resuscitation until "the child sneezed seven times, and the child opened his eyes." In boundless gratitude the mother fell at the prophet's feet.

Need a Miracle Be Spectacular?

Everywhere Elisha went miracles flourished, a phenomenon made possible in part, no doubt, by the fact that the people expected miracles. They believed that the power of God was available through Elisha, while he believed both in himself as channel and in God as source. Reports spread, perhaps exaggerated, but too many to be totally discredited. When a band of prophets made a stew which proved poisonous, Elisha threw a handful of meal into the pot and removed the poison. When one of his followers lost his axhead in the river Elisha caused the metal to float. When a farmer brought him the first fruits of his harvest, barley loaves and ears of grain, Elisha ordered the small offering given to the hundred hungry workmen around him. ". . . thus says the Lord, 'They shall eat and have some left.' . . . And they ate, and had some left, according to the word of the Lord."

Tales of Elisha traveled to foreign lands. To Syria, for instance, where the commander of the king's forces, one Naaman, had contracted the dread disease leprosy and a young Israelite slave girl passed on to the commander's wife the report of Elisha's peculiar powers. Perhaps Elisha might be able to cure the general. The king of Syria himself sent a letter to the king of Israel, along with expensive presents, asking that Israel's prophet cure Syria's commander. Upon reading the letter the king of Israel was aghast; was the Syrian king, expecting failure, hunting an excuse for war? But Elisha himself heard of the king's dismay and suggested that the Syrian be sent to him. "So Naaman came with his horses and chariots" but Elisha merely sent out word that he should wash seven times in the Jordan River and he would be clean. Naaman was incensed, humiliated. Syria had larger, cleaner rivers than the Jordan, and certainly more respect for the king's military. "So he turned and went away in a rage." But his servants, having no face to save, reminded Naaman that if the prophet had named some spectacular task he would have performed it; why not try the prophet's suggestion?

> So he went down and dipped himself seven times in the Jordan, according to the word of the man of God; and his flesh was restored like the flesh of a little child, and he was clean. 5:14

The refreshing touch to the story is that Elisha refused the general's gifts. Amazed—who wouldn't be—the commander asked a gift instead; two mule loads of the earth of Israel upon which he would stand, once he returned home, to offer his daily prayers, "For henceforth your servant will not offer burnt offering or sacrifice to any god but the Lord." The matter of holy ground (the place where it happened) is commentary on humankind's proclivity for reliving sublime moments, recapturing meaningful symbols, rededicating sluggish wills, reconsecrating high intentions.

Israel's Central Intelligence

Elisha was in touch with Syria's king clairvoyantly and was able to warn his own king when it was to Israel's advantage to change the place of the army's encampment. Acting on Elisha's foreknowledge, the king of Israel constantly outwitted Syrian plans, so the Syrian king suspected a betrayal among his own staff. But one of his servants quickly fixed the blame for the leak. "Elisha, the prophet who is in Israel, tells the king of Israel the words you speak in your bedchamber." Incensed, the Syrian king sent a great army to surround the place where Elisha lived and take the prophet. Next morning, Elisha's servant reported seeing Syrian horses and chariots coming their way.

> . . . And the servant said, "Alas, my master! What shall we do?" He said, "Fear not, for those who are with us are more than those who are with them." 6:15–16

The servant watched as Elisha prayed and forthwith he saw "horses and chariots of fire round about Elisha." Concurrently the Syrian soldiers who arrived to arrest Elisha suffered a distortion of vision so that they failed to recognize him and he was able to lead them to Samaria, Israel's own capital, where they regained their sight and realized they were trapped! The king of Israel deferentially asked Elisha if he should not now slay the bewildered Syrians. Instead, Elisha ordered that food be given them, after which amazing experience "the Syrians came no more on raids into the land of Israel."

What kind of prayer was Elisha's? A "spell" cast by mass hypnosis? A contagion of fear on the part of the Syrians as they felt the impact of Elisha's faith? Who of us knows how the prayer of faith operates? The documentation on prayers of faith is too slight for widespread study, because faith so often gives way at the height of a crisis.

Famine Reversal

Some time later, King Ben-hadad of Syria, deciding to attack Israel after a period of prolonged famine, mustered his entire army to besiege the city of Samaria. The king of Israel, desperate and in sackcloth, assessed the scarcity of food among his people (doves' dung selling for food and mothers eating their own children). He decided that since it was Elisha who had foretold the famine as God's punishment for Israel's derelict ways, the famine might lift if Elisha were disposed of. Fortunately Elisha himself, sitting with the elders in his own house, picked up the king's plan to destroy him. Almost immediately the king arrived with soldiers. Elisha greeted them with the astounding promise that by the same hour the next day the famine would be over and "a measure of fine meal shall be sold for a shekel" at the city gate. A captain standing by the king expressed his scornful doubt, to which Elisha answered that what he had foretold would come to pass all right but the captain would never see it.

That evening, four lepers realizing they were going to die of starvation anyway, decided to defect to the prosperous Syrians, by whom their lives might be spared for charity's sake. But when they reached the Syrian encampment no one was there! The Syrians had routed.

For the Lord had made the army of the Syrians hear the sound of chariots, and of horses, the sound of a great army, so that they said to one another, "Behold, the king of Israel has hired against us the kings of the Hittites and the kings of Egypt to come upon us." So they fled away in the twilight. . . . 7:6–7

The astounded lepers entered the silent camp, ate their fill, and carried off fantastic loot. Then, feeling compunction for not letting their own king hear the great good news, they returned to the city and had him informed. The king, understandably skeptical, decided the empty camp was a ruse of the Syrians; with human perversity he could not believe his prayers had been answered. However, a scouting party soon reported that the Syrian tents did indeed stand empty. "Then the people went out, and plundered the camp of the Syrians," which caused prices to fall almost instantly, just as promised by Elisha. Only—alas!—the captain who had doubted Elisha's foresight was crushed to death by the mob pushing through the city gate.

Syria's King Betrayed

Elisha was not through dealing with Syria. He visited Damascus. King Ben-hadad, who was ill, immediately sent an influential representative named Hazael with forty camel loads of gifts to inquire whether he would live. Elisha answered that the Lord said the king would not die of the illness and then informed Hazael that nevertheless the king would soon die. The prophet stared so disconcertingly at the emissary that Hazael became embarrassed as "the man of God wept." Nervously Hazael asked why he wept and Elisha answered, "Because I know the evil that you will do to the people of Israel." And he outlined the cruelties which would accrue from a coup Hazael would soon instigate. Hazael backed away, returning quickly to the king to report that Elisha said his illness would not prove fatal—but the next day he smothered the king with a wet blanket and usurped the throne.

Entanglements of Israel and Judah

The whole of this depressingly exciting book of Second Kings needs to be read, intrigue by intrigue, in order to understand in what manner the Hebrew people felt that the hand of God moved through human affairs.

While Joram, son of Ahab, was king of Israel, Jehoram, son of Jehoshaphat, whose wife was a daughter of Ahab, began to reign in Judah. Both "did what was evil in the sight of the Lord" and it was for that reason, as the historian saw it, that they had constant trouble. Edom revolted from Judah and the army of Israel joined Judah in an attack on Edom but the Israelite infantry deserted Joram and his chariot commanders when the outcome looked doubtful, with the result that Judah lost the vassalage of Edom. In due time Ahaziah, the twenty-two-year-old son of Jehoram, took over Judah's throne and went with his uncle Joram of Israel to attack Hazael of Syria but Joram was wounded and returned to his own town of Jezreel to recuperate. Soon Ahaziah went to Jezreel to pay a sick call on King Joram.

Now Elisha, for his part, saw no hope in either of the two kings, so he fomented a conspiracy to overthrow Joram of Israel by sending one of his own staff to Ramoth-gilead, where a group of officers of the Israelite army were on guard duty, to anoint their commander, Jehu, the new king of Israel. Elisha's deputy found the Israelite officers in council, called out Jehu and privately anointed him, at the same time prophesying the destruction of the house of Ahab and the grizzly death of Jezebel, whose blood would be licked up by dogs. Returning to the council, Jehu told his comrades that he had just been anointed king, and they quickly swore fealty.

In Jezreel, where King Joram lay recovering from his wound in the company of his friendly relative King Ahaziah of Judah, a watchman on the tower saw the approach of a company of soldiers. The king promptly sent a horseman to find out the soldiers' business but the horseman joined the soldiers instead of returning with the message. A second emissary did the same thing. Then the watchman on the tower recognized Commander Jehu by his furious driving. Quick action was called for and both kings climbed into their chariots and went to meet Jehu, hoping to avert trouble. But the meeting culminated in the death of both kings, and the body of Joram was thrown aside on the plot of ground which his father, Ahab, had stolen from his neighbor Naboth.

Back at the palace, when Jezebel heard that Jehu was approaching she "painted her eyes, and adorned her head," then—royal to the last minute—she leaned out the window and called to him insolently, "Is it peace, you Zimri?" referring to an infamous assassinator. Jehu's prompt answer was to call two eunuchs to throw her off the upstairs portico, and ". . . her blood spattered on the wall and on the horses, and they trampled on her." Unmoved, Jehu went inside to eat, ordering the queen buried. "But when they went to bury her, they found no more of her than the skull and the feet and the palms of her hands." Many onlookers recalled the prophesy of Elisha that Jezebel's blood would be licked up by dogs.

History has justifiably given Jezebel a bad name; she was arrogant, highhanded, callous about other people's suffering, determined to have her own way at all costs. But there is another aspect of her life scheme. She was a foreigner in a strange land, transferred like any other piece of property from her father's court in Tyre to Ahab's court in Israel. She had one thing of her own to cling to: her gods. And she treated them with due honor, building them altars on hilltops, paying Baal's priests from her own pocket, besides wheedling support from Ahab. In return she expected her gods' protection. Now why couldn't she have seen that Israel's God was superior to hers? Probably because the lives of the people around her did not appear all that persuasive. Most of the people at court apparently took their religion the way we take ours—for granted. The lives of her neighbors had no clear message. And from that day to this, many Jezebels go unchallenged and unredeemed for the same reason.

The Habit of Slaughter

Jehu developed a habit of slaughter. At some time in his life there must have been a moment of hesitance to kill, a moment when the primitive awareness of the oneness of all life gave pause to the murderous hand, but under the drive for power his spirit grew calloused. After an act of death is repeated many times the nervous system no longer appears to register. Jehu had no compunction in ordering the slaughter of Ahab's seventy sons along with their elders, guardians, friends and priests; then the forty-two kinsmen of Azariah of Judah.

After such carnage the people of Israel must have expected a purge of the priests of Baal formerly subsidized by Jezebel but Jehu's edict indicated exactly the opposite course. He proclaimed wholehearted worship of Baal and invited all the priests of Baal and their followers to gather at Baal's temple. Festive garments were provided for everyone and Jehu himself went in to offer the sacrifices. However, he had previously stationed eighty armed men outside the temple ready to kill every Baal worshiper at a given signal. The wholesale slaughter was accomplished, after which the temple itself was demolished. Thus was the worship of the God of Israel restored! But fanaticism seldom stays long in the saddle. Jehu overmassacred and found himself without adequate leadership when it came to dealing with Hazael of Syria. To bolster his position he paid tribute to Shalmaneser, of Assyria. When it came to religious preferences he gave priority to Yahweh but he did not stamp out Baalism. The compilers of the record comment that he "was not careful to walk in the law of the Lord," and after a twenty-eight-year reign he died, turning over to his son Jehoahaz a kingdom greatly reduced in size by the depredations of Syria.

A Designing Queen

Southward, in Judah, conditions were also chaotic. Queen Athaliah, mother of the slain king Ahaziah, attempted to keep the royal power in her own hands by killing off the rest of the royal family. However, a half sister of Ahaziah saved Ahaziah's seven-year-old son, Jehoash, by hiding him for six years until her husband, a highly placed priest named Jehoiada, managed to stage a *coup d'état* and crown the young king. Then, after eliminating the royal grandmother, Queen Athaliah, the priest Jehoiada felt free to dedicate himself to the Lord's more peaceful interests. In those days people saw no incongruity in a few slayings as a dedication of their purposes to the Lord. "And Jehoiada made a covenant between the Lord and the king and people, that they should be the Lord's people . . ."—the first covenanted coronation mentioned in the Bible record. The ensuing slaying of the priests of Baal in Judah was quicker than converting them and much the same euphoria seems to have resulted: ". . . all the people of the land rejoiced."

A Credit to Sound Upbringing

Jehoash did "what was right in the eyes of the Lord all his days, because . . . the priest instructed him." Nevertheless, few people today remember there ever was a priest named Jehoiada whose faithful teaching gave Judah four decades of honorable rule. The special interest of Jehoash was the repairing and refurbishing of the temple, to which he gave personal attention. His major difficulties were with his neighbors. Hazael, king of Syria, exacted such heavy tribute that the gold and votive gifts belonging to the temple had to go as levies. Eventually a conspiracy of Jehoash's own disgruntled servants caused his death.

A Family Failing

It should be no surprise that in the north both Jehu's son and grandson "made Israel to sin. . . . And the anger of the Lord was kindled against Israel." The demands of Syria depleted Israel's resources; the cavalry was almost wiped out and the army reduced to ten chariots.

Elisha's Dream

When word went out that the old prophet Elisha was ill and approaching death, Joash, king of Israel, hastened to him, weeping. "My father, my father! The chariots of Israel and its horsemen!" —referring to the fiery chariot which had taken away Elijah. Elisha's last act was one of sympathetic magic. He ordered the king to open an eastern window and shoot an arrow while he kept his hands on the king's hands, "The Lord's arrow of victory, the arrow of victory over Syria," he pronounced.

"So Elisha died, and they buried him," but even after his death power was said to cling to his bones. Sometime later a funeral was in process when a band of marauding Moabites appeared and the corpse was quickly thrown into Elisha's grave; immediately the corpse, touching Elisha's bones, revived "and stood on his feet." The historian does not record the elation of the revived individual but he must have had a story to tell his grandchildren—which may be the reason the legend is preserved.

The Fortunes of Kings

In 800 B.C. a new king of Judah, Amaziah, began his twenty-nine-year reign. "And he did what was right in the eyes of the Lord." Being successful in fighting the Edomites, he decided to court the friendship of Israel's king Jehoash, grandson of Jehu, and proposed a meeting but Jehoash rebuffed the idea, calling the suggestion a thistle's presumption in addressing a cedar, since Israel was the larger, stronger country. True to kingly nature (of that time, of course) Amaziah could not accept an insult and promptly called out his troops. The two kings "faced one another in battle," Amaziah was defeated, and the northerners carried off gold and silver treasures from the temple and palace, as well as hostages. War was definitely the game of kings (and neither king guessed that in this field of games war was being challenged across the Mediterranean, in Greece, by a new kind of contest called the Olympics [776 B.C.]). Eventually Amaziah was assassinated and his son Azariah—also called Uzziah—reigned for forty-one years. The first fact reported about him was his restoration of Elath, that important port on the Red Sea which has been coveted by princes and prime ministers from Solomon's day to the present.

In Israel Jeroboam II came to the throne in 786 B.C., reigning until 746 B.C., during which time the kings of Assyria grew stronger but were largely occupied on other fronts so that Israel had relative peace. (Watch out, though, big and little kings, for Rome was founded in 753 B.C.) Jeroboam extended Israel's borders farther north than at any time since Solomon. Economically the country also prospered. Caravans from Phoenicia carried goods brought in from foreign ports and Israel collected profitable tolls. Cities rapidly grew larger and more prosperous but there was slavery for debt, and for the poor a shortage of food amid plenty. In other words, unregulated inequities. However, religious practices flourished, because the priests played on the theme that all this prosperity was a sign of Yahweh's approval. It obviously paid to keep up one's temple dues, make the expected special offerings, and remain on the right side of God. Nothing so old-fashioned about the eighth century B.C.

This is the place in the story of the divided kingdoms to pause to read the eighth-century prophets: Amos, Hosea, Micah and Isaiah of Jerusalem. To be sure, only Isaiah is mentioned in Second Kings, the others appearing among the minor prophets (who come last in the English Revised Standard Version), but it is these prophets who demonstrate the corrective power of the prophet on Hebrew life. Because of them, kings are seldom left without a mentor, nor the people without counsel. Not that all kings were grateful for public admonitions said to come directly from the Lord, nor that all profiteers appreciated public exposure. Nor, for that matter, that all the people were willing to forsake foreign gods and their supposed blessings because some prophet went up and down the streets proclaiming the ire of Yahweh. But the prophets kept on speaking out. Even though the editors who finalized the books of Kings did not specify what prophet was declaring what message to each king, they did appraise each reign in terms of its loyalty to the covenant between God and his people, and it was the prophets who constantly saw to it that the country's leadership knew what those requirements were.

Chaos

In Judah, Azariah's son Jotham ruled as regent for his leprous father, then as king himself (750–735 B.C.). In Assyria, Tiglath-pileser III broke the advance of the people of Uratu, now modern Armenia, and began to collect tribute from scores of cities, among them Tyre (which later proved a challenge to Alexander the Great), Kue Gebal (later called Byblos, from which the word Bible is derived), Damascus and Samaria.

In the next fifteen years after the Assyrian campaign, four kings of Israel were murdered. Zechariah followed his father, Jeroboam II, but reigned only six months before he was killed by Shallum, who reigned one month and was murdered by a usurper named Menahem, whose cruelties included ripping up "all the women . . . who were with child." While Menahem's advisers were in daily executive session their bewildered uncertainty was matched by the apprehensive fear of the king's subjects. The king exacted heavy taxes in silver shekels from the wealthy and paid Tiglath-pileser so handsomely that the Assyrian king turned back; after all, Menahem alive was the source of more negotiable wealth than his death could provide. Menahem may have felt relieved when he finally "slept with his fathers, and Pekahiah his son reigned in his stead." But for only two years until a usurper named Pekah, the son of his captain, killed him.

Deportation

The recorder mentions "Pul the king of Assyria," but Pul was another name for Tiglath-pileser, whose conquests relentlessly expanded until they included much of the northern part of Israel, "and he carried the people captive to Assyria," the beginning of the Israelite deportation. "Hoshea . . . made a conspiracy against Pekah . . . and struck him down . . . and reigned in his stead," Israel's last king (732–721 B.C.). He remained loyal to Assyria until Tiglath-pileser's death but once Shalmaneser succeeded, he joined the revolution spreading through the west, encouraged by So, king of Egypt. Without the benefit of modern communications the people of Israel must have lived in daily uncertainty and confusion, scarcely knowing who was fighting whom until king Hoshea was captured and imprisoned by Shalmaneser, followed by Assyria's final siege of Samaria. Three long years of suffering ensued—hunger, constant fighting, ever-lessening hope of aid from Egypt, until finally the city capitulated to Shalmaneser's successor, Sargon.

The day of final tragedy came in 721 B.C., when the citizens of Samaria along with most of the rank and file of Israel were herded into caravans, most of the people walking, and driven by curses, promises and whips into exile all the way to Media and Assyria. It was the Assyrian way not to exterminate rebellious peoples and certainly not to try to police them in their own home territory, which was an expensive and uncertain way of keeping order, but to move them to a distant scene where their labor would still be useful to the empire. This calamitous mass deportation marked the end of the Northern Kingdom.

From that time on, the people of Israel have been known as the lost ten tribes, for they were unable to maintain their identity and never returned to their homeland. "And this was so, because the people of Israel had sinned against the Lord their God."

New Life in Samaria

To replace the Israelites in their old territory, immigrants were brought in from other areas. As strangers in a strange land the new people did not honor Israel's God; "therefore the Lord sent lions among them, which killed some of them." When the situation was reported to Assyria the king sent back a priest of Israel to "go and dwell there, and teach them the law of the god of the land." In line with tradition each locality supposedly had its own god who remained deity-in-charge, guarding both land and religious rites. So when a priest of Israel came back to Bethel the Assyrian authorities expected the newcomers to honor Yahweh. But the newcomers, far outnumbering the remaining Israelites, "feared the Lord but also served their own gods." Even the name Israel to designate the Northern Kingdom passed from use and the mixture of people around Samaria began to be called Samaritans. However, the term Israel slowly came back into use to designate the surviving Jewish people as a whole. This was the name the Lord had given their ancestor, Jacob.

Good King Hezekiah

In 715 B.C., while Sargon was still ruling Assyria, Hezekiah came to the throne of Judah. Here was a king of whom the historians really approved. "He trusted in the Lord the God of Israel; so that there was none like him among all the kings of Judah after him, nor among those who were before him." His twenty-nine-year reign began with the destruction of the high places used by foreign cults; he then took over improving Jerusalem, especially in the matter of increasing the water supply by having a tunnel dug to bring in water from beyond the wall. A fearless young king who intended to be independent, he rebelled against Assyria and also "smote the Philistines as far as Gaza and its territory, from watchtower to fortified city."

But Sennacherib came to Assyria's throne and almost immediately marched across to Judah and captured all the fortified cities so that Hezekiah had to sue for peace, strip the temple of its treasures, and pay tribute. Emissaries arrived from Assyria chiding the citizens of Jerusalem for false confidence in Hezekiah, as if Judah could remain an independent state. Did Judah expect to rely on Egypt, a broken reed, or on the ineffective god Yahweh?

Hezekiah took the burden of his people upon himself. Rending his clothes and covering himself with sackcloth, he sent two officials to the prophet Isaiah for direction. Isaiah assured the emissaries that the king of Assyria was about to hear a rumor of insurrection at home and return to his own country to fall by the sword without capturing Jerusalem.

It is here that the prophet Isaiah of Jerusalem comes on scene. Isaiah loved his home city; he knew its triumphs, its dire shortcomings. To him righteousness was not an abstraction but a social necessity. God was the lord of time but long-run purposes had to be underwritten in the present tense. His tone was often stern, even threatening, but kings listened.

> . . . cease to do evil,
> learn to do good;
> seek justice,
> correct oppression;
> defend the fatherless,
> plead for the widow. Is. 1:16–17

In his extremity Hezekiah had two choices; he could lose faith and await Assyria's onslaught or he could turn where he was accustomed to turn—to the Lord. Habit stood him in good stead. With Sennacherib's letter in hand, he "went up to the house of the Lord, and spread it before the Lord." In a very moving prayer filled with awe at the majesty of God he asked that Jerusalem be sustained.

Reprieve

Isaiah answered Hezekiah in behalf of the Lord in stately verse, addressing the king of Assyria and assuring him that all things were known to God: "I planned from days of old what now I bring to pass . . . and I will turn you back on the way by which you came." The Lord himself would defend Jerusalem and save an eventual nucleus of his people.

That night on the border of Egypt 185,000 Assyrians died in their camps. Herodotus, a non-biblical historian, ascribes the sudden defeat of Assyria to the fact that their bowstrings and other leather equipment were eaten by mice, and mice may have been carriers of the plague. Sennacherib, his army sick and sadly depleted, returned home without attacking Jerusalem. And in his own temple he was killed by two of his sons, and a third son, Esarhaddon, then reigned in his stead.

Hezekiah became ill; very ill indeed, so that Isaiah came to sustain him and to tell him sorrowfully to set his house in order because he would not recover. The king turned his face to the wall and prayed, weeping bitterly as a man may when he feels his assignment on this earth is not finished and he must leave too soon. Before Isaiah had passed from the courtyard he again heard the word of the Lord telling him to return and assure the king that his prayer of faith had been heard and the Lord would add fifteen years to his life. Moreover, the Lord himself would defend Jerusalem. Elated at relaying the good news, Isaiah called for a cake of figs to be made into a poultice to lay on the boil which was threatening the king's life.

While Hezekiah was convalescing he received letters and presents from Merodach-baladan, king of Babylonia, whose country was growing stronger. Few dreamed it then, but a new world power was rising. Hezekiah welcomed the Babylonian ambassadors and showed them his treasures, a generous hospitality for which Isaiah rebuked him, telling him that he foresaw a day when both treasures and people would be carried off to Babylon —instead of Assyria—where Hezekiah's own sons would become eunuchs in the Babylonian palace. Judah would still have to pay for its sins even though temporarily reprieved.

A Long Reign

Manasseh succeeded his father, Hezekiah, and reigned for forty-five years, as wicked as his father had been good, rebuilding the altars to Baal and adding new altars in honor of the various planets. So far did his apostasy take him that "he burned his son as an offering." The Lord sternly rebuked him, promising he would "wipe Jerusalem as one wipes a dish, wiping it and turning it upside down." Manasseh's son Amon, when he came to the throne, was no better than the father, so his own servants killed him.

Josiah's New Day

". . . and the people of the land made Josiah his son king instead" (640–609 B.C.). Josiah "walked in all the way of David his father, and he did not turn aside to the right hand or the left." Here began a new chapter in the life of the kingdom of Judah— one of the most exciting chapters of the whole Old Testament story. Reform was the order of the day. When Josiah had reigned eighteen years he ordered the rebuilding of the house of the Lord and, in the course of overseeing the pulling out of old timbers for replacement, the high priest found a Book of the Law. A forgotten book; a forgotten law. Or perhaps a book strategically placed there by priests who knew of its existence but had not previously felt the time propitious for revealing it. This was the book of Deuteronomy, at least the core of it, possibly written and compiled as early as Manasseh's reign but kept back by the priests until a king receptive to its teaching would be on the throne.

Discovering the Book of the Lord

The scroll was read to the king. Josiah was dismayed: the word of the Lord had been so far lost that neither he nor the people knew of it! Many individuals since the day of Josiah have had this same astounding experience—discovering for themselves the word of the Lord. How could the king reorder his kingdom in line with the laws of God? (This is the place to reread the book of Deuteronomy, through the eyes of Josiah.)

Hilkiah the priest and his associates went to Huldah, the prophetess, for direction. She answered that Jerusalem had indeed done evil in the sight of the Lord, and that evil begot its own consequence, which would one day fall heavily on Jerusalem. But because Josiah was penitent for breaking the laws of God, which he had not known, he would be allowed to go to his grave in peace and not witness the desolation of Jerusalem.

> Then the king sent, and all the elders of Judah and Jerusalem were gathered to him. And the king went up to the house of the Lord . . . and the priests and the prophets, all the people, both small and great; and he read in their hearing all the words of the book of the covenant. . . . And the king stood by the pillar and made a covenant before the Lord, to walk after the Lord and to keep his commandments and his testimonies and his statutes, with all his heart and all his soul, to perform the words of the covenant . . . and all the people joined in the covenant. 23:1–3

Reform

So then the reform movement swept the land and out went the false gods. After the re-establishment of approved temple worship by "all the people, both small and great," the Passover was kept with fervor. "For no such passover had been kept since the days of the judges . . . or during all the days of the kings of Israel or of the kings of Judah."

Josiah did not know that Assyria's permanent decline was under way. In 612 B.C. Nineveh went down before the Medes and Chaldeans; Babylon was growing more assertive, which was a thing Egypt did not like to see, so Pharaoh Neco allied himself with the Assyrians and turned his army northward to help block further Babylonian expansion. Since Josiah had always suffered from Assyrian aggression, Neco automatically became his enemy also, and he led his army out to meet the Egyptians at Megiddo. There he was killed and his body brought back to Jerusalem. This was certainly one royal funeral at which the show of grief was more than perfunctory.

Eulogy

All lives come under the judgment of time. The historian wrote:

> Before him there was no king like him, who turned to the Lord with all his heart and with all his soul and with all his might. . . . 23:25

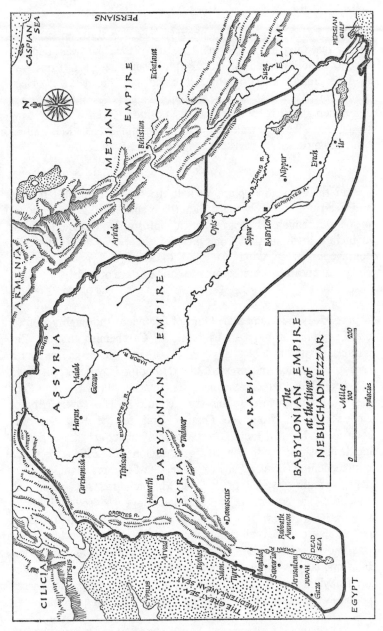

The
BABYLONIAN EMPIRE
at the time of
NEBUCHADNEZZAR

Hard Days

After Josiah, his son Jehoahaz reigned for three months, an ineffective king in a difficult situation; then he was deposed by Neco and carried off to Egypt, where he died. Preferring to keep Judah intact so that it could pay heavy taxes, Neco made Josiah's eldest son, Jehoiakim, king (609–598 B.C.) but Jehoiakim failed to bolster Judah's position. Even a strong king would have been stymied by the uncertain international situation. His most astute adviser was the prophet Jeremiah.

Jeremiah

And this is a good place to halt the story of Judah's decline and read the book which bears the name of that exceptional prophet Jeremiah. He was practical, informed on current affairs, invincibly loyal to the promptings of the Lord, and fanatically courageous in speaking his mind to kings and policy makers. His pronouncements lend drama to the last days of Judah.

The Rise of Babylon

In 605 Nebuchadnezzar king of Babylon thoroughly routed the Egyptians at the famous battle of Carchemish, on the Euphrates. From a tablet now in the British museum we learn how the Babylonians pressed the retreating Egyptians who had not been killed at Carchemish, slaughtering them so that "not a single man escaped to his own country." The sovereignty of Nebuchadnezzar from the Persian Gulf to the Red Sea was soon an undisputed fact. The splendor of his court, the engineering feats which made the city of Babylon militarily strong, the unprecedented development of trade, the fabulous Hanging Gardens, seventh wonder of the world, built for his queen, all enhanced his reputation. The Aramaic language used in Babylon was on its way to becoming the dominant speech of the common people in an ever-widening area. Moreover, Nebuchadnezzar was known as a religious man, devoted to the Babylonian deities. It is not surprising that Jehoiakim felt he had to make a place for Babylonian deities in Judah, even in the temple. Conquered peoples were expected to revere the gods of their conquerors.

Seventh-century Prophets

The seventh-century prophets—although not mentioned here by name—continued in the tradition of their predecessors, correcting kings, castigating the people for their sins, foretelling disaster, promising both the Lord's sure punishment and his faithful care. Zephaniah, a contemporary of Jeremiah, lambasted the king's treacherous counselors. Nahum spent his ire foretelling doom for Assyria and rejoicing in it. Habakkuk, just after the Chaldeans had defeated the Egyptians in 605 B.C., interrogated the Lord as to why the wicked dominated the righteous and justice was perverted, adding five famous "woes" assuring the oppressor that the suffering he inflicted on others would turn back on him. Here again the true state of affairs in Judah is highlighted by the pronouncements of these spokesmen commissioned by the Lord to speak forth his word.

Rebellion

After three years of vassalage Jehoiakim rebelled against Nebuchadnezzar, which must have appeared a fatal move to his neighbors, for bands of Chaldeans, Syrians, Moabites and Ammonites all set upon Judah, hoping for a slice of territory. The historian tries to perceive some reason for this run of disaster and concludes, "Surely this came upon Judah at the command of the Lord" because of the overwhelming sins of Manasseh and Judah's participation in them. It was probably one of these roving bands which killed Jehoiakim, "and Jehoiachin his son reigned in his stead," but only for three turbulent months. The Babylonian army besieged Jerusalem and when Nebuchadnezzar himself arrived, Jehoiachin gave himself up, along with his household and officials. Then ". . . the king of Babylon brought captive to Babylon all the men of valor, seven thousand, and the craftsmen and the smiths, one thousand, all of them strong and fit for war." This first great wave of exiles left Jerusalem depleted of leadership but still unsubdued.

Final Tragedy

Another of Josiah's sons, Zedekiah, came to the throne (597–587 B.C.), another inept king who dithered into disaster. In the ninth year of his reign he rebelled and Jerusalem withstood Babylon's siege for two years—thanks to Hezekiah's water tunnel, which brought in fresh water from outside the walls. Then famine forced Zedekiah to give up and flee by night with his "men of war." He was soon captured. "They slew the sons of Zedekiah before his eyes, and put out the eyes of Zedekiah, and bound him in fetters, and took him to Babylon." There was no world press to decry such savagery.

Final Days

After this final debacle a contingent of the Babylonian military returned to Jerusalem, broke down the walls, burned Solomon's magnificent temple, the palace, chief dwellings and public buildings, then carted off to Babylon most of the rest of the populace except "some of the poorest of the land." The chief priests, temple dignitaries and men of importance were slaughtered on the way. This was "the Exile," the moment of complete ignominy and heartbreak which forever after stood—and still stands—as the watershed of Hebrew history.

A capable native governor was appointed over what remained of Jerusalem and Judah, a nobleman named Gedaliah. He tried to restore the land and to pacify the remaining populace but within two years he was murdered. His friends, fearing Nebuchadnezzar's vengeance although they had not been involved, were afraid to stay and try to maintain order in the city. Against the judgment of the prophet Jeremiah, who had remained in Jerusalem, they decided to leave. "Then all the people, both small and great, and the captains of the force arose, and went to Egypt. . . ." The exile was complete.

Hope

In Babylon King Jehoiachin was suddenly freed and given a seat at the Babylonian king's table "above the seats of the kings who were with him in Babylon." No longer in prison garb, "he dined regularly at the king's table . . . and a regular allowance was given him by the king, every day a portion, as long as he lived." This kindly attention may have been a reward for good behavior on the part of the internees from Judah. The Babylonian king could scarcely have failed to note the character of this captive people who maintained their worship of their God and practiced the laws of their covenant with him. Thus the author of the books of Kings ended his record on a note of hope.

First Chronicles

The books of the Chronicles need to be read in double focus. In content, they retell in a highly selective way much of the story of Second Samuel and the books of Kings but they tell it from the vantage point of a much later date, perhaps as late as 250 B.C. Where Second Kings left off with the Jews having just been taken into captivity in Babylon, with their future highly uncertain, the Chronicles were written after they had spent a half century in Babylon, returned to Jerusalem, rebuilt the city walls, reconstituted the life of Judah, and—most important— rebuilt the temple and established its centrality in Jewish life. Originally, the books of Ezra and Nehemiah, which follow the Chronicles, were a part of the same scroll as the Chronicles but were lopped off by later editors and incorporated in accepted Hebrew scripture without the Chronicles, because they were the only history of the Jews in the period immediately following the exile. The Chronicles were the last books admitted to the canon, since they contributed little historically that was not already known.

So—if the reader is primarily concerned with acquiring an over-all view of the consecutive history of the Jews, then the books of Ezra and Nehemiah should be read immediately following Second Kings, leaving the Chronicles to serve as a refresher course in Jewish history with an emphasis that reflects the thinking at least a century or two later. By that time the position of rebuilt Jerusalem had stabilized. Babylonian control had given way to Persian dominance, then Persian control had given way to Greek dominance; Alexander the Great had made, or was about to make, his swing through Phoenicia and Syria; Hannibal was a force in North Africa; Egypt was independent; Rome had become a well-established republic probably not yet sacked by the Gauls. South of Palestine the Nabataeans were establishing themselves but not threatening the trade routes severely enough to be written into the record. But whatever was going on in the outer world was not greatly troubling the Chronicler. He was no real internationalist, nor was he ever as much interested in writing linear history as in drawing lessons from history. So he lifted from the record the outstanding events and personalities which gave support to his chief concern: the centrality of the temple in Jerusalem, the position of the priests and Levites with their proper ritual, and the necessity of the people's support of the system—the priorities of his own place and time.

Where the earlier account, in Samuel–Kings, presented fairly detailed history from Moses to the Exile, the Chronicler skipped over the conquest of Canaan, so that a reader who knew only his version might almost conclude that Moses handed his scepter to Joshua, who handed it to David, who promptly ordered the temple built. Where the earlier books presented a convincingly lifelike portrait of the warrior-king David delineated by someone who knew him intimately, regarded him highly and saw no reason to cover his faults, the Chronicler idealized David to the point of leaving out every derogatory incident. In the earlier account the kings of both Judah and Israel were presented in contemporary context, constantly fighting their enemies and often each other, maneuvering for power, improving their political position, meeting the ups and downs of complicated family life, trying to be loyal to their God only to defect, suffer, and reach out for restoration to favor. But the Chronicler wanted his heroes to be towering and flawless. He enjoyed embroidering his big scenes and he never skimped on figures. One wonders at his discrepancy in reporting figures. (But even today such discrepancy is a tendency of everyday speech. One individual reports to his friend, "There was a huge crowd," meaning a thousand people showed up. The friend who thinks of a huge crowd as ten thousand people reports that he heard there were ten thousand people at the celebration. Unwittingly he has distorted the report but made the point that there were a lot of people.) The Chronicler was more concerned with the impact of an important event or speech than with verbatim accuracy.

A modern student of ancient historians could have himself a field day comparing the Greek historian Thucydides, who wrote about the Peloponnesian War not too long before the Chronicler began his chronicling. Thucydides maintained that he did not feel at liberty to present any incident as fact if what he knew was based on conjecture or hearsay, and that he exercised close scrutiny of his source material although he found the process of research laborious. He says he always tried to convey the personality and conviction of the speaker, not his own point of view. But the Chronicler was a protagonist for his own convictions no matter whom he was quoting. As a theologian he also took for granted that he expressed the Almighty's point of view—as theologians often tend to do. However, he did stack his arguments on the firm foundation of God's expectation of his people's righteous conduct. To him God was no abstraction but a transcendent fact of daily life. Behind the perils of famine, pestilence, war, weather, and shifting population, through defeat as well as victory, the Hebrew people experienced a firsthand relationship to a reality they called God, to which—they came to say to *whom*—they were morally responsible. God was not a something they predicated but Someone they discovered, experienced, found *there,* within and without, inescapable. The Chronicler entered into this experience; he felt his people's yearning, their upreach, their affirmation of themselves, their fellows, and this Other. As a historian he presented them living forward but looking back to appraise the path they had traveled.

The Authority of Genealogy

Evidently feeling the need of the authority of honorable forebears, the Chronicler gave his convictions a running start by going back to Adam. Trunk, branches and every significant twig were fitted onto the schematic family tree. Let no honorable Jew feel he lacked respectable ancestry. Since the living descendants of David were particularly important—who knew when the monarchy might be restored?—their entire line was traced and the twelve tribes carefully located and characterized. All these genealogies and enumerations are likely to bore a here-and-now reader, who could scarcely care less whether a given singer in the temple choir was a descendant of Levi or of some other of Jacob's twelve sons. But here and there a phrase offers an illuminating sidelight. Isaac, the recorder reminds his audience, was the progenitor of the Edomites, whom the Israelites detested, as well as of the Israelites; and Isaac's half brother Ishmael, whom Abraham once banished to the wilderness, was the progenitor of the Arabs. The Edomites instituted kingship "before any king reigned over the Israelites."

"Jair, who had twenty-three cities in the land of Gilead." Cities? Towns, in modern terminology, and not very large towns, but often walled and fortified, ". . . and Seled died childless," a tragedy in his culture. "Now Sheshan had no sons, only daughters" but he gave one daughter to his Egyptian slave and they produced a longed-for son; an Egyptian slave might have been culturally way above the daughter. No small amount of Egyptian blood flowed in Hebrew veins. "Shimei had sixteen sons and six daughters," whom someone had to feed; it is to be hoped Shimei's crops were good. A pastoral scene: "They journeyed . . . to the east side of the valley, to seek pasture for their flocks, where they found rich, good pasture, and the land was very broad, quiet, and peaceful." Protocol prevailed even in this short record: "These are the sons of Bithiah, the daughter of Pharaoh, whom Merod married"—a daughter of Pharaoh evidently outranked her husband and so was mentioned first. Another woman made the genealogical list, a granddaughter of Ephraim and ancestress of Joshua, "Sheerah, who built both Lower and Upper Bethhoron, and Uzzensheerah"—or was it actually her descendants who did the building? Some figures appear magnified; for instance, the Benjaminites "valiant men—who carried shield and sword, and drew the bow, expert in war, forty-four thousand seven hundred and sixty, ready for service"—and, being ready, they went forth to fight.

> . . . they cried to God in the battle, and he granted their entreaty because they trusted in him. They carried off their livestock: fifty thousand of their camels, two hundred and fifty thousand sheep,

two thousand asses, and a hundred thousand men alive. For many
fell slain, because the war was of God. 5:20–21

The author forgot to ponder how much grassland that many
animals would need for grazing, and if the animals were grazing
how the warring Israelites ever rounded them up; and what the
Israelites did with a hundred thousand captives; and who made
that judgment about its being God's war.

Jabez

Poignant among the mini-biographies is the brief story of Jabez.

Jabez was more honorable than his brothers; and his mother called
his name Jabez, saying, "Because I bore him in pain." Jabez called
on the God of Israel, saying, "Oh that thou wouldst bless me and
enlarge my border, and that thy hand might be with me, and that
thou wouldst keep me from harm so that it might not hurt me!"
And God granted what he asked. 4:9–10

Since the father of Jabez is not named, his name had probably
been stricken from the temple register, so Jabez was without
family pedigree. His older brothers must have connived with the
father in whatever sin was committed. The family land had probably been confiscated, since Jabez prayed that his coast might be
enlarged. Such an earnest prayer! Where else could Jabez turn except to God whose mighty hand he needed to make his path
straight. His was a prayer of pure intent because, commented the
recorder, "God granted him what he asked." Later in the record,
a phrase appears: "The families of the scribes that dwelt at
Jabez. . . ." Evidently at some later time there was a town
which may have developed from a land development of Jabez's,
or from a school he started, since the families of scribes are
mentioned. Many Israelite towns were called after their founder or
leading citizen.

Names strange to us appear in the genealogy but someone must
have used them in birth registrations and in calling children from
their play: Sabta, Serug, Molid, Pelet, Jalon, Elioenai, Bukki,
Gog, Uzzi, Libni, Zuph, Jattir, Hod, Zur, Ir, Likhi, and scores
more. It was a sister of Gilead who had the name really worth
remembering: Hammolecheth. "So all Israel was enrolled by
genealogies." Nine chapters of the Chronicler's book.

Accouterments of Worship

Since worship in the temple was central to Israel's life, a sizable staff was needed, and the Chronicler was acquainted with all the positions and their requirements. To him the protocol of worship was intrinsic to worship itself, as is likely to be the case in an institutionalized church where authority comes down from the top. Established decorum guaranteed the kind of worship which would elicit a faithful response from God.

Where in the books of Kings the sounds of war, the clashing of swords and the zing of arrows seems forever in the background, in the Chronicles it is the music of harps, timbrels, lyres, and the singing of trained choruses which furnishes the background accompaniment. Indeed, the elaborate musical documentation suggests that the author himself may have been a Levite and musician, perhaps the one mentioned as the Levite who "should direct the music, for he understands it." (Mr. Chronicler, not so far from you in time, the Chinese philosopher Mencius was commenting that if the king's love of music were very great the kingdom would be near to a state of good government.)

By way of authority for the importance of the Levites and musicians, King David was credited with having instituted the temple's musical service in the very order in which the Chronicler knew it.

Everyone Accounted For

Occasionally an individual singer is singled out: "Heman the singer, the son of Joel, son of Samuel" along with his brother Asaph, "who stood on his right hand. . . . On the left hand were their brethren. . . ." Again, "Now these are the singers . . . dwelling in the chambers of the temple free from other service, for they were on duty day and night." No one's position was left out of the listing: ". . . the priests, the Levites, and the temple servants," among whom are listed the gatekeepers, two hundred and twelve of them: "David and Samuel the seer established them in their office of trust." Then came those in charge of the chambers and treasuries, the utensils of service, the furniture, the foods, fine flour, oil, wines, spices, and preparations of the showbread—

the twelve uniform cakes which stood in rows on a table in the inner sanctuary and were replaced with fresh cakes each Sabbath, "the bread of the Presence." The Chronicler overlooked nothing that maintained the propriety of worship.

Saul's Mini-biography

For this historian the important chapter in the story of Israel began with the kingship of Saul. But the account is truncated, opening at the point where the Israelites, led by Saul, fled before the Philistines, whose trade routes they had cut off. The rest of Saul's story follows the older record and his epitaph is the unctuous comment that "Saul died for his unfaithfulness." A less opinionated writer might have more sympathetically appraised Saul's struggle with himself, as well as against his neighbors, when he was precipitated to the unprecedented position of kingship and had to compete with a subordinate like David who was vastly more gifted than he.

Enter David

Where Second Samuel details "a long war between the house of Saul and the house of David," the Chronicler crisply reports, "Then all Israel gathered together to David at Hebron," with the elders effecting an immediate covenant and enthusiastically anointing David king, after which they turned eagerly toward the capture of Jerusalem—that challenging stronghold 2,500 feet above sea level, supposedly impregnable and already historic.

The Chronicler seems to have admired the military, especially David's "mighty men," who formed an invincible circle around him. The Secret Service of ancient Israel. Joab, being the first to smite an inhabitant of Jerusalem, was made top general and the armed forces expanded daily until there was a great army, "like an army of God." Various companies were mentioned for their special excellencies, such as the contingent who "were bowmen, and could shoot arrows and sling stones with either the right or the left hand."

According to this account David's first act after capturing the city was to bring up the ark. Again reading back into history an attitude current in his own time, the Chronicler has David commanding the Levites "to appoint their brethren as the singers who should play loudly on the musical instruments, on harps and lyres and cymbals, to raise a sound of joy." At least he had the right idea as to what guaranteed fervent participation in services of worship. The procession which brought the ark to Jerusalem was a gala of galas but proper in all its appointments. David's wife Michal does not berate him for showing off in public; a woman berate *David*? After the ark of God came safely into its tent David distributed his own largess. Levites and musicians were promptly appointed "to invoke, to thank, and to praise the Lord." As things should be, so they must have been! For climax the Chronicler inserts a long psalm, whether drawn from an ancient text or composed (expost facto) for the occasion, no one knows. The effect on the audience was the same. And on us.

O give thanks to the Lord, call on his name,
  make known his deeds among the peoples! . . .
He is the Lord our God . . .
He is mindful of his covenant for ever,
  of the word that he commanded, for a thousand generations. . . .
Sing to the Lord, all the earth!
  Tell of his salvation from day to day. . . .
Deliver us, O God of our salvation,
  and gather and save us from among the nations,
that we may give thanks to thy holy name,
  and glory in thy praise.
Blessed be the Lord, the God of Israel,
  from everlasting to everlasting! 16:8, 14–15, 23, 35–36

Unlike some modern music festivals, this one encompassed young and old and came to a peaceful termination. Finally "all the people departed each to his house, and David went home to bless his household." We can almost see King David's upraised hand and then his laying aside of the royal role as he retired wearily to his dressing room to have his tired feet massaged—but the Chronicler would never have mentioned that.

Since David was the man who honored the Lord by envisioning the temple and planning every detail, he could not be presented as the same man who tricked Uriah and stole his wife, the man whose favorite son turned against him, split the army and almost took over the throne; he could not be seen as the king whose subservience to his general, Joab, was at times less than royal, whose killing of Saul's descendants was petty and vengeful. The Chronicler determinedly refused to expose his hero's feet of clay. And he had a practical ethic behind his attitude. If a man of David's distinguished achievement could take as many liberties with the verities as he did and still be acclaimed for his spiritual leadership, what was to keep an ordinary man from allowing himself a little ethical leeway? Better that people should look up to David as a man of unflinching integrity in all circumstances. The Chronicler's stance raises interesting questions for our day, when some among us are concerned with allowing the media to expose freely whatever facts they find and others are concerned to keep the eyes of the rank and file on the achievement of their leaders and not on the occasional lack of integrity involved in producing the achievement.

". . . and so David reigned over all Israel; and he administered justice and equity to all his people." But he still had battles to fight, fighting being the avocation of ancient kings: "In the spring of the year, the time when kings go forth to battle. . . ." He had the descendants of the giants of Gath to overcome. For his honor and the honor of Israel and all that.

The Census

In chapter 21 David decides to "number Israel, from Beersheba to Dan." There was a popular attitude, not confined to Israel, that only God, or the gods, should know how much temporal power was available; Yahweh could augment or increase an army's might or a nation's power as he saw fit. His was the all-knowledge a census implied. And there may have been a disturbing memory of the census reported in the book of Numbers, when each person of proper age gave a half shekel to the sanctuary and it was the shekels which were counted. (A neat way to pay for the next all-American census.)

Satan

So why did David go ahead with the census? Satan prompted it. This is the first mention of Satan in the Bible. If the book of

Job was written before the Chronicles, then Satan's first appearance in the canon is at the heavenly court with other celestial beings or "sons of God." The Chronicler regards Satan as an independent agent, suggesting the dualism of Zoroastrianism, which no doubt seeped into Jewish thought under Persian influence. From here on, the theory of Satan develops in both Jewish and Christian thought as a part of the general concept of demonology and angelology.

After the census the story follows the general outline in Kings. David was offered his choice of three punishments, and the death from plague of seventy thousand men of Israel ensues. When God repented of the evil and stayed the hand of the destroying angel, "David lifted his eyes and saw the angel of the Lord standing between earth and heaven, and in his hand a drawn sword stretched out over Jerusalem." With the elders, clothed in sackcloth, David fell on his face and the angel commanded him to rear an altar right there on the threshing floor of Ornan the Jebusite, where they were standing. Ornan and his four sons had also seen the angel and when David asked to buy the site immediately, at full price, Ornan offered it free along with the oxen for a burnt offering. But David insisted on paying "six hundred shekels of gold by weight," rather than the fifty shekels of silver mentioned in Kings. A modern reader cannot help admiring the generous spirit of the Chronicler; nothing was too big or too brave for the heroes of the Lord, and the Chronicler wanted to express largess of spirit in terms the people of his own day would understand.

The Temple

David decided then and there to build a temple on that very spot and orders went out immediately for all the necessary building material, from dressed stone to iron for nails. Although David knew that the actual construction of the temple must be Solomon's, the Lord having withheld the privilege from him because of his much warring, the Chronicler has him going as far as he can.

For David said, "Solomon my son is young and inexperienced, and the house that is to be built for the Lord must be exceedingly magnificent, of fame and glory throughout all lands; I will therefore make preparation for it." So David provided materials in great quantity before his death. 22:5

Assembling the craftsmen, he gave his son a final admonition: "Arise and be doing! The Lord be with you!" (A wonderful text for any church-building enterprise.) All that was left for Solomon, according to this report, was to follow the blueprint. Solomon might go down in history as the king over Israel at the time of its greatest extent and renown but the Chronicler made sure that David was acclaimed the real instigator of the temple; also the one who organized the priests and Levites, and gave prominent place to the musicians.

After David had organized both civil and military affairs—the report being 288,000 men in the king's bodyguard alone—he called together in Jerusalem "all the officials of Israel" and commanded them to fulfill their obligations. Handing Solomon the plans for the temple, he presented the weight in gold of all the necessary temple vessels, adding silver, bronze, onyx, antimony, marble and many varieties of precious stones. Realizing the influence of example, he added his own personal gifts, including "three thousand talents . . . of the gold of Ophir." After that, practical man that he was, he passed the collection plate: "Who then will offer willingly, consecrating himself to the Lord?" The people responded, as he knew they would, making "their free will offerings," every man of them. "Then the people rejoiced because they had given willingly, for with a whole heart they had offered freely to the Lord."

David's farewell prayer is worthy of the great king whom the Chronicler revered:

> Thine, O Lord, is the greatness, and the power, and the glory, and the victory, and the majesty; for all that is in the heavens and in the earth is thine; thine is the kingdom, O Lord, and thou art exalted as head above all. . . . But who am I, and what is my people, that we should be able thus to offer willingly? For all things come from thee, and of thy own have we given thee. . . . O Lord, the God of . . . our fathers, keep for ever such purposes and thoughts in the hearts of thy people, and direct their hearts toward thee. 29:11, 14, 18

Public worship followed, with sacrifices "in abundance," after which—as has been the case at most religious festivals through the years—"they ate and drank before the Lord on that day with great gladness." Refreshed of soul and body, in that order.

The Succession

All that was left for David to do was to die, which he did regally "in a good old age, full of days, riches, and honor."

Second Chronicles

Since First and Second Chronicles were originally one book and share the same background, the historian moves on with his story. Solomon takes up the actual building of the temple and the first nine chapters are devoted to him. No mention is ever made of any lapse on his part from high moral conduct, nor are the initial difficulties of his reign rehearsed. In the Chronicler's mind, his reign should proceed with decorum, since he was God's anointed, and so it did.

> Solomon the son of David established himself in his kingdom, and the Lord his God was with him and made him exceedingly great. 1:1

The account of his reign does not open with his going to a high place to offer sacrifice—a procedure quite acceptable in Solomon's time, when the crest of a hill was often the site of an altar upon which a king or priest might offer sacrifice, but not at all acceptable in the Chronicler's time. The latter account opens with Solomon's going to Gibeon to offer sacrifice, because the tent of meeting was kept there. (This is the last mention of the tent of meeting.) In a profoundly reverent attitude, probably an accurate surmise, Solomon then began to build the temple.

> The house which I am to build will be great, for our God is greater than all gods. But who is able to build him a house, since heaven, even highest heaven, cannot contain him? 2:5–6

Details of the project are carefully recounted. His was a time of fine craftsmanship, mostly brought in from outside Judah, and also a time when all Jews believed in the God they were honoring.

While the king's orders were compulsory and workmen might have no choice but to comply, they shared the nation's regard for their accomplishment.

Finally the temple was ready for dedication, and the event loses nothing in the Chronicler's description. Solomon's prayer of dedication as "he knelt upon his knees in the presence of all the assembly of Israel, and spread forth his hands toward heaven" is the prayer of a king who feels himself responsible to God for the well-being of his people. For him God was an immediate presence.

> When Solomon had ended his prayer, fire came down from heaven and consumed the burnt offering and the sacrifices, and the glory of the Lord filled the temple. And the priests could not enter the house of the Lord, because the glory of the Lord filled the Lord's house. When all the children of Israel saw the fire come down and the glory of the Lord upon the temple, they bowed down with their faces to the earth on the pavement, and worshiped and gave thanks to the Lord, saying,
>> "For he is good,
>> for his steadfast love endures for ever." 7:1–3

On the whole, Solomon's career is portrayed much as in First Kings, including his building of store cities and fortifications, his forced levy of non-Jews, his military expeditions, his extension of trade, his reception of tribute, and the visit of the queen of Sheba. Only his misdeeds remain unrecorded. "Thus King Solomon excelled all the kings of the earth in riches and in wisdom." For forty years he reigned over Israel and then when he "slept with his fathers" his son Rehoboam came to the throne.

The division of the kingdom follows the earlier record, except that the kings of Israel are played down as far as possible and the acts of the kings of Judah are amplified. To the Chronicler any king or any group which failed to worship in the temple in Jerusalem was not worthy of much attention. For instance, the northern king Jeroboam, who was primarily responsible for the division of the kingdom, is described only enough to make clear the acts of Rehoboam, Solomon's successor in Judah. When Shishak of Egypt "came up against Jerusalem with twelve hundred chariots and sixty thousand horsemen," followed by his mercenaries from

Libya and Ethiopia and the Sukkiim, the prophet Shemaiah reproaches Rehoboam for forsaking the law of the Lord. The prophet delivers the Lord's word: "You abandoned me, so I have abandoned you to the hand of Shishak." But when Rehoboam and his princes humbled themselves, the Lord again spoke through Shemaiah, promising deliverance although not without penalty. Shishak of Egypt "took away the treasures of the house of the Lord and . . . of the king's house." Apparently the Chronicler had additional sources of factual material, for he observed, "Now the acts of Rehoboam, from first to last, are they not written in the chronicles of Shemaiah the prophet and of Iddo the seer?"

In order to underscore the importance of the priests and Levites, a battle not mentioned in the books of Kings is described: When Abijah, Rehoboam's son, began his reign he continued the war of Judah against Jeroboam, in Israel, who had "eight hundred thousand picked mighty warriors," twice the size of Judah's army. He stood on a hilltop and addressed—or dressed down—Jeroboam for taking advantage of Rehoboam when he was inexperienced, and for casting golden calves for worship. "Whoever comes to consecrate himself with a young bull or seven rams becomes a priest of what are no gods. But as for us, the Lord is our God, and we have not forsaken him. . . . Behold, God is with us at our head." When the actual fighting began Abijah may have had his moment of doubt, because he was ambushed from behind as well as facing a huge army in front, but his soldiers "cried to the Lord, and the priests blew the trumpets" and "God defeated Jeroboam and all Israel before Abijah and Judah." This splendid victory would not be known without the account in Chronicles.

The triumph of Asa, son of Abijah, is elaborated. Having destroyed all foreign altars and commanded the people of Judah "to seek the Lord, the God of their fathers, and to keep the law and the commandment," Asa led a great rebuilding program, which was blessed, he declared, because the people of Judah had sought the Lord, who "has given us peace on every side." So when "Zerah the Ethiopian came out against them with an army of a million men and three hundred chariots," Asa confidently cried to the Lord for help and "the Lord defeated the Ethiopians," who fled and "fell until none remained alive." Appropriately, at this time the spirit of God came upon Azariah the prophet to review the situation and call for fidelity, a persuasive reminder which gave Asa courage to clear the land of all idols.

In order to make a point, the Chronicler retells the story of Asa's seeking aid from the king of Syria at Damascus in fighting Baasha of Israel, who was blocking Judah's important commercial routes. Asa paid Damascus with treasures from the house of the Lord, and the combined armies of Syria and Judah defeated Israel. But instead of being congratulated for his victory Asa was promptly castigated by the seer Hanani for having relied on Syria instead of on the Lord. "You have done foolishly in this; and from now on you will have wars." Asa had the seer put in stocks for his bold words and "inflicted cruelties upon some of the people"; perhaps on those who applauded the seer. In the Chronicler's eyes it was this shift in Asa's loyalties which accounted for his becoming "diseased in his feet." Moreover, when the disease became severe Asa "did not seek the Lord, but sought help from physicians"! Whether gangrene or cancer, whatever, the diseased feet must have become unpleasant for those nearby, because the record has it that at Asa's death "They laid him on a bier which had been filled with various kinds of spices prepared by the perfumer's art."

At the Chronicler's hand the stature of Jehoshaphat is enhanced. The new king "walked in the earlier ways of his father. . . . Therefore the Lord established the kingdom in his hand." He sent five princes along with nine Levites and two priests "to teach in the cities of Judah. . . . having the book of the law of the Lord with them. . . . And the fear of the Lord fell upon all the kingdoms of the lands that were round about Judah, and they made no war against Jehoshaphat." An advanced idea—preventing war by teaching. And yet—and yet—his impressive military strength may have added a certain persuasion, because the Chronicler credits him with an army of 1,160,000 men, a highly exaggerated figure but awesome for the record.

The military venture of Jehoshaphat after he allied himself with Ahab of Israel follows the story in Kings, including the forecast by the prophet Micaiah that the army would be "scattered upon the mountains, as sheep that have no shepherd." (There is sometimes poignant poetry in the descriptive phrases of a pastoral people; anyone who has watched sheep in strange, rocky terrain when there is no shepherd to lead them can sense Micaiah's sadness for the scattered, disorganized foot soldiers.) Condemned for his alliance with Israel, Jehoshaphat returned to Jerusalem and "brought [the people] back to the Lord," appointing priests and Levites as judges—a commission not mentioned in Kings but in line with the standards of the Chronicler's day. Jehoshaphat learned from his mistakes and the next time he was attacked— this time by his neighbors the Ammonites and Moabites—he fasted, clearing his mind and cleansing his spirit. Confidently he called on the Lord: "We do not know what to do, but our eyes are upon thee." With the men of Judah standing in anticipation of the Lord's answer, "with their little ones, their wives, and their children," the spirit of the Lord came upon a man named Jahaziel, who sustained the crowd with the Lord's reply: "Fear not, and be not dismayed at this great multitude; for the battle is not yours but God's."

And so events proved. The people of Judah met the dawn in the wilderness of Tekoa with songs of praise for the Lord, which so confused the attacking armies that they shot their arrows wildly and destroyed each other. Jehoshaphat's army, swords still sheathed, marched back to Jerusalem "with harps and lyres and trumpets, to the house of the Lord." Eventually, no doubt, singing crusaders *shall* overcome and no one will be less surprised than the music makers. We would have missed this heartening episode if it had not been for the Chronicler's interest in music as intrinsic to worship and worship as a spontaneous factor in daily life.

Unfortunately Jehoshaphat later made an economic alliance with Israel's king, Ahaziah, "who did wickedly" in building ships for the Tarshish trade and was rebuked by the prophet Eliezer. "And the ships were wrecked and were not able to go to Tarshish."

The next digression from the report in Kings is the elaboration of Joash's refurbishing of the temple. Here the Levites are appointed trustees of the temple and honor guard to the king. The point is stressed that all the days of the priest Jehoiada (he lived to be one hundred thirty) Joash remained faithful, but later, without the good priest's salutary influence (meaning, probably, that the Chronicler felt kings needed priests as much as anybody) he let the heathen cults seep in. For this act Zechariah, son of Jehoiada, prophesied his downfall and for the prophecy was stoned. "And when he was dying, he said, 'May the Lord see and avenge.'" The army of Syria took care of the revenge, wounding Joash in battle, and his own servants "slew him on his bed."

The Chronicler adds to the history of Amaziah of Judah an episode in which he hired a hundred thousand mercenaries of Israel to join his three hundred thousand soldiers and prepared to fight Seir (the mountainous section of Edom) but a man of God warned him that God would not bless an alliance with Israel. Dismayed, Amaziah dismissed the mercenaries, who were understandably furious and turned to looting while Amaziah led his own army "and smote ten thousand men of Seir. The men of Judah captured another ten thousand alive, and took them to the top of a rock and threw them down . . . and they were all dashed to pieces." Incredible cruelty, all the more ghastly because neither Amaziah's contemporaries nor the Chronicler seem horrified by the deed. Evidently ours is not the only age which can be made callous to cruelty. Corrupted by his own violence, Amaziah later adopted the gods of Seir, which brought strong condemnation from a local prophet. Finally he was defeated by Israel, betrayed by a conspiracy in Jerusalem, and slain in Lachish, where he had fled. The high rate of death by murder for kings must have dampened some of the elation a royal family might be expected to feel at a coronation.

Uzziah, aged sixteen, is introduced as a good king "and as long as he sought the Lord, God made him prosper. . . . But when he was strong he grew proud, to his destruction." The Chronicler's interest is in the fact that he usurped the prerogatives of the priests by burning incense on the altar, an act which brought down the wrath of the priest Azariah, whose temerity in expressing his ire to the king made the king furious ". . . and when he became angry with the priests leprosy broke out on his forehead." To the Chronicler sickness was a sign of sin.

Uzziah's son Jotham "did what was right in the eyes of the Lord," taking care not to "invade the temple. . . . So Jotham became mighty, because he ordered his ways before the Lord his God." Seal of approval from the Chronicler. Uzziah's successor,

Ahaz, however, was particularly despicable in the eyes of the Chronicler because he made images of foreign gods and burned his sons as an offering. The account follows the story in Kings except that the author does not allow so evil a king as Ahaz to be buried in a royal tomb.

The story of good King Hezekiah is much expanded, and an elaborate celebration of the Passover, not even mentioned in Second Kings, is presented in full and impressive dignity. Remaining partial to the Levites, the Chronicler comments that "the Levites were more upright in heart than the priests in sanctifying themselves." During the week-long celebration of the Passover, the whole assembly of Judah, including sojourners from Israel and foreigners, "rejoiced." Such a great verb to express a great occasion—rejoiced!

In the account of the reign of Manasseh, the Chronicler unprecedentedly presents him as less evil than he is depicted in Kings, affirming that when the king found himself bound with fetters in Babylon he heartily repented "and God received his entreaty . . . and brought him again to Jerusalem. . . . Then Manasseh knew that the Lord was God." The reign of Josiah, the reformer king, follows the record in Kings with special emphasis on cult procedures. Here is a king in full stature, dedicated, inspiring enthusiasm, leading in reform. Expectedly, when he died at the end of a beneficent reign of thirty-one years, "All Judah and Jerusalem mourned for Josiah." Even the prophet Jeremiah lamented, followed by "all the singing men and singing women."

The final reckoning of Chronicles follows the earlier account, a sad tabulation for any historian who must recount the doom of a nation. Condensed into a few sentences are the basic facts: the triumph of the Chaldeans, who killed young and old, carried off to Babylon the treasures of the house of God and of the palace, burned the temple of Solomon, broke down the walls of Jerusalem, and finally herded into exile "those who had escaped from the sword," thus fulfilling "the word of the Lord by the mouth of Jeremiah." The last, hopeful paragraph, noting the proclamation of Cyrus some forty years later allowing the Jews to return to Judah, belongs rightfully to the book of Ezra, where it also becomes the opening sentences.

Ezra

Return from Babylon

At some period in assembling the record of the Jewish people—history and prophetic insight—the books we know as Ezra and Nehemiah were cut off from the original scroll of Chronicles to become independent documents, no doubt because the Chronicles rehearsed the same story as the books of Kings while Ezra and Nehemiah furnished the primary account of the return of the Jews from exile in Babylonia. The book of Ezra leads off with an account of the first return under an official named Shesh-bazzar appointed by Cyrus about 538 B.C. Shesh-bazzar set earnestly to work to rebuild the temple but met so much opposition that he had to give up for the time being. At least a quarter century later, in the reign of Darius I, a second contingent of returnees was led by Zerubbabel and Jeshua, who completed the temple under the challenge and encouragement of the prophets Haggai and Zechariah. Then, some time around the mid-fifth century, while Artaxerxes was king, Nehemiah came and in spite of continued opposition built the walls of Jerusalem. Still later, Ezra the scribe, a man of enormous determination, led another group of Babylonian Jews back to their homeland.

The final editor of the whole scroll Chronicles-Ezra-Nehemiah apparently tried to preserve as much as possible of the early first-hand documents but he was certainly thrown off stride as to chronology. Or it may have been later copyists who jumbled part of the Ezra story into Nehemiah's account of building the city wall.

Ezra's Intent

Ezra had learned firsthand in Babylon how difficult it is to maintain true worship in the midst of foreigners with strange gods, and he knew that the Jews who had remained behind in Jerusalem at the time of the great deportation had become careless about the rites and practices centering in the temple. He intended that traditional Judaism should cohere and flourish. *Pure, secure,* and *endure* might be called his key words. He would have been pleased to see his name in the canon!

The Return

The first half dozen chapters of Ezra tell the exciting story of the first return of Jews from Babylon. The great Cyrus, king of Persia and a farsighted ruler, decided that the restive conquered peoples in Babylonia who still resented their uprooting, clung to their native gods, and lived for the day they could go home, had just as well get up and go home. To be sure, they would still have to pay tribute but if they were more contented back wherever they came from, he could save a considerable degree of both civil and military surveillance. And he implemented his decision in generous fashion. The Jews, for one, were not only free to return to Judah but free to "rebuild the house of the Lord, the God of Israel—he is the God who is in Jerusalem." Not only could the Jews return but Cyrus urged their Babylonian neighbors to give them beasts, sustenance and gifts for their undertaking.

Led by the priests and Levites, supported by "everyone whose spirit God had stirred," a sizable portion of the Jewish population prepared to leave. It was not just a poor, scraggly group of captives returning to their own land but a well-organized contingent bearing among their own belongings the temple vessels which Nebuchadnezzar had purloined: ". . . all the vessels of gold and silver were five thousand four hundred and sixty-nine." With typical Hebrew thoroughness Shesh-bazzar had the returnees listed by tribe, family and individual name—including priests, Levites, singers, gatekeepers and temple servants. Anyone who could not produce an adequate genealogy was excluded from partaking of holy food until a priest could be found capable of operating the Urim and Thummim in his behalf. The cavalcade included 42,360 registered Jews besides 7,337 servants along with horses, mules, camels and asses. (The Chronicler's figures are always on the generous side.)

The trek from Babylon back to Jerusalem is much less famous than the migration from Egypt to Canaan but it must have been a tremendous venture. First there was the parting of the patriotic Jews from members of their families who, for reasons of business, health or divided allegiance, remained in Babylon. Many families probably parted with mutual assurances that those left behind would follow as soon as the advance guard rebuilt homes, put in crops, and found jobs. Centuries later European Jewish émigrés leaving Europe for Israel had to deal with some of the same problems.

Home Again

Once back in Jerusalem, the first sight of their old homes must have been a joyous but traumatic experience. In some neighborhoods not a trace remained of the olden days. Strangers lived where neighbors should be; such public buildings as remained were either in disrepair or housed a new brand of bureaucrats; farms lay fallow or were tilled by alien hands. Local Jews who had not been carried into captivity had adjusted to life with peoples brought in from other countries and had often married alien wives; their children and grandchildren spoke foreign tongues. Traditional Hebrew patterns of worship had been hybridized. Restructuring the national life would not come easily. But Shesh-bazzar must have had his plans well in hand because he proceeded at once to the first business of the day—looking to the welfare of the temple. Spurred by his enthusiasm, heads of families "made freewill offerings for the house of God, to erect it on its site; according to their ability they gave to the treasury. . . ." Freewill—a tremendous word in temple building.

"The priests, the Levites, and some of the people lived in Jerusalem and its vicinity"; the rest, including the singers, lived in the towns round about. The Chronicler must indeed have had a hand in compiling the book of Ezra because the singers, with whom he seemed to identify, are mentioned recurrently.

Joy with Tears

With some textual interruption and misplacement the narrative continues. Under the leadership of the priest Jeshua and a man named Zerubbabel, "the altar of the God of Israel" was rebuilt and the ritual of morning and evening burnt offerings was reinstated. The people were then ready for a festival as of old. "And they kept the feast of booths," that ancient celebration of the ingathering of the crops.

Construction of the temple began! As when building Solomon's temple, they went to Sidon and Tyre for cedar trees to be delivered at the port of Joppa. Overseers and contractors were appointed; workmen were hired. At last the foundations were completed, and that called for proper celebration, with "the priests in their vestments" coming forward with trumpets, the Levites with cymbals, "and they sang responsively,"

> For he is good,
> for his steadfast love endures for ever toward Israel. 3:11

Almost too much joy. The oldsters wept; ". . . so that the people could not distinguish the sound of the joyful shout from the sound of the people's weeping."

Trouble Looms

But all was not serene. Some Jews from around Jerusalem, as far as Samaria, claimed to have followed orthodox Jewish practices ever since they had been left behind at the time of the Babylonian captivity and they now wanted to join in the temple project. The returnees would have none of them; they alone had withstood the hardships of Babylon and they wanted no augmented forces. "You have nothing to do with us in building a house to our God; but we alone will build to the Lord. . . ." As decisive and divisive words as Jews ever spoke. *We alone.* Only partially recognized, a theological question was thus posed: If Yahweh was indeed a universal God, should not all who wished to acknowledge him be included in the worshiping-serving community? Especially if they advocated the same views and practices. On the other hand, there might be tighter solidarity if the worshiping community were carefully screened as to forebears and mutual experience.

Turned away, "the people of the land discouraged the people of Judah," frustrating them wherever possible. Their dignitaries wrote a letter to Artaxerxes accusing the returned Jews of rebuilding Jerusalem, "that rebellious and wicked city," for their own divisive purposes. They insinuated that the next step would be refusal to pay "tribute, custom, or toll, and the royal revenue will be impaired." Did the king want to lose possession of "the province Beyond the River"?—the river being the Euphrates and the province Judah. The king did not. Posthaste he replied that the work must be stopped, and just as fast the recipients of the letter showed it to the Jewish authorities in Jerusalem. "Then the work on the house of God which is in Jerusalem stopped."

In the next incident, the resumption of the building of the temple, Darius is king of Babylonia, but whether the first or second Darius is not stated. Darius II ruled until 405. This scrambling of sequence in no way affects the meaning of events but it confuses the logical historian.

Renewed Building

When building began again, the governor of the province Beyond the River wrote to Darius, now king of Persia, that he had gone "to the province of Judah, to the house of the great God" and seen it being rebuilt with huge stones and timber; "this work goes on diligently and prospers in their hands." The Jews, he said, claimed permission from Cyrus. Would Darius please have the records checked? Darius found that the truth lay with the Jews, so since the edicts of a Persian king could not be altered, he returned word that the building of the temple in Jerusalem should continue *and* that the cost should come from the royal revenue; likewise that the day-by-day need of animals for sacrifice be met. Thus the faith and determination of the Jews paid off—which was nothing new in their history. Finally the temple was finished and the Passover was celebrated, complete with paschal lamb and the seven-day feast of unleavened bread. Celebrated "with joy; for the Lord had made them joyful."

Ezra

In chapter 7 Ezra himself comes into the story, again in misplaced material which should follow the seventh chapter of Nehemiah. More than a century has gone by but Jews are still returning from Babylon, among them this scribe Ezra, who was accompanied by more priests, Levites, singers and gate-keepers. Ezra had a special purpose in returning:

> For Ezra had set his heart to study the law of the Lord, and to do it, and to teach his statutes and ordinances in Israel. 7:10

In other words, he was bent on reform down to the last letter. He brought along a communication from King Artaxerxes—probably Artaxerxes II by then (405–359 B.C.)—indicating that anyone who wished might accompany Ezra and that he should carry the gifts of gold already received and buy offerings for the temple. "Whatever seems good to you and your brethren to do with the rest of the silver and gold, you may do, according to the will of your God." Moreover, the treasurer was instructed to supply further support for the work of God "lest his wrath be against the realm of the king and his sons." Priests, Levites, singers, doorkeepers and temple servants were to live tax-free!

Ezra was satisfied. "I took courage, for the hand of the Lord my God was upon me, and I gathered leading men from Israel to go up with me." That is, leading Israelites in Babylon. Again the roll of returnees was tabulated and Ezra discovered there were "none of the sons of Levi," so he sent out a request "to send us ministers for the house of our God. And by the good hand of our God upon us, they brought us a man of discretion" —along with kinsmen and servants. He was fortunate to have his prayer answered by the arrival of this "man of discretion"; many leaders do not have as much. Before leaving Babylon Ezra called for a general fast "that we might humble ourselves before our God, to seek from him a straight way for ourselves," because their route led through hazardous territory and they carried considerable treasure.

> For I was ashamed to ask the king for a band of soldiers and horse-men to protect us . . . on our way; since we had told the king,

"The hand of our God is for good upon all that seek him. . . ." So we fasted and besought our God for this, and he listened to our entreaty. 8:22–23

No ambushes; no enemies; a safe journey. Their treasure was duly delivered in Jerusalem. And tabulated. The king's commissions to the satraps and governors were handed over, and the authorities proffered the expected aid.

But now Ezra met a challenge of a different sort. His attention was called to the fact that, since the first Jews had returned from Babylon, there had been widespread intermarriage of Jewish priests, Levites, and general population with neighboring peoples —Canaanites, Hittites, Perizzites, Moabites, Egyptians and their ilk—"so that the holy race has mixed itself with the peoples of the land." Said Ezra, "When I heard this, I rent my garments and my mantle, and pulled hair from my head and beard, and sat appalled." At the time of the evening sacrifice he prayed aloud—while the faithless and their families listened in.

O my God, I am ashamed and blush to lift my face to thee, my God, for our iniquities have risen higher than our heads, and our guilt has mounted up to the heavens. 9:6

Some of the wives and children, previously happy and contented, must have been thoroughly dismayed to find they were guilty of anything which could make this earnest and devoted man so ashamed of them.

So far as feeling guilty was concerned, Ezra's overreaction was a new experience for Jewish men. Previous to the Exile, intermarriage had not been particularly discouraged, but while in Babylon the Jews had learned the hard way that purity of worship depended to a considerable extent upon keeping themselves set apart from alien customs. If they were to be Yahweh's people, under his protection, then they would have to eliminate outside alliances. A modern reader might quickly ask about the alternate possibility of Ezra's instructing these outsiders, teaching the wives, indoctrinating the children in the true faith. But the concept of conversion had not yet taken root and proselytizing was a vocation of the future. It seems never to have occurred to Ezra to put the burden of example on the faithful Jewish husbands and fathers.

He was a spiritual surgeon and he saw only one method of purification: excise the gentile wives. And children. The fact that
Jewish men had begot the children was canceled out by the
undue influence which mothers have on the young. Ezra was
sternly persuasive. Weeping, the Jewish males made their vow
to disown non-Jewish wives and children. The purity of the
culture was saved.

What the women and children were doing while Ezra wept
and grieved is not recorded by the male scribes, except that
"the people wept bitterly." Ezra himself, faithful to the light he
had, "spent the night, neither eating bread nor drinking water;
for he was mourning over the faithlessness of the exiles."

A decision having been made, it was implemented promptly.
All Jews were ordered to gather in Jerusalem within three days
if they did not want to forfeit their property. One wonders if
maybe some did forfeit their property and ignore the summons.
But in the main, the Jewish males maintained the solidarity which
had bound them together through generations and gathered in
Jerusalem as ordered. It was a sad gathering; a tragic time. "And
all the people sat in the open square before the house of God,
trembling because of this matter and because of the heavy rain."
It must have seemed to many as if the heavens also wept. According to custom, a roll was taken. Names were tabulated of all the
men who had married foreign women "and they put them away
with their children."

Away where? Looking back, we can hope there were grand-
parents around, even if they were "heathen." There must have
been a lot of lonely men that night in Israel and chances are
that Ezra fasted and prayed again. If he had not been a man of
intense integrity, willing to fast and pray in behalf of his convictions, he could never have exerted so powerful an influence
in behalf of single-minded devotion to Israel.

But—but marriage is also a covenant, most fundamental of
human relationships. Those disrupted families were bound to
each other in love and trust. Would it be possible for a man
who could not be faithful to his family to be faithful to his
God? Is law more important than the spirit? Generations of
Jews have worked at these questions and some different con-

clusions have emerged over the by-line of later Jews. Questions and answers still haunting society. The deep impression of the book of Ezra on the reader is the utter devotion of the man and his willingness to put all he had behind his convictions.

Nehemiah

The Author

The book of Nehemiah has an individuality all its own. And for the best of reasons: The man Nehemiah kept his own record of his governorship in Jerusalem, making forthright entries more for his own eye than for any other's. All the book's editor had to do—presumably he was the same man who compiled the Chronicles—was to incorporate the shorter record into his own longer account. In the course of the editing he managed to confuse Nehemiah's narration somewhat. Or it may have been a copyist who inserted some of the Ezra episodes out of context. In spite of the editing, however, Nehemiah himself comes through clearly as a highly intelligent official; independent, stern, determined, capable, farsighted, wealthy and nothing-withholding toward whatever he thought the Lord required of him.

Artaxerxes

The first seven chapters are written in the first person at a time when Nehemiah was cupbearer to King Artaxerxes, probably Artaxerxes I, whose reign covered the years 465–424, but possibly Artaxerxes II, 404–358. Before Nehemiah's day, Jerusalem had seemed on its way to reconstruction; now the reports coming in told of broken walls, of gates destroyed by fires, and of the Jews who had never been in exile "in great trouble and shame." Had there been an attack of some kind? No one knows. Someday archaeological records of the period may turn up and biblical specialists around the world will have another scholarly field day dating Nehemiah.

Nehemiah's position as cupbearer put him in a very personal relationship to the king. He would not have had the appointment if he had not been an astute man with whom the king could converse profitably. There must have been mutual respect and genuine friendship between the two because the king immediately noticed when one day Nehemiah appeared sad. And when the king asked the reason, Nehemiah told him that distressing news had come from Jerusalem, the city of his forebears. He did not explain that he had wept for days over the news and had confessed the sins which must have been Israel's to have come to so dire a situation, then had begged the Lord to bless this very interview. Instead he boldly asked for permission to go to Jerusalem to see for himself what could be done. He knew, of course, that the king might feel affronted—a cupbearer who would rather be somewhere else? On the other hand, the king might respect Nehemiah's loyalty and his determination to move in on the problem. His majesty's answer was to ask Nehemiah how long he would be gone. Perhaps the king was influenced by the queen's presence. (Who was she? Did she understand Nehemiah's need? Had she heard of the God of Israel? Did she look expectantly at her royal husband? Women whose names remain unrecorded in Jewish history have often influenced its course.)

While his courage was up, Nehemiah set a date to leave and also asked for letters of safe-conduct to "the governors of the province Beyond the River" (the Euphrates) and for a letter to the keeper of the royal forest for timbers "to make beams for the gates of the fortress of the temple, and for the wall of the city, and for the house which I shall occupy." Apparently Nehemiah was accustomed to taking care of important affairs in adequate fashion. If he had asked too little he might have got nothing. The king acquiesced and, Nehemiah records, "the good hand of my God was upon me." However, in spite of the king's sanction, which included an impressive contingent of "officers of the army and horsemen," all did not go smoothly. Not just because they had a thousand miles of desert, mountains and rivers to cross but also because neighboring big shots turned obstructionist. Particularly Governor Sanballat of Samaria. (We know his position from a citation in the Elephantine papyri, a sizable collection of more or less official documents written in Aramaic at Elephantine, in Egypt, by members of a colony of Jewish mercenaries employed by the Persian Government in the fifth century B.C.; their discovery in 1907 lent proof to the surmise that after the Exile the Jews were more widely scattered than the Bible story suggests, and also records their orthodoxy to the point that animal sacrifices were performed locally when the temple at Jerusalem was inaccessible.) Tobiah, an influential Ammonite official in the Persian service, was also antagonistic. These dignitaries were greatly displeased "that someone had come to seek the welfare of Israel." But Nehemiah proceeded to Jerusalem, according to his own plan and disposition.

Rebuilding the Walls

After he had been in Jerusalem for three days—without divulging his position or intentions—Nehemiah decided that his best course was to inspect the city wall firsthand unaccompanied by officials, so he picked a handful of his own deputies to make the rounds of the city wall with him in the night. Nothing escaped his keen eye. After he had the facts from observation and not from hearsay, he called together the priests, nobles, officials and common people, reviewed the situation, expressed his enthusiasm for rebuilding the walls and climaxed his pep talk with the assurance that he had come as governor with the approval of Artaxerxes himself. The people were probably astounded, then relieved, and finally eager. "And they said, 'Let us rise up and build.'" (A great slogan for city planners in any age.)

Neighboring governors continued to be suspicious; Jerusalem made strong would be a threat to them. Besides, the Jews might mount an insurrection against Persia. Let Nehemiah cease and desist. In reply Nehemiah assured them coldly that his work was God's business; certainly not theirs. While they grumbled he kept his attention on his complicated job, deploying his forces carefully, every man of them accounted for. Tasks were apportioned out to various groups. The priests, including the high priest, rebuilt the famous old Sheep Gate. Guild by guild, gate by gate, all was on assignment. As usual there were a few slackers. ". . . the Tekoites repaired; but their nobles did not put their necks to the work of the Lord." But most people pitched in loyally, including goldsmiths and perfumers. Hallohesh, the son of the "ruler of half the district of Jerusalem, repaired, he and his daughters." (Sic!) Doors, bolts, bars, stairs, the entire wall was gradually building up. Accompanied by cheers of encouragement? Not exactly, with angry Governor Sanballat sending derisive onlookers to make fun of these amateur bricklayers who thought they could rebuild a city. Nevertheless the work went on. "For the people had a mind to work." (Another slogan for determined urbanite constructionists.)

So now the irate neighboring officials, their derision having failed, threatened to resort to arms. At the same time, they hired prophets to prognosticate doom. The sight of enemy archers in the distance along with the prophetic warnings were too much for some of the Jewish construction superintendents, who reported to Nehemiah, "The strength of the burden-bearers is failing, and there is much rubbish; we are not able to work on the wall." Nehemiah looked at the rubbish, both material and human, and "set a guard as a protection . . . day and night." Families with bows, spears, swords kept watch behind the workmen, encouraged by Nehemiah's reminder, "Remember the Lord, who is great and terrible. . . ." In time of crisis, "Those who carried burdens were laden in such a way that each with one hand labored . . . and with the other held his weapon."

When their threats failed, the opposing governors tried ruse. They invited Nehemiah to a conference, most deadly of restraining actions once a project is under way. Distrusting its purpose, Nehemiah pleaded lack of time. "I am doing a great work and I cannot come down." Four times he refused their invitation. Then the high priest, Shemaiah, sent word to Nehemiah that his life was in danger; he had better take sanctuary in the temple quickly. Sensing that the high priest was a hired stooge, Nehemiah promptly put him in his place. "Should such a man as I flee?"

The last stretch of wall was the hardest, because crops were failing for lack of attention. People were hungry, small businessmen were borrowing heavily to keep from bankruptcy, rich Jews were enslaving poor Jews, bankers were charging one per cent per month interest of fellow Jews. Nehemiah called a town meeting. With stinging accuracy he rehearsed the shameful practices, turning searing scorn on those who profited from the necessities of the times. His words struck home; contrition and reform ensued and the building continued "day and night and half of them held the spears from the break of dawn until the stars came out." Nehemiah and his assistants slept in their clothes.

Finally Nehemiah could record: "The wall was finished . . . in fifty-two days."

> And when all our enemies heard of it, all the nations round about us were afraid and fell greatly in their own esteem; for they perceived that this work had been accomplished with the help of our God. 6:16

It was also fortunate that God had had on call this capable, highly trained, determined administrator, Nehemiah. (God, listen: do you have in mind another Nehemiah to tackle urban reconstruction?)

Dedication of the Wall

Dedication of the city wall was one celebration in which everyone—except the jealous dissenters—could participate with pride, joy and relief. Pride in their own handwork and courageous determination; joy in having something worthy of presenting to the Lord; relief to be living again in a stoutly walled city. A day was set for the festivities. (We have now moved from chapter 7 to chapter 12, because in the book's present form other incidents have been interpolated in the report about the wall.) For the great celebration, the Levites were rounded up to lead the thanksgiving "with singing, with cymbals, harps, and lyres." After the customary purification ceremonies, Nehemiah himself "brought up the princes of Judah upon the wall." Two great companies were formed, led by priests, men of distinction and trumpeters, the companies marching in opposite directions until they had encompassed the wall. Then the whole assembly went to the temple. "And they offered great sacrifices that day and rejoiced, for God had made them rejoice with great joy." Later, recording the occasion, Nehemiah had an afterthought: "the women and children also rejoiced." Maybe their treble voices gave the jubilation traveling power, for ". . . the joy of Jerusalem was heard afar off."

Nehemiah's Governorship

(Now we are back in chapter 5.) Here was one governor who did not live off taxes exacted from the people. He says that from the time he was appointed until the end of his twelve-year term neither he nor his relatives "ate the food allowance of the governor," as had been the case with former governors whose servants "lorded it over the people." At his own table Nehemiah fed one hundred fifty lesser officials as well as all foreign envoys. He lists one day's average consumption of food, which must have strained even his ample exchequer. And on that point he asks the Lord to look favorably on his honest accounting.

The outer defenses of the city having been taken care of, Nehemiah of the orderly mind then decided to tabulate the human resources by conducting a census. "Then God put it into my mind to assemble the nobles and the officials and the people to be enrolled by genealogy." The onus seems to have been lifted from census taking or this tabulation was considered merely a matter of bringing the genealogical record up to date. The enumeration turned up the list of persons who had returned with the first exodus from Babylon.

Now that the city was safe it needed more inhabitants. Leading men of surrounding Judean towns were invited to move into the city, then lots were cast "to bring one out of ten to live in Jerusalem the holy city." There must have been a flurry of building, for practically no new houses had been built while the walls were in disrepair. The treasury had to be replenished; ". . . some of the heads of fathers' houses gave to the work"—generously; the governor himself gave "a thousand darics of gold, fifty basins, five hundred and thirty priests' garments." The total amount raised was not small and the country's economy picked up as spirits picked up; nor was the order rescinded.

Ezra Again

The record of Nehemiah's achievements is interrupted at chapter 8 by the reappearance of Ezra in the story! Where he came from is any scholar's guess but apparently some editor incorrectly placed a section of the Ezra manuscript here. Ezra began by reading the law to "all the people gathered as one man . . . before the Water Gate. . . . And he read from it facing the square before the Water Gate from early morning until midday, in the presence of the men and the women and those who could understand; and the ears of all the people were attentive to the book of the law." Standing on a wooden pulpit, he was banked by a committee of experts who helped to expound the law clearly "and they gave the sense, so that the people understood the reading." Sensing how far they had strayed from the rectitude demanded by the law, "all the people wept," and Ezra declared the day of their repentance "holy to our Lord." The next day, after a period of rejoicing because they now "understood the words that were declared to them," they came together "in order to study the words of the law."

Reminded by the reading that there was a proper protocol for keeping the feast of booths, the people immediately decided to reestablish the festival. "They kept the feast seven days; and on the eighth day there was a solemn assembly, according to the ordinance." A résumé of their history under God was a part of the ritual but Ezra's way of reminding the people of their heritage was no mere oration. He addressed his remarks directly to the Lord in the form of a long prayer rich in contrition and grateful awe.

". . . our fathers . . . stiffened their neck and did not obey thy commandments. . . . But thou art a God ready to forgive, gracious and merciful, slow to anger and abounding in steadfast love. . . ." 9:16–17

Also he did not hesitate to remind the Lord, in the people's presence, of the hardship they had suffered under the Almighty's just punishment.

Covenant

With the last verse of chapter 9 the focus shifts again to the Nehemiah story. Apparently some later editor did his best to make the broken record fit together, for it continues: "Because of all this we make a firm covenant and write it, and our princes, our Levites, and our priests set their seal to it." The names of the signers were

appended, names strange to a modern tongue but nevertheless individuals bound by a holy bond—among them Hattush, Mijamin,
Pahath-moab, Zattu, Azgad, Magpiash, Hallohesh, Baanah. The
rest of the people joined with them in "a curse and an oath" to
observe all the laws ordained by God through Moses. No more
giving of daughters or sons "to the peoples of the land," no more
buying from non-Jews on a holy day, no more skimping on temple support; instead, a firm promise to give to the house of the
Lord their first sons, first fruits, first-born of herds and flocks, a
portion of each man's meal, wine and oil. "We will not neglect the
house of our God."

Nehemiah's Second Term

After twelve years of governorship Nehemiah returned to Persia, perhaps at the request of Artaxerxes, perhaps on his own
initiative, to pay his respects to the king and look after his own
estates. "And after some time" he again asked leave to return to
Jerusalem, evidently to his old position, since he began at once to
issue orders. He found that the high priests who administered temple affairs had given a wealthy landowner named Tobiah—the
same one who had tried to obstruct his building of the city walls—
a large room in the temple for his own use. Tobiah was related to
people in high places but his impressive connections did not deter
Nehemiah from promptly ousting him and his belongings and ordering the room returned to its intended use as a storehouse for
tithes of cereal, wine, oil, frankincense and all such donations to
the Levites, singers and gatekeepers.

Also during Nehemiah's absence the Levites and singers had
not been given their proper portions, so they had gone back to
their former homes in the villages and countryside where they
could make a living. Nehemiah moved in on that situation too,
bringing back the displaced Levites and singers, appointing new
treasurers and overseers, and getting both the city and the temple
schedules operating again. Apparently he enjoyed his own efficient
administration—who doesn't?—and he nudged God for approval.
"Remember me, O my God . . . and wipe not out my good
deeds. . . ."

Inspiring himself as well as his fellow citizens, Nehemiah continued his reforms. Shocked to see the desecration of the Sabbath —men treading the wine presses, bringing produce into the city for sale, and bartering for fish from Tyre—he stopped the trade short, reminding the merchants that such action on the part of their forebears had brought down the wrath of God. To support his position he stationed guards at the city gates to insure the sanctity of both the gates and the Sabbath.

Moving about freely among the people, he found that half the city's children spoke the language of their non-Jewish mothers, for intermarriage with the women of Ashdod, Moab and Ammon was common. After all, these were related peoples. But this devoted Jew would have none of that sort of laxity. "And I contended with them and cursed them and beat some of them and pulled out their hair. . . ." If children ran at the sight of him it is not recorded, but there must have been some shocked non-Jewish mothers. It was the fathers, though, whom he most blamed, reminding them that even Solomon could not withstand the wiles of foreign women, who "made even him to sin." When it came to repudiating their marriage to foreign women, pressure was put on men in high places as well as on the lowliest. The grandson of the high priest, who was also son-in-law of Sanballat, governor of Samaria, was deported. Nehemiah intended that nobody, but nobody, was going to take the fundamental practices of Judaism lightly. "Remember me, O my God, for good"—the last words of the book which bears his name.

By the first century A.D. Palestinian Jews held the position that divine inspirations had come to an end with the books of Ezra and Nehemiah. Accepted books written before theirs might be admitted to authorized scripture but works written later, however valuable in their way, were not to become canonical. Around A.D. 90 in the town of Jamnia, in Palestine, a gathering of rabbis made once and for all the list of authoritative books. On the other hand, the Alexandrian Jews, in a predominantly Greek culture, believed the spirit of the Lord continued to inspire writers after Nehemiah's day but the best they could do for the canon was to get fourteen other books included in a separate section of scripture soon called the Apocrypha.

Outside Palestine the early Christians used the apocryphal

books in worship and instruction because the books were included in the older Greek texts, which were older than any complete Hebrew text. In fact, there is no complete Hebrew text earlier than the ninth century A.D. Jerome, in the fourth century A.D., and still later Luther, followed the tighter Jewish text. In 1546 the Roman Catholic Church at the Council of Trent again included the apocryphal books. And so the discussion continued. But, for official Judaism, Nehemiah marked the end of the epoch of holy inspiration.

Esther

Melodrama or serious comedy? It depends upon whether one reads the book of Esther as a rollicking story of adventure with emphasis on plot and counterplot or sees the plot as subsidiary to character portrayal. Was Queen Esther a social climber, wittingly or under family duress willing to become the concubine of a Persian king for the sake of privileges bound to accrue to her family, or was she a pawn of fate who later used her position with noble disregard of self in order to help her people? Was Mordecai a political maneuverer, a canny wheeler-dealer, or was he a devoted Hebrew dedicated to the idea that even in extremity the Jews must remain true to their God?

Is this a "religious" story? No mention is made of God; the prayers included in the authorized text were apparently inserted by some later priest or copyist who felt Esther should have prayed such prayers. Certainly the book is not comparable in intent or content to the books of prophecy or wisdom; so why was it included in the canon? Many scholarly commentators and rabbis have felt it should have been omitted. Martin Luther among them.

But a people is made by its literature as well as by its religion and as literature the book of Esther can hold its own alongside the Arabian Nights and the Vetalapanchavimsati of Somadeva (and who hasn't read *that?*). If it was originally a harem story of the Persian court it has been lifted into a Jewish context and used with religious intent to authenticate a festival which the Jews were already observing. There is nothing unusual about a religious minority's sharing a festival of the dominant cultural group and slowly adapting it to their own purposes. The early Christians took over a pagan spring festival, name and all, and elevated it to the celebration of the resurrection of their Lord. Probably today some current religious festivals—Jewish and Christian—could stand an infusion of relevancy.

Act One, Exit Queen Vashti

King Ahasuerus, or Xerxes I, who "reigned from India to Ethiopia over one hundred and twenty-seven provinces," decided to give a banquet for all his princes, nobles, governors and satraps in order to display "the riches of his royal glory and the splendor and pomp of his majesty for many days." One hundred and eighty days, in fact, which probably meant that his guests came for successive nights or weeks according to their rank. The celebration was climaxed by a superfestival lasting seven days. (The book is replete with that lucky number seven.) The dining couches were "of gold and silver on a mosaic pavement of porphyry, marble, mother-of-pearl and precious stones. Drinks were served in golden goblets, goblets of different kinds, and the royal wine was lavished according to the bounty of the king." At the same time Queen Vashti gave a banquet for the women. Quite possibly by the seventh day the guests were rather in their cups.

At the final banquet the king decided to exhibit his beautiful queen, Vashti. This kind of display was not according to custom —bringing a virtuous woman before a huge roomful of men guests —and it must have astounded the queen. If she remained properly veiled, which was the least respect a Persian king could have shown her, then the guests could not see her beauty. Commanded to appear without a veil was tantamount to presenting a dancing girl. Queen Vashti was not about to be displayed and she refused to come.

The king was upset; "his anger burned within him"; this was a slap in his august face. He conferred with his councilors, the seven princes, "who saw the king's face and sat first in the kingdom." To see the king's face was a particular honor because, as anyone knows, an individual exposes his soul when he opens his mouth, even to eat. The princes, aware of their importance, called attention to the fact that they also had been insulted by Queen Vashti's refusal to obey her husband's order, and through them all the men of the kingdom were insulted. The news of her recalcitrance would leak into every harem in the country.

> This very day the ladies of Persia and Media who have heard of the queen's behavior will be telling it to all the king's princes, and there will be contempt and wrath in plenty. 1:18

Could the king risk national insubordination? Better dispense with the queen and "give her royal position to another who is better than she." That would teach the women throughout the land who was boss at home. Forthwith the king dictated letters announcing "that every man be lord in his own house."

So now, in the realm of Ahasuerus, man had redeemed his rightful eminence and the king got over his anger. He may even have been a little sad, for the record says, "he remembered Vashti and what she had done and what had been decreed against her." However, life must go on and he needed a queen. Concubines were not enough. There were official functions to think of and he did not wish to sit on his throne looking at the empty seat belonging to a queen whom many women throughout the land privately admired for putting her honor above her position.

Act Two, the Power of Beauty

The second act of the drama opens with the king's officials scouring the country for the most beautiful virgins for the king's harem in Susa. The prize for the maiden the king considered most pleasing: the throne. Enter a lovely Jewish girl named Hadassah, meaning *myrtle;* later her name was changed to Esther, meaning *star.* In a land where numerology was a science of prediction, names were important because of the numerical value of each letter. "The maiden was beautiful and lovely." She was the adopted daughter of an older cousin named Mordecai, grandson of a Benjaminite who had been carried into captivity by Nebuchadnezzar; a kindly man who had adopted her because she was an orphan.

Once admitted to the harem, the chosen girls spent a solid year undergoing beauty treatments; massage with fine oils and perfumes, hair care, great attention to toes and fingernails, and the best of food in order to produce a finely textured body and heighten sexual charm. The eunuch in charge of the harem was chosen for his position because of his ability to instill the graces of the court into his protégées. This eunuch, named Hegai, admired the girl Esther and gave her the best of everything, including *seven* maids. Esther made no mention of being Jewish, this crucial fact being saved for the denouement, later in the tale.

Esther's Banquet

In the *seventh* year of Ahasuerus' reign the time came for Esther to spend a night with the king.

> . . . the king loved Esther more than all the women, and she found grace and favor in his sight more than all the virgins, so that he set the royal crown on her head and made her queen instead of Vashti. 2:17

Then he gave a sumptuous banquet for all the notables. Says the record, ". . . it was Esther's banquet." It was indeed, but her cousin Mordecai, who regularly sat at the king's gate in order to catch the news of the day and watch over the well-being of Esther, must have had a pretty satisfactory evening too.

Evidently Mordecai had contrived a string of informers, because one day he found out about a plot in which two angry eunuchs "who guarded the threshold" planned to murder the king. He got prompt word to the new queen, who told the king and thereby got Mordecai's name to the royal ear. The plot was verified, the men hanged, and the incident recorded "in the Book of the Chronicles in the presence of the king." Thus two Jews, Esther and Mordecai, merited the king's favor.

Act Three, Introducing the Villain

Now the king appointed as his grand vizier a man named Haman and immediately everyone "did obeisance to Haman; for the king had so commanded concerning him." Everyone but Mordecai. Perhaps, as a Jew, Mordecai felt this exaggerated obeisance was too close to worship. Anyway, he let it be known that he was a Jew—which gave Haman an idea. "Haman was filled with fury. But he disdained to lay hands on Mordecai alone." He may have feared the reaction of other Jews, so he thought of something much more satisfactory than beheading one Jew. He devised a lottery, probably under direction of the court necromancers, to name a propitious day for presenting the king with information about "a certain people scattered abroad" in all the provinces, who followed their own laws instead of the king's laws. Ought they not be destroyed? The king agreed and handed Haman his signet ring to affix royal approval to such a decree. Then, just to prove he did not want the king to lose tax money, Haman offered the king ten thousand talents of silver. What was $18 million to the king? He told Haman to divide the money between himself and the people, not specifying the terms for division.

> Letters were sent by couriers to all the king's provinces, to destroy, to slay, and to annihilate all Jews, young and old, women and children, in one day . . . and to plunder their goods. . . . And the king and Haman sat down to drink; but the city of Susa was perplexed. 3:13, 15

The Jews went into mourning, "fasting and weeping and lamenting, and most of them lay in sackcloth and ashes," in true Jewish fashion. Mordecai managed to get a letter through to Esther explaining the predicament of the Jews, and beseeching her to go to the king and beg him to save her people.

Esther quickly reminded Mordecai that no one, not even a queen, went into the inner court without being called by the king, and she had not been called for a month; the penalty was death, unless it pleased the king to hold out his golden scepter. Mordecai's reply was that the queen herself could not hope to escape the pogrom; this was her one opportunity. His final word must have searched her heart. "And who knows whether you have not come to the kingdom for such a time as this?" (A question most of us have to answer in some time of need.)

Esther replied with the request that all the Jews in Susa fast for three days on her behalf. "Then I will go to the king, though it is against the law; and if I perish, I perish." Mordecai fasted with her. People accustomed to fasting in times of great need seem to find that mind and body are strangely purified so that the impossible often becomes possible.

Then Esther went to the king and he held out the golden scepter, spontaneously offering to grant her request, "even to the half of my kingdom." But Esther did nothing so simple as to present the predicament of her people. Instead, with one eye on Haman, she asked the two men to come to dinner that very day. The king agreed and Haman was delighted, for this was the kind of public recognition he relished. Only he and the king as the queen's private guests!

Act Four, Reprisal

In fine mood the two men arrived for dinner. Again, but in a different way, it was Esther's banquet. For a second time the king offered to grant her request "even to the half of my kingdom . . ." but again Esther postponed her desperate proposal. Maybe she felt that Haman's influence was still too strong, or that the king was not yet completely under her spell, so she asked the two men to come to dinner again the following day.

Haman left the palace "joyful and glad of heart"; that is, until he saw Mordecai at the king's gate busily ignoring him as he passed by. Then "he was filled with wrath against Mordecai. Nevertheless Haman restrained himself, and went home." First he told his wife and friends about the honors bestowed on him by the king.

> And Haman added, "Even Queen Esther let no one come with the king to the banquet she prepared but myself. And tomorrow also I am invited by her together with the king. Yet all this does me no good, so long as I see Mordecai the Jew sitting at the king's gate." 5:12–13

His guests had a suggestion: build a good tall gallows—say fifty cubits (87 feet) high—and tomorrow tell the king to hang Mordecai on it. "Then go merrily with the king to the dinner."

Who knows how news gets from one man's strong intent to another man's listening subconscious? The king had a sleepless night. Something prompted him to have the book of memorable deeds read to him. Thus he was reminded that a Jew named Mordecai had saved his life when a plot by a couple of eunuchs would have ended it. He asked the secretary, "What honor or dignity has been bestowed on Mordecai for this?" Nothing, exactly nothing. By that time it was morning, and, bright and early, Haman appeared at the palace. The king asked him, "What shall be done to the man whom the king delights to honor?" Thinking that of course the king meant him, Haman suggested that such a man be clothed in the king's own royal robes, wear the royal crown, ride on the royal horse and parade through the city while a prince preceded him announcing the king's honor. The king beamed. Exactly thus should it be done for good old Mordecai, who have saved his life— and Haman himself must look after the matter at once. Which he did—and then rushed home to report his ignominy. His wife and friends had no comforting words but assured him dolefully that the Jewish people would now rally around Mordecai toward no good end for Haman.

Came the queen's banquet; came the king and Haman; came the wine and the mellow moment when the king reminded his queen she had not yet expressed her wish—"even to the half of my kingdom." So Esther gave the moment all she had and practically laid her threatened people at his royal feet. When the ireful king asked who had perpetrated this ghastly deed, Esther was quick with the accusing finger. "A foe and enemy! This wicked Haman!"

. . . Then Haman was in terror before the king and the queen. 6:6

Right here at its climax the drama is slowed down for a few minutes because the king's physiological processes were only human and he had drunk a lot of wine. The palace having no inside plumbing, the king "went into the palace garden." Haman lost no time in begging for his life. In final desperation he fell on the couch where Esther was sitting. And just at that moment the king re-entered, reacted, and shouted, "Will he even assault the queen in my presence, in my own house?" A eunuch immediately covered Haman's face, and ingratiated himself with the king by announcing that Haman had prepared a gallows in his own yard to hang Mordecai. "Hang him on that," ordered the king. And it was done.

"Then the anger of the king abated." And in the emotional swing from dark hatred to bright good will, the king gave Esther Haman's house, sent for Mordecai and presented him with his own signet ring, which he had no doubt ordered snatched from

Haman at the moment of parting, and let Esther set her beloved elder cousin over the house of Haman.

Nevertheless, Esther was not diverted from the main point of her confrontation with the king. She fell at his feet in tears, beseeching him to avert Haman's evil designs against all the kingdom's Jews. The king extended his golden scepter, the queen rose and pressed her point. The king turned the matter over to Mordecai: ". . . write as you please in regard to the Jews, in the name of the king, and seal it with the king's ring."

Out went another royal order to "the satraps and the governors and the princes of the provinces from India to Ethiopia," the couriers being sent forth "on swift horses that were used in the king's service, bred from the royal stud."

Act Five, an Ethical Slump

And right at this point the romantic tale drops back to the age of vindictiveness and loses its charm for a modern reader struggling to live out the concept of mercy in place of eye-for-eye retribution. Mordecai's order permitted the Jews everywhere "to destroy, to slay, and to annihilate" those who would have destroyed them.

> Then Mordecai went out from the presence of the king in royal robes of blue and white, with a great golden crown and a mantle of fine linen and purple, while the city of Susa shouted and rejoiced. The Jews had light and gladness and joy and honor. And in every province and in every city, wherever the king's command and his edict came, there was gladness and joy among the Jews, a feast and a holiday. And many from the peoples of the country declared themselves Jews, for fear of the Jews had fallen upon them. 8:15–17

Slaughter and pillage ensued; five hundred killed in Susa alone, including Haman's ten sons. The next day the king reported the number to Esther, adding in consternation, "What then have they done in the rest of the king's provinces!" Nevertheless he asked her if she had any further petitions, and she did. Let the next day be a repetition of the slaughter and let the bodies of Haman's sons hang on the gallows. This time only three hundred were killed in the capital but seventy-five thousand in the provinces. It was a time of wild retribution.

Afterward Mordecai sent letters to all the Jews everywhere

advising them to celebrate these joyous events forever and ever: a day for feasting and gladness, a day for sending "choice portions to one another."

So what do the modern man and woman of good will do with the story? Make a celebration of it because of its long tradition, emphasizing the noble characteristics of Esther and Mordecai and sliding lightly over the ruthless reprisals? Turn it into a farcical festival, encouraging children to masquerade as the various characters—ten thousand beautiful Esthers in home-sewn finery, ten thousand noble Mordecais in dime-store beards, ten thousand wicked Hamans to be hissed at! Utilize it to intensify the cult spirit? Truncate the final episode, allowing the story to end with the vindication of the Jews and Esther's happy rise to power? Overlook the fact that the book poses a moral problem in our own age? How disturbing that man is a thinking animal, who keeps on pondering the meaning of the play after the curtain goes down!

Wisdom Literature

Israel had two sources of religious authority rooted in the priests, the prophets and the men of wisdom. Jeremiah used the phrase ". . . for the law shall not perish from the priest, nor counsel from the wise, nor the word from the prophet." Where the priests and prophets called to the nation, "Hear, O Israel, and be good," the wise men said, "Hear, my son, and be wise," an individual matter. For the priests and the prophets reform was corporate and action social; for the wise men the reiterated theme was: this is the way for *you* to act advantageously.

Although largely written by Jews, the wisdom literature of Israel was not entirely original. Every country in the ancient world had its wisdom literature, which the Jews appropriated freely. Egypt was the center from which the pronouncements of the wise spread around the Mediterranean border. *The Instructions of Ptah-hotep,* written around 2400 B.C.—sometimes called the oldest book in the world—and *The Dispute with His Soul of One Who Is Tired of Life,* produced before 2000 B.C., made their way across boundaries. The Babylonians had their *Book of Proverbs* and a philosophical poem titled *The Righteous Sufferer,* a Babylonian Job. (The book of Job itself gives no indication of being a Hebrew production, not even in the names of the people involved nor in the word commonly used for God.) Traces of Persian wisdom also reached Palestine. Closer to home, Israel's neighbor Edom, just south of the Dead Sea, was famous for its men of wisdom referred to by several Old Testament writers. Greek philosophy made its way into Palestine before the fourth century B.C., emphasizing universality.

These observations of the wise traveled largely in the form of proverbs, riddles, short verse, and the pronouncements of personified Wisdom, who declaimed both in prose and poetry. Job alone is a full-length, fully realized drama, the high point of Hebrew wisdom literature. The formal body of wisdom literature preserved in the Old Testament includes the books of Job, Psalms, Proverbs, Ecclesiastes and the Song of Songs, but in the Apocrypha —the group of books declared useful but not inspired—are two delightful works, The Wisdom of Solomon and The Wisdom of Sirach. However, for a complete anthology on wisdom in the Old Testament, excerpts from several other books would have to be included.

Because wisdom sayings were the fruit of practical life, even women of insight were sometimes sought out. A brave and canny woman of Tekoa was called by Joab to reason with David about forgiving his son Absalom; Canaanite wise women figure in the Song of Deborah, who was also a wise woman as well as a judge; a wise woman of the city of Abel, famous for its wisdom in settling disputes, arranged a compromise with Joab which saved her city; for practical advice in the reign of David, "the counsel which Ahithophel gave was as if one consulted the oracle of God."

Unless one watches for references to these men and women of wisdom and notes the fables, riddles, proverbs and folk epigrams which intersperse history and prophecy, it is easy to bypass some of the best examples of Hebrew insight. In fact, one of the delights of reading the Old Testament cover to cover is coming upon typical and topical bits of practical wisdom which could well go into a modern anthology titled *This is the Way It Is*.

A glance at a modern English version of the books of wisdom shows what a sizable proportion is poetry, although much earlier versions in a variety of languages printed the poetry as prose. Nothing, however, kept the poetry from sounding like poetry when read aloud. Indeed, one third of the entire Old Testament is estimated to be poetry of various types; only epic poems seem to be missing. The Babylonians, Canaanites, Sumerians and Greeks produced the sweeping epics; the Hebrews spoke to more immediate occasions. A reader does not have to be able to scan in terms of iambic feet or to distinguish hexameters from octameters to enjoy the stately flow of phrases. It is no wonder that people who listened to the psalmists and song writers remembered their words. Not that all a prophet had to do was to tell himself to speak in verse. He had first to have content, and, second, he had to have the poet's gift for simile and metaphor.

Much of the wisdom literature has a pragmatic realism to which modern thought is hospitable. We have our hours of special concern when we act out the fact that reform is corporate but we also listen avidly to those who tell us the way to act advantageously for ourselves. And it is this honest self-interest which the wisdom purveyors played on, even when delivering what might pass for exalted counsel. They taught their listeners to be self-conscious about their actions and attitudes, which was certainly a step ahead of unmindful emotional reaction even though self-consideration might be dominant. Wisdom literature survives because it proved useful to the individual struggling with everyday life.

Job

No Old Testament character is more widely misunderstood than Job. To begin with, he was not a patient man, as the proverbial expression has him; he railed against his fate and flung challenges right in the face of God. Neither was he an old man, as artists present him. He was a man struck down in his prime, a deduction supported by the fact that he had ten more children after he recovered from his affliction. Nor is the book which bears his name filled with philosophical abstractions; the questions he poses are personal and direct, even when their import is theological, and the speeches are reflections of the kind of characters who make them. Job's is a highly personal story and his friends react with scorn, anger, supercilious moralizing and self-righteous superiority, just the way most of us tend to react in a tight place. The fact that their talk is sometimes hard to unravel rests on the muddling of the text by a succession of copyists and editors rather than on original composition. Like other literary masterpieces to which the book is often compared—Milton's *Paradise Lost* and Dante's *Inferno*—the book is a cross section of life at the point where meaning and action cut deepest, so the reader cannot escape personal questions: is it true for *me,* would *I* react the same way, does the answer satisfy *my* needs? As with some very modern plays, the audience participates.

Author

The author is unnamed. To some degree the book's argument is bound to be autobiographical and the author is surely a Middle East savant but not necessarily Jewish, since none of his characters is Jewish and the locale of the story is Edom, southeast of Palestine, famed for its men of wisdom. Patently the author was acquainted with the wisdom literature of surrounding countries, for the text contains Egyptian loan words and more uncommon expressions than any other book of the Old Testament. His keen observation of nature was a trait also common among Israel's neighbors.

Date

The prologue and the epilogue retell an old tale reflecting the patriarchal age (which is also the Middle Bronze Age, roughly 2100 to 1500), when wealth consisted primarily of cattle and slaves, when men were supposed to have long lives, when large families signified God's favor. The basic tale could have been drawn from an Ugaritic epic about a King Keret, whose entire family was wiped out in a series of catastrophes while he himself became the victim of a disease, then later—with the favor of the god El—acquired a new wife and second family. Or it could derive from a Sumerian version of the general Job motif compounded around 1700 B.C., a story pieced together by modern scholarship from fragments of manuscripts which for some years lay unrecognized in museums hundreds of miles apart. (Part of the excitement of scholarship.) On the other hand, the full work, much as we have it today, could have been written as late as the fifth or fourth centuries influenced by Persian literature, since the character of Satan in the heavenly assembly suggests Persian influence. The dramatic structure also raises the possibility of fifth-century Greek influence. Manuscripts found at Qumran, especially portions of a Targum—Aramaic free translation of the Old Testament—indicate that the book of Job had been in circulation for some time before the first century B.C., perhaps since the third century.

The Prologue

There was a man in the land of Uz, whose name was Job; and that man was blameless and upright, one who feared God, and turned away from evil. 1:1

He had seven sons and three daughters, the ideal number in his day, sons being more important than daughters but daughters a comforting adjunct to the household; a rich man with thousands of sheep, camels, asses, oxen and servants, "so that this man was the greatest of all the people of the east." Job's was a feasting family with many celebrations in the houses of his sons, and Job as head of the family always took great pains to offer sacrifices lest in their revelry someone might offend God. A careful cultist.

The action begins in the Heavenly Court. "Now there was a day when the sons of God came to present themselves before the Lord, and Satan also came among them." When Satan mentioned that he had really been covering the ground in his peregrinations on earth, God asked him if he had noted his servant Job, for when it came to righteousness "there is none like him on the earth." Agreed, said Satan, but why shouldn't Job be upright since he had been blessed with every good thing? Just remove all that good luck and see how upright he would remain. God felt so sure of Job's character that he told Satan to go ahead and deprive him of as many of his blessings as he saw fit, except that he must not take Job's life. So Satan set forth to test Job.

Immediately trouble descended. The Sabeans swooped down on his oxen and asses, killed the herdsmen and drove away the animals. Lightning burned up his sheep and shepherds; the Chaldeans raided the camels and killed the camel drivers. Most dire of all, a cyclone struck the house of his eldest son while the brothers and sisters were feasting and all were killed. Stricken, Job put on the garments of mourning, shaved his head, and fell to the ground in a daze of submission to God's will. Not a word of accusation against God.

Again the sons of God convened and God called Satan's attention to Job's continued blamelessness. "He still holds fast his integrity." Unimpressed, Satan retorted that Job's own skin had not been threatened. "All that a man has he will give for his life"; but just endanger Job's own flesh and see a different reaction. God's reply was, "Behold, he is in your power; only spare his life." So Satan went to work on Job, who broke out "with loathsome sores from the sole of his foot to the crown of his head." Maybe boils, as tradition has it; maybe yaws; certainly some painful disgusting disease so that Job, whose servants were soon unwilling to look after him, sat among the ashes and tried to scrape himself clean with a piece of broken pottery.

His wife could not stand his suffering; with all that punishment why on earth was he still loyal to God? "Curse God, and die." There is a time when an individual would rather give up a loved one than see him suffer further; there is also a time when predicating a good God seems a delusion. Job reproved his wife; should he accept good fortune from God's hand and expect to experience no setback? So he suffered on and soon the news of his misfortune brought three of his friends to see for themselves what had befallen this previous fortunate potentate. They were Eliphaz from Teman, Bildad the Shuhite, and Zophar the Naamathite, all from different areas but arriving simultaneously. When they saw Job's actual condition they wept and tore their garments, which was eastern polite custom; then they sat silent for seven days, no doubt trying to think up appropriate comment for a situation in which no comment was adequate.

This is the story's setting, the end of the prologue, and from here the author turns to philosophical dialogue rooted in experience and expressed in poetry.

The Dialogue

Finally, taking the long silence of his friends for accusation, Job curses the day of his birth, bemoaning the fact that life was given at all to one who must eventually become bitter in soul, able only to dig for death as for a treasure.

> "For the thing that I fear comes upon me,
> and what I dread befalls me." 3:25

He may have meant that he had always feared a state of affairs he could not cope with, even while he prided himself on being equal to life's exigencies. Stung by his outburst of bitterness, his friends counter with moral pronouncements. Their debate with him has three rounds. In the first, Eliphaz replies to Job's diatribe and Job then replies to Eliphaz; Bildad offers his comments and Job replies; Zophar gives an opinion, which Job refutes. In the second round each of the three friends makes further comments, to which Job responds with mounting anger, anxiety and stubborn self-affirmation. The third round breaks down so far as schematic arrangement goes. Apparently at some time there was a scrambling of the text, especially in chapters 24 and 25. Some of the misconstruing may be purposeful emendation by later editors whose conventional theology could not countenance the impiety of so influential a figure as Job. Or there may be inadvertent miscopying. Besides, we have to remember that Westerners look for logic where Easterners are often satisfied to open shutters and let the light fall as it will.

Eliphaz politely asks to venture a word, recalling that Job has often instructed other people. He should know that the upright are not struck down; God is just; there is a reason for his suffering. Eliphaz himself once had a mystical experience, hearing a voice which observed:

> "Can mortal man be righteous before God?
>   can a man be pure before his maker?" 4:17

He waxes eloquent over his own superior insight into the nature of God, who sends the rain, "sets on high those who are lowly," "frustrates the devices of the crafty," but saves "the needy from the hand of the mighty." In fact, philosophizes Eliphaz, who hasn't a boil on his body and whose fortunes are still intact, ". . . happy is the man whom God reproves."

Job does not bother to thank him for his piety. He feels that what he is currently suffering is beyond any sins he could have committed even unwittingly. All he now asks of God is to be crushed permanently, because he has no more resources within himself, and his friends are as treacherous as freshets dark with ice. But he is still willing to be genuinely instructed.

> "Teach me, and I will be silent;
>   make me understand how I have erred." 6:24

His longing is desperate and wistful and honest and heavy with grief.

> "But the night is long,
>   and I am full of tossing till the dawn.
> My flesh is clothed with worms and dirt;

> my skin hardens, then breaks out afresh.
> My days . . . come to their end without hope. . . .
> I will speak in the anguish of my spirit. . . ." 7:4–6, 11

Then, with wry humor, he asks if he is a sea monster to be guarded because he threatens evil. Why should God make so much of man, constantly testing him?

> "If I sin, what do I do to thee, thou watcher of men?
> Why hast thou made me thy mark? . . .
> Why dost thou not pardon my transgression . . . ?" 7:20–21

He had expected understanding of God, even compassion. There is a ring of amazed disillusionment in his voice.

Without polite preamble Bildad jumps into the argument. He must know that God does not pervert justice and if he can find no sin in himself then it must be his children who have sinned. He quotes a pair of proverbs to prove his point:

> "Can papyrus grow where there is no marsh?
> Can reeds flourish where there is no water?" 8:11

Neither can suffering afflict a man who has not sinned. "Behold, God will not reject a blameless man."

Instead of replying point by point, Job pushes his own argument that it is impossible for a man to be just before God, who is "wise in heart, and mighty in strength," who in anger can overturn mountains, command the sun, seal up the stars, stretch out the heavens, set in place the Bear and Orion and the Pleiades, who does "marvelous things without number." God is indeed too mighty to fit the small scale of justice his friends describe. Nevertheless (we can almost see his chin tighten) he would like to bring God into court and confront him. The big question is whether his suffering means that God declares him guilty. An umpire is needed but God is both accuser and arbiter.

Zophar, who hears Job's words but fails to recognize his courage, tries to shame Job for insisting he is blameless. Let God set Job's heart right, then his life will be "brighter than the noonday." (There are no stage directions but we can practically see Zophar smugly clasping his hands across his ample midriff.)

As the second round of speeches begins, Job's sarcasm comes to his aid.

> Then Job answered:
> "No doubt you are the people,
>   and wisdom will die with you.
> But I have understanding as well as you;
>   I am not inferior to you." 12:1–3

Certainly he knows he is a laughingstock, but God is not as predictable as they make him out; he makes fools of judges, strips priests, "pours contempt on princes." Having delineated the unassailable attributes of God, half in wonder, half in scorn, he defies the Almighty in what has long been a piously mistranslated verse (13:15). He does not affirm that he will trust God even though God slay him, as the King James version has it, but rather states flatly:

> "Behold, he will slay me; I have no hope;
>   yet I will defend my ways to his face." 13:15

Then he seems suddenly to turn inward, submerged in the common life of man, identifying with all mortals likewise unable to understand their situation (chapter 14). He is no longer the only afflicted one, nor even the principal sufferer at the hands of God. Humanity shares a common lot; defeated hopes come as they come, individually experienced but not unique. Man comes forth like a flower only to wither; he disappears like a shadow. Nevertheless God brings this fleeting creature into judgment. For what purpose? Since man's days and potentialities are both predestined, could not God absorb himself in other business than troubling man, and let man "enjoy, like a hireling, his day"? Like a river dried up, man will not waken from his inevitable last unconsciousness "or be roused out of his sleep." And yet—and yet—"If a man die, shall he live again?" Is there an eventual hope, an ultimate justification?

> ". . . the torrents wash away the soil of the earth;
>   so thou destroyest the hope of man.
> Thou prevailest for ever against him, and he passes. . . ." 14:19–20

All an individual really knows is the pain of his own body, "and he mourns only for himself."

Having now moved into the second round of speeches, Eliphaz announces that Job's own words condemn him and his talk is blasphemy; nobody—not even the angels—could be as innocent as Job portrays himself. He admits that the wicked occasionally do seem to prosper but they suffer in their conscience and know their inevitable doom.

Bored and disgusted, Job turns on his "miserable comforters," asking, "Shall windy words have an end?" but he is no longer interested in their answers. "God has worn me out. . . . shriveled me. . . . gnashed his teeth at me. . . . set me up as his target. . . . runs upon me like a warrior. . . . although there is no violence in my hands, and my prayer is pure." He begs the earth to let his blood cry out for him, since his day is past. His cry is the cry of the individual who sees no light ahead. Is God this unjust, this impersonal, this unhearing?

Actually Job is asking a very modern question, although obviously he never names it the mechanical theory of the universe. There are moments when he is skirting the idea of impersonal forces as the origin, continuum, and end of man's being. He gets as far as asking what use is God if he is callously indifferent to the fact of man and his fate, but he never gets as far as eliminating God as creator and sustainer of the universe.

Bildad takes a second aim right at the center of Job's misery. Who does Job think he is, asking God to change the order of things? Job is experiencing a foretaste of his eternal fate, including no descendants, most dire of fates to an Eastern patriarch.

Job answers across a void, realizing his isolation from his fellows. "I am repulsive to my wife. . . . Even young children despise me. . . . All my intimate friends abhor me. . . . and I have escaped by the skin of my teeth."

> "Have pity on me, have pity on me, O you my friends,
>   for the hand of God has touched me!
> Why do you, like God, pursue me?" 19:21–22

But, he insists, time at last will justify him. If he could, he would write his words on a copper scroll or engrave them on the face of a rocky cliff. Someday God must vindicate him. A welling up of faith lifts him for a moment above his puny friends. "For I know that my Redeemer lives!"

Zophar is evidently disturbed by Job's remarks; perhaps Job's searching integrity has stirred some guilt in his heart, because he unctuously warns Job that people who treat the poor unfairly or seize houses they did not build will never really profit. Nonsense, answers the disillusioned Job. The wicked often live happily, reach old age, grow powerful; their children are well established; "They spend their days in prosperity. . . ." But what difference does it make? Whether men die in bright prosperity or in bitterness of soul, "They lie down alike in the dust, and the worms cover them."

Eliphaz opens the third round of argument with the question "Can a man be profitable to God?" The impassive deity has no need of Job's righteousness even if Job were indeed righteous.

> "Agree with God, and be at peace;
>   thereby good will come to you. . . .
> If you return to the Almighty and humble yourself, . . .
> then you will delight yourself in the Almighty,
>   and lift up your face to God." 22:21, 23, 26

Ignoring such trite advice, Job again turns toward God:

> Oh, that I knew where I might find him,
>   that I might even to his seat!
> I would lay my case before him. . . .
> Would he contend with me in the greatness of his power?
>   No; he would give heed to me.
> There an upright man could reason with him,
>   and I should be acquitted for ever by my judge . . .
>   when he has tried me, I shall come forth as gold. 23:3–4, 6–7, 10

These are the quiet words of a man who is sure of both his intentions and his record. But God makes no answer and Job admits he is terrified of him; "and thick darkness covers my face."

Bildad apparently feels someone should break in on Job and he does it, reminding Job that dominion and fear are with God, before whom even the moon and stars pale. But Job does not care for Bildad's moralizing and turns caustic sarcasm on him:

"How you have helped him who has no power!
How you have saved the arm that has no strength!" 26:2

In scorn of little-minded men and still confused by the Almighty,
he affirms again:

". . . as long as my breath is in me,
    and the spirit of God is in my nostrils;
    my lips will not speak falsehood. . . .
Far be it from me to say that you are right." 27:3–5

In the middle of the argument, at a place where the text is confused, a great poem on wisdom is inserted (chapter 28). Although
it is put into the mouth of Job it is not correlated with the rest of
the argument. An affirmation by Wisdom declares that wisdom
far exceeds in value any fine metal or precious stone: gold, silver,
coral, crystal, pearls, topaz, onyx, sapphires.

"Man puts his hand to the flinty rock, . . .
    and his eye sees every precious thing. . . .
But where shall wisdom be found?
    And where is the place of understanding? . . .
God understands the way to it. . . .
When he gave to the wind its weight,
    and meted out the waters by measure;
when he made a decree for the rain . . .
then he saw it and declared it . . .
'Behold, the fear of the Lord, that is wisdom;
    and to depart from evil is understanding.'" 28:9–10, 12, 23, 25–28

For a final time Job turns to the contrast between his happy
past and his undeserved present. Taking sixteen oaths on the
integrity of his life, he spreads his record before God. He has not
only acted justly toward the people around him but he has dealt
generously with his servants, recognizing their humanity. "Did not
he who made me in the womb make him?" (A genuine insight
into the brotherhood of all men.) In final desperation he cries
out:

> "Oh, that I had one to hear me!
> (Here is my signature! Let the Almighty answer me!) . . .
>   like a prince I would approach him." 31:35, 37

It is at this dramatic climax that the Lord's answer would be expected to come. Job's longing to be understood by God has finally rent the veil and made it possible for God to respond. But there is an intrusion in the text. A younger man, named Elihu, comes on the scene and takes up the accusations against Job and also against the inadequacies of his friends' arguments. He speaks in a different vocabulary, using many Aramaic words and a different style, suggesting a late editorial intrusion.

The newcomer, Elihu, speaks:

> Behold, my heart is like wine that has no vent;
>   like new wineskins, it is ready to burst.
> I must speak, that I may find relief. . . . 32:19–20

Not that Job might find relief, but that he himself might exercise his own pomposity. Most of his words are redundant, but he makes one sound comment that God does answer through dreams and visions, then piously appends that a sufferer may draw to himself an angel to act as mediator so that even at the moment of death, a bewildered man may at last understand God's purposes and rejoice. Neither righteousness nor evil affect God, and if Job were truly a righteous man he would acknowledge God's impartiality in allowing both the good and the bad to suffer.

Job does not answer him. There is silence—finally. An end both to Job's probing and to his friends' circuitous reasoning. Then, strangely, Job becomes aware of Something which had hitherto eluded him. From that point of balance where insight and feeling flow into each other, Job senses the Presence! "Then the Lord answered Job out of the whirlwind." How else describe a theophany, a divine disclosure? God now takes up the question, compounding Job's irony:

> "Who is this that darkens counsel
>   by words without knowledge?
> Gird up your loins like a man,
>   I will question you, and you shall declare to me.

Where were you when I laid the foundation of the earth? . . .
when the morning stars sang together,
  and all the sons of God shouted for joy?" 38:2–4, 7

How could God speak in less than poetry? He reviews his own involvement in creation: the earth, the heavens, the sea; time, light and darkness; it is he who tutored the elements: snow, rain, hail, dew, hoarfrost, ice, clouds, lighting, and at the same time taught the earth's creatures their art of survival. Can Job instruct the lion how to hunt its prey, or provide food for the young ravens? Does Job know the ways of mountain goats, of calving hinds, of wild asses and oxen? Can he understand the nature of the ostrich, give the horse his might, dispense wisdom to the hawk and eagle? Can the questioner also answer? God does not condemn Job's moral performance, only his temerity, his rashness, in attempting to judge a God whose actions he cannot begin to comprehend.

Job covers his mouth with his hand, abashed, as before royalty.

The Lord continues lest Job be silenced only for lack of counterargument. Must Job, in order to justify his own innocence, censure God himself? Does he think God could not control the forces of evil? Take. the hippopotamus; who but God could restrain him? Or Leviathan, monster of the smoking nostrils; could Job subdue him? But to God, Leviathan is only another of his creatures. God is the Lord of all nature!

At last Job's restless questioning heart is stilled in wonder. This is the Lord, the very God, whom he has been challenging. A God of purposes beyond his comprehension, a God of the long run; God of the universe who sees man in true proportion without demeaning him. Job's suffering is now set in a larger framework. He confesses:

". . . Therefore I have uttered what I did not understand,
  things too wonderful for me, which I did not know." 42:3

He will continue questioning but now as a pupil, no longer asking for vindication, because at best human righteousness must fall far short of divine attainment. (Need a lonely child ever ask compassion from a parent whose hand he is holding?)

"I had heard of thee by the hearing of the ear,
>   but now my eye sees thee;
> therefore I despise myself,
>   and repent in dust and ashes." 42:5–6

The "cloud of unknowing" between the two, God and man, had lifted. Job's questions of his suffering had not been answered, but trust had replaced resentment.

There the poem ends and the prose of the folktale takes over. The Lord has a word for the three friends; Elihu he ignores. To Eliphaz he states flatly, "My wrath is kindled against you and against your two friends; for you have not spoken of me what is right, as my servant Job has." Let them therefore make a burnt offering and let Job intercede for them. So Job prays for his friends—for forgiveness of their servility in not standing up to the Almighty who had made man in his own image. Perhaps—we can at least hope—he also prayed for forgiveness of their pious platitudes, of which the Almighty must get almighty tired. ". . . and the Lord accepted Job's prayer."

After his prayer for his friends, which bound Job back into the bundle of humanity, "the Lord restored the fortunes of Job." We ponder whether complete well-being may not always depend upon an individual's willingness to become surety for his fellows; coming before the Lord in behalf of another may be the hallmark of a life tuned in to the infinite compassion.

No explicit mention is made of Job's disease being cured, but since his brothers and sisters and friends all invited themselves to dinner again, each bringing him "a piece of money and a ring of gold," the deduction seems logical that Job's loathsome sores disappeared. His fortune in sheep, camels and asses doubled. Again he had seven sons and three daughters. "And in all the land there were no women so fair as Job's daughters," which must have pleased Job a lot, because he gave them the same inheritance he gave his sons. (He really had learned something during his long affliction.) What happened to his wife does not seem to have interested the author, nor is Satan mentioned; having lost face, he probably also lost interest in the Heavenly Court. Job himself lived another one hundred and forty years and saw four generations of his family thrive.

The purpose of appending this second round of good fortune is open to debate. Perhaps the epilogue is an attempt to speak allegorically to the reader, affirming that whatever is most needful will be made possible. The point remains that Job's honest searching elicited experience of both the reality and the transcendence of God. We stand tall beside him, oblivious of the stretch of time between us, sensing our kinship with him and with the unfolding universe, humble but unabashed.

The Psalms

Examining the psalms critically is a good deal like analyzing a Beethoven symphony; for the non-specialist it is better to listen to the music. And any attempt to concentrate on the language, style and content of the psalms comes off about like dissecting motherhood and patriotism; it can be done, but who cares? Even though psalms are constantly read in public and add dimension to almost any kind of religious service, they remain private in their connotation. Indeed, just because they have been a part of so many shared experiences, they personalize in memory. One psalm may bring to mind a service when a new church was being dedicated and one's own grandfather, perhaps, led the responsive reading of the eighth psalm, or maybe the twenty-eighth. Or someone starts to repeat the twenty-third psalm and the voice we hear is our minister's saying the words softly by the bedside of someone we loved who was soon to leave us. Or maybe we hear in memory the happy voices of children at their first Communion —the nineteenth psalm; or the earnest voices of a group unjustly imprisoned as they repeat over and over the first seven verses of the seventeenth psalm; or the hoarse voices of passengers at sea repeating the affirmation of the one man who has remained unafraid in the tempest—"he made the storm be still, and the waves of the sea were hushed"; or the jubilant voices of a family reunited after years of separation in far places—the one hundred forty-seventh psalm. Multiplied thousands of individuals have memories hallowing their favorite psalms and all are personal.

And yet thoughtful perusal does enhance appreciation. Literally, there is a psalm for every occasion. Generations have found it so. Some psalms are joyous, some dismal, some filled with praise and some, alas, given to vilification of current enemies. Not all ancient poets were filled with sweetness and light, and occasional righteous souls felt justified in asking the Lord to deal with their enemies the way they would themselves like to deal if their sword were longer and sharper. Which only proves how human were the singers of Israel. How human, but how near to the divine when exultant hearts overflowed with adoration and gratitude. In the psalms the inner life of the Hebrew people is revealed, and behold, it is our inner life also.

To appreciate the importance of the psalms in Hebrew life we have to relive the great festivals such as Passover, when all Jews who could possibly get to Jerusalem streamed in from every direction. Blithe pilgrims, often piped along their way, sang out their hearts as they recalled their history, both their days of discouragement and their times of triumph. Finally they converged on the temple, toward which they customarily turned when they prayed, the temple where dwelt the Most High. And there the priests waited, and the choirmasters with their choirs, the orchestra conductors with their men and instruments, and certainly the city dignitaries, who at the right moment would include attentive royalty. No wonder we find the psalms particularly suitable for religious celebration; they were written as part of the matrix of religious life.

Themes

The themes explicate the human situation. So there are psalms of thanksgiving, eulogies to the Most High for acts of deliverance or simply for the blessings of nature and daily life; hymns of praise in honor of God's mercy, his attentiveness, his forethought, his miraculous powers; hymns of faith in which the singer expresses confidence founded on experience; psalms of wisdom reviewing God's demand for righteousness on the part of his people; songs of Zion largely nationalistic in their regard for the capital city, which is also the holy city; royal psalms written in honor of a coronation or a regal wedding or the birth of a prince; psalms of enthronement ascribing to God the rulership of the world and all that dwells therein; liturgic psalms composed for special services; didactic psalms teaching regard for the divine government of the universe and extolling God's judgment of the acts of all men, good and bad; songs of contrition reminding both singer and listener of the need for forgiveness and the need to forgive. There are even psalms celebrating the law.

Authors, Editors, and Dates

Some psalms fit into two or more categories, sometimes because they express more than one mood and sometimes because they are a composite of the work of more than one author. All down the line, editors made free with older works, omitting lines that once referred to some specific event in order to give the psalm more general use or, conversely, adapting an old psalm to a new occasion. Theories on dates and authorship shift as more records of contemporary cultures come to light. Discovery of an enormous quantity of Ugaritic documents on the northern Syrian coast has brought to light legends and historical and mythological poems written in an ancient Canaanite dialect, which indicates that some of the Hebrew psalms may be very old, either in their derivation or as expressions of an attitude common in the same general period.

There never has been agreement among editors and scholars as to numbering the psalms or finalizing their exact content. Greek and Hebrew editors combined psalms differently; old manuscripts have variations; modern scholars scrutinize and delineate the various collections by approximate dates and periods. But the average one of us is only casually interested in knowing whether a given psalm was originally part of the Asaph Psalter or came from an appendix to the Korah Psalter!

Scholarly commentaries also discuss the musical settings. The instruments which accompanied the choir are listed in psalm 150 as the trumpet, lute, harp, timbrel, strings, pipes and cymbals, both the "sounding cymbals" and the "loud clashing cymbals." In great temple services there was apparently more than one choir, and on occasion choirs were massed on the city wall or on both sides of a great city gate through which a triumphal procession was about to enter.

Old manuscripts have musical directions most of which have to be guessed at. As often as the word *selah* occurs, no one knows exactly what it indicates; perhaps the place for an instrumental interlude, or for the prostration of the priests. What is the meaning of *miktam, maskil, shiggayong?* Many scholars conjecture but no one knows except that they must have been directions to the choirmaster. The word *lamenasseah* is appended to fifty-five psalms and is usually translated "for the chief musician" but that is a half guess. Right in line with a modern hymnbook, however, are the indications as to which tune should be used. Psalms 45 and 69 are to be sung according to *shoshanim,* meaning the tune "Lilies"; while the tune for psalm 22 is "The Mind of the Dawn." Not all the music was for singing; some was composed for the dancers, who also had an important part in processions.

57

While no psalm can be credited to King David beyond dispute, there are portions of psalms that could well have been his. Psalm 57, for instance, may have come to him when he was fleeing from Saul and pleading for the mercy of the Lord in the shadow of whose wings he must take refuge, then suddenly realizes that he can trust in God! His anxiety changes to reassurance and he breaks into ecstasy, realizing he need never more waver.

> My heart is steadfast, O God,
>   my heart is steadfast!
> I will sing and make melody!
>   Awake, my soul!
> Awake, O harp and lyre!
>   I will awake the dawn! . . .
> Be exalted, O God, above the heavens!
>   Let thy glory be over all the earth! 57:7–8, 11

In modern life everybody edits his own book of Psalms. For all practical purposes some psalms disappear from our personal collection because we feel no need for them. Others we memorize and no extremity could take them from us. One great experience in editorship which can come anyone's way is to be part of a committee to compile a small book of psalms to be used by some special group—for explorers setting off on a trek, or the armed forces, or patients in hospitals, or children in kindergarten, busy house-wives, harried businessmen. Which are *their* special psalms? Probably those that are *our* special psalms.

Songs for All Seasons

Even to try to indicate typical psalms in different categories is a disheartening task, because an amateur editor, which means most of us, is bound to leave out lines someone else cherishes. But categorizing the psalms does sharpen our mood.

Praise 136

One of the great songs of praise is psalm 136. This God we turn to is God of the universe, no less; but still his heart beats in steadfast love for his children.

> O give thanks to the Lord of lords,
>   for his steadfast love endures for ever; . . .
> to him who spread out the earth upon the waters . . .
>   . . . who made the great lights . . .
> the sun to rule over the day . . .
> the moon and stars to rule over the night . . .
> to him who led his people through the wilderness. . . .
> It is he who remembered us in our low estate. . . .
> O give thanks to the God of heaven,
> for his steadfast love endures for ever. 136:3, 6–9, 16, 23, 26

95

Psalm 95 celebrates the kingship of God, whose majesty elicits songs of praise. Probably no psalm more often serves as the introit at a service of worship, especially the first seven verses.

> O come, let us sing to the Lord;
>   let us make a joyful noise to the rock of our salvation!
> Let us come into his presence with thanksgiving;
>   let us make a joyful noise to him with songs of praise!
> For the Lord is a great God,
>   and a great King above all gods.
> In his hand are the depths of the earth;
>   the heights of the mountains are his also.
> The sea is his, for he made it;
>   for his hands formed the dry land.

> O come, let us worship and bow down,
>> let us kneel before the Lord, our Maker!
> For he is our God,
>> and we are the people of his pasture,
>> and the sheep of his hand. 95:1–7

117

Psalm 117 is a hymn of pure praise; also the shortest psalm (and the middle verses of the entire Bible).

> Praise the Lord, all nations!
>> Extol him, all peoples!
> For great is his steadfast love toward us;
>> and the faithfulness of the Lord endures for ever.
> Praise the Lord! 117:1–2

150

The doxology which marks the end of the psalter is another all-encompassing call for praise.

> Praise the Lord!
> Praise God in his sanctuary;
>> praise him in his mighty firmament!
> Praise him for his mighty deeds;
>> praise him according to his exceeding greatness! . . .
> Let everything that breathes praise the Lord!
> Praise the Lord! 150:1–2, 6

Laments 89

The long, eighty-ninth psalm is a king's prayer for deliverance from enemies who are overwhelming him. As a descendant of David he rehearses God's former faithfulness in dealing with David as if to persuade himself that a God of that proven magnanimity would surely not fail one of David's line. But he is now having a very hard time.

The heavens are thine, the earth also is thine;
 the world and all that is in it, thou hast founded them. . . .
Righteousness and justice are the foundation of thy throne;
 steadfast love and faithfulness go before thee. . . .
How long will thy wrath burn like fire?

Remember, O Lord, what the measure of life is. . . .
Lord, where is thy steadfast love of old,
   which by thy faithfulness thou didst swear to David?
Remember, O Lord, how thy servant is scorned;
   how I bear in my bosom the insults of the peoples. . . . 89:11, 14
     46–47, 49–50

22

Particularly treasured by Christians because its opening words
were repeated by Jesus on the cross is the lament for God's apparent absence in time of trial:

> My God, my God, why hast thou forsaken me? 22:1

The author of the psalm, however, is speaking of his own condition and explains that he is so nearly dead that his relatives have
already begun to divide his property, but he vows that if the Lord
heals him, he will testify before the congregation:

I will tell of thy name to my brethren. . . .
All the ends of the earth shall remember
   and turn to the Lord . . .
   men shall tell of the Lord to the coming generation
and proclaim his deliverance to a people yet unborn. . . . 22:22, 27,
   30–31

137

This most nostalgic of psalms, the one hundred thirty-seventh,
recalls the lonely days of the captivity of the people of Judah in
Babylon.

> By the waters of Babylon,
>   there we sat down and wept,
>   when we remembered Zion.
> On the willows there
>   we hung up our lyres. . . .
> How shall we sing the Lord's song
>   in a foreign land?
> If I forget you, O Jerusalem,
>   let my right hand wither! 137:1–2, 4–5

But just when a modern reader is caught up in the poet's homesick grief the writer turns vindictive and prays for the destruction of his enemies, including rasing their cities. These are scalding words which present the naked soul in unquestioning anger, the kind of anger mankind still finds it difficult to temper.

> Happy shall he be who takes your little ones
> and dashes them against the rock! 137:9

Songs of Faith

In moments of faith poets of insight raised the sights of the whole community of Israel, shedding a warm light down the centuries. Some of the psalmists had a genius for expressing the trusting confidence of the people, making it plain that they have faith in God because they have had experience of God. Knowing well who was the arbiter of their destiny, they could attest that their God of unlimited power is honorable and trustworthy. More, he is a God who tends his people as a shepherd his flock, as a host his guests; the one who never fails even in the moment of death. Probably no poem in any language is recited from memory by as many people as the twenty-third psalm. It holds open the doors of faith and love to all who wish to enter.

23

> The Lord is my shepherd, I shall not want;
>   he makes me lie down in green pastures.
> He leads me beside still waters;
>   he restores my soul. . . .
> Even though I walk through the
>   valley of the shadow of death,
>   I fear no evil;
> for thou art with me. . . .
> Surely goodness and mercy shall follow me
>   all the days of my life;
> and I shall dwell in the house of the Lord
>   for ever. 23:1–6

Justice 62

Close to faith is the sense of God's justice. Several psalms make the point underscored in psalm 62:

Once God has spoken;
  twice have I heard this:
that power belongs to God;
  and that to thee, O Lord, belongs
    steadfast love.
For thou dost requite a man
  according to his work. 62:11–12

Songs of Zion

Jerusalem was more than the capital city and the center of national life. Other countries had busy capitals. Jerusalem was the Lord's city, the home of the temple, which contained the holy of holies, wherein the Lord dwelt. Psalm 122 speaks for the heart of the nation:

122

I was glad when they said to me,
  "Let us go to the house of the Lord!"
Our feet have been standing
  within your gates, O Jerusalem!
Jerusalem, built as a city
  which is bound firmly together,
to which the tribes go up,
  the tribes of the Lord. . . .
Pray for the peace of Jerusalem!
  "May they prosper who love you!
Peace be within your walls,
  and security within your towers!" . . .
For the sake of the house of the Lord our God,
  I will seek your good. 122:1–4, 6–7, 9

84

Psalm 84 sings praise to Zion as the goal of the pilgrims; the poet envies even the birds and the servants, who live permanently in the temple courtyard.

How lovely is thy dwelling place,
  O Lord of hosts!
My soul longs, yea, faints
  for the courts of the Lord. . . .

> Even the sparrow finds a home,
>> and the swallow a nest for herself.
> Blessed are those who dwell in thy house,
>> ever singing thy praise! . . .
> I would rather be a doorkeeper in the house of my God
>> than dwell in the tents of wickedness. . . .
> No good thing does the Lord withhold
>> from those who walk uprightly. 84:1-4, 10-11

Royal Psalms 110

Possibly composed for a coronation, psalm 110 is one of the oldest in the collection; its images and parallelisms closely resemble corresponding phrases in Bronze-Age Canaanite texts. Apparently it was written by a king who was also a priest, as was Melchizedek, the eighteenth-century B.C. king-priest of Salem (possibly Jerusalem) mentioned in Genesis. Behind and above the king was the Lord, maker and preserver of kings.

> The Lord says to my lord:
> "Sit at my right hand,
>> till I make your enemies
>>> your footstool." . . .
> Your people will offer themselves freely
>> on the day you lead your host
>> upon the holy mountains. . . .
> The Lord has sworn
>> and will not change his mind,
> "You are a priest for ever
>> after the order of Melchizedek." 110:1, 3-4

2

Psalm two is another royal psalm, composed for another early coronation. Let other nations try to conspire against Jerusalem if they are so rash, but the power of the Lord is behind Zion.

> He who sits in the heavens laughs;
>> the Lord has them in derision.
> Then he will speak to them in his wrath. . . .
> "I have set my king
>> on Zion, my holy hill." . . .

"Ask of me, and I will make the nations your heritage,
    and the ends of the earth your possession. . . ." 2:4–6, 8

Liturgic Psalms 24

Some liturgic hymns were meant for festive occasions, such as psalm 24, which may have marked the return to the city of victorious armed forces; especially appropriate if the ark, containing the Ten Commandments on their tablets of stone and Aaron's rod which sprouted, had accompanied the soldiers. The majesty of the words matches the solemnity and joy of the occasion. It is easy to imagine antiphonal choirs at the gates of Jerusalem, with throngs of people responding.

> Who shall ascend the hill of the Lord?
>   And who shall stand in his holy place?
> He who has clean hands and a pure heart,
>   who does not lift up his soul to what is false,
>   and does not swear deceitfully. . . .
> Lift up your heads, O gates!
>   and be lifted up, O ancient doors!
>   that the King of glory may come in.
> Who is the King of glory?
>   The Lord, strong and mighty,
>   the Lord, mighty in battle! . . .
>   The Lord of hosts,
>   he is the King of glory! 24:3–4, 7–8, 10

Wisdom Psalms 119

Psalm 119, the longest in the collection, is a soliloquy on the laws of God and man's response. Its form is an acrostic, each stanza made up of eight lines beginning with the same letter of the (Hebrew) alphabet; 176 lines in all. Commentary on the demands of God and the willing response of man discloses Israel's persecution and the people's acknowledgment that justice is sure.

> Give me understanding, that I may keep thy law
>   and observe it with my whole heart. . . .
> This is my comfort in my affliction
>   that thy promise gives me life. . . .

> Thy word is a lamp to my feet.
>> and a light to my path. . . .
> Great peace have those who love thy law;
>> nothing can make them stumble. 119:34, 50, 105, 165

139

The author of Psalm 139 ponders the wisdom of God, his knowledge of the mind and heart of man and his dominion over nature. Here for the first time a poet expresses the thought that God is in Sheol, the Pit, as well as in heaven.

> O Lord, thou hast searched me and known me! . . .
>> thou discernest my thoughts from afar. . . .
> Even before a word is on my tongue,
>> lo, O Lord, thou knowest it altogether. . . .
> Such knowledge is too wonderful for me;
>> it is high, I cannot attain it.
> Whither shall I go from thy Spirit?
>> Or whither shall I flee from thy presence?
> If I ascend to heaven, thou art there!
>> If I make my bed in Sheol, thou art there!
> If I take the wings of the morning
>> and dwell in the uttermost parts of the sea,
> even there thy hand shall lead me,
>> and thy right hand shall hold me. . . .
> even the darkness is not dark to thee. . . .
> How precious to me are thy thoughts, O God!
>> How vast is the sum of them! . . .
> Search me, O God, and know my heart!
>> Try me and know my thoughts!
> And see if there be any wicked way in me,
>> and lead me in the way everlasting! 139:1–2, 4, 6–10, 12, 17, 23–24

Gratitude 30

Gratitude is native to the human heart and thankfulness comes spontaneously to those who are alert to the manifold disclosures of God. Psalm 30 is a hymn of pure gratitude, probably for healing an illness in which the sufferer had known the despair of long nights of pain and the relief of finding himself still alive in the morning, facing a brighter future.

O Lord my God, I cried to thee for help,
  and thou hast healed me. . . .
Weeping may tarry for the night,
  but joy comes with the morning. . . .
Thou hast turned for me my mourning into dancing. . . .
  O Lord my God, I will give thanks to thee for ever. 30:2, 5, 11–12

3

Depths of gratitude, almost an awed gratitude, are expressed in the third psalm, supposedly composed by David when he was fleeing from his son Absalom and had to sleep in the open country knowing there were thousands of people who, he felt, "have set themselves against me round about."

But thou, O Lord, art a shield about me,
  my glory, and the lifter of my head.
I cry aloud to the Lord,
  and he answers me from his holy hill. 3:3–4

Wonder 8

Some of the psalms express a kind of astounded wonder that God *is*. They are hymns of personal discovery. For the poet, God was not just invented to fill a longing, or predicated as a regulatory force, or dramatized as an anthropomorphic father figure. He was *found*. He was detected in the workings of the universe and disclosed within the individual soul.

Each man makes his own discovery. If we who read these ancient attestations have made the same discovery, then we share a common awe. If we have not made the personal discovery, then we have to close the book sorrowfully, because the upper ranges of human experience have not yet been put to trial by us. The eighth psalm celebrates man's dignity as he shares God's dominion.

O Lord, our Lord,
how majestic is thy name in all the earth! . . .
When I look at thy heavens, the work of thy fingers,
  the moon and the stars which thou hast established;
What is man that thou art mindful of him,

and the son of man that thou dost care for him?
Yet thou hast made him little less than God,
  and dost crown him with glory and honor.
Thou hast given him dominion over the works of thy hands;
  thou hast put all things under his feet. . . .
O Lord, our Lord,
  how majestic is thy name in all the earth! 8:1, 3–6, 9

One closes the book of Psalms pondering, for they raise questions which each of us has to answer for ourself. They may leave us wistful because the psalmist's assurance of God's availability is greater than our own; or they may leave us exultant because we see that, age by age, people make the same transforming discoveries. At any rate, the more the psalms are read the more clearly their moods and meanings are disclosed. New significance steps out suddenly. A psalm which has been read a hundred times without emotion may all at once appear to be printed in boldface, a personal answer to a deep need.

Proverbs

Proverbs have always been the shorthand of wisdom. In any culture, they pass on standards of felicitous conduct, comment on foibles of human nature, offer pertinent advice in pithy form easier to remember than a sermon. A man who can coin quotable proverbs is surely as useful in his day as a politician or a teacher. He is also a maker of fame for himself, at least for as long as people remember who said it first. Benjamin Franklin could have harnessed electricity, invented the printing press, influenced the formation of the new republic, and never have been half so well known if he had not also been Poor Richard, prime contriver of American proverbs. (An empty barrel makes the most noise; he that lieth down with dogs shall rise up with fleas.) On the other hand, many proverbs which are coin of the realm have no signature. (A stitch in time saves nine; a bird in the hand is worth two in the bush.)

A nation with a low literacy rate is more likely to be a proverb-quoting people than a nation with high standards of literacy. The Hebrews produced the most proverbs before the rank and file could read. The Chinese likewise coined proverbs of remarkable pertinence through three thousand years of illiteracy, which may have given them their facility for quoting the current aphorisms of their leadership. Anybody who can quote a proverb to clinch an argument has the edge on his opponent and basks in a moment's illusion that he is a philosopher. Among the Hebrews of that day, servants, slaves and women did not enter into weighty discussions with their betters, meaning the male heads of the household, but if they just happened to toss in a proverb in support of the right argument they certainly merited a nod of approval.

But the book of Proverbs does not consist entirely of proverbs. There are also discourses by Wisdom, who is personified discernment-judgment-knowledge, both timeless and pertinent to the immediate situation. Wisdom speaks in both general and specific terms, some of the observations being apposite today, which for the modern reader redeems their tendency toward clichés. There are also personal observations by individual commentators speaking to given situations.

It was inevitable that there should be a compilation of this highly regarded collection of wisdom. The book we call Proverbs is really a collection of collections, an anthology of anthologies, gathered together at various times, the earliest probably in the sixth century B.C., three hundred years or so after Solomon, to whom the book is ascribed. Some of the proverbs may well have been his, handed down for generations. The last collection was produced before 180 B.C., because Sirach, a man of wisdom, second century B.C., quoted from it.

An Explicit Title

The book of Proverbs boasts the longest title of any book in the Old Testament. Evidently its final editor had the same idea held by some modern publishers that a non-fiction title should indicate what a book is about.

> The proverbs of Solomon, son of David, king of Israel:
> That men may know wisdom and instruction,
>   understand words of insight,
> receive instruction in wise dealing,
>   righteousness, justice, and equity;
> that prudence may be given to the simple,
>   knowledge and discretion to the youth—
> the wise man also may hear and increase in learning,
>   and the man of understanding acquire skill,
> to understand a proverb and a figure,
>   the words of the wise and their riddles. 1:1–6

Who Could Disagree?

The first part of the collection (1:1 to 9:18), edited around the fourth century B.C., has three sections, the first made up of a

dozen discourses admonishing the hearers to walk in the way of
sound instruction. Some of the instruction sounds as if it might
have been delivered in public to the equivalent of a commence-
ment audience or a community picnic. All of it is conventionally
acceptable home training; none is socially challenging. For instance:

> Hear, my son, your father's instruction,
>   and reject not your mother's teaching;
> for they are a fair garland for your head,
>   and pendants for your neck. 1:8–9

The youth of the current generation might be glad to wear the
garlands and pendants but less likely to stand respectfully for
their father's instruction, which may be a reflection on the kind of
instruction—spoken and acted out—which their fathers sometimes administer.

In the second discourse Wisdom is personified as a prophetess:

> Wisdom cries aloud in the street;
>   in the markets she raises her voice. . . . 1:20

and goes on to threaten those who do not listen. In those days, in
spite of braying donkeys and squeaky carts a voice delivering an
oration on wisdom would be listened to on the street. (In Greece
or Egypt as well as in Israel, a crowd would gather, taking notes,
and go home and repeat the gist of the discourse.) A quotable
phrase insured the speaker's reputation.

Successive discourses pointed the way in which making the
ears "attentive to wisdom" promoted understanding of "the knowledge of God," which in turn led to spiritual and physical health,
the true wealth that brings lasting peace of mind. An attentive
pupil, it was pointed out, could profit by the wisdom toward
which even his teacher was once directed by his own parents.
Marital unfaithfulness and sexual indulgence lead only to grief;
"at the end of your life you groan." Quotable lines about rash
pledges and lazy ways keep even a modern reader nodding his
head in agreement and some of the quick illustrations from nature still capture attention, including the well-worn admonition:

> Go to the ant, O sluggard;
>   consider her ways, and be wise. 6:6

The ant, who without any ruler "prepares her food in summer" and "gathers her sustenance in harvest," while the sluggard folds his hands until poverty comes upon him "like a vagabond."

A poem in which Wisdom speaks as a prophetess (chapter 8) includes some of the finest lines in the entire collection; stately phrases depicting Wisdom as the master workman who helped to sustain the Creator in his initial act of creation:

> The Lord created me at the beginning of his work,
>   the first of his acts of old. . . .
> Before the mountains had been shaped. . . .
> When he established the heavens, I was there,
>   when he drew a circle on the face of the deep . . .
> when he marked out the foundations of the earth,
>   then I was beside him, like a master workman;
> and I was daily his delight . . .
> rejoicing in his inhabited world
>   and delighting in the sons of men. 8:22, 25, 27, 29–31

Wishful Thinking

However, there were some wishful thinkers who overaffirmed and held to untenable premises in the name of Wisdom, carrying a banner for the rosy half-truth that the good will be rich and healthy, a standard around which the spiritually anemic rally in any generation. Says Wisdom:

> Riches and honor are with me,
>   enduring wealth and prosperity. . . .
> I walk in the way of righteousness,
>   in the paths of justice,
> endowing with wealth those who love me,
>   and filling their treasuries. 8:18, 20–21

There must have been a good many close observers, some of them teen-agers, who questioned the cheerful premise that those who turn to God and live moral lives will be rewarded with health, wealth, and happiness. In real life the price of unselfishness is sometimes penury, and there are men and women who give themselves so completely to the world's needs that worldly riches, perhaps even assurance of the next day's meals, never come their way; and those who share wisdom abundantly both in word and deed may never find good health or fame. Or even safety. Instead, they find something more satisfying. However, Wisdom happily contradicted her claims about goodness producing tangible wealth:

> Take my instruction instead of silver,
>   and knowledge rather than choice gold;
> for wisdom is better than jewels,
>   and all that you may desire cannot compare with her. 8:10–11

In an allegory (chapter 9) Wisdom, the personification of gracious rectitude, scores over the noisy wanton, Folly. Where Wisdom calls to the untaught:

> "Come, eat of my bread
>   and drink of the wine I have mixed . . .
>   and walk in the way of insight." 9:5–6

Folly, noisy and wanton, calls to the passer-by:

> "Stolen water is sweet,
>   and bread eaten in secret is pleasant." 9:17

According to Solomon

Book Two (10:1 to 22:16) and Book Four (25:1 to 29:27) have the same intriguing title: *Proverbs of Solomon.* According to the book of First Kings, Solomon "also uttered three thousand proverbs." Many of these proverbs are presented as couplets, or distichs, some of their clauses being synonymous:

> A liberal man will be enriched,
>   and one who waters will himself be watered. 11:25

Close to three hundred of the sayings are antithetical and could be called the *but* proverbs:

> The fear of the Lord prolongs life,
>   but the years of the wicked will be short. 10:27

> A soft answer turns away wrath,
>   but a harsh word stirs up anger. 15:1

In some couplets the second clause completes the thought of the first:

> The mind of the wise makes his speech judicious,
> and adds persuasiveness to his lips. 16:23

> When a man's folly brings his way to ruin,
> his heart rages against the Lord. 19:3

> Discipline your son, and he will give you rest;
> he will give delight to your heart. 29:17

Largely from these books Two and Four, come the proverbs which comment on an individual's firsthand relationships.

Family

> Hearken to your father who begot you,
> and do not despise your mother when she is old. 23:22

> Train up a child in the way he should go,
> and when he is old he will not depart from it. 22:6

> He who finds a wife finds a good thing,
> and obtains favor from the Lord. 18:22

> Grandchildren are the crown of the aged,
> and the glory of sons is their fathers. 17:6

> A wise son makes a glad father,
> but a foolish man despises his mother. 15:20

Friend

> A friend loves at all times,
> and a brother is born for adversity. 17:17

Woman

> It is better to live in a corner of the housetop
> than in a house shared with a contentious woman. 21:9; 25:24

> Like a gold ring in a swine's snout
> is a beautiful woman without discretion. 11:22

Enemy

> If your enemy is hungry, give him bread to eat;
> and if he is thirsty, give him water to drink. 25:21

> Do not rejoice when your enemy falls,
> and let not your heart be glad when he stumbles. 24:17

Food and Drink

Better is a dinner of herbs where love is
    than a fatted ox and hatred with it. 15:17

Do not look at wine when it is red,
    when it sparkles in the cup
    and goes down smoothly.
At the last it bites like a serpent,
    and stings like an adder. 23:31–32

Work

He who is slack in his work
    is a brother to him who destroys. 18:9

Wealth

Riches do not profit in the day of wrath,
    but righteousness delivers from death. 11:4

Better is a little with righteousness
    than great revenues with injustice. 16:8

Medicine

A cheerful heart is a good medicine,
    but a downcast spirit dries up the bones. 17:22

Kings

Take away the dross from the silver,
    and the smith has material for a vessel;
take away the wicked from the presence of the king,
    and his throne will be established in righteousness. 25:4–5

Do not put yourself forward in the king's presence
    or stand in the place of the great;
for it is better to be told, "Come up here,"
    than to be put lower in the presence of the prince. 25:6–7

When you sit down to eat with a ruler,
    observe carefully what is before you;
and put a knife to your throat
    if you are a man given to appetite.
Do not desire his delicacies,
    for they are deceptive food. 23:1–3

Morals

A man without self-control
  is like a city broken into and left without walls. 25:28

A good name is to be chosen rather than great riches,
  and favor is better than silver or gold. 22:1

He who keeps his mouth and his tongue
  keeps himself out of trouble. 21:23

He who is slow to anger has great understanding,
  but he who has a hasty temper exalts folly. 14:29

A righteous man has regard for the life of his beast,
  but the mercy of the wicked is cruel. 12:10

The Lord

He who is kind to the poor lends to the Lord,
  and he will repay him for his deed. 19:17

The name of the Lord is a strong tower;
  the righteous man runs into it and is safe. 18:10

Commit your work to the Lord,
  and your plans will be established. 16:3

Book Three (22:17 to 24:22) contains a collection of a teacher's instructions to his pupils, whom he calls his son. The compiler borrowed freely from an Egyptian source known as *Teaching for Life and Instruction for Prosperity,* written by the "Overseer of Grains," Amenemope, composed for his son in order to "lead him aright in the ways of life." The Egyptian author had thirty sections to his book and the Hebrew author also mentions:

Have I not written for you thirty sayings
  of admonition and knowledge,
to show you what is right and true,
  that you may give a true answer to those who sent you? 22:20–21

Discipline is a responsibility of both parent and teacher:

Do not withold discipline from a child;
    if you beat him with a rod, he will not die.
If you beat him with a rod
    you will save his life from Sheol. 23:13–14

First Appendix

The first of five appendixes is attached to Book Three, titled "These also are sayings of the wise." These appendixes are documents of unknown origin which some early editor felt should not be left out of a Hebrew collection of quotations about wisdom. Typical of the first appendix:

Fair Play

Be not a witness against your neighbor without cause,
    and do not deceive with your lips.
Do not say, "I will do to him as he has done to me;
    I will pay the man back for what he has done." 24:28–29

Then comes Book Four, already discussed with Book Two, followed by four more appendixes.

Appendix Two

The second appendix (30:1–9) is called the *Oracle of Agur Son of Jakeh of Massa,* Massa being an Arabian tribe. Whoever Agur may have been, he knew humility and wonder, two excellent traits for an orator.

Surely I am too stupid to be a man.
    I have not the understanding of a man.
I have not learned wisdom,
    nor have I knowledge of the Holy One. 30:2–3

But he longs to be kept from extremes lest he wander from God.

Remove far from me falsehood and lying;
    give me neither poverty nor riches;
    feed me with the food that is needful for me,
lest I be full, and deny thee
    and profane the name of my God. 30:8–9

Appendix Three

Appendix three (30:10–33) contains both admonitions and numerical proverbs.

Three things are too wonderful for me;
    four I do not understand:

the way of an eagle in the sky,
   the way of a serpent on a rock,
the way of a ship on the high seas,
   and the way of a man with a maiden. 30:18–19

Four things on earth are small,
   but they are exceedingly wise:
the ants are a people not strong,
   yet they provide their food in the summer;
The badgers are a people not mighty,
   yet they make their homes in the rocks;
the locusts have no king,
   yet all of them march in rank;
the lizard you can take in your hands,
   yet it is in kings' palaces. 30:24–28

Three things are stately in their tread;
   four are stately in their stride:
the lion, which is mightiest among beasts
   and does not turn back before any;
the strutting cock, the he-goat,
   and a king striding before his people. 30:29–31

It was not only the numerical proverbs that sometimes expressed a wry sense of humor:

If you have been foolish, exalting yourself,
   or if you have been devising evil,
   put your hand on your mouth.
For pressing milk produces curds,
   pressing the nose produces blood,
   and pressing anger produces strife. 30:32–33

Appendix Four

The fourth appendix incorporates a queen's advice to her son, the king. The tenor of the advice leads one to suspect that the king was young and had sowed a few wild oats, or else that the queen felt his father may have been somewhat less than circumspect, which prompted her to try to save her son from temptation and folly. Cautioning King Lemuel not to waste his strength on women, she also reminds him that "it is not for kings to drink wine." Instead, let him give the wine to the poor so that they will "remember their misery no more." There is poignancy in her comments and it may have been her eloquence on her son's responsibility to judge righteously in order to "maintain the rights of the poor and needy" which accounted for her words having been preserved. In the eyes of the final editors of the canon not many women were deemed worthy of being quoted.

Appendix Five

The final appendix (31:10–31) is a panegyric to a noble wife who is thrifty in the care of her household. Written in the form of an alphabetical acrostic poem, it is by all odds the most quoted chapter in the book of Proverbs, probably having been read at more funerals of highly respected wives than any other chapter in the Old Testament except the twenty-third psalm.

Appropriately the ode of honor opens with a question: "A good wife who can find?" Supposedly the author had found her, because he appears to know her actions around the clock—and she wastes small time in sleep.

> She rises while it is yet night
>   and provides food for her household
> and tasks for her maidens. . . .
>   Her lamp does not go out at night. 31:15, 18

She spins and weaves—and apparently dyes her own fabrics, since "all her household are clothed in scarlet" and, for herself, "her clothing is fine linen and purple." Best of all, says the man who wrote of her charms,

> The heart of her husband trusts in her,
>   and he will have no lack of gain. 31:11
>
> Her husband is known in the gates,
>   when he sits among the elders of the land. 31:23

Small wonder he declares that "She is far more precious than jewels." Moreover he respects her financial acumen:

> She considers a field and buys it;
>   with the fruit of her hands she plants a vineyard. . . .
> She makes linen garments and sells them;
>   she delivers girdles to the merchant. 31:16, 24

Having prospered, she is also benevolent:

> She opens her hand to the poor,
>> and reaches out her hand to the needy . . .
>> and the teaching of her kindness is on her tongue. 31:20, 26

Expectedly, she is also a fine mother:

>> Her children rise up and call her blessed. . . . 31:28

Then lest anyone think he is talking about good women in the abstract, he allows himself a couplet of direct address:

>> "Many women have done excellently,
>>> but you surpass them all." 31:29

It is to be hoped that he was speaking to the living lady herself and not looking down on her open coffin. At the end he moralizes:

> Charm is deceitful, and beauty is vain,
>> but a woman who fears the Lord is to be praised. 31:30

All in all, she—whoever the prototype may have been—deserved to make the canon and find her place in Hebrew wisdom literature.

Today sections of this library of wisdom known as the book of Proverbs may appear a shade on the trite side, somewhat simplistic in theology, certainly more concerned with individual satisfaction than with meeting the needs of others, but on the whole the book discloses insight into the whole human problem of people getting along with people where they are. Proverbs live, of course, because they jog our minds to attention and ours is a generation whose minds tend to drift. Incorporated into Holy Writ, these particular proverbs take on some of the authority of the voice of the Lord.

Ecclesiastes

Who Says?

The trouble with the book of Ecclesiastes is not that so much of it is pessimistic but that so much of it is true.

> What does man gain by all the toil
>> at which he toils under the sun?
> A generation goes, and a generation comes. . . .
> The wind blows to the south,
>> and goes round to the north;
> round and round goes the wind,
>> and on its circuits the wind returns. . . .
> What has been is what will be,
>> and what has been done is what will be done;
> And there is nothing new under the sun. 1:3–4, 6, 9

And does it ever sound futile when set down in print! That is Koheleth, also spelled Qoheleth, and in English "the Preacher," the author of this acid, heretical, pessimistic, cynical and sometimes amusing book. The Greek translated his name Ekklesiastes, meaning "one who speaks to the assembly," and tradition equated him with Solomon, who "assembled the elders of Israel and all the heads of the tribes" and made a long and prayerful speech to them—and God. The author himself says he was a son of David, king in Jerusalem; and it could have been Solomon although if Solomon had exemplified such extreme pessimism it would have been natural for the book of Kings, or of some of the sources on which Kings drew, to have mentioned the fact. King David had many sons. If one of the others was philosophically inclined and a popular speaker besides, it must have galled him to have word go out that his production came from his famous half brother, Solomon.

Whoever he was, he had some motivating reason for taking as his main theme: all striving is futile. Futile or not, he apparently enjoyed discussing the matter. And in estimating his own achievements he appears honest if not modest.

> I said to myself, "I have acquired great wisdom, surpassing all who were over Jerusalem before me; and my mind has had great experience of wisdom and knowledge." 1:16

But he felt that increasing knowledge merely increased sorrow. So it does, in a way. If a man knew the whole of any one of the world's problems—hunger, say—he would have a vast store of knowledge but he could easily break his own heart. That was the point of view of Koheleth.

Just too Bad

At some time Koheleth took a fling at pleasure, which also proved to be rank futility. "What use is it?" And laughter, he said, was mad. He tried to cheer his body with wine, but without going to excess, and reported his alcoholic bout with the judicious phrase "my mind still guiding me with wisdom." He took up public works, built houses, planted vineyards, developed gardens and parks, had pools dug, bought slaves, herds and flocks "more than any who had been before me in Jerusalem," amassed silver and gold, collected singers and concubines, and says that he enjoyed everything he did. So? So nothing! (He anticipated the same findings as Shakespeare's lady lawyer named Portia: ". . . they are as sick that surfeit with too much as they that starve with nothing.") Koheleth summed it up: ". . . all was vanity and a striving after wind, and there was nothing to be gained under the sun."

Nevertheless, he felt there was something to be said for wisdom, which "excels folly as light excels darkness. The wise man has eyes in his head, . . ." but lest he cheer himself up he quickly reminded himself, "What befalls the fool will befall me also. . . . How the wise man dies just like the fool!"

Who can argue with that?

The Koheleth had a really depressing thought: the next generation is going to garner what *he* sows and who knows what they will be like? Deserving? A man who dwelt on the thought could drive himself crazy; "even in the night his mind does not rest." Better just to eat and drink. All experience is "from the hand of God." Oh, yes, there *is* God, he acknowledged, but who can understand him?

Whose Time Do We Live In?

One of the most famous passages from the book is the commentary on time. Not time in the broad philosophical sense, but time broken into man-sized pieces—*times*.

> For everything there is a season, and a time for every matter under heaven:
> a time to be born, and a time to die:
> a time to plant, and a time to pluck up what is planted;
> a time to kill, and a time to heal;
> a time to break down, and a time to build up;
> a time to weep, and a time to laugh;
> a time to mourn, and a time to dance;
> a time to cast away stones, and a time to gather stones together;
> a time to embrace, and a time to refrain from embracing;
> a time to seek, and a time to lose;
> a time to keep, and a time to cast away;
> a time to rend, and a time to sew;
> a time to keep silence, and a time to speak;
> a time to love, and a time to hate;
> a time for war, and a time for peace.
> What gain has the worker from his toil? 3:1–9

God, with all that time which he "has given to the sons of men to be busy with," has also "put eternity into man's mind." Still, how much can man find out about what time means to God "from the beginning to the end"? Time always has the upper hand. For Koheleth time circles; he sees no spiraling toward meaning.

God proposes and disposes; he tests men, but only in order to show them they are no better than beasts: same breath, same death.

Koheleth did admit, however, "better is a poor and wise youth than an old and foolish king, who will no longer take advice."

And he admitted that two persons were better than one, because if one failed the other could lift him up.

Then God comes into the discourse again. The Preacher could not omit God because, as he saw it, God *is*. He exists. There is no way to escape considering him, since it is he who causes everything to happen, and yet there is no use expressing opinions about him. Then hastily he added, "but do you fear God." Either Koheleth was a fairly orthodox gentleman at heart or he became a shade cautious as he thought about who might be listening in.

> Guard your steps when you go to the house of God. . . . Be not rash with your mouth, nor let your heart be hasty to utter a word before God, for God is in heaven, and you upon earth; therefore let your words be few. 5:1–2

God the inscrutable, the wholly other, before whom man stands in awe, silenced by his own finite limitations. It is this sort of sudden insight embedded in an oracle on futility which helped to authenticate the book of Ecclesiastes for the canon.

Reading this discourse intently, one is caught by a certain undertow of longing in this distinguished man's disillusionment, as if he were waiting for someone to disprove his conclusions. Then he rallies his pessimism and seems to enjoy shocking his listeners as if he would startle them into *thinking* rather than merely reacting. Sometimes he barely misses being flippant but he does not numb himself to man's ultimate test: an appraisal of God and an appraisal by God. He turns toward a light too bright to bear and when it becomes blackness he still searches for the light behind God's darkened face. Apparently none of his listeners confronted him with an *experience* of God. What he could not know intellectually he might have found experientially if someone had challenged him to transcend himself in meditation or in vicarious suffering. Then the God he predicated intellectually might not have seemed entirely incomprehensible.

Whose Fault Is Futility?

Whatever Koheleth lacked it was not honesty. If he saw life as stark, he so reported it. At time he expressed his conclusion in proverbs:

He who loves money will not be satisfied with money; nor he who
loves wealth, with gain; this also is vanity. . . .
Sweet is the sleep of a laborer, whether he eats little or much; but
the surfeit of the rich will not let him sleep. 5:10, 12

He affirmed that, all in all, riches were a curse but if one had
them he had better enjoy them. Rich or poor, however, life is futile.

For who knows what is good for man while he lives the few days
of his vain life, which he passes like a shadow? 6:12

He must have held his listeners under a spell, for someone took
down his aphorisms.

> A good name is better than precious ointment;
>   and the day of death, than the day of birth. . . .
> It is better for a man to hear the rebuke of the wise
>   than to hear the song of fools. . . .

Surely there is not a righteous man on earth who does good and
never sins. 7:1, 5, 20

Women were not his open admiration; apparently he had had
disillusioning experiences:

And I found more bitter than death the woman whose heart is
snares and nets, and whose hands are fetters; he who pleases God
escapes her, but the sinner is taken by her. 7:26

There is a way to deal with kings:

Keep the king's command, and because of your sacred oath be not
dismayed; go from his presence, do not delay when the matter is
unpleasant, for he does whatever he pleases. For the word of the
king is supreme, and who may say to him, "What are you doing?"
8:2–4

Death

Death haunted the Preacher. He could neither understand it
nor leave it alone. Was he getting old and feeling nonplused with
the awareness that death must soon be dealt with firsthand; or
was he young, brilliant and fearful?

But he who is joined with all the living has hope, for a living dog is
better than a dead lion. For the living know that they will die, but

the dead know nothing, and they have no more reward; but the memory of them is lost. Their love and their hate and their envy have already perished, and they have no more for ever any share in all that is done under the sun. 9:4–6

Nevertheless a man should enjoy his bread and wine, his clean clothes, his wife, his work. He should live with zest:

Whatever your hand finds to do, do it with your might; for there is no work or thought or knowledge or wisdom in Sheol, to which you are going. 9:10

Chance

Every man needs to know that life's rewards are not dealt out on the basis of just expectations.

Again I saw that under the sun the race is not to the swift, nor the battle to the strong, nor bread to the wise, nor riches to the intelligent, nor favor to the men of skill; but time and chance happen to them all. 9:11

However melancholy life seemed, Koheleth did at least thoroughly enjoy reporting his reactions:

> Bread is made for laughter,
>   and wine gladdens life,
>   and money answers everything. . . .
> Cast your bread upon the waters,
>   for you will find it after many days. . . .

Rejoice, O young man, in your youth, and let your heart cheer you in the days of your youth; walk in the ways of your heart and the sight of your eyes. But know that for all these things God will bring you into judgment. 10:19; 11:1, 9

Old Age

The first seven verses of chapter 12 paint a highly graphic picture of old age. Scholars have pointed out that the opening phrase, "Remember also your Creator in the days of your youth," seems strange counsel coming from Koheleth, and that since a Hebrew word similar to "creator" means "grave," the passage may have been "Remember also your grave in the days of your youth." But the familiar expression is:

Remember also your Creator in the days of your youth, before the evil days come, and the years draw nigh, when you will say, "I have no pleasure in them"; before the sun and the light, and the moon, and the stars are darkened and the clouds return after the rain; in the day when the keepers of the house tremble, and the strong men are bent, and the grinders cease because they are few, and those that look through the windows are dimmed, and the doors on the street are shut; when the sound of the grinding is low, and one rises up at the voice of a bird, and all the daughters of song are brought low; they are afraid also of what is high, and terrors are in the way; the almond tree blossoms, the grasshopper drags itself along and desire fails; because man goes to his eternal home, and the mourners go about the streets; before the silver cord is snapped, or the golden bowl is broken, or the pitcher is broken at the fountain, or the wheel broken at the cistern, and the dust returns to the earth as it was, and the spirit returns to God who gave it. Vanity of vanities, says the Preacher; all is vanity. 12:1–8

And so, remembering all the dear familiar things and admitting that the cord which binds the living spirit to the body is growing tenuous, he faces eternal pointlessness. (Not for him William Cullen Bryant's youthful courage in looking at death "like one who wraps the drapery of his couch / About him, and lies down to pleasant dreams.")

Postscript

Almost at the end of the discourses there is a lift to the Preacher's message, sustaining to the spirit only as raw honesty has a certain challenge about it. But someone who knew him well, perhaps a former student or close observer, added a footnote to Koheleth's pronouncements which brought him to life as a man of unsparing uprightness:

Besides being wise, the Preacher also taught the people knowledge, weighing and studying and arranging proverbs with great care. The Preacher sought to find pleasing words, and uprightly he wrote words of truth. 12:9–10

The two closing comments, probably the emendations of a pious editor, may be the precepts which saved the book for posterity:

The end of the matter; all has been heard. Fear God, and keep his commandments; for this is the whole duty of man. For God will bring every deed into judgment, with every secret thing, whether good or evil. 12:13–14

Song of Solomon

No book in the Bible has occasioned more argument as to how it got into a canon of sacred scriptures than the Song of Songs. To an uninstructed ear the poems which make up the book sound like a collection of love poems, nothing more. Charming and exotic love poems. Delicate and passionate expressions of a man and woman who love each other. As fresh and frank as any modern lyrics but a great deal more poetic than most which make the discs. The poems do not appear to have religious connotation in the usual sense of honoring the power and majesty of God, or even in mentioning his name. The earliest editors pondered the problem of the book's inclusion when the canon was being formed and scholars have discussed it ever since.

Allegory

The probability is that at the time of the selection some theologian with literary leaning pointed out what appeared to him to be a deeper meaning than met casual appraisal. The love expressed so fervently was not that between a man and a woman but, figuratively, between God and man. In other words, an allegory. King Solomon had risen above cold facts to present this extended metaphor of the ardent heart of God longing for his chosen people as a groom longs for his bride. Acceptance of the book as allegory was also the theory of the early Christians except that they conceived the symbology as Christ's love for his church. Still others saw the rapture of intellect for the soul, and who better than Solomon, wisest of men and most prolific of Israel's poets, could write on *that* subject?

Authorship

The fact that the poems were ascribed to Solomon also weighed in their favor. In the book of Kings Solomon is credited with 1,105 poems, and his distinction as a lover, what with seven hundred wives and three hundred concubines, was proverbial. Moreover, it was Solomon who built the temple, a fact not very relevant to the poetry, but an impressive credential. To be sure, there is no textual evidence that Solomon wrote the poems, but from ancient days to the Middle Ages it was customary to accredit a literary production to a famous name if possible.

Content

Modern scholars view the book as a collection of folk poems assembled and edited in the third century B.C., as is indicated by their linguistic variations, including Aramaisms and Persian derivatives. Although the form of the text presents the work as one long poem, the internal evidence suggests several shorter poems, possibly of various dates. Both Egyptian and Syrian poetry utilizes some of the same figures of speech, even some of the same phrases. And there are precedents of custom in dramatizing royal nuptials. In certain localities of Syria and Lebanon the groom and bride become, figuratively, king and queen during the days of wedding festivities. In derivation the poems may be survivals of ancient Canaanite liturgies recited at New Year festivals, a dialogue between the deity and the cult prostitute who symbolized the consort of the deity, necessary for reproduction. Derivations are lost in conjecture.

Attempts have also been made to construct a drama of the poems with dialogue to be read by the groom, his bride and their attendants. Unfortunately, there is no plot, no movement of characters through a problem toward any kind of solution. But distinct characters there are, although their identification has to be deduced from their lines.

The reader is probably on soundest ground when he reads the poems as exactly what they appear to be: expressions of young love. To the Hebrew mind that would be no reason to exclude them from the scriptures, for the Jews never drew the sharp distinction between body and spirit that some of their contemporary cultures adduced. If life lived to the glory of God is all one piece, both times of worship and times of work, temple life and family life, citizenship in the political state and in the kingdom of heaven on earth, altruistic love for one's fellows and sexual love for one's mate, why should not poems of love be included in the canons? The conclusion may have been more felt than stated but the poems were given their place.

The Song of Songs lives not because it can be construed as a religious allegory but because poetry by its very nature lends itself to the binding of the generations in common experience. Read aloud or scanned silently, these poems are lyrically satisfying. The joy and thrill of life they reflect are reason enough to make us thankful they found their way into the canon, where they would not be lost from sight.

First Poem

The separate poems do not follow chapter divisions but are not difficult to distinguish. In the first poem the bride addresses her absent lover in the presence of her attendants. A modern presentation would probably depict her holding her lover's photograph while she apostrophizes his virtues so clear to the eyes of love. Some critics suggest that the bride has been taken into the king's harem to await his approval and is urging her lover to hasten to rescue her. Do something!

> O that you would kiss me with the
>   kisses of your mouth!
> For your love is better than wine,
>   your anointing oils are fragrant,
> your name is oil poured out;
>   therefore the maidens love you.
> Draw me after you, let us make haste.
>   The king has brought me into his chambers. 1:2–4

Her attendants, who take much the same part as the chorus in Greek drama, reply to her:

> We will exult and rejoice in you;
>   we will extol your love more than wine;
>   rightly do they love you. 1:4

The bride looks at herself with the searching eyes of one who is loved. Her olive skin makes her think of the tents of Kedar, made of soft leather.

> I am very dark, but comely,
>> O daughters of Jerusalem,
> like the tents of Kedar,
>> like the curtains of Solomon. 1:5

All at once she decides she is too dark; her brothers should not have let her work in the vineyards. She wishes she had taken better care of herself; kept her own vineyard.

> Do not gaze at me because I am swarthy,
>> because the sun has scorched me.
> My mother's sons were angry with me,
>> they made me keeper of the vineyards;
>> but, my own vineyard I have not kept! 1:6

She then wonders what is delaying her lover's arrival and she addresses his absence:

> Tell me, you whom my soul loves,
>> where you pasture your flock,
>> where you make it lie down at noon;
> for why should I be like one who wanders
>> beside the flocks of your companions? 1:7

The attendants respond:

> If you do not know,
>> O fairest among women,
> follow in the tracks of the flock,
>> and pasture your kids
>> beside the shepherds' tents. 1:8

Second Poem

It may well be a different pair of lovers presented in the second poem. The groom has arrived and speaks with his sweetheart, delighted by her radiance and pleased with her festive attire, her "neck with strings of jewels."

> Behold, you are beautiful, my love;
>> behold, you are beautiful;
>> your eyes are doves. 1:15

To which she replies:

> As an apple tree among the trees of the wood,
> so is my beloved among young men. 2:3

Third Poem

Beginning with verse 8, chapter 2, and continuing to the end of
the chapter, the third poem presents a groom arriving to summon
his bride. Phrases well known to modern playgoers are inter-
spersed:

> Catch us the foxes,
> the little foxes,
> that spoil the vineyards. . . . 2:15

Also some of the most lovely lines of the entire book.

> . . . for lo, the winter is past,
> the rain is over and gone.
> The flowers appear on the earth,
> the time of singing has come,
> and the voice of the turtledove
> is heard in our land.
> The fig tree puts forth its figs,
> and the vines are in blossom;
> they give forth fragrance. 2:11–13

Fourth Poem

The fourth poem, chapter 3, depicts the bride, or bride-to-be,
lying on her bed at night, dreaming that she is hunting for her
lover but cannot find him. Then she does find him! Perhaps she
has wakened and is imagining the scene. He is arriving like a
procession of Solomon with his attendants and wedding gifts.

> What is that coming up from the wilderness,
> like a column of smoke,
> perfumed with myrrh and frankincense,
> with all the fragrant powders of the merchant?
> Behold, it is the litter of Solomon!
> About it are sixty mighty men. . . .
> Go forth, O daughters of Zion,
> and behold King Solomon,

with the crown with which his mother crowned him
    on the day of his wedding,
    on the day of the gladness of his heart. 3:6–7, 11

Oriental Figures of Speech

A modern poet is scarcely apt to compare the flowing dark hair
of his sweetheart to "a flock of goats, moving down the slopes of
Gilead," even if he knows where Gilead is; but then, goats do not
much figure in our culture. Actually the sight of the black goats on
a hillside in the fresh breeze of morning—preferably in the distance—is a beautiful picture. Nor is a modern swain likely to
compare his love's cheeks to the "halves of a pomegranate," but
the modern swain probably never saw a freshly cut ripe pomegranate; nor would he compare the breasts of his love to the twin
fawns of a gazelle that fed among lilies. The reader has to enter
the Eastern poet's domain, where nard and saffron, calamus and
cinnamon, trees of frankincense, myrrh and aloes, spice the night
air. These are poems to be read with abandon, a lilt in the heart.
It helps also to have some background of geography and folklore;
how else could one know that the peaks of Amana, Senir and
Hermon were the mountain dwellings of a Syrian goddess?

Return, return, O Shulammite,
    return, return, that we may look upon you. 6:13

Shulammite—was this a family name, or an inhabitant of a local
village, or was the word intended for Shunammite, indicating the
beautiful Abishag, who was brought to King David to keep his poor
old bones warm on a cold night, devotion which casts a May-and-
December wistfulness? For the modern reader the poem has ambiguities, which is certainly a characteristic shared by much modern
verse, and ambiguities seem to multiply in translation.

However, there is nothing ambiguous or dated in such phrases
as: "a king is held captive in [your] tresses," "Set me as a seal
upon your heart," "turn away your eyes from me, / for they disturb
me," "I slept, but my heart was awake." And then these lines
which have spanned time:

Many waters cannot quench love,
    neither can floods drown it.

> If a man offered for love
>   all the wealth of his house,
>   it would be utterly scorned. 8:7

August Appreciation

History, law, wars, theology, customs, arguments—all the facets of early Hebrew life are in the books of the Old Testament. And then there is this lyrical poetry. The renowned second-century Jewish scholar Akiba ben Joseph, who has been called the father of rabbinical Judaism and was an authoritative voice in fixing the Old Testament canon, not only defended the inclusion of the Song of Songs in accepted scripture but expressed his personal appreciation: "The entire world, from the beginning to the end, does not outweigh the day on which the Song of Songs was given to Israel; all Scripture is holy, but the Song of Songs is the Holy of Holies."

Isaiah

Isaiah of Jerusalem

Isaiah—the name evokes the picture of a venerable prophet with flowing beard and eyes so piercing that they penetrate not only the sins of his generation but also of ours. Awed by his moral grandeur, the great painters have so pictured him. Actually, according to the book which bears his name, Isaiah was a young man of twenty when he experienced the revelation of God's holiness which elicited his total dedication. He was already married and had a small son. Moreover, he was a sophisticated member of the nobility, at ease at court. Jerusalem was his home city; Jerusalem, where trade flourished, where foreign envoys were constantly coming and going, where religious beliefs and practices were syncretized, where styles of dress and social standards were set and national policies promulgated.

Jerusalem had seldom been so prosperous. Uzziah had been king since 783 B.C. and a strong king he was. He had secured his borders, demanding loyalty from the Bedouin Ammonites on the eastern frontier and erecting watchtowers in strategic places where the nomadic Arabs based their raids. Along the western border he had built cities in Judea in place of the old fortified towns of the Philistines. In the south he had recovered Elath, the most important port on the Red Sea, where caravan routes terminated. To the north he kept close watch on Israel, while streamlining Judah's army and using it when necessary to safeguard the extended landholdings of the rich, whose poor tenants provided food for the city. If the courts were sometimes corrupt it was no more than could be expected in so prosperous and cosmopolitan a society. Sadly, in 750 B.C. Uzziah had developed leprosy and was confined to quarters while his son Jotham acted as co-regent for the ensuing eight years but Uzziah's was the powerful and respected name. And then, in 742 B.C., King Uzziah died.

Isaiah's Vision

It may have been the occasion of his lying in state in the palace and the respectful mourning of the city which took Isaiah to the temple. The temple King Solomon had built! Thinking on King Uzziah's death as he entered the temple, Isaiah may have felt the heavy hand of history upon him. Where was his country headed now? What about the talk that a powerful usurping soldier called Tiglath-pileser III was bulwarking Assyrian power? What was the will of Yahweh for Israel? God the eternal, God the covenanting ruler of his chosen people, God the just who countenanced no brooking of his holy will. Was Yahweh truly *here,* indwelling the temple, available in time of need?

Standing rapt in the inner court Isaiah watched a shaft of light as it struck the temple wall. What others, great in Jewish history, had stood as he was standing in overwhelming reverence? Amos surely; and Hosea—towering prophets whose pronouncements had influenced his boyhood. Yahweh always seemed to provide his people with a prophet. Suddenly wonder gave way to amazement, reality to Reality.

> In the year that King Uzziah died I saw the Lord sitting upon a throne, high and lifted up; and his train filled the temple. Above him stood the seraphim; each had six wings: with two he covered his face, and with two he covered his feet, and with two he flew. And one called to another and said:
> > "Holy, holy, holy is the Lord of hosts;
> > the whole earth is full of his glory." 6:1–3

The foundation of the temple shook. A tremor of earthquake, perhaps, which heightened the sense of the immanence of the Holy. Isaiah was transfixed, revealed to himself. The chasm between him and the utterly pure, the transcendently radiant, was too wide. He knew himself for a lost soul, "a man of unclean lips," living among people likewise unclean. The holiness of God!

But the real miracle was still to come. A seraph took up tongs from the altar and lifted one of the white-hot stones used to transfer the altar fire; with it he touched Isaiah on the lips, his trembling human lips. "Behold . . . your guilt is taken away, and your sin forgiven." Unbelievable! But it happened to *him*. Only a very great soul can accept absolute forgiveness. The rest of us return again and again, often in agonizing regret, to the memory of our sin. For Isaiah a total cleansing had occurred. Life was made new. And he was only twenty.

The next experience followed inevitably. He sensed the need around him. "And I heard the voice of the Lord saying, 'Whom shall I send, and who will go for us?' Then I said, 'Here I am! Send me.'"

His Commission

Of course! Naturally! Details of the commissions were for the Lord to disclose. "Go, and say to this people . . ." but instead of encouraging Isaiah the Lord cautioned him that although the people had normal eyes and ears they were currently unable to see or hear. They did not understand, which meant that they could not turn to be healed. To be given a message and then forewarned that it would not be heeded—this was a tough assignment. How long could Judah's lack of comprehension last? The answer was doleful: it would last until the cities were laid waste and the land made utterly desolate. Isaiah knew he faced cause for discouragement. But that coal which had touched his lips had also nerved his soul. He could deliver whatever message the Lord gave him for as long as the Lord continued to speak.

From that day on, Isaiah's message proved time-transcending and one reason for its far-reaching vitality is the fact that he was not only a prophet of stature but a poet of equal stature. A large part of his message is recorded as poetry, stirring to read aloud, easy to memorize, quotable. Through the centuries the music of synagogue and church has incorporated many passages; and preachers seem always to have had a fondness for lifting texts from his discourses. Perhaps the taproots of religion and poetry draw from the same springs.

The Book of Isaiah

Because Isaiah's calling came at an early age and he continued to speak out for more than forty years does not mean that his book is a coherent composition written in time sequence. Actually it is an anthology not all written by the same man or even in the same century. Scholars agree that there was a prophet named Isaiah living in Jerusalem in the troubled last half of the eighth and early-seventh centuries B.C. To him belong the first thirty-nine chapters of the book. But there was also a prophet, unnamed, who reflects the time of the Persian King Cyrus in the sixth century. Because his pronouncements were later recorded on the same scroll with the pronouncements of Isaiah of Jerusalem, scholars call him Deutero-Isaiah and credit him with at least chapters 40 through 55. Many students of the text also predicate a third Isaiah, called for purposes of identification Trito-Isaiah, indicating the writer or writers of the miscellaneous final eleven chapters of the book. The political background of the book we know as Isaiah covers more than two centuries and has had many corrections as disciples and scribes underscored and updated the messages they were copying and promulgating.

His Message

Although the book of Isaiah is an anthology, there is continuity of message. One way and another the poet-prophets kept saying that it is God who controls events and uses them for his purposes; that when his people stray he will utilize whatever means he needs—even foreign conquest and exile—for their chastening; that he is relentlessly just but also compassionate. Much of the early part of the book is given to oracles of woe, to dire foresight and an almost cosmic sense of reprisal. Later portions are more joyous. A reader cannot lay the book down without feeling that the door will one day open on a bright new world.

First Isaiah

First Isaiah's collection of pronouncements is captioned with an introductory statement:

> The vision of Isaiah the son of Amoz, which he saw concerning Judah and Jerusalem in the days of Uzziah, Jotham, Ahaz, and Hezekiah, kings of Judah. 1:1

His Oracles

Five chapters of oracles follow, the first calling on Judah to remember that they are the people of the Lord, who does not need their offerings but awaits their justice and righteousness.

> ". . . The ox knows its owner,
>   and the ass its master's crib;
> but Israel does not know,
>   my people does not understand." . . .
> "What to me is the multitude of your sacrifices?"
>   says the Lord;
> "I have had enough of burnt offerings of rams
>   and the fat of fed beasts. . . .
> Wash yourselves; make yourselves clean . . .
> cease to do evil,
>   learn to do good;
> seek justice,
>   correct oppression;
> defend the fatherless,
>   plead for the widow . . .
> though your sins are like scarlet,
>   they shall be as white as snow;
> though they are red like crimson,
>   they shall become like wool. . . ." 1:3, 11, 16–18

The second oracle stresses the new age, which shall be the age of peace, following the judgment of the Lord.

> He shall judge between the nations . . .
>   and they shall beat their swords into plowshares,
>   and their spears into pruning hooks;
>   nation shall not lift up sword against nation,
>   neither shall they learn war any more. 2:4

The third describes anarchy in Jerusalem, with "the mighty man and the soldier, / the judge and the prophet, / the diviner and the elder," the men of distinction, all taken away by conquerors and only the inexperienced left in control. What else could the corruption of Judah have produced except ruin?

". . . What do you mean by crushing my people,
   by grinding the face of the poor?" says the Lord God of hosts. 3:15

Evidently Isaiah also had small regard for the society dames and damsels who joined the afternoon parade of fine clothes, those who

>   . . . Walk with outstretched necks . . .
>   mincing along as they go,
>   tinkling with their feet. . . . 3:16

All that finery, the pendants and bracelets, armlets, sashes, amulets, signet rings and nose rings, festal robes, mantles, cloaks and handbags, turbans and veils will be lost to them.

Song of the Vineyard

The fifth chapter, an allegory known as the song of the vineyard, is Isaiah's love song for the vineyard he himself had planted and tended, anticipating a yield of fine grapes but harvesting only small, wild grapes. Then his call to become a prophet of the Lord picks up the story of his life when he took his young son and went to caution King Ahaz against joining with the kings of Israel and Syria in defying Assyria. Ahaz, both afraid to join the alliance and afraid not to join; "his heart and the heart of his people shook as the trees of the forest shake before the wind." Isaiah admonished him that he must not fear Israel and Syria, for both countries were doomed and within sixty-five years Ephraim—a name often used for Israel—"will no longer be a people." Let Ahaz ask for a sign from the Lord. But Ahaz piously refused to "put the Lord to the test," whereupon Isaiah continued his dire prognostications including the fact that the land before whose two kings Ahaz was in dread would be deserted and Assyria would dominate Judah. But eventually the way of the Lord would prevail and the "land beyond the Jordan, Galilee of the nations," would become a glorious place.

> The people who walked in darkness
>   have seen a great light. . . .
> For to us a child is born,
>   to us a son is given;
> and the government will be upon his shoulder,
>   and his name will be called
> "Wonderful Counselor, Mighty God,
>   Everlasting Father, Prince of Peace."
> Of the increase of his government and of peace
>   there will be no end. . . . 9:2, 6–7

The messianic king would reign!

Events moved on and Isaiah's messages of woe increased. Tiglath-pileser III captured Carchemish in 738 B.C., Damascus in 732 B.C.; Israel's King Menahem paid tribute. But the Lord had punishment in store for "the arrogant boasting of the king of Assyria and his haughty pride." Far in the future Isaiah again saw a brighter time, when a descendant of David would lead his people.

> And the spirit of the Lord shall rest upon him . . .
> with righteousness he shall judge the poor. . . .
> The wolf shall dwell with the lamb,
>   and the leopard shall lie down with the kid,
> and the calf and the lion and the fatling together,
>   and a little child shall lead them . . .
> for the earth shall be full of the knowledge of the Lord
>   as the waters cover the sea. 11:2, 4, 6, 9

An oracle against Babylon is apparently an insertion, because the new Babylonian power had not yet risen but a time was foreseen when even Babylon would have become "a possession of the hedgehog . . . and I will sweep it with the broom of destruction." Oracles follow against Assyria, Moab, Damascus, Egypt, Babylon, Edom, Arabia, Tyre and Sidon. Three chapters, 24 to 27, are often referred to as the "Isaiah apocalypse" because they depict the time when universal judgment would be meted out and Judah would again sing praises.

> Thou dost keep him in perfect peace,
>   whose mind is stayed on thee,
>   because he trusts in thee. 26:3

Relevance to History

A factual outline of the rise and fall of nations during the troubled times of Isaiah reveals the astonishing relevance of his pronouncements. People who heard him must have marveled and quaked at his foresight. The women of Jerusalem were probably furious when their husbands brought home his latest pronouncements, copied and distributed by the student scribes who followed him about, for some of the husbands took Isaiah seriously, or anyway fearfully, unable to laugh off a man whom kings called in for advice. He talked to people of all walks of life with equal scorn and equal concern. For instance, the men in the king's merchant marine and the war fleet: "Your tackle hangs loose; / it cannot hold the mast firm in its place, / or keep the sail spread out."

But just when he had frightened half of Jerusalem, including the men in high places who had to make final judgments as to allies and the collection of taxes and tribute, he went apart for a quiet appraisal of the future and reported that a time was coming when even the desert would rejoice and blossom. The wonderful thirty-fifth chapter of Isaiah! Let the people who knew all too well what drought and intense heat could do to their crops, what wild beasts when hungry could do to their flocks, what it meant to go to bed in fear and waken to the new day still in fear, sing of their future. A day would arrive when the desert would blossom, the lame walk, the blind see.

> And the ransomed of the Lord shall return,
>   and come to Zion with singing . . .
> they shall obtain joy and gladness,
>   and sorrow and sighing shall flee away. 35:10

Chapters 36 to 39 constitute a historical appendix, duplicating the story in Second Kings; a story too climactic not to be retold by some of Isaiah's followers, especially when it was Isaiah whom the king called on when the outlook was darkest. It is all here, a recapitulation of these troubled times and Isaiah's participation in them.

By the time the messages of this first Isaiah ceased, the venerable prophet was an old man, just as the artists have depicted him; a wise, courageous, undiminished man of God who had devoted his whole lifetime to his commission. And throughout, a poet. So does the word of God indwell the words of men.

Second Isaiah

It was in the twelfth century A.D. that a scholarly rabbi first questioned the unity of the book of Isaiah, and in the eighteenth century that two German scholars pointed out the differences in political background, style, thought, and vocabulary between the first thirty-nine chapters and the rest of the book. Where Isaiah of Jerusalem concerned himself with Assyria and its conquests, Second Isaiah referred to Cyrus, king of Persia, who had conquered Babylonia—where the people of Judah were interned —in the sixth century B.C. Dating the three sections of the book with relative accuracy enhances the meaning of the messages to the people who heard them but does not change their amazing relevancy for our day.

The relevancy of Isaiah to the continuing problems of man in a changing society has been underscored by the Qumran Scrolls, another example of the way in which modern scholarship and skillful archaeological research have increased our understanding of the Bible. The Qumran Scrolls are an unprecedentedly large collection of whole and fragmentary scrolls, more than six hundred, found between 1947 and the mid-fifties in caves near the Dead Sea, where they were hidden in pottery jars during the threatening last days before the final fall of the Temple in A.D. 70. About a quarter of the find consists of copies of Hebrew scripture, the rest being liturgical works, a *Manual of Discipline,* theological commentaries, eschatological surmises, all tinged with a note of joy rising from the dedication of the monastic community of Essenes—a Jewish sect—then living at Qumran. All the books of the Old Testament except Esther are represented in whole or part, with more copies of Isaiah than of any other book; some of them fragmentary and with some textual variation. One copy of Isaiah is a twenty-four-foot scroll of fifty-four columns. Over all, the Qumran findings are probably the most significant contribution to biblical scholarship in this century. And the impression which the book of Isaiah made on the Qumran community in their own perilous times speaks for the invincible spirit with which Isaiah has inspired succeeding generations, including our own.

When Second Isaiah wrote, Jerusalem was practically an abandoned city. The mood of the exiled people was not one of hope, and any confidence they tried to summon as to their ultimate return was strictly a matter of faith. Where the prophet delivered his pronouncements is problematical. In Babylon a Hebrew prophet would not be likely to speak in the courtyard of the conqueror's temple, or in the palace domain.

Facing the Future

The theme of his message was that the people of Israel had brought the punishment of exile upon themselves, since Yahweh was a just God, but he was also a God of mercy and forgiveness who intended their ultimate liberation. It was this consolation that highlighted his first message, the famous fortieth chapter. The scene depicted is the council of heaven, from which voices are heard.

> Comfort, comfort my people,
>   says your God.
> Speak tenderly to Jerusalem,
>   and cry to her
> that her warfare is ended,
>   that her iniquity is pardoned,
> that she has received from the Lord's hand
>   double for all her sins. 40:1–2

Pardon—an incredible relief to anyone who has ever felt estranged from his God; a restoration to an open relationship. Understandably, great souls of many centuries have turned to this chapter. John Brown read it in his prison at Harper's Ferry; Luther pored over it in his fortress at Salzburg; Oliver Cromwell turned to it for strength; Daniel Webster sought its comfort when he was broken in spirit; Tennyson claimed it as one of the five great classics of the Old Testament; both Wordsworth and Tennyson referred to its influence on their styles; Handel opened his oratorio

The Messiah with the tenor voice singing out, "Comfort ye, comfort ye my people, saith your God."

Conditions are soon to be changed, Isaiah affirmed,

> ". . . And the glory of the Lord shall be revealed,
>> and all flesh shall see it together,
>> for the mouth of the Lord has spoken." . . .
> He will feed his flock like a shepherd,
>> he will gather the lambs in his arms,
> he will carry them in his bosom,
>> and gently lead those that are with young. . . .
> He gives power to the faint,
>> and to him who has no might he increases strength . . .
> but they who wait for the Lord shall renew their strength,
>> they shall mount up with wings like eagles,
> they shall run and not be weary,
>> they shall walk and not faint. 40:5, 11, 29, 31

Embedded in the eleven chapters, 43 to 53, are four dissertations known as the "servant songs," in which the figure of a servant of God (in the sense of one who waits upon the Lord's direction) accepts and carries out his appointment. In the first song it is Yahweh who speaks in regal dignity and loving encouragement. In the second and third servant songs it is the servant who speaks. Aware that he was called to his task from his very inception, he accepts his calling in awe and wonder, incredulous that it should be he to whom the Lord has made his promises known. He knows, too, he can speak to those in need because he himself has been answered.

> "I will give you as a light to the nations,
>> that my salvation may reach to the end of the earth." . . .
> Sing for joy, O heavens, and exult, O earth;
>> break forth, O mountains, into singing!
> For the Lord has comforted his people. . . .
> The Lord God has given me
>> the tongue of those who are taught,
> that I may know how to sustain with a word
>> him that is weary. . . .
> How beautiful upon the mountains
>> are the feet of him who brings good tidings,
> who publishes peace. . . . 49:6, 13; 50:4; 52:7

In the fourth servant song the speaker is unidentified. He may be Israel itself personified, or a literal person, past or future. He has suffered for his very faithfulness; he has accepted the wounds of others.

> He was despised and rejected by men;
>   a man of sorrows, and acquainted with grief. . . .
> But he was wounded for our transgressions,
>   he was bruised for our iniquities. . . .
> All we like sheep have gone astray . . .
> and the Lord has laid on him the iniquity of us all. 53:3, 5–6

Chapter 54 is a hymn of encouragement and assurance to Israel. God's people must not think of themselves as small just because their number is few and their present position ignominious; nor dare they allow the gods of their conquerors to appear mightier than Yahweh, who is the God of both past and future. (This is the chapter which gave William Carey his world vision.)

> Enlarge the place of your tent,
>   and let the curtains of your habitations be stretched out;
> hold not back, lengthen your cords and strengthen your stakes. . . .
> For the mountains may depart and the hills be removed,
>   but my steadfast love shall not depart from you. . . . 54:2, 10

Chapter 55, a hymn of triumph and joy, follows; some of its passages are as often set to music as any verses in the entire scripture, a fact which would surely not seem strange to Second Isaiah.

> "Ho, every one who thirsts, come to the waters;
> and he who has no money,
>   come, buy and eat! . . .
> Behold, you shall call nations that you know not. . . .
> Seek the Lord while he may be found,
>   call upon him while he is near;
> let the wicked forsake his way,
>   and the unrighteous man his thoughts;
> let him return to the Lord, that he may have mercy on him,
>   and to our God, for he will abundantly pardon. . . .
> For as the heavens are higher than the earth,
>   so are my ways higher than your ways
>   and my thoughts than your thoughts. . . ." 55:1, 5–7, 9

Throughout his writing, which may originally have been spontaneous preachments and odes of exultation, Second Isaiah is the most enthusiastic of prophets; never dull or wordy, always forceful; insistent in his joy, contagiously triumphant in spirit. Moreover, he felt the universality of God. For him Yahweh was no longer a Hebrew God but the God of all peoples, whose tenderness was alert to all who turned to him.

". . . for my house shall be called a house of prayer
    for all peoples. . . .
I dwell in the high and holy place,
    and also with him who is of a contrite and humble spirit. . . .
Fasting like yours this day
    will not make your voice to be heard on high.
Is such the fast that I choose,
    a day for a man to humble himself? . . .
Is it not to share your bread with the hungry,
    and bring the homeless poor into your house . . . ?
Then shall your light break forth like the dawn,
    and your healing shall spring up speedily. . . .
Then you shall call, and the Lord will answer;
    you shall cry, and he will say, Here I am." 56:7; 57:15; 58:4–5, 7–9

Some of these latter postulates are credited by careful analysts to the third author, Trito-Isaiah, for the substance of the last eleven chapters seems to belong to the postrestoration period, when the Hebrews were back in their home country, rebuilding the temple. It was then all the nations, not only Israel, whom God was calling to repentance. These latter oracles need to be read entire, because their spirit is cumulative.

Arise, shine; for your light has come,
    and the glory of the Lord has risen upon you. . . .
And nations shall come to your light,
    and kings to the brightness of your rising . . .
you shall call your walls Salvation,
    and your gates Praise.
The sun shall be no more
    your light by day,
nor for brightness shall the moon

give light to you by night;
but the Lord will be your everlasting light. . . . 60:1, 3, 18–19

The prophet constantly felt both his own inadequacies and the wonder of the Lord's response:

Yet, O Lord, thou art our Father;
we are the clay, and thou art our potter;
we are all the work of thy hand. 64:8

He heard and reported the Lord's answers.

". . . Before they call I will answer,
while they are yet speaking I will hear. . . .
As one whom his mother comforts,
so I will comfort you. . . ." 65:24; 66:13

Then in swift prose sentences he pictured the Lord revealing his glory to the nations who would one day assemble in Jerusalem, where even some gentiles might be accepted as priests! Then . . . "all flesh shall come to worship before me, says the Lord."

Jeremiah

Anyone who expects to make time-place sense of the book of Jeremiah at first reading has to be either a scholar, a psychic, or disappointed. The facts as he faced them are largely incorporated into his text but not always in sequence. Every political move seems to have provoked from him either brokenhearted protestations or wrathful accusations. His secretary, Baruch, took notes and eventually compiled them but the task was not easy, because Jeremiah's mind operated on two levels of consciousness: he had symbolic visions and veridical premonitions, and he also had an astute analytical approach to political affairs along with unusual common sense. Moreover, some of his pronouncements were made in vigorous prose but others in lyrical poetry. In either case he used telling figures of speech and was adept with historical allusions. His moods were mercurial. While the armies of the ancient world were traveling rough terrain, the roughest terrain was mapped across the mountaintops and depressions of this dedicated prophet's mind.

Political Background

Jeremiah lived in the last half of the seventh century B.C. and the first quarter of the sixth century, when the whole world as he knew it was in crisis. On every side the great political powers were changing position, shifting dominance. When he began his career the Assyrians were at the peak of their power, with the Chaldeans edging toward the second dominance of Babylon; the Egyptians were determined to lose neither territory nor prestige;

the Medes, south of the Caspian, were already extending their territory and making alliance with Lydia, which would lead eventually to a much more advantageous coalition with Persia. Obviously none of these moves was mapped in advance, so Jeremiah had to guess and deduce just as kings and their advisers were doing.

His Call

Jeremiah was born into a priestly family in Anathoth, a town a few miles northeast of Jerusalem, and probably expected to become a priest himself. He must have heard the words of the prophets Amos, Hosea and Micah read aloud and occasionally have gone to the temple in Jerusalem for festivals. The year 621 B.C. probably had considerable impact on his life because that was the year King Josiah instituted his great reforms based on the discovery of the main portions of Deuteronomy and a renewal of commitment to the law of Moses. Jeremiah's was the kind of mind which would look searchingly at reform, question motivations, and finally stake his life on his convictions. When not yet twenty he realized he was called to a prophet's career.

He recorded simply that the word of the Lord came to him in the thirteenth year of Josiah's reign (627 B.C.). It came with that awesome impact familiar to "the called" in every generation. The Lord reminded him that he had been consecrated even before his birth but Jeremiah, at nineteen, was afraid of his youth: how could one so inexperienced speak out and be heard?

Reassurance from the Lord came quickly. "See, I have set you this day over nations and over kingdoms, . . . to destroy and to overthrow, to build and to plant." Not only to overthrow—a calling congenial to the young—but "to build and to plant." So there he was—dedicated, doubting, ready to follow, afraid he was overestimating himself, waiting. His eye caught sight of a branch of flowering almond, popularly called the wakeful tree because it was the first to bloom in the spring. Even so, said the Lord, the wakeful one, "I am watching over my word to perform it." (Centuries later, St. Francis observed, "I said to the almond tree, 'Speak to me of God,' and the almond tree blossomed.")

Jeremiah's Visions

Almost at once, a test came to Jeremiah in the form of an awareness of coming events. This kind of subjective discernment comes in various ways to some perceptive individuals. To those who have it, the past, present and future become curiously concurrent, so that on occasion they can sense the direction events are taking. In this instance Jeremiah fell into a reverie and watched pictures forming: a boiling pot, facing away from the north, a symbol which he took to mean that trouble was coming from the north (Assyria); punishment for the people of Judah because "they have burned incense to other gods, and worshiped the works of their own hands." (A threat which hangs over successive generations.) Jeremiah was instructed to stand strong, like an iron pillar, in order to hold out against the disbelief and antagonism of kings, princes, priests and people. Strength flowed into him and he was ready when the Lord added a command, "Go and proclaim in the hearing of Jerusalem . . ." followed by a moving reminder of the Lord's past leading and present dependability. He realized that a hard life lay ahead; a lonely life, a daring life, a defeated life, a fruitful life. Time played out his premonition against a cyclorama of fast-moving international events.

Cyclorama of International Events

The politically incredible happened. In 614 B.C. the great city of Ashur, just south of Nineveh, fell to the advancing Medes; in 612 invincible Nineveh surrendered to the Medes and Chaldeans, now more commonly called the Babylonians, as they moved toward the city of Babylon. In 609 Pharaoh Neco started north to reinforce the Assyrian army. King Josiah misread the situation, met Neco at Megiddo and in the fierce fighting was killed. Jeremiah had warned him against the venture and pressed for keeping Judah out of the struggle but his pronouncements were ignored. At Haran, north of Nineveh, the Babylonians soon defeated both the Egyptians and the Assyrians. As a world power, Assyria was finished.

All the rest of Jeremiah's career has to be seen against the international background outlined in the book of Second Kings and against the theology of Second Kings, for Jeremiah was convinced that the Lord used the great nations to chastise his own people for their apostasy. Yahweh was the God whose might was matched by his holiness, whose people were made in his likeness and were expected to remain true to their heritage. They had failed, and if they continued to follow lesser gods, who demanded lesser rectitude, then they would fall to the conqueror who acted as the scourge of God. By word and deed and daring, Jeremiah reiterated his message.

Events moved fast in the next twenty years as Judah's independence oozed away with the decadence of religion and the drain of tribute. King after bewildered king—five in all—proved unequal to the leadership of Judah, until in July 587 B.C. the walls of Jerusalem were breached and Zedekiah fled in the night only to be overtaken, blinded and carried in chains to Babylon. A month later, the city was put to the torch, its walls leveled, important officials executed, and the rest of the population, except for the most menial and the very poor, deported to Babylon. All during this mounting political turmoil Jeremiah preached, prophesied, lamented, threatened, promised and hoped.

The first twenty-five chapters to the book of Jeremiah are mainly an anthology of the prophet's oracles, or communications of divine will, many of them in poetic form. The next twenty chapters, 26–45, tell the story of his life in prose. The final six chapters, 46–51, which may or may not be Jeremiah's, constitute a collection of oracles—largely threats and promises—addressed to surrounding nations.

The pictorial quality of his communications must have helped to hold his audiences. When passers-by heard him call the Assyrians lions roaring down upon them, they stopped, laid down their burdens and listened. When he compared the listeners themselves, often apostate worshipers of Baal, to "a wild ass used to the wilderness, in her heat sniffing the wind," unable to restrain her lust, they became fearful. And when he accused them of supporting temple prostitution, preparing offerings for Baal, and looking to cultic deities less morally demanding than Yahweh to monitor their crops and prosper their bargains, they either cringed or resented the prophet bitterly.

> "Return, O faithless sons,
>   I will heal your faithlessness." . . .
> "Circumcise yourselves to the Lord,
>   remove the foreskin of your hearts,
>   O men of Judah and inhabitants of Jerusalem;
> lest my wrath go forth like fire,
>   and burn with none to quench it,
>   because of the evil of your doings." 3:22; 4:4

Those were hard words to hear but harder to forget. Men went home and looked apprehensively at the offerings their wives were preparing for the lesser gods; they themselves scurried to the temple. But Jeremiah followed them there thundering out that a gesture of obeisance and an offering to Yahweh were not enough. There was the matter of honesty, integrity, faithfulness.

> Run to and fro in the streets of Jerusalem,
>   look and take note!
> Search her squares to see
>   if you can find a man,
> one who does justice
>   and seeks truth. . . . 5:1

If such a one could be found the Lord would pardon the iniquities of the people. But Jeremiah has to report failure.

> Then I said, "These are only the poor . . .
> for they do not know the way of the Lord. . . .
> I will go to the great,
>   and will speak to them. . . .
> But they all alike had broken the yoke,
>   they had burst the bonds. . . ." 5:4–5

Therefore they should be slain by beasts of prey: the lion, wolf and leopard. Jeremiah knew the animals of the region. Judah was primarily farming country, herdsmen's land, bordered by a desolate wilderness of crags and rocks, sand and untillable open stretches where nothing more succulent than stubby camel grass would grow. The animals and birds he mentioned are indicative of the countryside around Jerusalem: lions, camels, wild asses, cattle, sheep, lambs, heifers, bulls, eagles, leopards, serpents, jackals, hinds, wild dogs, storks, turtledoves, swallows, eagles, cranes, speckled birds of prey, doves, locusts, gadflies; even scarecrows in the cucumber fields! And of course horses of war and the "well-fed lusty stallions."

Parables in Action

Jeremiah was quick to see parables both in nature and in the human scene. Sometimes he acted out the parables. Desperate to make the people understand the inviolability of the Lord's commands and the inexorableness of the doom of those who forsook the right way, he demonstrated the import of his message. At the Lord's behest, he bought a loincloth, put it on, then traveled all the way to the Euphrates River, where he hid it in the cleft of a rock, allowed it to remain for several days, then removed it and found it mildewed and half rotten. The Lord's pronouncement was that the people "who stubbornly follow their own heart and have gone after other gods . . . shall be like this waistcloth, which is good for nothing." Judah was meant to cling to the Lord "as the waistcloth clings to the loins of a man . . . that they might be for me a people, a name, a praise, and a glory, but they would not listen." Sheer poetry, those words, as well as stinging rebuke—"be for me a people, a name, a praise, and a glory."

On another occasion Jeremiah was directed by the Lord to go down to a potter's house, where he watched a skilled workman turning out an ornamental jar probably intended for temple use, but the potter's hand slipped and the jar was spoiled. Unperturbed, the potter kept the wheel whirring and changed the shape of the vessel. Jeremiah turned to the crowd. In the same way, said the Lord, God could remake his errant people if they would only put themselves wholly and repentantly in his hands.

The Lord next put it into Jeremiah's mind to buy an earthen flask fresh from the potter's hand and call together "some of the elders of the people and some of the senior priests" at a certain city gate, then smash the vessel before their eyes. "Thus says the Lord of hosts: So will I break this people and this city, as one breaks a potter's vessel, so that it can never be mended." The ring of pottery breaking against stone was dramatic, frightening. The priest Pashhur, chief officer of the temple, had Jeremiah beaten and put in stocks. But as soon as he was released the uncowed prophet announced the priest's own fearful future when the king of Babylon would eventually take over the temple and Pashhur and all his house would be taken into captivity. The story of that broken potter's flask, its meaning and the public threat to the priest got around.

Much later, when King Zedekiah was planning to revolt against the suzerainty of Babylon, the Lord instructed Jeremiah to make it clear to the people that they would suffer not only for Zedekiah's mistaken actions but for their own sins. By way of illustration, Jeremiah made himself yoke-bars and fastened them about his own neck with thongs as a sign of the yoke of Babylon. Incensed, the popular prophet Hananiah grabbed the yoke-bars and broke them, swearing that within two years the yoke of Babylon would likewise be broken. No doubt the people cheered Hananiah and Zedekiah beamed but Jeremiah decreed, on behalf of the Lord, that Hananiah himself would die within the year. Which he did. And Jeremiah made himself a new yoke of iron to stress his warning.

Temple Sermon

The intent of Jeremiah's sermons was to reveal the people to themselves and then to reveal God's revulsion at what was transpiring. In chapters 7 and 8 the discourse known as his temple sermon is recorded—whether all one discourse or related discourses editorialized into one is not important. The Lord instructed Jeremiah to "Stand in the gate of the Lord's house, and proclaim there this word . . ." which included a warning against the people's trusting in the presence of the temple among them as if it were their safeguard, when actually their only safety lay in reforming their conduct. Desecrated by idolatry, the temple itself would be destroyed.

> "Will you steal, murder, commit adultery, swear falsely, burn incense to Baal, and go after other gods that you have not known, and then come and stand before me in this house, which is called by my name, and say, 'We are delivered!'—only to go on doing all these abominations? Has this house, which is called by my name, become a den of robbers in your eyes? Behold, I myself have seen it, says the Lord." 7:9–11

Jeremiah evoked so strong a sense of the presence of the Lord
that his listeners feared lest the temple actually be destroyed. They
would gladly have removed him from the scene permanently. In
another sermon, however, he tempered his threats of disaster with
a tremendous peroration on the nature of the truly wise man,
whom the Lord unfailingly blesses.

> Thus says the Lord: "Let not the wise man glory in his wisdom, let
> not the mighty man glory in his might, let not the rich man glory in
> his riches; but let him who glories glory in this, that he understands
> and knows me, that I am the Lord who practice steadfast love, jus-
> tice, and righteousness in the earth; for in these things I delight,
> says the Lord." 9:23–24

> "But this command I gave them, 'Obey my voice, and I will be your
> God, and you shall be my people; and walk in all the way that I
> command you, that it may be well with you!' " 7:23

Laments

In spite of his insight Jeremiah was an altogether human
prophet, a lonely man, sometimes melancholy in his desire for
companionship and approval. Having been instructed by the Lord
not to take a wife, he knew that sons and daughters would never
be his. He must be the Lord's instrument, instantly available. So,
having no one else to whom to turn when his best efforts failed,
he turned directly to the Lord. Six of his very personal prayers,
commonly called Jeremiah's laments, are recorded. In the first, he
expressed his astonishment to discover a plot against his life when
he knew himself to be "like a gentle lamb"; why then should he
be led to slaughter? In the second, he regretted having been born;
his was a life of rectitude, he affirmed, so that the Lord's words
"became to me a joy and the daylight of my heart"; why then
did his pain increase? Is God a deceitful brook, whose waters fail?
To his agony of frustration the Lord replied with reassurance that
if he continued to speak "what is precious, and not what is worthless," he would be as the Lord's own mouth. "And I will make
you to this people a fortified wall of bronze." Promise enough; also
a supreme demand for constancy.

In his third lament Jeremiah bypassed the need of lesser comfort and pleaded:

> Heal me, O Lord, and I shall be healed;
>   save me, and I shall be saved;
>   for thou art my praise. 17:14

In the fourth lament he again resented the people's recompense of evil for good. The fifth followed a literal beating and a night spent in the stocks, while the sixth curses the day on which he was born.

> Why did I come forth from the womb
>   to see toil and sorrow,
>   and spend my days in shame? 20:18

All the laments called down vengeance on his enemies. In his discouraged moments he was sometimes an angry prophet, not only angry in behalf of the Lord but angry in his own proud masculine heart because he was constantly mistreated for doing his duty. Let those who persecuted him suffer!

> O Lord of hosts, who triest the righteous,
>   who seest the heart and the mind,
> let me see thy vengeance upon them,
>   for to thee have I committed my cause. 20:12

Personal forgiveness was at such times beyond his thinking.

Occasionally, mercurial King Zedekiah begged Jeremiah to intercede with the Lord for Judah. The prophet's response was that the Lord had decreed the victory to Babylon, as God's instrument of chastisement. "Thus says the Lord: Behold, I set before you the way of life and the way of death." Those who stayed in the city would die by sword, famine, pestilence; those who accepted God's punishment and surrendered to Babylon should have life as their prize of war.

Later, after Nebuchadnezzar had taken King Jeconiah to Babylon in the first contingent of exiles, "together with the princes of Judah, the craftsmen, and the smiths," Jeremiah had a vision of two baskets of figs placed before the temple, one containing good, ripe figs, the other spoiled figs. The good figs represented the exiles, he interpreted, whom God would eventually bless, "and they shall be my people and I will be their God," but the bad figs represented those who held out against Babylon as God's instrument of punishment.

To the first exiles already in Babylon he wrote a letter exhorting them in the name of the Lord to make the most of their situation:

". . . Build houses and live in them; plant gardens and eat their produce. Take wives and have sons and daughters . . . multiply there, and do not decrease. But seek the welfare of the city where I have sent you into exile, and pray to the Lord on its behalf, for in its welfare you will find your welfare. . . . For thus says the Lord: When seventy years are completed for Babylon, I will visit you, and I will fulfil to you my promise and bring you back to this place. . . . You will seek me and find me; when you seek me with all your heart . . . and I will bring you back to the place from which I sent you into exile. . . ." 29:5-7, 10, 13-14

This farsighted letter brought a scathing response from a prominent exile name Shemaiah to the general secretary of the temple in Jerusalem, calling on him to put the madman Jeremiah in stocks and collar. The temple official, friendly to Jeremiah, read him the letter. Jeremiah's response was a second letter to the exiles, expressing the Lord's decree that Shemaiah would not have a single descendant who would live to see the glad day of the return.

Gradually Jeremiah's preaching was curtailed and he was not allowed to enter even the temple courtyard. So, at the suggestion of the Lord, he wrote a book! When the papyrus roll was completed his loyal secretary Baruch bravely took it to the temple and read it aloud to an assembly of dignitaries who had been summoned to consider some way out of the country's desperate situation. Jeremiah's words were barbed. Accusations against Judah's leadership were documented, hard to sidestep, impossible to deny. The listeners were shaken. Such talk was treason. Or was it—could it be—the actual mind of the Lord! The scroll was reported to the princes also in plenary session and they also listened to its reading. Their first reaction was to warn Baruch and Jeremiah they had better go into hiding; their next, that the scroll must be read to the king. So the scroll was read to Zedekiah as he sat by a brazier of fire in his elaborate winter palace. He listened in scorn and as each section of the scroll was finished he took his own penknife, cut the section off and in spite of the protestations of his Cabinet threw it into the fire. Then he ordered the arrest of Jeremiah and Baruch, but how could men be arrested when they had taken the advice of the temple dignitaries and disappeared? The destruction of the scroll should have been discouragement enough for both Jeremiah and Baruch but neither they nor the Lord were about to be defeated by one weak king. The Lord ordered the book rewritten and rewritten it was, possibly being finished after Jeremiah was carried off to Egypt.

It was while the siege of Jerusalem was temporarily suspended that Jeremiah decided to go home to Anathoth to receive his share of an inheritance; strictly his private business. But when he went to pass through the city gate he was arrested, accused of deserting to the Babylonians, flogged and jailed. Surreptitiously King Zedekiah sent for him, pleading for an oracle concerning the city's fate. The answer was assurance that the king would be delivered into the hands of Babylon. Even in custody Jeremiah continued to advocate surrender to the Babylonians, until finally some of the princes demanded his death as a traitor. Reluctantly consenting, Zedekiah ordered him thrown into a deep pit, where he sank in the mire.

Then comes one of the most poignant and memorable incidents of his entire career. A black man, an Ethiopian, named Ebedmelech—let his name be remembered!—a member of a foreign embassy, whether as an official or a servant we do not know, took it upon himself to do what no Hebrew official was courageous enough to do. He went to the king and reported that Jeremiah was going to die at the bottom of the old cistern. His tone of voice must have been sufficient accusation, because the king ordered that Jeremiah be got out of the cistern. In an old storehouse of the palace Ebed-melech quickly found "old rags and worn-out clothes" which he instructed the prophet to wad under his armpits while he was pulled out with a rope.

It was while Jeremiah was still confined to the court of the guard that an enormously sustaining revelation came to him, growing out of a business transaction. His cousin Hanamel came from Anathoth to request him to buy his field. Now why should

Jeremiah of all men invest in a field when he was the proclaimer of the forthcoming desolation of the land? But Jeremiah also believed in the far day when Judah would again be, under the Lord's direction, a free country with a viable economy.

> "And I bought the field at Anathoth from Hanamel my cousin, and weighed out the money to him, seventeen shekels of silver. I signed the deed, sealed it, got witnesses, and weighed the money on scales. Then I took the sealed deed of purchase . . . and I gave the deed of purchase to Baruch . . . in the presence of witnesses . . . and in the presence of all the Jews who were sitting in the court of the guard. I charged Baruch in their presence, saying, 'Thus says the Lord of hosts, the God of Israel: Take these deeds . . . and put them in an earthenware vessel, that they may last for a long time. For thus says the Lord of hosts, the God of Israel: Houses and fields and vineyards shall again be bought in this land.'" 32:9–15

The people were obviously impressed, and Jeremiah was lifted into a state of prayer.

> "Ah Lord God! It is thou who hast made the heavens and the earth by thy great power and by thy outstretched arm! Nothing is too hard for thee. . . ."

A moving prayer follows, reviewing God's leading, his inexorable justice, and mentioning this small practical transaction to authenticate his promise, "for I will restore their fortunes, says the Lord."

In the fourth month of the eleventh year of Zedekiah, the Babylonians breached the walls of Jerusalem, the city fell, and the king fled in the night only to be taken prisoner, blinded and carried captive to Babylon. The rest of the story of the deportation we know from Second Kings, how Jeremiah chose not to go to Babylon, where he would have been treated with respect, but stayed with the remnant in Jerusalem under the sponsorship of Gedaliah, the newly appointed governor of Judah, friendly to him. There seems to have been a period of steady recovery for the ravaged country and then a member of the deposed royal family, named Ishmael, murdered Gedaliah and his entourage. Officials who tried to avenge Gedaliah's murder feared that Babylonian deputies, when they arrived, would not believe them. It might be better to escape while they could. After ten days of waiting for God to speak, Jeremiah received a message direct from the Lord that the loyal citizens should remain where they were; to leave would bring only suffering. But nervous and uncertain, afraid to accept the oracle, the men decided to go to Egypt, taking Jeremiah and Baruch along. They may have wanted to be sure they could receive the Lord's counsel through Jeremiah even if they were not presently following it. And the word did continue to come to Jeremiah in Egypt, although mainly to declare that Egypt was not safe from the power of Nebuchadnezzar and that punishment would come as surely in Egypt to those who sought foreign gods as it had in Judah. Oracles against various foreign nations followed: Egypt, the Philistines, Moab, Ammon, Edom, Damascus, Kedar and Hazor, Elam, and finally Babylon.

The final chapter of the book is an historical appendix reviewing the last days of Judah before the Exile and the good fortune of Jehoiachin in Babylon in being released from prison and given a seat at the table of Babylon's new king. Presumably Jeremiah died in Egypt and his faithful secretary Baruch saw to it that both his biography and his inspired poetry were saved for posterity.

Lamentations

Whose Holy City?

A Jew lamenting the ill fortune of Jerusalem was—and is—
one of the world's sorriest figures. For a loyal Jew in the sixth century B.C. the most tragic event imaginable was the desecration of
Jerusalem at the hands of invading armies. This was the city of his
soul, the city of his God, the city of God's people. In Jerusalem
was his safety; he was guarded by its high walls, its enormous
gates, its soldiers as good as any in the world with the bow and
arrow, the long spear, the short spear, sword, dagger, on up to
the heavy battering ram. Unless the odds were completely over-
powering, the walls of Jerusalem stood.

Not only was Jerusalem the city of the Jew's safety but it was
the city of his pride. There sat Solomon's temple, high on the hill,
a symbol of national aspiration, political and spiritual. To it came
a constant stream of Jews from outlying areas, some for trade but
most in order to celebrate national festivals and holy days; no
sacrifice was so effective, so worthy, as sacrifice offered in the
temple of Jerusalem. A modern Westerner can scarcely imagine
how a Jew felt about Jerusalem. Perhaps a European can identify
with the city in which his family has lived for at least five hundred years—Genoa, say, or Prague—but a citizen of Chicago
whose family arrived six months ago—or six years—and who will
probably be transferred to Detroit next year, what can he know
of such personal devotion? Chicago is St. Louis is Jersey City is
Birmingham is Sacramento.

Another drastic difference: when cruel circumstances devastated

Jerusalem the people fundamentally blamed themselves. The Eternal City which housed the temple which housed God could not be destroyed as long as God's people stood foursquare. For a Jew, Jerusalem was never taken by the enemy until it was first lost by its own sons and daughters. To see Jerusalem sacked and burned was to be personally desecrated; God would have protected his city if his people had proved worthy. In their minds whatever was, was of God; both reward and punishment. To be sure, punishment could be inflicted by their enemies, but it was "allowed" by God because of their own unworthiness. But—if the people were proving faithless to their God, where had the priests been all this time? Where were the prophets? Why had they allowed the people to go astray so that their disgrace was plain for their enemies to gloat over? Priests and prophets must also be called to account.

Modern cities can, and do, also fall into disaster. When culture fails, whatever seems to be destroying the people evokes anger, frustration, resentment, maybe even mob action, but not much in the way of ardent self-condemnation and not drastic recrimination of the priests and prophets. Why do we know only the transferable blame?

Poetry of Grief

Out of an unrepentant people come no such poetry as came from the author of these ancient lamentations; poetry with a note of heartbreak which spans the long years because it mourns the breakdown of character. Not the world's greatest poetry from a literary point of view, but among the most moving.

Traditionally Jeremiah has been taken to be the author of this book called Lamentations; even now in the Revised Standard Version, as well as in the King James, Jeremiah is given the credit line. But modern scholarship points out that neither the style nor the vocabulary are Jeremiah's; nor the basic ideas. Nor would he have been likely to lament the cessation of prophecy when he himself was a practicing prophet. Nor did Jeremiah seem primarily concerned about the status of the temple, or of the priests and the monarch, while the author of Lamentations is much burdened.

Actually, however, there is no proof that the author of these

poems was lamenting the destruction of Jerusalem by the Babylonians, as has been supposed. Sometime between the dedication
of the new temple, in 516 B.C., and the time of Nehemiah, the
middle of the next century, dire things happened in Jerusalem. We
know because Nehemiah, over in Susa, the capital of Elam, reported that one of his people brought news that survivors in
Jerusalem were "in great trouble and shame" and that "the wall
of Jerusalem is broken down, and its gates are destroyed by fire."
Nehemiah was so overwhelmed that he "wept, and mourned for
days." But what happened, perpetrated by whom, we do not
know. Also in Lamentations Edom is bewailed as an enemy, but
according to Jeremiah Edom was conquered by the Babylonians
along with Judah and was a friendly country when the Jews fled,
in 587 B.C. Later, however, Obadiah was very angry with the
Edomites for joining the siege of Jerusalem. What siege? Was
there another, later attempt to wreck the restored city? All in all,
Lamentations *may* be describing a second, partial destruction of
Jerusalem sometime during the blank period in Jewish history of
which we have neither scriptural nor secular accounts. Someday
more scrolls or artifacts may be uncovered by archaeologists which
will fill this gap in historical evidence.

Grief, Suffering and Sin

The book consists of five elegies, the first four written as alpha-
betic acrostics and the fifth not, although it has as many verses as
there are letters in the Hebrew alphabet. Poems 2 and 4 appear
to be the oldest; the third the poorest from a literary standpoint,
although it has the most intricate scheme with each of the three
verses of each stanza beginning with the same letter. The fifth
poem is really a prayer. The writer was a professional poet and
handled the elegiac meter capably.

In the first poem Jerusalem is personified as a recently bereft
widow grieving over her fate:

> How lonely sits the city
>   that was full of people!
> How like a widow has she become,
>   she that was great among the nations!

> She that was a princess among the cities
>   has become a vassal.
> She weeps bitterly in the night,
>   tears on her cheeks. . . .
> Jerusalem remembers
>   in the days of her affliction and bitterness
> all the precious things
>   that were hers from days of old. 1:1–2, 7

But the city accepts basic blame for its own condition! Jerusalem has sinned grievously.

> All her people groan
>   as they search for bread;
> they trade their treasures for food
>   to revive their strength. . . .
> The Lord is in the right,
>   for I have rebelled against his word. . . . 1:11, 18

Nevertheless, although Jerusalem accepts blame for her own condition she still realizes it was her enemies who brought it to pass, and any hardship the Lord can think up to visit on them will be just all right with Jerusalem.

> ". . . All my enemies have heard of my trouble;
>   they are glad that thou hast done it. . . .
> Let all their evil doing come before thee;
>   and deal with them
> as thou has done with me
>   because of all my transgressions. . . ." 1:21–22

In the second poem that poet laments the Lord's anger in setting "the daughter of Zion under a cloud." He feels the Lord has reduced the kingdom to ruins; he has shown himself alien to its rulers' cause.

> The Lord has become like an enemy,
>   he has destroyed Israel . . .
> and in his fierce indignation has spurned
>   king and priest. 2:5–6

Saddened in his heart the poet looks at a desolate people who cannot find the inspiration to begin again:

> . . . and her prophets obtain
> no vision from the Lord. 2:9

This is the point of no return, when a people have lost faith in themselves and in the concerned attention of their God. The poet breaks into a prayer of desperation:

> Look, O Lord, and see! . . .
> Should women eat their offspring,
>   the children of their tender care?
> Or should priest and prophet
>   be slain in the sanctuary of the Lord? 2:20

If priests cannot be safe in the sanctuary, where under heaven would anyone be safe? This is a plea of a people completely stymied, unable to flee, unable to remain and escape starvation. And unsure that Heaven is hearing their cries.

The third poem is a first-person testimony, divided between description of the city's desperate state and pleas for reassurance. The poet leads off from a solid first-person stance:

> I am the man who has seen affliction
>   under the rod of his wrath. . . .
> He has made my flesh and my skin waste away,
>   and broken my bones. . . .
> He is to me like a bear lying in wait,
>   like a lion in hiding;
> he led me off my way and tore me to pieces;
>   he has made me desolate;
> he bent his bow and set me
>   as a mark for his arrow. 3:1, 4, 10–12

Suddenly he reassures himself. Looking back on the history of his people, remembering the long way they have been led, he strikes an affirmative note:

> But this I call to mind,
>   and therefore I have hope:
> The steadfast love of the Lord never ceases,
>   his mercies never come to an end; . . .
>   great is thy faithfulness.
> "The Lord is my portion," says my soul,
>   "therefore I will hope in him." 3:21–24

Admittedly, it *is* the Lord who sees, understands, rewards and punishes; for the Jew, there was no going around that fact.

> Who has commanded and it came to pass,
>   unless the Lord ordained it?
> Is it not from the mouth of the Most High
>   that good and evil come?
> Why should a living man complain,
>   a man, about the punishment of his sins? 3:37–39

But then again, even though the punishment is decreed by God, the nation's enemies wrought the havoc and the poet is very inventive in suggesting to the Lord what might now be done to them. As in many a modern prayer, the Lord is reminded of conditions he must already know about:

> . . . Thou hast seen all their vengeance,
>   all their devices against me. . . .
> Thou wilt requite them, O Lord,
>   according to the work of their hands. . . . 3:60, 64

The fourth poem, which has only two verses to each stanza, describes the terrors of the siege, how the holy stones are scattered, how people who formerly feasted on dainties are now perishing in the streets, the princes once "whiter than milk," their bodies more ruddy than coral, now blacker than soot. This is stark verse.

> The tongue of the nursling cleaves
>   to the roof of its mouth for thirst;
> the children beg for food
>   but no one gives to them. . . .
> Happier were the victims of the sword
>   than the victims of hunger. . . .
> The hands of compassionate women
>   have boiled their own children. . . .
> The Lord gave full vent to his wrath,
>   he poured out his hot anger. . . . 4:4, 9–11

Why? Israel's questing soul was always asking: Why did it have to happen to us? Ah yes, we have sinned; we have sinned.

> This was for the sins of her prophets
>   and the iniquities of her priests. . . .

> Our eyes failed, ever watching
>   vainly for help;
> in our watching we watched
>   for a nation which could not be saved. 4:13, 17

The poet then turns on Edom, assuring the Edomites, "to you also the cup shall pass"; Edom shall have its sins uncovered.

The final prayer-poem, judging by its historical references to Egypt and Assyria, must have been written half a century after the other four poems. Here the entire congregation beseeches the Lord to take note of their plight and offer deliverance.

> Our inheritance has been turned over to strangers. . . .
> We must pay for the water we drink,
>   the wood we get must be bought.
> With a yoke on our necks we are hard driven;
>   we are weary, we are given no rest. . . .
> The old men have quit the city gate,
>   the young men their music.
> The joy of our hearts has ceased;
>   our dancing has been turned to mourning. 5:2, 4–5, 14–15

The final note is a prayer for divine remembrance.

> . . . Restore us to thyself, O Lord, that we may be restored!
>   Renew our days as of old!
> Or hast thou utterly rejected us?
>   Art thou exceedingly angry with us? 5:21–22

With that all but helpless question the poet lays down his pen.

Ezekiel

The book of Ezekiel was written by a priest of that name who was exiled to Babylonia, beginning his ministry to his fellow Jews around 593 B.C. and continuing for thirty years. Apparently he had been deported with that first group of distinguished court personnel and prominent persons carried off by Nebuchadnezzar when King Jehoiachin surrendered to Nebuchadnezzar on March 16, 597 B.C. Ezekiel might be living in the city of Babylon but plainly his mind was on his compatriots in Jerusalem. He must have followed the letters and messages from Judah with much anxiety, aways hoping of course that the complete destruction of Jerusalem might be averted. Since he had a certain amount of clairvoyance and was able in spite of distance to pick up impressions of affairs in Jerusalem it is sometimes difficult to determine how much of what he described was objective reporting and how much was mediated through his inner vision.

The Text

Ezekiel's book is one of the longest in the Old Testament and one of the hardest to follow in spite of its relatively reliable chronology. It is not just the strangeness of his visions which makes it difficult but the Hebrew text is not well preserved. Some verses are unintelligible even to scholars who will wrestle with almost any enigma; words are omitted, misspelled, inserted. Copyists were either careless or confused, perhaps because they did not always understand what Ezekiel was talking about. His symbolism is sometimes esoteric and even when he does explain a vision his explanation may lack clarity. The quality of his poetry is disputed, some scholars insisting it is downright poor while others call is magnificent. Judgment of its excellence probably depends on the response it elicits from individual readers. The thirty-seventh chapter, which is in prose, inspired a great Negro spiritual about dry bones and the power of the Almighty to restore life.

Outline of the Book

The author had a logical mind along with his gift of visions and meaningful dreams. His book has a definite outline. Chapters 1 to 24, written before the main exile of 587 B.C., delineate a series of anticipatory visions—oracles of warning—pertaining to the forthcoming destruction of Jerusalem. Chapters 25 to 32 are given over to a resounding and detailed denunciation of foreign nations, stressing the fact that Israel is not alone in coming under God's judgment. Chapters 33 to 39 ease the burdens of Israel's sins and punishment by describing its future re-establishment. Chapters 40 to 48 depict a detailed restoration of the temple in Jerusalem.

Ezekiel's Call

Ezekiel was in Babylonia sitting by the grand canal known as the river Chebar, a branch of the Euphrates, when his first great vision "happened," as visions will. The date was July 21, 593 B.C.; he was just that definite about it—although, obviously, he used an ancient calendar. To understand the authority of a major vision, one almost has to have had one. Isaiah knew; Paul and John knew; Joan of Arc knew; Swedenborg knew. On the other hand, deranged people have visions; so do some geniuses; and some very ordinary persons. People around those thus gifted often consider them queer, or inspired, or both. Ezekiel knew this fact of life. He says the Lord instructed him to ignore resentment, scoffing and indifference, and keep on speaking out. His calling was to proclaim.

First Vision

He saw a storm come out of the north flashing fire, emanating a luminosity which disclosed four creatures, each with four faces and two pairs of wings. The four flew in a straight line. (Many primitive cultures hold that malicious spirits move in a straight line.) Near each creature a wheel spun and within each wheel whirred another, smaller wheel, the rims ornamented with eyes and the wheels lifting as the creatures moved. And "the spirit of the living creatures was in the wheels" and "the sound of their wings [was] like the sound of many waters." Over their heads "was the likeness of a throne" made of lapis lazuli and above the throne a human form surrounded by a peculiar brightness—"the likeness of the glory of the Lord." Ezekiel fell on his face. The figure said, "Son of man, stand up on your feet, and I will speak with you." A tremendous form of address, "Son of man," as if to emphasize the humanhood of the hearer of God's transcendent word. The phrase occurs ninety-three times in this book. "Stand upon your feet"—no cringing before the Most High; only man on his two firm feet can collaborate with God. "Son of man, I send you to . . . Israel, to a nation of rebels . . . open your mouth, and eat what I give you." A hand unrolled a scroll inscribed on both sides with words of lamentation and mourning. Ezekiel found the message sweet as honey. This was the communication he was to speak forth. Having made the command plain, the Spirit left with a sound like an earthquake, the creatures following. Ezekiel, lifted up by the Spirit, then went to the exiles who dwelt by the Chebar but he was still overwhelmed by the vision and sat speechless for seven days. (An excellent precedent for anyone reporting visions; spiritual revelation often requires lengthy meditation.)

Strange Prophecies

At the end of the seven days of pondering, the Lord reminded Ezekiel, "Son of man, I have made you a watchman for the house of Israel." (A term indicating the Jewish people.) Then, to dramatize the fate coming to Israel, he was told to lie on his left side for the number of days of Israel's punishment, then to lie on his right side for the number of days of Judah's punishment. The days, equated with years, indicated the length of their estrangement. During his confinement Ezekiel was commanded to eat sparse amounts of a vegetable bread baked on a fire of human dung, a sentence later commuted to cow dung to prevent ritual uncleanness. He was also ordered to cut off his hair and beard, divide the hair into three parts, one part to burn in Jerusalem when the siege was over, one part to strike with the sword around the city (an emblem of military defeat), one part to scatter to the wind, with a few hairs set afire to represent the fire which would "come forth into all the house of Israel." God's judgment would not be denied.

In Jerusalem

He must have kept a diary, the way he pinpointed the exact date of his most overwhelming experience. On September 17, 592 B.C., he was addressing a meeting of the "elders of Judah" in his own house in Babylon when he saw the form of a hand which grabbed him by his hair and appeared to hoist him through the air to the temple in Jerusalem, where he beheld the radiance of the Most High. He saw heathen rites being performed, including ritual weeping for Tammuz, god of spring, killed each year by the advent of summer heat. A man clothed in linen, probably signifying a priest, was instructed to mark the head of every onlooker who remonstrated against the heathen worship. Everyone else—men, women, children—must be slain. When the man in linen reported he had carried out his commission Ezekiel saw again "the brightness of the glory of the Lord," the throne borne by the cherubim, the whirling wheels "like sparkling chrysolite," the four faces. Even God himself left the desecrated sanctuary.

Ezekiel's warnings, probably plain to his hearers, are less plain to modern readers even though we follow his account with the help of scholarly footnotes. But their import is plain: the Lord continues with his scattered people, who will one day be returned to Israel, where he will give them "one heart, and put a new spirit within them . . . and they shall be my people, and I will be their God." Again Ezekiel was lifted up and returned to Babylon to deliver his warnings.

In spite of definite dates it is often difficult to decide whether a given vision comes before or after certain historical events. Also the historical incidents are sometimes difficult to identify; it is not easy to discriminate between what was Ezekiel's actual prophecy in the sense of foretelling and what was written in as prophecy by later interpolators. But it is not at all difficult to identify his desperate concern. Throughout the remainder of the first twenty-four chapters his visions proliferate as he passes on "the word of the Lord," denouncing those who cry " 'Peace,' when there is no peace." Retribution will be sure for the land which transgresses. Erring inhabitants shall be treated like the wood of the vine, meaning the thick stems good for nothing but burning. Even Judah's pride, Jerusalem, is likened to a foundling nurtured in a loving adopted family until she "grew exceedingly beautiful, and came to regal estate," only to play the harlot. Jerusalem's older sister is Samaria, her younger sister Sodom, but Jerusalem herself has become more corrupt than either. Nevertheless the Lord will forgive all that has been done.

Vision Follows Vision

A dramatic allegory of two eagles and the Lord's planting of "a sprig from the lofty top of the cedar" illustrates a contemporary state of affairs. The great eagle denotes Nebuchadnezzar, while the house of David is represented by the top of the cedar, of which the young twig is Jehoiachin; the city of trade is, of course, Babylon and the land of trade, Babylonia. King Zedekiah is indicated by the term "seed of the land" and the second eagle refers to Psammetichus II, who rounded up Zedekiah and Judah's neighboring countries in an attempt to rebel against Babylonia. Zedekiah, when "planted," or made king, could not withstand the east wind, Nebuchadnezzar. The purpose of the allegory is to dramatize the fact that both men and events are the Lord's creatures.

"And all the trees of the field shall know that I the Lord bring low the high tree, and make high the low tree, dry up the green tree, and make the dry tree flourish. I the Lord have spoken, and I will do it." 17:24

Responsibility

In chapter 18 Ezekiel introduces an emphasis upon individual responsibility, which was the heart of his message. If not a new concept for Judaism it was at least a note seldom sounded and never stressed. Former prophets emphasized ethical conduct on the part of the tribe and nation. A whole family, or even a tribe, might be punished for the sins of one member. The exiled Jews thought of themselves as suffering for the sins of their forebears. But the Jews in captivity lived where crosscurrents of thought and culture blew in on them. Even though Greek political dominance was two centuries in the future, Greek philosophy and Greek stress upon the importance of the individual were already pressing questions on other cultures. Ezekiel's insight extended the concept of individual responsibility. No more quoting of the proverb "The fathers have eaten sour grapes, and the children's teeth are set on edge." Rather, sons shall not suffer for the iniquity of the father, ". . . the soul that sins shall die." (In that time/place the sins of the mother as an influence on posterity did not merit consideration, because *self*-awareness, self-determination, self-accountability were still masculine prerogatives.) But Ezekiel was a forerunner in the march toward nondiscriminatory democracy.

Chapter 19 is composed of two poetic laments. In the first, Judah is compared to a lioness both of whose whelps—Jehoahaz and Jehoiachin—had been taken away; in the second, to a fruitful vine which is picked up and transplanted in the wilderness. Occasionally a personal message to Ezekiel himself intrudes, as when the Lord instructs him not to mourn the death of his wife publicly but to remain silent until word of the fall of Jerusalem reaches him.

Surrounding Countries

Chapters 25 to 32 are given over to oracles against surrounding countries: Ammon, Moab, Edom, Philistia, Tyre, Sidon, Egypt. Sometimes in prose, sometimes in sweeping poetry, history is rehearsed, both political and economic. Trade comes to life as the products of Mediterranean ports are named: silver, iron, tin, lead, war horses and mules, ivory tusks and ebony, emeralds, purple embroidered work, fine linen, white wool, coral and agate, wheat, olives, early figs, honey, oil and balm, wine, wrought iron, cassia, calamus, saddle cloths; lambs, rams and goats; all kinds of spices, all precious stones, and gold; choice garments, carpets of colored stuff. In poetic cadence ships again sail the high seas; winds, oarsmen, mariners, shipwrecks sound contemporary. Names of jewels seem all but transmuted into tangible gems as the people of Jerusalem are reminded of their former blessings.

Some oracles are dated, as for instance the oracle of latest date, April 26, 571 B.C., which mentions the booty Nebuchadnezzar would receive from Egypt to compensate for what Tyre had failed to yield. Egypt's Pharaoh is likened to a great cedar of Lebanon in whose boughs the birds made nests until its pride brought it low. Lament is made for him because he thought himself a lion, while in the eyes of the Lord he was a sea monster to be captured in a net. Egypt must go down to the underworld with the uncircumcised, the executed, and those who die untimely deaths.

Future Restoration of Israel

The theme changes and the future restoration of Israel becomes the subject of chapters 33 to 39. The end of chapter 18 is repeated, probably intentionally, a good deal as a modern minister may find himself quoting himself because his original remarks made a telling point. Ezekiel wanted his hearers to take in the fact indelibly that where formerly the Lord had covenanted with his people Israel, he now had to disown them as a group because so many had proved unworthy. Nevertheless, each individual still has his own opportunity to live righteously. Each one is now called to account. Happily, when a wicked man reforms, his former sins shall not be remembered against him.

Fall of Jerusalem

In 585 B.C. Ezekiel, still living in Babylon, had a nerve-wracking experience not uncommon to perceptive persons who sense trouble in the air. He felt agitated, sure that trouble was happening somewhere and that it mattered to him, but what? He had no explanation for his anxiety. Next morning a messenger came from Jerusalem announcing that the city had finally fallen. Catastrophe enough! But now his tongue was freed and he could pour out his insights. Most important was the assurance that in spite of current catastrophe God would eventually restore his people. Just as the present punishment of Jerusalem was God's, even so, the initiative for restoration is also his. Salvation is not alone a matter of repentance, forgiveness, and renewal but also of God's love eliciting his children's loyalty, which must be freely given.

Dry Bones

Best known of Ezekiel's visions is the one of the valley of dry bones. Many bones, very dry. Could they be brought to life again? Ridiculous. But God commanded, "Prophesy to these bones, and say to them, O dry bones, hear the word of the Lord." Then—just as the spiritual has immortalized the miracle —the dry bones began to come together; they hooked up, put on sinew, flesh and skin, began to breathe. They lived! Moreover, this God who restored dry bones would also revive his people! "And I shall put my Spirit within you, and you shall live, and I will place you in your own land; then you shall know that I, the Lord, have spoken. . . ."

Sweeping apocalyptic oracles describe the coming of foes from the north. Gog, king of Magog, will come against Israel with hordes of soldiers, but God himself will lead his people against united heathendom and cause the enemy to fall in the open field to be devoured by wild beasts and birds of prey. Their spears, bows and arrows, shields, all their weapons shall be burned, enough fuel to last for seven years. A great sacrificial feast will follow. "And I will set my glory among the nations. . . ."

The New Temple

How are the people of God to live together when finally restored to their own land? In former years they had profaned Jerusalem; what was to keep them from backsliding again? In Ezekiel's last nine chapters he develops specifications for a new temple, for the priests and Levites who should attend it, for the cultic practices necessary to save a nation which must be guarded from mistakes. In trance he even discerns the measurements of the temple, walled and set on a high hill, isolated from the palace, situated more than a mile from the city. Details are sketched in from staircase to paneling. New rules are promulgated, the most innovative being the new position of the Levites. Back when the Hebrews left Egypt, all the descendants of Jacob's son Levi were designated a priestly class. As time went on, only the descendants of Levi who were also descendants of Aaron could become officiating priests; the rest of the males of the tribe of Levi, although still set apart as a priestly class, became servants of the priests and did not enter the sanctuary. By the time the Chronicles were written the Levites had been granted a higher position and put in charge of the musical services. Ezekiel defines their role more specifically, emphasizing with Ezra and Nehemiah the importance of rules and regulations for all matters pretaining to the temple.

In spite of Ezekiel's concern for individual responsibility he believed firmly in controls and practices which would keep the whole Jewish people in line. He thought in terms of a closed community with male Jews born to their religious inheritance. The river which he envisioned flowing from the temple, purifying the Dead Sea, watering the wilderness so that fruit trees could grow in the desert, was for the refreshment of the Jews returning from captivity.

Why did Ezekiel's visions—bizarre, magnificent, strange, cryptic, authoritative—make such an impression on his hearers? And on generations after him? Probably because he was a man of known integrity and faithfulness in a city where many captives must have faced constant temptation to compromise; he was a man of fearless oratory when outspoken denunciation must have been unpopular. He sustained his discouraged countrymen with his insistent trust in God's continuing love even though the calamity of bondage was decreed by God. And then there was a luminous quality about him. Even the vicissitudes of transcribing, editing, translating and interpreting his message have not tarnished his spiritual impact. Evidently he radiated, as well as colorfully reiterated, his message.

Daniel

The book of Daniel takes its name from the chief character in a collection of stories and visions dealing with the final outcome of history—the latter days, the culmination of present events. Hence the term apocalyptic writing. The book was a publication with a purpose. Its author wanted to encourage, warn, and advise the Jews living in his own time, which was the decade between 175 and 164 B.C., when Antiochus Epiphanes was king of Syria and had jurisdiction over Palestine. (His name meant Antiochus the Illustrious but later rabbinical commentators called him Antiochus the Wicked.) Since the return of the Jews from Babylon they never had a more difficult time. In fact, up to Antiochus the Great, father of Antiochus Epiphanes, Palestine had known comparative peace, mostly because major powers were occupied with each other. But now the situation of the Jews seemed desperate.

The Seleucid kings, to whose line Antiochus Epiphanes belongs, are important to a modern reader of Daniel for two reasons: first, because it was their machinations which made life so dangerously difficult for the Jews; second, because the book of Daniel is so cryptic and ambiguous that the reader needs some factual knowledge of the political situation it addresses, some fact upon which to hang his interpretations. No Jewish author would have dared to comment directly on current political matters; he had to disguise his opinions as historical commentary so that non-Jewish readers would not catch on.

The Seleucids were a Syrian dynasty whose founder, Seleucis I, had been a powerful general under Alexander the Great; his victories in the latter part of the fourth century B.C. secured the dominance of Babylonia for him, to which was later added much of Syria, Persia and Bactria. It was he who, around 300 B.C., founded the city of Antioch, some sixty miles west of Aleppo on the Orontes River; hence the honorary title Antiochus. From the city's founding, many Jews lived in Antioch. Antiochus II is the first of the line referred to in the Bible, an indirect comment in Daniel 2:6. A harried man, he fought Egypt; then, when peace was declared, divorced his wife to marry the daughter of the pharaoh; two years later he remarried his first wife, who poisoned him and his Egyptian wife and had their son executed. Next on the throne was Antiochus III, 242–223 B.C., called the Great; referred to in Daniel 2:10–21. Many but not all Jews preferred this Syrian rule to Egyptian dominance because of Egypt's heavy hand with taxes. The Roman-Jewish historian Josephus calls the Palestine of those days a storm-tossed ship, buffeted as it was between Egyptian influence and Hellenistic culture.

Antiochus Epiphanes (IV) took over the throne after his father's death and his brother's murder. He proved an extravagant, ostentatious king who put on a show of geniality with his officers and with the populace while highhandedly promoting his often tyrannical rule. Since Greek culture flourished throughout most of the Mediterranean area, the more urbane Jews favored the language and general philosophy of the Greeks but conservative Jews held to strictly traditional Hebrew customs. Rivalry for the high priesthood developed between the two factions. Onias II, the recognized priest, represented the party of strict observance, while his brother Jason led the dissenters who favored Greek culture. Bribery brought Jason his brother's position but subsequent bribery lost it for him, and a third contender, Menelaus, took over, after which Onias was assassinated and Jason fled. Then, while Antiochus Epiphanes was again off at war against the Egyptians, Jason gathered enough troops to oust Menelaus, but only until Antiochus returned and reinstated him.

By that time Antiochus had had enough of the wrangling and

declared for Greek cultural uniformity throughout the realm, not because he cared for Greek culture but because he was intent upon denationalizing contentious subjects, chief among them the Jews. In token of his determination he consecrated the temple in Jerusalem to Zeus, offered pork on its altars, and made capital offences of circumcision, owning Jewish books of law, and honoring the Sabbath. He thought he had permanently chastened the Jews but it was his severity which later led to the incredibly successful Maccabean revolt, after which the temple was cleansed, refurbished and rededicated. In honor of that joyous event the celebration known as Hannukah, or the Feast of Lights, was instituted.

However, during the reign of Antiochus Epiphanes the political position of the Jews was highly precarious. They questioned among themselves: Would God remain their protector? Were they worthy of his favor? Did they have the faith to claim his support? What did the future hold? Uncertainty wracked the whole Jewish community. It was then that some Jewish writer, whose name we do not know, decided to speak to the situation by authoring the book of Daniel.

The Text

His protagonist is an ancient hero, perhaps the same Daniel mentioned by Ezekiel, although in Hebrew the spelling differs. And Ezekiel's Daniel may be the one referred to in the Ras Shamra tablets, found in 1930 but written some 1,500 years earlier. There is no sufficient reason to suppose, as some scholars do, that the tales could not be basically factual. Hero tales seldom materialize out of thin air and no legends are more likely to survive than those stamped with the charisma of a gifted man of remarkable character such as Daniel. The first six chapters of the book were written in Aramaic, the popular spoken language of Antiochus Epiphanes' time. The rest of the book dealing with Daniel's visions is in Greek and incorporates a number of Persian loan words.

Daniel: His Story

When King Jehoiakim and the treasures of the temple fell into the hands of Nebuchadnezzar, in 597 B.C., the Babylonian king ordered that royal and noble "youths without blemish," competent and knowledgeable, be brought to Babylon, where they should be taught the language and culture of the Chaldeans and join the palace entourage. Among the transplanted youths were Daniel and three friends whose names were changed to Shadrach, Meshach and Abednego. The best foods and wines were ordered for them but such rich fare was contrary to Jewish dietary law, so Daniel begged that they be allowed simpler food. Skeptically the eunuch in charge agreed to a trial period and at the end of it the young Jews proved more alert and healthier than their comrades. "As for those four youths, God gave them learning and skill in all letters and wisdom; and Daniel had understanding in all visions and dreams." When finally presented to Nebuchadnezzar they were found to be "ten times better than all the magicians and enchanters that were in all his kingdom."

A time of testing came. King Nebuchadnezzar was a great dreamer. Modern psychiatrists would probably assure him that he was fortunate, because his unconscious was able to use his dreams to disclose his problems. But the king had one dream which disturbed him greatly, as major dreams may. Unfortunately he forgot the content of the dream, remembering only that it was highly disturbing. At once he called together the court diviners and ordered them to explain his dream to him. But first they would have to tell him what he had dreamed. If they did not perform satisfactorily they should be "torn limb from limb." The diviners were stymied; interpretation, yes, but to read the king's mind to determine what he had dreamed—"none can show it to the king except the gods. . . ." Irate, the king ordered all dream interpreters promptly slain. The edict included the four Hebrew youths. So? Daniel requested an appointment with the king, then asked his three friends to pray for him, which they probably did with all the faith they could muster. Finally Daniel felt he had caught a glimpse of the king's dream and promptly "blessed the God of heaven."

Half a century ago this insight of Daniel's was either gulped down as a miracle or dismissed as fiction, but in this day of controlled dream laboratories researchers have recorded other incidents of two persons dreaming the same dream at the same time, and at least one skilled trance subject has been able to recover someone else's dream. Evidently Daniel's ability to handle "deep and mysterious things" was not necessarily fictitious.

Confronting the king, Daniel described the dream. The king had seen an image "mighty and of exceeding brightness," frightening because its head was of fine gold, its breast and arms of silver, its legs of iron, its feet of clay. A stone "cut out by no human hand" smote the image on its clay feet until it crumbled away, while the stone became "a great mountain and filled the whole earth." The interpretation, said Daniel, signified that Nebuchadnezzar, "to whom the God of heaven has given the kingdom, the power, and the might, and the glory," was the head of gold, while less-powerful kings who would succeed him were merely silver, bronze, and iron mixed with clay. All would be broken into pieces. However, the stone which filled the earth represented a final kingdom which would never be destroyed.

The king was impressed. He made Daniel "chief prefect over all the wise men of Babylon" and then at Daniel's request made his three friends viceroys. (Nobody dreamed that "feet of clay" would become an idiom in the English language.)

The Fiery Furnace

As time went on, Nebuchadnezzar felt his power and had an image sixty cubits high made of pure gold set up on the plain of Dura, then ordered all the officials of the provinces to come to the dedication. At "the sound of the horn, pipe, lyre, trigon, harp, bagpipe, and every kind of music" the people must fall down and worship the golden image or be cast into a fiery furnace. This was the moment for which the rivals of the Hebrew viceroys had waited. Promptly they informed the king that the Hebrews whom he had honored did not bow to the image but went on praying to their own God. Having his favorites ignore his order publicly was too much for the king and in a rage he "ordered the furnace heated seven times more than it was wont to be heated" and had the three men bound and cast into flames so scorching that those who threw them in were also seared. The king himself peered into the furnace, then turned in astonishment to his counselors. "But I see four men loose, walking in the midst of the fire, and they are not hurt; and the appearance of the fourth is like a son of the gods." Awed, the king called the young men forth; their hair was not singed, their clothes did not smell of fire. The king blessed their astounding God—and promoted them.

Who was that fourth man? Was he an apparition of the king's distraught mind, or a celestial figure such as is reported in other biblical incidents, or a psychic projection of the concentrating mind of Daniel? To make a sound deduction we need more experience with fiery furnaces, faith, and with Daniels, but we do have reliable documentation on Taoist priests walking on red-hot coals without being burned. However, even if some do indeed perform these exceptional and well-attested acts, is anything to be gained thereby? A demonstration of faith? Faith in what? Does faith release energies as yet uncharted which may have enormous relevance for human behavior in days to come? The book of Daniel has to be read with an open mind.

A King's Madness

Nebuchadnezzar had a third dream and again called for interpreters. He had seen a great tree whose top reached to heaven so that all the world could see both its abundant fruit and the birds and beasts which enjoyed its shade. A celestial being ordered that it be hewn down but that its roots be left in the earth bound with a band of iron and bronze. An order was given that the mind of the tree, called "him," should be changed to the mind of a beast while "seven times pass over him." The purpose of the image was "to the end that the living may know that the Most High rules the kingdom of men, and gives it to whom he will, and sets over it the lowliest of men."

Daniel interpreted the dream to signify that the tree was the king, whose dominion had spread to the ends of the earth, while the message from the celestial being meant that the king would suffer a form of insanity in which a man acts like a beast (zoanthropy); the king would try to eat grass like an ox and live in the open for seven seasons. Having faithfully interpreted the vision, Daniel begged his majesty to practice righteousness, show mercy to the oppressed and thereby lighten his sentence.

Within the year Nebuchadnezzar, walking on the flat roof of his royal palace glorying in his power, was suddenly struck by the madness and shortly afterward was turned out into the field "till his hair grew as long as eagles' feathers, and his nails were like birds' claws." The story then shifts to the first person and Nebuchadnezzar tells of his own recovery, when he blessed the Most High and knew himself subject to the Almighty's will. When his reason and the glory of his kingdom returned, he continued to "praise and extol and honor the King of heaven; for all his works are right and his ways are just; and those who walk in pride he is able to abase."

Belshazzar

The account moves on to a later ruler, Belshazzar, who gave a state banquet for a thousand of his lords and ordered that the gold and silver vessels taken from the temple in Jerusalem be brought forth for his guests' use. Libations were poured to heathen deities and defiant merriment reigned. Suddenly, at the height of the revelry, a hand materialized on the wall, writing mysterious words: *mene, mene, tekel, parsin.* The king, so frightened that "his knees knocked together," called for his wise men, diviners and astrologers. Not one could decipher the meaning. Then the queen remembered there was one man in whom dwelt "the spirit of the holy gods," a man who had been chief of diviners at Nebuchadnezzar's court. Daniel was immediately brought into the banquet hall and explained that Belshazzar was being warned as Nebuchadnezzar had been; he would likewise be brought low in order to cure his sacrilege and pride. The words meant that he had been weighed in the balance and found wanting; his days were numbered; his kingdom would be divided between the Medes and Persians.

Notwithstanding the dire nature of the interpretation Belshazzar remembered the reward he had offered and had Daniel clothed in fine purple with a chain of gold about his neck and commissioned him as third ruler in the kingdom. "That very night

Belshazzar the Chaldean king was slain. And Darius the Mede received the kingdom. . . ."

Daniel in the Lions' Den

Darius, when he came to the throne, made Daniel one of three presidents who presided over one hundred twenty satraps and soon he became top man, which did not set well with the natives. Attempting to devise his downfall, they concluded it could come only "in connection with the law of his God"—a tremendous tribute to the impression Daniel's life must have made upon them. Surreptitiously they persuaded the king to pass an edict that for a month no prayer or petition should be made to any god or man except to his royal highness on pain of the culprit's being thrown into a den of lions. Daniel heard the edict but continued to pray facing Jerusalem "and gave thanks before his God, as he had done previously." (Those are important words: "as he had done previously"; his praise rose from a proven faith.) Of course he was reported and the reluctant king was forced to order him thrown into the den of lions, adding a personal prayer to the sentence he had passed: "May your God, whom you serve continually, deliver you!" Then a stone was rolled in place to close the opening of the cave "and the king sealed it with his own signet. . . ." Poor, torn king; he had either to lose face or lose Daniel. He returned to his palace to fast and remain awake all night. At dawn he went anxiously to the lions' den, ordered the stone rolled back, and called out to Daniel, "servant of the living God," to see if he had met miraculous deliverance. Daniel himself answered!

He was quite unharmed, "because he had trusted in his God." Naturally he was quickly brought forth and, just as naturally for those times, the men who had accused him—along with their wives and children, alas—were thrown to the same lions, who "broke all their bones in pieces." No question is raised by the historians as to why a God powerful enough to deliver Daniel did not also deliver those innocent wives and children. One cannot ask twentieth-century questions of the second century B.C. And goodness knows what questions the twenty-second century will ask of our insensitive age. Anyway, the whole incident so impressed the king that he wrote "to all the peoples, nations, and languages that dwell in all the earth," urging them to "tremble and fear before the God of Daniel," who "delivers and rescues" even from the jaws of hungry lions. His prayer was answered in at least one way he never dreamed of: centuries later, some unnamed Negro slave in democratic America, home of the free and the brave, wrote a spiritual which has raised the hearts of thousands: "Didn't our Lord deliver Daniel, Daniel?"

These days, who believes that folk tale about Daniel and the lions? Maybe a few seasoned lion tamers . . . or those occasional stalwart Arab nomads who never eat flesh but cultivate concentration and can walk into a cave of hyenas and cow the lot of them . . . or maybe an exceptional practicing mystic. Anyway, a den of lions is a place for an expert who has previously tested his theories.

The Visions

The next six chapters are given over to four visions said to have come to Daniel "as he lay on his bed," visions definitely relevant to the time in which the author of the book lived. They are cryptic, symbolic foretellings of future political developments up to and including the reign of Antiochus Epiphanes with emphasis beyond that time on the final day when God's kingdom on earth will be manifest. The visions pass their own judgments.

The first vision is typical. Daniel perceived four beasts coming up out of the sea: a lion with eagles' wings which were plucked off as it was made to stand on two feet like a man and given a man's mind; a bear with three ribs in its mouth "and it was told, 'Arise, devour much flesh' "; a leopard with four wings and four heads "and dominion was given to it"; a fourth beast "terrible and dreadful and exceedingly strong," with great iron teeth and ten horns, among which there developed a small horn with eyes like a man and a speaking mouth. Three horns were plucked out by the roots while the little horn described the placing of several thrones, one of which was a fiery throne occupied by "the Ancient of Days," in raiment white as snow, who judged ten thousand times ten thousand standing before him. As the horn was speaking, the beast itself was slain but the lives of the other three beasts were spared for a time. Then, emerging from the clouds, appeared "one like a son of man," to whom the Ancient of Days gave dominion over all nations for time everlasting.

Alarmed, Daniel asked for an interpretation of his vision, which he received in detail nearly as confusing as the vision. The winged lion stood for the Babylonian empire, the bear for the Medes, the leopard for the Persians, and the ten-horned beast for the Greeks, whose kingdom, after the mighty Alexander, fell to ten rulers. The small horn stood for Antiochus Epiphanes, who became powerful by uprooting other horns. The Ancient of Days, representing God, made the judgment that eventually a messianic king, God's anointed, would reign for all time.

This vision of the final triumph of the kingdom of God has furnished prophetic inspiration for many a later sermon. The early church claimed that in the one "like a son of man" Daniel was foreseeing the coming of Jesus as the Messiah. Today both Jews and Christians reinterpret the vision variously, some claiming the fall of the Vatican is indicated, or the demise of communism, or the eventual triumph of whatever sect they currently see as all-saving. But the fact that cryptic prophecy can lend itself to farfetched interpretation does not indicate it was useless to those for whom the book was written.

Daniel's second vision came two years later, when he was in Susa, the Persian winter capital. Again animals held a central place, with a ram and a strangely behorned he-goat rampaging until "truth was cast down to the ground." When he asked for an interpretation he was answered by Gabriel, one of the seven archangels in the Hebrew hierarchy, here mentioned for the first time in the Bible record, "Understand, O son of man, that the vision is for the time of the end," whose approach was signaled by further interpretation of the behavior of the animals.

Daniel's own reaction to his vision was inconclusive. He knew he had seen something significant but its meaning was unclear in detail—like half catching onto a coded message when time was running out. He said frankly, "And I, Daniel, was overcome and lay sick for some days; then I rose and went about the king's business; but I was appalled by the vision and did not understand it." All visionaries do not have the common sense to arise and go about the king's business.

Ultimate Deliverance

Evidently the writer of the book of Daniel had read the prophet Jeremiah, because Daniel is presented as pondering the seventy years' desolation prophesied by Jeremiah before the ultimate restoration of Jerusalem. Daniel wanted God's direction and he wanted it with all his heart. He prayed; he fasted; he confessed his own wrongdoing and the waywardness of his people.

> "To us, O Lord, belongs confusion of face, to our kings, to our princes, and to our fathers, because we have sinned against thee. To the Lord our God belong mercy and forgiveness . . . we do not present our supplications before thee on the ground of our righteousness, but on the ground of thy great mercy." 9:8–9, 18

If all the rest of the book of Daniel were lost this prayer would make the book worthwhile.

It was Gabriel who again appeared in answer to Daniel's prayer for guidance. He interpreted Jeremiah's seventy weeks as "weeks of years"—490 years. Any student of history can apply the figures and come out with something more or less meaningful if he picks a careful starting date. Some interpretations seem reasonable to some—and some seem insufferably authoritarian, but then, even Daniel was mystified. His one certainty was that the heavenly host were involved in the affairs of men. Encouragement enough.

For a further disclosure, Daniel prepared himself by sparse diet and dedication. The vision came in "the third year of Cyrus king of Persia," 515 B.C., when he was standing on the bank of a river. All at once his companions were struck down by the impact of a presence they could not see but felt so that "a great trembling fell upon them." Daniel, himself, beheld a being from the world of angels who said, "Fear not, Daniel, for from the first day that you set your mind to understand and humbled yourself before your God, your words have been heard, and I have come because of your words"—not an uncommon experience for those who believe their prayers are heard and attended.

Even in the celestial realm, however, there can be delays.

Gabriel, again the protagonist of the message, had had to contend for three weeks with the angel who was the guardian of Persia until Michael, ever the Jews' patron angel, came to help him so that he might descend to make explanation of what was yet to befall the Jews. All we know for sure is that Daniel felt he had been addressed by Gabriel and that Gabriel strengthened him. "O man greatly beloved . . . be strong and of good courage." So Daniel was strong and of good courage.

A detailed vision of future kingships follows, also open to differing interpretations but definitely apocalyptic in intent: there will be a time of final reckoning, an ultimate disclosure of divine purpose.

> And many of those who sleep in the dust of the earth shall awake, some to everlasting life, and some to shame and everlasting contempt. And those who are wise shall shine like the brightness of the firmament; and those who turn many to righteousness, like the stars for ever and ever. 12:2–3

Finally Daniel was asked to "shut up the words, and seal the book." When he pleaded to know "the issue of these things" he was told that "the words are shut up and sealed until the time of the end," but he was promised that at the final consummation he should stand in his own allotted place.

A book devoted to miraculous happenings and prescient prognostications may impress some readers as belonging to the field of abnormal psychology, but to others the record presents authentic spiritual venturing on the part of a dedicated man. However footnoted, Daniel has become for many seeking souls a challenging exemplar. He sought the best interests of his people through a maze of inner and outer events and meanings such as have often summoned and lifted up the practicing mystic.

The Minor Prophets

The term Minor Prophets can be misleading if it is taken to suggest the quality of their message. Rather, it derives from the length of their recorded contributions. When the prophetic books were first brought together for publication the twelve shorter books fit on one scroll, which came to be called The Book of the Twelve. The messages of the twelve were, of course, written in Hebrew but by the middle of the third century B.C. so many Jews were scattered throughout the Greek world, speaking and writing Greek, that a Greek translation of the Hebrew scripture seemed in order. Made during the reign of Ptolemy II supposedly by seventy-two scholars, the Greek translation came to be known as the Septuagint (the seventy). In it, and in most subsequent translations, the Minor Prophets were grouped at the end of the compilation.

Hosea

Besides Isaiah of Jerusalem the eighth-century prophets were Amos, Micah and Hosea. Only Hosea lived in Israel, probably in the southern part, because he constantly uses the term Ephraim for Israel. From the mid-century on, the political fortunes of Israel were definitely on the downgrade. Currently Assyria and Israel were allies but Israel had already begun to sell oil, one of its most valuable exports, to Egypt, then Assyria's enemy. Hosea's reaction to the maneuvering of Israel's kings was reflected in his questioning as to why his country's leaders constantly shopped around for foreign help, always precarious, instead of turning directly to the Lord, who had never failed them. The first verse of his book places his calling to become a prophet "in the days of Uzziah, Jotham, Ahaz, and Hezekiah, kings of Judah, and in the days of Jeroboam the son of Joash, king of Israel."

The Text

Not a small portion of the Hebrew text of the book is garbled, which has necessitated educated guesses as to intended meaning. Differing opinions account for the divergence of certain passages in various translations, including English. But the thrust of the book is clear: Israel has played the harlot and would have to be dealt with accordingly.

Religious Corruption

Debased religious practices met Hosea's eye on every side. Idolatry marked both wayside shrines and temples. On festival occasions temple priestesses were offered as prostitutes in a participatory rite in honor of Baal, who was conceived as dying and descending to the underworld when the dry season blighted the fields, only to return and marry the earth goddess when the autumnal rains assured ample crops of grain, grapes and olives. Rituals and ceremonies became a mixture of Hebrew and Canaanite custom.

Parable of a Broken Marriage

Hosea is the only one of the prophets whose life is a parable of his prophecy. Using his own unhappy marriage as an example of a broken relationship between two who should remain eternally faithful, he pointed out the defection of Israel and the sorrowing compassion of God, who hated sin but continued to love the sinner. If the reference to his marriage is taken as factual as well as symbolic, the story is that the Lord told him to take "a wife of harlotry . . . for the land commits great harlotry by forsaking the Lord." Apparently he married a temple prostitute, a woman named Gomer, who bore him three children. Later, Gomer returned to her old life but Hosea still loved her and in spite of the public disgrace she had brought on him, he bought her back. The price was high: fifteen shekels plus ten bushels of barley. But God also expected to pay a great price for Israel. Hosea was keenly aware of the high cost of redemption.

The words of the Lord to Israel, as recorded by Hosea, have become through the centuries a part of the orthodox Jewish wedding ceremony. "And I will betroth you to me for ever; I will betroth you to me in righteousness and in justice, in steadfast love, and in mercy. I will betroth you to me in faithfulness; and you shall know the Lord."

Hosea's account of his own experience in forgiving Gomer is one of the few places in the Old Testament where an understanding of personal forgiveness comes to the fore. (Joseph's forgiveness of his brothers is another.) Tremendous passages of supplication for forgiveness from the Lord mark the sweep of Hebrew religious thought. Also magnificent passages in which the Lord himself offers forgiveness. But Hosea must have stimulated some long thoughts about forgiveness applying to those who have personally wronged us, for the idea surfaces in the teaching of Jesus and leads to animated discussion. How much forgiveness? How long? Why? Hosea had hurled a barbed question into the field of ethics.

The Oracles

Only the first three chapters of Hosea's book are devoted to his own tragic story. The following eleven chapters are his pronouncement against Israel, broken occasionally by a few words of condemnation of Judah. Throughout, he speaks in vivid phrases of a poet; perhaps a greater prophet for being so good a poet. A strong tragic poet.

The Land

He had the ancient poet's awareness of the land, its ways and rhythms, and felt himself a part of the land and of the people he was upbraiding.

> Therefore the land mourns. . . .
> They sacrifice on the tops of the mountains,

> and make offerings upon the hills,
> under oak, poplar, and terebinth,
>   because their shade is good. . . .
> A wind has wrapped them in its wings. . . .
> And now they sin more and more. . . .
> Therefore they shall be like the morning mist
>   or like the dew that goes early away,
> like the chaff that swirls from the threshing floor
>   or like the smoke from a window. . . .
> Like a stubborn heifer,
>   Israel is stubborn;
> can the Lord now feed them
>   like a lamb in a broad pasture? . . .
> With their flocks and herds they shall go
>   to seek the Lord. 4:3, 13, 19; 13:2–3; 4:16; 5:6

Because much of the country was wild, predatory animals lived in the outlying areas and domestic animals had to be guarded. Hosea's figures of speech are based on the daily life of the countryside.

> For I will be like a lion to Ephraim,
>   and like a young lion to the house of Judah,
> I, even I, will rend and go away,
>   I will carry off, and none shall rescue. . . .
> Ephraim is like a dove,
>   silly and without sense,
>   calling to Egypt, going to Assyria.
> As they go, I will spread over them my net;
>   I will bring them down like birds of the air. . . . 5:14; 7:11–12

Lack of Understanding

The harlotry which cast a shadow over his own life also darkened his diatribes as he bitingly chastised his people for their apostasy. But why denigrate only the women, when it is the men who have led them into evil?

> I will not punish your daughters when they play the harlot,
>   nor your brides when they commit adultery;
> for the men themselves go aside with harlots,
>   and sacrifice with cult prostitutes,
> and a people without understanding shall come to ruin. 4:14

That was the nub of the matter, the lack of understanding; ignorant shortsightedness. However, repentance, at once so hard and so easy, would lead to restoration.

> For I desire steadfast love and not sacrifice,
>> the knowledge of God, rather than burnt offerings. 6:6

Hosea looked out on a world at war and its futility numbed him, yet his confidence welled up through his discouragement, heartening his people.

> Because you have trusted in your chariots
>> and in the multitude of your warriors,
> therefore the tumult of war shall arise among your people,
>> and all your fortresses shall be destroyed. . . . 10:13–14

> Let us know, let us press on to know the Lord;
>> his going forth is sure as the dawn;
> he will come to us as the showers,
>> as the spring rains that water the earth. 6:3–4

Nothing in the entire canon throbs more hauntingly with eternal love than Hosea's perception of God as father.

> When Israel was a child, I loved him,
>> and out of Egypt I called my son. . . .
> Yet it was I who taught Ephraim to walk,
>> I took them up in my arms. . . .
> I led them with cords of compassion,
>> with the bands of love . . .
>> and I bent down to them and fed them. . . .
> I will not execute my fierce anger . . .
>> for I am God and not man,
>> the Holy One in your midst. . . .
> I am the Lord your God . . .
>> you know no God but me,
>> and besides me there is no savior. 11:1, 3–4, 9; 13:4

Reconciliation

The last chapter of his oracles, known to most Jews today because it is read in the synagogues on the Sabbath of Repentance, the Sabbath between Rosh Hoshana and Yom Kippur, opens with the lines:

> Return, O Israel, to the Lord your God,
>> for you have stumbled because of your iniquity. . . .
> I will heal their faithlessness;
>> I will love them freely. . . . 14:1, 4

At the end of the book a later editor has added as a postscript, an editorial blessing.

> Whoever is wise, let him understand these things;
>> whoever is discerning, let him know them;
> for the ways of the Lord are right,
>> and the upright walk in them. . . . 14:9

Joel

Background

Joel is not liberal in presenting his personal background, saying only that his father's name was Pethuel but neglecting to give the locality where he lived. His time was probably around 350 B.C., almost certainly the fourth century. He does mention the temple on Mount Zion and the city wall, already rebuilt.

Plague of Locusts

The event which precipitated Joel's exhortations was a plague of locusts, pests which came periodically to Palestine—and still do. Formerly they caused widespread crop failure, sometimes inducing starvation. Wonderful lines to read when the so-called seventeen-year locusts start chewing up our own trees.

> Has such a thing happened in your days,
>> or in the days of your fathers?
> Tell your children of it,
>> and let your children tell their children,
>> and their children another generation.
> What the cutting locust left,
>> the swarming locust has eaten.
> What the swarming locust left,
>> the hopping locust has eaten,
> And what the hopping locust left,
>> the destroying locust has eaten. 1:2–4

It is as if a foreign nation had attacked his people; a nation with teeth like lions'—the vines are wasted, the fig trees splintered, stripped of their bark and left with white trunks.

> Awake, you drunkards, and weep;
>   and wail, all you drinkers of wine,
> because of the sweet wine,
>   for it is cut off from your mouth. 1:5

His hearers knew the ritual of wailing for the loss of the wine. The Canaanites had a practice of ritual wailing at the time the vines ceased to bear, their cries being expected to waken the god of fertility, and Joel was satirizing this ritual ululation; and if the people are bewildered by their losses, how much more the dumb animals who depended on the land. There were plenty of losses to the farmers: wheat and barley gone; pomegranate, palm and apple withered; "and gladness fails from the sons of men."

> How the beasts groan!
>   The herds of cattle are perplexed
> because there is no pasture for them;
>   even the flocks of sheep are dismayed. . . .
> The sun and the moon are darkened,
>   and the stars withdraw their shining. 1:18, 2:10

There was widespread belief that the sun grew dim when tragedy struck a powerful leader. (When Julius Caesar was assassinated the sun was said to have suddenly dimmed. And at the time of the death of Jesus, Luke has it that "It was now about the sixth hour, and there was darkness over the whole land until the ninth hour, while the sun's light failed. . . .") Seeing portentous signs, the people identified with nature which was sharing their grief. To Joel, when the land was stricken Israel was stricken. But the people had themselves to blame. They had broken their rapport with the Lord and confidence had to be restored.

Sackcloth for All

> Gird on sackcloth and lament, O priests. . . .
> Go in, pass the night in sackcloth,
>   O ministers of my God! . . . 1:13

Again, this ceremony of lamentation was well known to some of the cults in Jerusalem. At the time of the winter solstice the non-Jewish priests retired to an underground chamber to emerge again at dawn carrying the image of a man-child, signifying that virility would return to the earth. So widespread and deep-rooted was some version of this ceremony that it carried over into Christianity: at Christmas in certain localities priests still emerge from a darkened room at dawn intoning, "The Virgin has given birth! Light shall increase!"

Repentance

For Judah the immediate experience of calamity had to be met; not just questioned. What should the Lord's true followers do? Joel suggested a course of overt action.

> Blow the trumpet in Zion;
>   sound the alarm on my holy mountain!
> Let all the inhabitants of the land tremble,
>   for the day of the Lord is coming, it is near. 2:1

Warming to his subject he developed the current calamity into a foretaste of the final day of the Lord, when the last reckoning would be made. Fire and flame spelled destruction. Like war horses and the rumbling of chariots, like a powerful army drawn up for battle, leaping upon the city and running upon the walls, climbing into homes, came the host of the Lord. He struck terror into the hearts of his listeners, then offered an answer to the faithful. Repentance!

> For the day of the Lord is great and terrible;
>   who can endure it?
> "Yet even now," says the Lord,
>   "return to me with all your heart,
> with fasting, with weeping, and with mourning;
>   and rend your hearts and not your garments."
> Return to the Lord, your God,
>   for he is gracious and merciful,
> slow to anger, and abounding in steadfast love,
>   and repents of evil. 2:11–13

Face-saving

Call a solemn assembly, Joel advised; sanctify the congregation; gather the children. Let the priests, weeping, cry to the Lord to spare his people. Then came a typical Eastern touch; he did not want the people of Israel to lose face because of their losses. If their God should not come to their rescue fast enough, the people around them were bound to jeer, "Where is their God?"

Prayers Answered

> The Lord answered and said to his people,
> "Behold, I am sending to you
>   grain, wine, and oil,
>   and you will be satisfied;
> and I will no more make you
>   a reproach among the nations. . . ." 2:19

Joel then addressed the land itself. One of the more winsome aspects of his prophecy is his identification with the land: It is his own land; its people are his people; so their land and everything it produces are his concern. And God's concern. God must surely care for his people's land.

> "Fear not, O land;
>   be glad and rejoice,
>   for the Lord has done great things!
> Fear not, you beasts of the field,
>   for the pastures of the wilderness are green;
> the tree bears its fruit,
>   the fig tree and vine give their full yield . . .
>   he has poured down for you abundant rain,
>   the early and the latter rain, as before." 2:21–23

The latter rain was an extra blessing for the land. The heavy rains usually came along in midwinter, but if the early rain was scant then there was the later, spring rain, which usually saved the crops. Even so, God was able to restore Israel.

> "I will restore to you the years
>   which the swarming locust has eaten. . . ." 2:25

What greater promise could there be? To have wasted years restored! This was more than a promise of food. Was Joel older now, that he could speak wistfully of having his years restored? ". . . the years which the swarming locust has eaten. . . ."

> "And it shall come to pass afterward,
>   that I will pour out my spirit on all flesh;
> your sons and your daughters shall prophesy,
>   your old men shall dream dreams,
>   and your young men shall see visions." 2:28

Calamity for Judah's Enemies

Joel's final message is something of a tirade; the usual anathema against his country's enemies. In very human fashion the prophets sometimes bolstered their sense of their country's failure by pointing to worse sins on the part of their enemy. They shall surely face a day of ultimate reckoning when "The sun shall be turned to darkness," and the heavens and earth yield portents of "blood and fire and columns of smoke." The enemy nations must be brought down in the valley of Jehoshaphat.

> "What are you to me, O Tyre and Sidon, and all the regions of Philistia? . . . For you have taken my silver and my gold, and have carried my rich treasures into your temples. You have sold the people of Judah and Jerusalem to the Greeks. . . . I will sell your sons and your daughters into the hand of the sons of Judah, and they will sell them to the Sabeans, to a nation far off; for the Lord has spoken." 3:4–6, 8

Warming to his theme, he calls for a holy war.

> Beat your plowshares into swords,
>   and your pruning hooks into spears. . . .
> Multitudes, multitudes,
>   in the valley of decision!
> ". . . And Jerusalem shall be holy
>   and strangers shall never again pass through it." 3:10, 14, 17

Honest, earnest, patriotic Joel, great enough to catch a vision of the restoration of his people but not of the regeneration of his enemies.

Amos

Background

Tekoa is not much of a place, really; not the kind of locality one would expect to produce a renowned social reformer and certainly not a place to draw scores of scholars and pilgrims yearly, as it does. Perched on the edge of the "wilderness" of rocky hills which stretch eastward toward the Dead Sea, the limestone subsoil nourishes such nondescript growth as has always marked the area. Scattered sycamore trees still grow there and gardeners still prune them in the hope of improving the rather tasteless figlike fruit. But modern farmers are also at work with modern fertilizers, and if Amos does stalk the hills at night, as some shepherds insist, he must feel that his faith in the restoration of Israel is being justified.

In Amos' day, around the middle of the eighth century B.C., the town was fortified. A century earlier, King Rehoboam had realized that Tekoa, being only six miles from Bethlehem, which was about the same distance from Jerusalem, could help to guard the approach to his capital city. Later Jehoshaphat had expected to meet the invading Ammonite and Moabite armies there at Tekoa, and Amos must often have heard the king's words to his army repeated when the elders gathered at the town gates: After encouraging his people Jehoshaphat had then ordered his singers to go before the army "to sing and praise the Lord," and so inspiring and unexpected were the songs that victory was assured; "the Lord set an ambush against the enemy," who turned and destroyed each other so that, without fighting, Jerusalem was saved.

Any boy growing up in Tekoa in Amos' day felt his share of responsibility for the safety of Jerusalem. Not only prosperity and goodness but the very righteousness of the Lord was expected to center there. In Tekoa most families in their workaday lives accepted as home the place assigned to them by birth but every male hoped to make at least one trip to Jerusalem, there to offer his sacrifices in Solomon's temple.

Good Times

In the first half of the eighth century B.C. there was peace in Judah. Up north, in Israel, there was also unprecedented prosperity. In fact, an economic boom. Merchants speculated on heavy imports and everyone seemed to profit; flourishing businessmen intended to keep it that way. High and low observed the festival days, and sacrifices at the temple were lavish. Let the whole world see that the God of Israel was mightier than the gods of its neighbors; were not his people unprecedentedly successful? Well, all but the poor.

Answering a Call

Up to the Northern Kingdom went Amos the herdsman, called of the Lord to preach reform. He was a natural orator and knew how to hurl an invective, to utilize figures of speech, satire, and scathing denunciation with biting simplicity. Only Isaiah among the prophets could equal his rhetoric. He knew Israel's history; he knew the current scene; he knew the attempted aggression of Israel's neighbors. What he had seen through the years yeasted uneasily in his soul. If *he* could see the ruthlessness, the ostentatious extravagance, the empty religious ceremony around him, how much more the Lord! Did the country not realize that the Lord would bring destruction on *every* people who flouted his laws? Amos was the first internationalist among the prophets, antedating Isaiah. He preached universal justice, impartial condemnation.

The prophet proceeded to Bethel, one of the three great sanctuaries of Israel, where Amaziah, the ranking priest, held sway. Declaring that the Lord had roared at him from Zion the way a lion of the hills roars in frustration, he called out so loudly that a crowd assembled and he hurled his oracles. "Thus saith the Lord"—he was sure for whom he spoke. And he promptly condemned not only Israel but Israel's neighbors—Damascus, Gaza, the Philistine cities, Edom, Tyre; then added that the cruelty of Ammonite soldiers would also be requited. "Because they have ripped up women with child in Gilead"—a sport many ancient armies enjoyed, betting on the sex of an unborn child and ripping open the expectant mother to prove the bet—"the King shall go into exile, he and his princes together." The same fate awaited Israel's ancient enemy Moab. "Says the Lord." Even Amos' homeland, Judah, would not escape judgment. But his full wrath—and the Lord's—was turned again on Israel:

> ". . . I will not revoke the punishment;
>   because they sell the righteous for silver,
>   and the needy for a pair of shoes—
>   they that trample the head of the poor into the dust of the earth,
>   and turn aside the way of the afflicted. . . ." 2:6–7

Recalling the Ways of God

They had become an immoral lot, both sexually and in the way they were taking a poor man's cloak as surety against a small loan and then ignoring the law of Moses that at sundown a man must be allowed to sleep in his cloak.

Cannot the people of God understand the undeviating ways of God? A covenanted people had to remember that a righteous God demands a righteous people. Let Assyria and the strongholds of Egypt observe that the Lord did not spare his own people when their righteousness did not exceed the morality of their sinful neighbors. (Even now one almost hears the grief which throbs through his stern reproval.) No one would be spared judgment, not even the most prosperous with their great houses, their summer and winter homes, their palaces with carvings of ivory; they would have no place to flee; the horns of the altar, which the worst of culprits could grasp and claim safety, would be denied them. The conduct of women as well as of men was reprehensible and he called the women who urged their husbands on to unjust profit so that they could buy finery "you cows of Bashan"; they had forgotten the nature of women: to pity and give nourishment. But

equally sinful were those who brought their sacrifices every morning, who counted up their tithes every three days, who let everyone
know how they honored the law of the temple; " 'for so you love
to do, O people of Israel!' says the Lord God."

God's Power

By way of emphasis Amos pointed out God's independence;
how he blessed with rain whom he pleased and when necessary
"smote you with blight and mildew," laid waste vineyards, let the
locusts devour the olive trees, and tried to bring Israel to its
senses. But so far even "pestilence after the manner of Egypt"
had failed to effect reform. Thinking on the might of the Lord,
he intruded a magnificent doxology. As a man of the open fields,
of the hills where the wind blows powerfully and storms shake
the sky, he felt the omnipotence, the sheer grandeur of this
God who made stern demands of his people. Let them note who
is speaking.

> For lo, he who forms the mountains, and creates the wind,
>   and declares to man what is his thought;
> who makes the morning darkness,
>   and treads on the heights of the earth—
> the Lord, the God of hosts, is his name! 4:13

Seek God and Live

It was no pleasure for Amos to publish his warnings; he called
them his lamentations. "Seek me and live," he pleaded in behalf
of the Lord, "O you who turn justice to wormwood." He realized
that powerful hate was turned toward anyone who "reproves
in the gate," where people gathered to hear the news of the day;
"they abhor him who speaks the truth." But he did not desist.
"For I know how many are your transgressions," and he named
them, but still urged, "Seek good, and not evil, that you may live."
Did they think the Lord delighted in their feasts in his honor when
they desecrated his principles? God was not listening to the melody
of their harps or the noise of their songs, because they were es-
sentially pretentious ritual rather than pure devotion. Then came
the heart of his message:

> "But let justice roll down like waters,
>   and righteousness like an ever-flowing stream." 5:24

This fresh voice from the hills was no respecter of persons. No more was God. Amos continued to proclaim that the rich pretenders were the worst of the lot. They were smug, and well-fed smug at that.

> "Woe to those who are at ease in Zion,
>   and to those who feel secure on the mountain of Samaria. . . .
> Woe to those who lie upon beds of Ivory . . .
> who drink wine in bowls,
>   and anoint themselves with the finest oils. . . ." 6:1, 4, 6

Vision of Reprisal

Amos thought it all over. He meditated. God had always answered with calamity when his people faltered. Would he send a plague of locusts to destroy the crops and throw the nation into hunger? He turned from the vision in anguish. Was God calling for a judgment of fire? Amos visioned it—"and it devoured the great deep and was eating up the land." Occasionally, devastating fires did sweep in from the sea. Vessels from enemy nations carrying slaves, gold, expensive cargo sometimes attacked each other as they met in the coastwise trade; one ship would catch afire from burning flares hurled by enemy ships and, out of control, drift against the shore in the night, setting fire to a field or a village.

> "O Lord God, forgive, I beseech thee!
> How can Jacob stand?
> He is so small!" 7:2

The Plumb-line Test

Again the Lord repented the reprisal he had planned but he held a plumb line against a wall and asked Amos what he saw. "A plumb line." Then the Lord announced—and Amos heard the words in despair—"Behold, I am setting a plumb line in the midst of my people Israel. . . ." Like a wall or a building, a nation must line up true to a plumb line, which for Israel was the law of the Lord.

Reaction of the Ranking Priest

This kind of talk was too much for Amaziah, priest of Bethel. The people were becoming fearful. Emotionally charged prophets had a way of causing events to materialize, and the danger Amos prophesied included the king and the whole economic structure. Amaziah sent a report to King Jeroboam advising him it was high time for the state to come to the aid of the church, as it were, and outlaw this prophet's speech. He ordered Amos out of town. "O seer, go, flee away to the land of Judah, and eat bread there, and prophesy there; but never again prophesy at Bethel, for it is the king's sanctuary, and it is a temple of the kingdom."

But Amos was not to be ordered off the premises. He replied that he was not a professional prophet, out for hire; he belonged to no prophets' guild. He was a herdsman called by God to prophesy. Then, to prove his gift as a seer, he told the high priest what was going to happen to him and his family, ending, "and Israel shall surely go into exile away from its land."

A fourth vision, about a basket of summer fruit quickly spoiled, represented Israel and its rotten economic order. (Nobody could pinpoint sins more graphically than Amos.)

> Hear this, you who trample upon the needy,
>   and bring the poor of the land to an end,
> saying, "When will the new moon be over,
>   that we may sell grain?
> And the sabbath,
>   that we may offer wheat for sale,
> that we may make the ephah small and the shekel great,
>   and deal deceitfully with false balances,
> that we may buy the poor for silver,
>   and the needy for a pair of sandals,
> and sell the refuse of the wheat?" 8:4–6

The Saddest Famine

> "Behold, the days are coming," says the Lord God,
>   "when I will send a famine on the land;
> not a famine of bread, nor a thirst for water,
>   but of hearing the words of the Lord." 8:11

And that would be the most disastrous famine of all, when the people did not know where to turn for spiritual food.

The theme changes abruptly as Amos declares that ultimately there will be a day of rebuilding, a true day of the Lord when the mountains will drip sweet wine and the fortunes of God's people will be restored. This final message of hope may have been appended by a later hand, for Amos himself was not one to equivocate or to offer a happy ending for sinful people. On the other hand, it was Amos who had pleaded with the Lord to avert the locusts and the fire because Israel was the Lord's own people.

One individual is always a lonely figure when measuring his message against the times. But Amos saw that one individual was all God needed if he was sure of his vision and of its Source. And Amos made himself that one individual in his day.

Obadiah

Twelve men mentioned in the Old Testament bear the name Obadiah, meaning "servant of God." Nothing is known of the background of the author of the book which bears the name, but he must have merited respect in his day or his pronouncements would never have survived to make the canon. Although his writing is run of the mill and his religious insight limited, he had the grace of brevity since his book is only one chapter in length. His driving idea is the destruction of Edom, that rocky tableland south of the Dead Sea which commanded the high caravan routes. Destruction at the hand of God.

The Edomites had been subjected by David and thereafter fluctuated between revolt with brief independence and subjugation by Judah, finally to become a vassal of Assyria and then of Babylon. In 586 B.C., when they might have been expected to aid Judah, likewise a small country straining to maintain independence against Babylonian dominance, they sided with Babylonia and looted Judah. Obadiah considered that betrayal in time of crisis the more dastardly because the original ancestor of the Edomites was said to have been Esau, brother of Jacob; thus they should have considered themselves kinsmen. Now oblivion was too good for them, Obadiah affirmed, and nothing was going to save them, not even their high and rocky setting.

> Though you soar aloft like the eagle,
>> though your nest is set among the stars,
>> thence I will bring you down, says the Lord. 4

Obadiah felt himself to be a spokesman for the Lord and expected his pronouncements to be respected by his countrymen and feared by his enemies. He rehearsed Edom's perfidy.

> . . . you should not have rejoiced over the people of Judah
>   in the day of their ruin . . .
> you should not have gloated over his disaster
>   in the day of his calamity. 12–13

Even the wise men of Edom, famous throughout the whole region for their insight, would be routed out.

> Will I not on that day, says the Lord,
>   destroy the wise men out of Edom,
>   and understanding out of Mount Esau? . . .
> For the day of the Lord is near upon all the nations,
> As you have done, it shall be done to you,
>   your deeds shall return on your own head. 8, 15

But Obadiah also glimpsed a brighter future. The time was close at hand, he affirmed, when the Lord and his people would win out "and there shall be no survivor to the house of Esau; for the Lord has spoken." Someday Israelite saviors would rule Edom "and the kingdom shall be the Lord's."

Whether he was wish-thinking, or speaking with prophetic vision, or making a statement of faith, the time did come when Edom was overrun by the great trading empire of the Nabataeans, who built the acropolis of Petra on the rocks of Edom's heights. Obadiah was a prophet of nationalism in the sense that Judah must eventually triumph because it was under the special direction and blessing of the Lord, but not until all nations had come under God's judgment, after which "the kingdom shall be the Lord's."

Jonah

The prophets of Israel were God-fearing men, out to stir the conscience of their countrymen, to blast their enemies, and to proclaim the word of the Lord. But there was one prophet, named Jonah, who himself disobeyed God, had a harrowing adventure, came through it amazed at the ways of the Lord, and then yielded to a second temptation. But he got the author's point of view across.

Date

This Jonah is presented as an historical figure, and Second Kings does report an eighth-century minor prophet named Jonah who came from a village near Nazareth to counsel Jeroboam II when the king was restoring the borders of Israel. His name may have been borrowed along with a few recorded or unrecorded traditions but the author's purpose is not so much to record history as to make the point that if Yahweh was God *at* all he was God *of* all. The time of writing was the postexilic period, possibly the fourth or third century B.C., when Alexander the Great was annihilating the Persian Empire in favor of Greek world domination, and ideas of tolerance and universalism were spreading rapidly. Too rapidly for the comfort of the strict constructionists of Israel who followed the precepts of Nehemiah and Ezra.

An Unwilling Envoy

The word of the Lord came to this man Jonah instructing him to go to Nineveh and cry out against the city's godlessness.

The author does not say how the word came. An inner voice, a dream, or a vision? Or as a rational deduction that, since Nineveh was said to be the world's wickedest city, surely the people ought to hear the judgment of the Lord and be given an opportunity to repent. Plenty of people came by their call that way, through plain ratiocination. A need is apparent, an individual with adequate qualifications is at hand; must God lean out of a cloud to call him or can he reason out his own response? However Jonah was called, he knew it was the Lord who was commissioning him to go to Nineveh, capital of Assyria on the Tigris. So— he quickly bought a ticket and boarded a ship for Tarshish, which may have been the Spanish city later known as Cádiz, to which the Phoenicians had already sailed. Definitely he was fleeing the prompting of the Lord.

> "But the Lord hurled a great wind upon the sea, and there was a mighty tempest on the sea, so that the ship threatened to break up." 1:4

The sailors were frightened and called on their god. (When would a modern sailor call on his God if not when frightened?)

The sailors threw the cargo overboard to lighten the ship. This was a desperate measure, because when they got to port they might well have to pay for that cargo if the consignee refused to believe their report of the storm and accused them of having smuggled the freight onto another ship for pay. As the cargo went overboard, everybody prayed. Except Jonah. Jonah had gone to his berth in the hold of the ship and fallen asleep. The captain was amazed; such indifference to danger was not natural for a sober man. He himself descended to the hold to interview Jonah.

> "What do you mean, you sleeper? Arise, call upon your god! Perhaps the god will give a thought to us, that we do not perish." 1:6

In a crisis it was certainly best to try all the gods. (Don't we all? We call on government agencies, private agencies, international agencies, and supernatural agencies.)

The sailors held that a wicked man aboard often jinxed a ship. That is, a really "unholy" man, not just an ordinary merchant expecting to cheat some foreign buyer, or a shipper with a half-spoiled cargo to dump on a poor market. However, confession of sin might save a ship. But no sailor was likely to confess his sins at the moment of danger, lest he be dropped overboard. The crew decided to cast lots, convinced that a lot could be depended upon to fall to the right man. The lot fell to Jonah—which Jonah may have expected and therefore influenced.

The sailors, aghast, asked the unfortunate passenger how his bad luck had come about. "What is your occupation? And whence do you come? What is your country? And of what people are you?"

Self-judgment

Jonah was honest with them, being at heart a good man. He told them he was a Hebrew who feared the Lord, "the God of heaven, who made the sea and the dry land." If he was about to be eliminated he was not going to let them think it was by the will of a mere sea-god such as the Greek Poseidon.

The crew were reluctant to hoist the honest passenger overboard but better one man should perish than all of them. They put it up to Jonah. "What shall we do to you, that the sea may quiet down for us?" Jonah could see that the waves were mounting.

> "Take me up and throw me into the sea; then the sea will quiet down for you; for I know it is because of me that this great tempest has come upon you." 1:12

It took a certain amount of conceit, no doubt, for a man to believe that the Lord God would whip up such a storm just to bring one individual to heel, but the Hebrews had figured out early in their career as a people that God's special care for them also presupposed his wrath for any defection. Back in the eighth century B.C. it was considered a major betrayal not to follow a course of action God had made plain.

The sailors really tried to save this honest wicked man.

> . . . the men rowed hard to bring the ship back to land, but they could not, for the sea grew more and more tempestuous against them. 1:13

So they called on Jonah's God not to blame them for what they were about to do; after all, the storm was *his* retribution. "So they took up Jonah and threw him into the sea; and the sea ceased from its raging"—which frightened the men even more. Here was a God who not only caused storms to blow but also stilled them. They offered a sacrifice and made vows. The author of the story does not say what their vows were but some of them may have kept their vows and became better men thereafter.

Jonah and the Whale

Right here the author makes a statement which has been a point of debate with thousands of believers and doubters through the centuries:

> And the Lord appointed a great fish to swallow up Jonah; and Jonah was in the belly of the fish three days and three nights. 1:17

Some earnest commentators have tried to sustain the plausibility of the story by explaining that the shock of having swallowed a live man whole caused the great fish's gastric juices to dry up so that it could not digest Jonah; one bishop had the inspiration that the fish was newly dead when Jonah was thrown overboard so that Jonah merely drifted down its gullet. More-sophisticated commentators call attention to other legends of like nature in other countries. Still others have felt the report to be allegorical. At any rate, the last thing Jonah remembered before losing consciousness was the gaping mouth of an enormous fish. Then, after three days, ". . . the Lord spoke to the fish, and it vomited out Jonah upon the dry land." There he was, conscious and on solid ground.

And what, after all, is so confounding about a wayward prophet's being lost in a cavern of darkness, given time to assay his actions, and then returned to his daily schedule only to find his appointment with life still waiting? It happens one way or another to most of us who feel called by God to a difficult job, then renege, ponder in agony, and finally come back to the assignment. Whether we spend those three days in hell, in delirium, or in a fish's belly, the experience is the same. An inward experience (and never mind the pun, because many Hebrew writers doted on puns). The miracle of the marvelous second chance is the real point.

Prayer in Extremity

Scholars deduce that the long prayer which Jonah prayed while inside the fish is a late emendation. If so, it only means that a later editor felt that Jonah must have prayed when he found himself in such an extremity, and so furnished the prayer. If we composed a prayer for Jonah what would we say?

Repent!

Finding himself spewed back on land, Jonah did exactly what most of us would do if we found ourselves miraculously given a second opportunity. He took off for Nineveh to warn the people, just as God had commanded in the first place. And he probably went with a much deeper understanding of what it meant to be commanded by God Almighty!

"An extremely great city, three days' journey in breadth," became Jonah's parish. His message was simple and direct. He told the people they were wicked and had better repent. In fact, they had just forty days in which to change their ways. Setting a deadline may have helped. Individuals who expect to change their ways eventually are not likely to change them at all. The case of the indefinite tomorrow clogs the heavenly courts of justice.

Forty days was not much time for corrupt city officials who had been cheating the people to take care of the slums of Nineveh with their putrid sewage problem, their cracked pipelines to fresh water, their bumpy streets knee-deep in mud; not to mention the triple taxes for king, temple and their own itchy palms. The city was not wicked in the abstract; it was wicked in the concrete.

And the people of Nineveh believed God; they proclaimed a fast, and put on a sackcloth, from the greatest to the least of them. 3:5

The king was impressed by this spontaneous demonstration of earnest repentance. Of course, kings, presidents, and such notables do tend to follow the people quite as much as they lead. So the king rose to heights of statesmanship he never knew he had and exchanged his fine purple for sackcloth, and sat in ashes also.

And he made proclamation and published through Nineveh, "By the decree of the king and his nobles: Let neither man nor beast . . . feed, or drink water, but let man and beast be covered with sackcloth, and let them cry mightily to God; yea, let everyone turn from his evil way and from the violence which is in his hands. Who knows, God may yet repent and turn from his fierce anger, so that we perish not?" 3:7–9

The inclusion of the animals may have contributed to the spiritual strength necessary for reform. The people realized that their destinies were one. Humility, regret, renewal drew the entire population into a circle of mutuality. God himself was moved to see this wonder of the changed heart!

When God saw what they did . . . God repented of the evil which he had said he would do to them; and he did not do it. 3:10

Around 800 B.C. it may have been too big an idea to conceive of a righteous God who did not mete out evil for evil but, on the other hand, did let the combination of circumstances, conduct, and intent come to focus so that his erring children would see the fruits of their evil and draw their own conclusions. At any rate, Nineveh was saved!

Wounded Pride

Was Jonah pleased at the success of his city-wide evangelistic campaign? He was not. He had prophesied doom and doom was what he wanted to see produced. In fact, he chided God for being so softhearted:

"I pray thee, Lord, is not this what I said when I was yet in my country? That is why I made haste to flee to Tarshish; for I knew that thou art a gracious God and merciful, slow to anger, and abounding in steadfast love, and repentest of evil." 4:2

So there *was* one theologian who had glimpsed the nature of the Eternal One—Jonah himself. However, the amazing fact that God's care extended to the wickedest people on earth did not fill Jonah with awe. Instead, ego pride blotted out the sun. He was no longer the powerful spokesman of the Lord, and instead of feting him for having saved them, the people were adoring God.

Jonah was extremely irate. He told the Lord frankly he would rather die than to have made such a fool of himself, arousing a city because of a fate that never befell. He went outside the city, built himself a lean-to, and felt sorry for himself. No doubt the lean-to was a modest structure but it would hold a lot of the rest of us who cannot countenance losing face.

It was hot out there in the open field. God felt sorry for his sulking son who had, after all, done such a good job of proclaiming his message. He sent a plant—probably, say scholars, the castor plant which has such huge, lovely leaves—to grow over the little booth and give his son Jonah some shade. "So Jonah was exceedingly glad because of the plant." People can become very fond of a plant; a psychological symbiosis. It was his friend. But God wasn't through with the plant or Jonah. ". . . when dawn came up the next day, God appointed a worm which attacked the plant, so that it withered." For good measure he also sent "a sultry east wind," the dryest, hottest wind of that area, "and the sun beat upon the head of Jonah so that he was faint; and he asked that he might die. . . ."

Then God asked Jonah if he thought self-pity was any proper reaction for a prophet. Fancy being that angry because a plant he had grown fond of happened to die. Jonah brushed him off. "I do well to be angry, angry enough to die." God had one more argument for Jonah:

> "You pity the plant, for which you did not labor, nor did you make it grow, which came into being in a night. . . . And should I not pity Nineveh, that great city, in which there are more than a hundred and twenty thousand persons who do not know their right hand from their left, and also much cattle?" 4:10–11

Universal Compassion

What a profoundly delicate touch on the part of the storyteller to include in God's pity the cattle. Centuries later another Jewish prophet was to make the falling sparrow famous as an illustration of God's care for all his creatures.

The author of this account did not point up his moral further. He did not need to, because the people for whom he was writing knew very well that they had been trying to claim God as their special protector, ignoring the fact that he might just possibly be interested in the welfare of all his children. They were struggling with the concept of a universal deity versus a national deity. And not only in terms of his jurisdiction but in the corollary belief: If their God was indeed the God of all mankind, then how could they ask for special preferment? To be prostrated by the challenge of such concepts seems almost absurd now, but in 800 B.C. when Jonah lived—and even in 300 B.C. when his historian lived—such philosophical considerations were devastating.

We do not know Jonah's final reaction, whether he went back to active evangelism, what he told his grandchildren. Maybe it was Jonah who *did* tell his grandchildren, so that a great-great-grand-son of his somewhere down the line could finally record his story. That bit about three days in the belly of a fish sounds as if some grandfather may have been very, very earnest about getting it into some grandson's head that it did not pay to flee from God's commands, spoken or implicit. Presumably some of the rest of us could do with the three-day fish treatment in the interest of expanding our horizons.

Micah

Occasionally in almost every nation's history someone comes along with the stalwart conviction that what should be, could be. This is one of humankind's blinding insights. Anybody can say the words, but actually to believe them is to embark on a transformed life of enormous impact. The prophet Micah was such a man. Some of his life must have overlapped Isaiah's, because he says he wrote while Jotham, Ahaz and Hezekiah were kings of Judah, which means that he saw the westward advance of Assyria. His home was the town of Moresheth, situated in the foothills of Judea southeast of Jerusalem.

Fearless Fulmination

He not only foresaw the threat of devastating defeat from outside but also the threat of internal disintegration in Jerusalem from acute economic inequalities. This was not the way God meant man to act toward man. There must be an agony at the heart of God. So he spoke out. Which was a dangerous thing to do, temporal power being what it was. And is.

> Hear, you peoples, all of you;
>   hearken, O earth, and all that is in it;
> and let the Lord God be a witness against you,
>   the Lord from his holy temple. 1:2

Graphically and in a voice to be heard, he pictured the descent of the Lord with mountains melting under him and valleys cleft like wax before fire. He did not care to what extent he had to go

to make his people understand—just so they finally took in what
he was telling them.

> All this is for the transgression of Jacob
>   and for the sins of the house of Israel. . . .
> For this I will lament and wail;
>   I will go stripped and naked;
> I will make lamentation like the jackals,
>   and mourning like the ostriches.
> For her wound is incurable. . . . 1:5, 8–9

Micah may have been speaking literally about going naked, because it was the way of some earnest prophets to dramatize their
message, even running naked through the streets as if actually
fleeing from the wrath of the Lord; he may also have covered
himself with ashes and wailed the cry of the jackal being closed
in by larger predators. In whatever way he could, he intended to
get through to his people the tragedy of their situation.

Especially he wanted to waken the rich and the powerful to a
realization of the prevailing economic injustice. They had a power
drive, he insisted; they lay awake nights plotting how to wangle
more fields and houses from the poor. They exploited the working class, drove the women out of their homes, deprived children
of their birthright. Child labor was a fact of daily life just as much
as the dawn-to-dark labor forced on captives. Those who heard
him knew too well what he was talking about, so men in power
tried to restrain his vehemence. "Do not preach," they threatened, "one should not preach of such things." His were no words
for the workers to hear. Micah's reply was the further accusation
that the affluent were practically eating the flesh of the people.

> . . . and flay their skin from off them,
>   and break their bones in pieces,
>   and chop them up like meat in a kettle,
>   like flesh in a caldron. 3:3

Ridicule

Lesser seers who sold their seership to the highest bidder, coun-
tered with more pleasant prophecies, foretelling a successful future
for Israel; prosperity written in the stars. They ridiculed this in-

sistent man—what better weapon than ridicule? So Micah answered them.

> Therefore it shall be night to you, without vision. . . .
> The sun shall go down upon the prophets,
>   and the day shall be black over them;
> the seers shall be disgraced . . .
> they shall all cover their lips,
>   for there is no answer from God. 3:6–7

As might be expected, the people knew the difference between true and false prophets. Micah was plainly filled with the power that comes from affirming justice. He knew the conditions he decried; he could name the fields, the mines, the seasonal crops. He knew the priests who "taught for hire," and he stood firm, confronting those who confused prosperity with God's approval. Zion was intended for worthier service and would again become a holy city in a nation at peace.

> For out of Zion shall go forth the law,
>   and the word of the Lord from Jerusalem . . .
> and they shall beat their swords into plowshares,
>   and their spears into pruning hooks;
> nation shall not lift up sword against nation,
>   neither shall they learn war any more;
> but they shall sit every man under his vine and under his fig tree,
>   and none shall make them afraid;
>   for the mouth of the Lord of hosts has spoken. 4:2–4

But this prophet from the small town did not see Israel's ultimate ruler as coming forth from the great city of Jerusalem. He turned to another small town.

Out of Bethlehem

> But you, O Bethlehem Ephrathah,
>   who are little to be among the clans of Judah,
> from you shall come forth for me
>   one who is to be ruler in Israel,
> whose origin is from of old,
>   from ancient days. 5:2

Portraying Israel as a culprit arraigned before a law court, Micah called on the people:

True Religion

> Hear what the Lord says:
> Arise, plead your case before the mountains,
>   and let the hills hear your voice.
> Hear, you mountains, the controversy of the Lord. . . .
> He has showed you, O man, what is good;
>   and what does the Lord require of you
> but to do justice, and to love kindness,
>   and to walk humbly with your God? 6:1–2, 8

Simple words. Inclusive doctrine. No place in Hebrew scripture is this definition of religion excelled. Isaiah, Jeremiah, Amos and others caught the implications for mankind of God's justice; Hosea knew the triumph of suffering love. Micah added tenderness and humility. Then he went on to lament the scarcity of honest and worthy men, "The godly man has perished from the earth," so that enmity existed in households, son against father, daughter against mother. But however dark the times, his final message was a hymn of praise.

> Who is a God like thee, pardoning iniquity
>   and passing over transgression? . . .
> He does not retain his anger for ever
>   because he delights in steadfast love. . . .
> Thou wilt cast all our sins
>   into the depths of the sea. 7:18–19

Thus he sent his hearers bravely into the new day, lifting their weight of guilt and turning their faces toward a better tomorrow.

Nahum

The book of Nahum is not prophetic in the usual sense of calling Israel or its enemies to account for their sins, nor is it particularly religious in upholding the power and holiness of God. But it is superb poetry. Its figures of speech are sharp, clear, almost onomatopoetic; its speech is terse, with an accumulative impact. Nahum is a poet of anger, magnificent anger, which rises to vindictive rejoicing as he sees the approaching devastation of the Assyrian Empire.

Author

Nothing is known of the author. His name means *comfort* or *comforter* but there is nothing soothing about his words except that he sees the assuagement of his country's hardship with the removal of Assyria from dominance. Even his home town, Elkosh, remains unidentified. His identity is lost in the poem, but not his personality. The date is approximately the time of the event he anticipates, close to the last decade of the seventh century.

The precipitating event is the imminent fall of Nineveh, Assyria's capital on the upper Tigris. After more than two centuries of relentless Assyrian domination of the whole area from Mesopotamia to the Mediterranean, now the Medes from the east and the Chaldeans from the southeast are closing in. Assyrian fighting had been particularly cruel. Hard-driven armies spared nothing and no one when they laid siege to an enemy city, and all the cities in the Assyrian path were enemy cities until they came under Assyrian rule. Protecting walls were battered down, and once a city surrendered it was sacked and burned, the leadership of resistance killed, and the people carried off for resettlement in some other area of the empire. So now it is the turn of Nineveh to meet reprisal. If Nahum had not felt Assyria's power definitely spent he would not have dared cry out in such blatant jubilation.

The Avenger

The first chapter expresses wonder at the sheer might of God and at his sovereignty over nature as well as over events. The theme is the Lord's avenging wrath. The might of the universe is his; he can hurl his vengeance where he will.

> His way is in whirlwind and storm,
>   and the clouds are the dust of his feet.
> He rebukes the sea and makes it dry. . . .
> The mountains quake before him,
>   the hills melt. . . .
> Who can stand before his indignation? 1:3–6

But the Lord is more than cosmic anger; he is a refuge to his people:

> The Lord is good,
>   a stronghold in the day of trouble;
>   he knows those who take refuge in him. 1:7

Assyria's downfall will soon be announced:

> Behold, on the mountains the feet of him
>   who brings good tidings,
>   who proclaims peace!
> Keep your feasts, O Judah,
>   fulfil your vows. . . . 1:15

Wages of Sin

To Nahum, Assyria succumbs because of its sins against God and man. The superpower deserves its punishment:

> Nineveh is like a pool
>   whose waters run away. . . .

Desolate! Desolation and ruin!
  Hearts faint and knees tremble. . . .
Woe to the bloody city,
  all full of lies and booty—
  no end to plunder! . . .
Horsemen charging,
  flashing sword and glittering spear,
hosts of slain,
  heaps of corpses,
dead bodies without end—
  they stumble over the bodies! 2:8, 10; 3:1, 3

Assyria's capital is a harlot "graceful and of deadly charms" who betrays nations and deserves the contempt it is now receiving. Nahum compares its forthcoming ruin to the fall of Thebes of the hundred gates, once all but totally destroyed by Assyria.

Are you better than Thebes
  that sat by the Nile,
with water around her,
  her rampart a sea,
  and water her wall? . . .
Yet she was carried away . . .
her little ones were dashed in pieces
  at the head of every street. . . . 3:8, 10

Nineveh will also seek in vain for a refuge from the enemy.

Behold, your troops
  are women in your midst. . . .
Your princes are like grasshoppers,
  your scribes like clouds of locusts
settling on the fences
  in a day of cold—
when the sun rises, they fly away;
  no one knows where they are. 3:13, 17

If the poet seems somewhat less than noble in his exultation over the agony of the people of Nineveh he is only identifying himself as a son of his times. Not just in rejoicing to see cruelty requited with cruelty but in freely expressing his elated rage as he watches an enemy who has hurt and demeaned his own people go down to defeat. Some of the impact of his poetry derives from its unrestrained candor. His final words are for Nineveh:

> All who hear the news of you
> clap their hands over you.
> For upon whom has not come
> your unceasing evil? 3:19

Habakkuk

This short book of Habakkuk, fifty-six verses, is one of the most
moving books among the Minor Prophets. The first part, Habakkuk's dialogue with God, seems to have been written during the
reign of Jehoiakim, in the troubled last decade of the seventh century B.C. The Medes and Persians were moving down on Nineveh,
whose fall shortly thereafter marked the end of Assyria's empire. Habakkuk had already experienced the rough years when
Judah had been under Egypt's suzerainty and then had seen
Egypt's defeat by Nebuchadnezzar at Carchemish. His description of the social chaos of his own country could scarcely be
matched in our day except by just such relatively small nations as
have seen their lands devastated by the superior armies of powerful nations struggling for dominance.

Violence, contention, destruction, injustice—Habakkuk names
them all—surround him and he cries out for an answer. Not for
him public accusation of his country's rulers, adding to the rebellious spirit of his people. He turned directly to the Lord. If God
was what he purported to be in relation to men—provisioner,
director, protector and support—and if he had indeed led his people to this point, then let him and no other explain the dire predicament in which they were trapped. Why, O God, why? Then,
having stated his question, Habakkuk waited for an answer.

The first of the book's three main divisions is made up of
Habakkuk's statement of his problem and God's reply.

> O Lord, how long shall I cry for help,
> and thou wilt not hear?

Or cry to thee "Violence!"
  and thou wilt not save? . . .
So the law is slacked
  and justice goes forth.
For the wicked surround the righteous,
  so justice goes forth perverted. 1:2, 4

The prophet's contemporaries knew exactly what he was talking about. The contention to which he referred was right in their own streets and affected their own households, their conscripted sons, their hungry children, their total livelihood. The justice which every Jew felt basic to corporate life was perverted by foreign overlords and by those members of their own race who toadied to their conquerors for the sake of gain.

God's answer was that the Chaldeans, "that bitter and hasty nation," were instruments of the Lord to drive out the Assyrian oppressors. Admittedly, they appeared to be a formidable counterthreat. "Dread and terrible are they." Although they served as avengers they were also a force to fear, with their horses "swifter than leopards, more fierce than the evening wolves," with men who "laugh at every fortress" and "sweep by like the wind and go on." But God would use them also for his own purposes.

Some time must have elapsed before the second section of the book was recorded, because Habakkuk cried out again against the cruelty of these very agents whom God was supposedly using. But he first reminded himself that God saw beyond the present hour.

Art thou not from everlasting,
  O Lord my God, my Holy One?
  We shall not die.
O Lord, thou hast ordained them as a judgment;
  and thou, O Rock, hast established them for chastisement. 1:12

An overwhelming chastisement! In fact, said Habakkuk, these Chaldeans, whom the Lord intended as his punitive agents, treated men as fish, collecting them in a sieve, while they lived in luxury and had rich food. He felt he could not go on without knowing the Lord's opinion of this further unjust state of affairs.

> I will take my stand to watch,
>   and station myself on the tower,
> and look forth to see what he will say to me. . . . 2:1

The Lord answered that Habakkuk must write the vision that he is to be given, making it plain on a tablet so that anyone who ran by would be able to read it; the vision might not come instantly, but if it tarried he must wait for it, for "the righteous shall live by his faith."

The prophet then spoke four *woes* against those who were oppressing his people, with a fifth *woe* directed especially against those who worshiped man-made idols.

> "Woe to him who heaps up what is not his own. . . .
>   Woe to him who gets evil gain for his house,
>   to set his nest on high,
>   to be safe from the reach of harm! . . .
>   Woe to him who builds a town with blood,
>   and founds a city on iniquity! . . .
>   Woe to him who makes his neighbors drink
>   of the cup of his wrath, and makes them drunk. . . .
>   Woe to him who says to a wooden thing, Awake;
>   to a dumb stone, Arise!
>   Can this give revelation?
> Behold, it is overlaid with gold and silver,
>   and there is no breath at all in it." 2:6, 9, 12, 15, 19

How different from the gilded wooden thing is the Lord!

> But the Lord is in his holy temple;
>   let all the earth keep silence before him. 2:20

The earth in silence. The ultimate praise. Anyone who has experienced the awe-full majesty of the Most High is surely unable to speak. But his heart can affirm the future:

> For the earth will be filled
>   with the knowledge of the glory of the Lord,
>   as the waters cover the sea. 2:14

The final section of this short, searching book is a prayer. Actually it is a liturgical hymn, perhaps older than Habakkuk, perhaps sung by him; definitely associated with his name. After the prayer he describes the Lord and his power over nature in strong anthropomorphic figures of speech.

> O Lord, I have heard the report of thee,
>   and thy work, O Lord, do I fear. . . .
> His glory covered the heavens,
>   and the earth was full of his praise.
> His brightness was like the light,
>   rays flashed from his hand. . . .
> He stood and measured the earth;
>   he looked and shook the nations;
> then the eternal mountains were scattered,
>   the everlasting hills sank low.
>   His ways were as of old. 3:2–4, 6

If God's justice is not apparent the reason must be that time does not press him. For Habakkuk, faith must and does suffice. Even if trees do not blossom and bear fruit, and fields fail to yield, and flocks and herds vanish, Habakkuk still will not doubt.

> God, the Lord, is my strength;
>   he makes my feet like hinds' feet,
>   he makes me tread upon my high places. 3:19

Sure now of his footing, he and all God's people can reach the high places, where offerings are made to the Lord, where men and God meet.

In spirit the book is not far removed from Job; in affirmation it is kin to Jeremiah. But this man Habakkuk was very much himself. His assurance was born of personal confrontation with God. Therefore, he could affirm steadfastly that even in the face of suffering and uncertainty, it is possible to be serene.

> . . . yet I will rejoice in the Lord,
>   I will joy in the God of my salvation. 3:18

Not surprisingly, at the close of the poem are the directions: "To the choirmaster: with stringed instruments." His was the kind of affirmative joy which could be set to music.

Zephaniah

Zephaniah was one of the minor Minor Prophets, not a literary giant or a particularly picturesque orator, but he could look at a situation and see it for what it was. He preached during the reign of King Josiah (640–609 B.C.) but evidently before Josiah discovered the Deuteronomic laws and carried out his reforms. He says he was a descendant (probably a grandson) of another of the reforming kings, Hezekiah (715–687 B.C.), who had been stirred to action by Isaiah and Micah, and his preaching shows that he did indeed know the court circles and had intimate knowledge of the city of Jerusalem. The predicament of the poor was not his chief concern, as it had been with Micah, but he was hot-and-bothered about the flagrant violations in the worship of Israel's God. If the persons responsible for religious irregularities right there in the capital would rectify the perversions they had allowed to develop, he affirmed hope for Israel. But redemption would not come easy. Nor include everybody.

> "I will utterly sweep away everything
>   from the face of the earth," says the Lord.
> "I will sweep away man and beast,
>   I will sweep away the birds of the air
>   and the fish of the sea.
> I will overthrow the wicked;
>   I will cut off mankind
>   from the face of the earth," says the Lord. 1:2–3

The whole earth would have to suffer, he felt, in order to clean up the accumulated moral debris. He looked at the Canaanite priests dominating the high places, the priests of Milcom, chief Canaanite god, parading the streets, and the Assyrian priests, who were the astrological necromancers holding forth on the very roof of Israel's temple, and he called time on them, climaxing his accusations with a magnificent pronouncement:

> Be silent before the Lord God!
>   For the day of the Lord is at hand. . . . 1:7

The Lord has prepared a banquet, he told whoever would listen; evidently referring to one of the feasts which followed a sacrificial offering. But at the Lord's feast anyone who came dressed in foreign attire, indicating that he was a follower of some other than the true God, or anyone who "leaped over the threshold" (gate crasher), or practiced fraud, would be punished.

> At that time I will search Jerusalem with lamps,
>   and I will punish the men
> who are thickening upon their lees. 1:12

A common feature of heathen festivals was a torchlight procession; the Lord, too, knew how to search Jerusalem with lamps, including the tiny clay lamps which men sometimes strapped to the toes of their shoes so that they could see the rough cobbled street and not step in dung. He also knew how gluttons drank their wine down to the thickened lees, or dregs, which also "thickened the men and made them indolent."

Nor was it any use to argue that current events, good or ill, were of no interest to God, as the free-thinkers held; as if God were an impersonal force of nature. They insisted:

> The Lord will not do good,
>   nor will he do ill. 1:12

Nonsense, answered Zephaniah irately; where did they ever get the idea that God was not in history while it was being made? If he had formerly led his people and directed his creation, then he was still involved in events as they happened, appearances to the contrary notwithstanding. And now events were on the march:

> The great day of the Lord is near,
>   near and hastening fast. . . .

A day of wrath is that day,
  a day of distress and anguish,
a day of ruin and devastation,
  a day of darkness and gloom,
a day of clouds and thick darkness. . . . 1:14–15

Jerusalem shuddered. High and low, the people grew nervous listening to a highborn, high-minded orator who took to the streets and thundered his message with such assurance.

Seek the Lord, all you humble of the land,
  who do his commands;
seek righteousness, seek humility;
  perhaps you may be hidden
  on the day of the wrath of the Lord. 2:3

After cautioning his own people he prophesied doom for every enemy of the Lord; Gaza deserted, Ashkelon a desolation, Ashdod's people driven out, Ekron uprooted, woes to the people of the seacoast, Moab become like Sodom, the Ammonites like Gomorrah, the Israelites plundering them all. The Ethiopians should be slain, Assyria destroyed, Nineveh made a desolation. Hebrew prophets could scarcely imagine God's having compassion on Israel's enemies; they imputed their own standards of ethics to him, evil for evil, and a lavish hand with destruction. How contemporary Zephaniah's anger against those who in any way demeaned his country.

When the prosperous idolatrous nations were wiped out by the wrath of God, said Zephaniah, then the beasts could take over Nineveh, who fancied herself the capital of the civilized world.

Herds shall lie down in the midst of her,
  all the beasts of the field;
the vulture and the hedgehog
  shall lodge in her capitals;
the owl shall hoot in the window,
  the raven croak on the threshold;
  for her cedar work will be laid bare.
This is the exultant city
  that dwelt secure,
that said to herself,
  "I am and there is none else." 2:14–15

Zephaniah preached over a number of years and the gist of his message was always clear and sustained: Jerusalem was the city of his forebears chosen by God to live uprightly and bear witness of him. He felt personally outraged and compared the city officials to roaring lions, the judges to the wolves that come in the evenings; the prophets were wanton; the priests profaned whatever was sacred. The Lord alone remained upright.

> The Lord within her is righteous . . .
> every morning he shows forth his justice,
> each dawn he does not fail. . . . 3:5

This ability to sense God still in the midst of his people in spite of their wickedness was the strength of the prophets, especially of the prophets who preached after the return of their people from exile. But they knew that no individual could be chastised to the point of utter defeat so that he could not rise to make a new start. Zephaniah saw beyond current devastation to an ingathering of the Jewish people and a return to the Holy Land, where the faithful, however few, would form the nucleus for a redeemed community under God's direction.

> "For I will leave in the midst of you
>   a people humble and lowly.
> They shall seek refuge in the name of the Lord,
>   those who are left in Israel;
> they shall do no wrong
>   and utter no lies,
> nor shall there be found in their mouth
>   a deceitful tongue." 3:12

And he had a special concern for the little people, often forgotten by those in power, the decrepit and the beggars.

> ". . . Behold, at that time I will deal
>   with all your oppressors.
> And I will save the lame
>   and gather the outcast. . . .
> At that time I bring you home,
>   at the time when I gather you together. . . ." 3:19–20

Haggai

Two chapters made up of five messages constitute the book of the prophet Haggai, a book which left a lasting impression on the Jewish people because Haggai was one of the prime instigators of the building of the temple after the return of the Jews from captivity in 536 B.C. When Cyrus, then king of Persia and Babylon, first gave permission for the return of the Jews to Jerusalem and for the rebuilding of their temple to Yahweh, they were in high spirits and no doubt intended to make the new temple their first concern. But once back in Jerusalem under the immediate leadership of Shesh-bazzar, curator of the temple treasures released by Cyrus, their intentions languished under pressure of daily needs. By 520 B.C. times were definitely difficult; rebuilding a city and reviving trade was a hard, slow job. Spirits began to lag and the prevailing poverty dampened religious zeal. Haggai and Zechariah turned their prophetic energies toward reviving the will of the people.

Haggai's messages are dated as to year, month, and day, all of them delivered between the sixth and ninth months of 520 B.C. First he addressed Zerubbabel, then governor of Judah and a descendent of David, and Joshua, the high priest, who shared leadership and responsibility. But he also included the dejected and disinterested, who felt "the time has not yet come to rebuild the house of the Lord," rebuking them sternly for dwelling in paneled houses while the Lord's house lay in ruins. No wonder they are in economic difficulty, he chided; they were not putting first things first.

Now therefore thus says the Lord of hosts: Consider how you have fared. You have sown much, and harvested little; you eat, but you never have enough; you drink, but you never have your fill; you clothe yourselves, but no one is warm; and he who earns wages earns wages to put them into a bag with holes. 1:5-6

Enough of this procrastination. The Lord's command was to "Go up to the hills and bring wood and build the house." The people took the words to heart and followed Haggai's directions. Then the prophet spoke again in behalf of God. "I am with you, says the Lord." So it was not Haggai another citizen of Jerusalem who was inspiring the building of the temple, but Haggai the spokesman for the Lord.

Haggai's third message is an admission that in the eyes of those who knew pre-exilic Jerusalem the present temple must seem as nothing compared to Solomon's temple. Nevertheless, "take courage, all you people of the land." The Lord's message was, ". . . for I am with you. . . . My Spirit abides among you; fear not." Moreover time was coming when the Lord would "shake all nations, so that the treasures of all nations shall come in, and I will fill this house with splendor. . . . The silver is mine, and the gold is mine, says the Lord of hosts."

The fourth message is an objection to the ritual uncleanliness of careless people. The earlier prophets had laid no such emphasis on ritual purification, but these are postexilic days, when the cult of Judaism was tightening its hold. An offering or sacrifice made by one who had ignored the taboos became defiled also. The community was held together partially through obligatory ritual. When the foundation of the temple was laid God's blessing would be ample.

The fifth message is addressed, at the behest of the Lord, to Governor Zerubbabel, promising that God was "about to destroy the strength of the kingdoms of the nations," after which he would make Zerubbabel "like a signet ring." In other words, the Lord's own representative.

The enthusiasm and reassurance of Haggai, conveyor and interpreter of the Lord's expectation, had their effect, for the temple was completed in 515 B.C.

Zechariah

As with the book of Isaiah, the book of Zechariah has two authors, the first from the Persian period and the second from the Greek period. Because the second author was not named but his writings were on the Zechariah scroll, he is commonly referred to as Deutero-Zechariah. The career of the Zechariah (520–518 B.C.) whose name titles the book overlapped Haggai's day of exhortation. While Zechariah also urged the rebuilding of the temple as an immediate task, his emphasis was on the life of faith and the eventual triumph of the Lord, which would outspan all temporal achievements. His theme is well stated in his fifth vision: Not by might, nor by power, but by my Spirit, says the Lord of hosts. (A great text for the United Nations!)

Repentance

Zechariah's first message to the people of Jerusalem, not long back from their captivity in Babylonia, was preceded by a call for repentance; they must not be like their fathers, who failed to heed the Lord and later suffered the consequences. Then he had a vision which he dated exactly as to day and month in the second year of Darius, king of Persia. He saw a horseman on a red horse followed by three more horses, and when he asked who these might be, an angel answered that they were patrolling the earth to keep it at peace. The angel asked the Lord how long he intended to remain indignant with Judah: after all, the people had had hard times for seventy years. "And the Lord answered gracious and comforting words," explaining that it was "the nations that are at ease" with whom he was most angry; he has "returned to Jerusalem with compassion," promising that his house shall indeed be built, his cities again overflow with prosperity, and Zion shall be comforted.

In the second vision Zechariah saw four horns representing the great powers which had shattered and scattered Judah—probably the Assyrians, Babylonians, Medes and Persians. Then four smiths appeared, intending to terrify the nations which had lifted up their might against Judah. In other words, imperialism was doomed.

The third vision disclosed "a man with a measuring line in his hand," intended for measuring Jerusalem, probably for the purpose of building its wall. But Zechariah insisted that the Lord was guardian enough; he saw no such necessity as Nehemiah saw to rebuild the fortified walls. "For I will be to her a wall of fire round about, says the Lord, and I will be the glory within her."

Oracles followed, short and forceful. The captives still in Babylon must return to Zion, because the nation which plundered them "shall become plunder for those who served them." God himself would dwell in Zion and "many nations shall join themselves to the Lord in that day, and shall be my people. . . ." This is a new note in prophecy—the conversion of non-Jews. "And the Lord will inherit Judah as his portion in the holy land. . . ." (The only place in the Bible where Israel is called the holy land.)

A fourth vision introduces another character new to the Old Testament—Satan. (We hear of Satan first in the Chronicles but that is because the order of the books in the canon put Chronicles ahead of Zechariah; both books were written after the religion of the Persians had permeated the common thought of the Jewish people, Satan being a common figure to the Persians. Satan had not yet taken on the character of "the devil" but was "the adversary," the one who accuses.) Zechariah visioned Joshua the high priest in "filthy garments," standing before the angel with Satan at hand to accuse him. The angel ordered the bystanders to remove the soiled garments, saying, "Behold, I have taken your iniquity away from you. . . ." The reference was to the lack of ritual cleanliness on the part of the priests; detailed refinements of the priest's role were not being meticulously followed, and if exceptions were made in small matters, major infringements were sure to follow. But the angel assured the priest on behalf of the Lord, "If you will walk in my ways and keep my charge, then you shall rule my house and have charge of my courts. . . ." Moreover, "the Branch" (sometimes translated "the Sprout"), meaning an offshoot of the house of David—in this case Zerubbabel—should be established, probably meaning he would be crowned king.

The fifth vision depicted a rather complicated lampstand whose lamps represented the eyes of the Lord, which surveyed the whole earth. The sixth vision portrayed a flying scroll bearing curses meant for those who broke various prohibitions. The seventh showed a cask with its cover lifted to disclose a woman called Wickedness, but Zechariah quickly thrust her back into the container and clamped the lid down. Immediately two female figures with wings like the stork's carried the container off to Babylon, where sins had been abundant. The implied moral was that such conduct did not belong to Israel.

The eighth vision disclosed four chariots drawn by horses of different colors representing—according to the interpreting angel —the four winds of heaven eager to patrol the earth for the Lord, whose day was coming. "And those who are far off shall come and help to build the temple of the Lord."

In a day which had few graphic arts, these pictorial oral presentations dramatically served to etch Zechariah's message into people's minds. A series of oracles followed, serving as warning not to accept form instead of right intent. Fasting, for instance, was not as important as rendering true judgments, showing mercy and kindness, not oppressing the needy. It was those who broke the laws of the spirit who incurred the wrath of the Lord. "'As I called, and they would not hear, so they called, and I would not hear,' says the Lord of hosts." When the Lord comes to dwell in Zion it will be safe for children to play in the streets. All of God's people shall be brought together "and they shall be my people and I will be their God, in faithfulness and in righteousness."

The next six chapters vary greatly in style, suggesting a different author. Two chapters are written as poetry, two are titled oracles, one is messianic, the last a description of final warfare and victory. The social and political climates have changed. Names mentioned by the first Zechariah are not mentioned here. The temple is no longer an issue, prophecy is suspect and prophets scorned, violence is underscored. The focus is on the eventual rulership of the world under Judah, with Judah under the hand of God. In a sense, it is not important who wrote these latter pronouncements because it was the messages themselves which mattered enough to their hearers for them to have been recorded and cherished.

Doom was pronounced on the great cities of the East, whom the house of Judah must not fear again.

> Rejoice greatly, O daughter of Zion! . . .
> Lo, your king comes to you;
>   triumphant and victorious is he,
>   humble and riding on an ass,
>   on a colt the foal of an ass. 9:9

Christians later saw the triumphal entry of Jesus into Jerusalem as fulfillment of this prophecy, although some suggest that, knowing the prophecy of Zechariah, Jesus purposefully dramatized its fulfillment. The oracle makes plain its point that the Lord's kingdom shall one day triumph.

> "Though I scattered them among the nations,
>   yet in far countries they shall remember me,
>   and with their children they shall live and return. . . .
> They will call on my name,
>   and I will answer them.
> I will say, 'They are my people';
>   and they will say, 'The Lord is my God.'" 10:9; 13:9

The good shepherd will be rejected by his disobedient sheep and afflicted for their sake, but a chastened remnant shall turn to him. Final warfare will be desperate and the Mount of Olives will split in two, but eventually a day of perpetual light will emerge.

And the Lord will become king over all the earth; on that day the Lord will be one and his name one. . . . there shall be inscribed on the bells of the horses, "Holy to the Lord." . . . And there shall no longer be a trader in the house of the Lord of hosts. . . . 14:9, 20–21

This unknown prophet caught the essential message that the line between the sacred and the secular, between religion and life, would eventually be erased as people learned to live totally dedicated to "the way of the Lord."

Malachi

Malachi is a great reference book for clergymen when they want to come down hard on members of their church who fail to put service to the temple at the top of the list—providing that the slack members happen to be *at* church to hear the sermon. To be sure, Malachi makes the Lord's blessings contingent upon the financial contributions received but he does promise big interest on the investment.

> Bring the full tithes into the storehouse, that there may be food in my house; and thereby put me to the test, says the Lord of Hosts, if I will not open the windows of heaven for you and pour down for you an overflowing blessing. 3:10

Another useful text to be recited as the priest holds in his hand a sparsely filled collection plate:

> And now entreat the favor of God, that he may be gracious to us. With such a gift from your hand, will he show favor to any of you? says the Lord of hosts. 1:9

Conversely, Malachi is also the prophet for the Board of Trustees when they think the clergy are performing their duties in a slipshod manner or failing to be exemplars. The question is: how can there be devotion in a church whose priests are lackadaisical?

> For the lips of a priest should guard knowledge, and men should seek instruction from his mouth, for he is the messenger of the Lord of hosts. But you have turned aside from the way; you have caused many to stumble by your instruction. . . . 2:7–8

A name may add weight to a message, as, for instance, the words of Moses witnessing across the centuries with added emphasis because the great deliverer of his people spoke them. But the book of Malachi has an anonymous author. All we know is that the name means "my messenger." Perhaps Malachi chose to be forgotten in the message. From the text, we deduce that his book was produced a generation before Nehemiah, around 460 B.C., after the rebuilding of the second temple while a Persian governor ruled the land. The style of presentation is question-and-answer but not in Socratic fashion; rather, a one-man dialogue. For instance: " 'I have loved you,' says the Lord. But you say, 'How hast thou loved us?' "

As with many of the prophets, Malachi was a master of powerful figures of speech which often put fear into the hearts of his listeners. Israel never produced great art in the way of painting and sculpture, and its greatest architecture was executed under the direction of imported artisans, but it did produce graphic poetry and masterful prose which served the same purpose in emotional involvement. With his own palate of colors Malachi presented the awful judgment of the Lord.

> For behold, the day comes, burning like an oven, when all the arrogant and all evildoers will be stubble; the day that comes shall burn them up, says the Lord of hosts, so that it will leave them neither root nor branch. But for you who fear my name the sun of righteousness shall rise, with healing in its wings. You shall go forth leaping like calves from the stall. 4:1–2

How Much Cult?

Malachi was another cultic prophet; that is, he emphasized the importance of form to conduct. Without rules for religious observance how could daily life be lined up with the requirements of a covenanted nation? A set of rites centering around an approved set of symbols seemed to him to be the guarantee of right conduct. The perennial controversy over custom and precedent! Can the life of a nation be made responsible without honoring the guidelines established by the fathers? Is it not dangerous to make changes?

Evidently in Malachi's day the people were acting out their answers. They had become indifferent to the temple sacrifices because the non-religious around them seemed to thrive just as prosperously as they did. What value then an expensive sacrifice? The priests too were in a state of apathy. To Malachi the temple was the heartbeat of the nation, only the beat had become erratic. He intended to cleanse the blood and steady the pulse.

The Church and Society

In Malachi's day temple life was not simple, even though carefully delineated. Often, in fact, it was as worldly as life at court. It had its economic investments: animals for sacrifice bought from those who raised them and sold at high profit to those who wished to offer them in propitiation for sin. Then there were food and maintenance for both animals and their keepers; living quarters for the priests, their food to buy, prepare and serve; guests to entertain; the poor to look after. There were tithes to be collected, apportioned, distributed. And liturgies which had to be learned and taught, also composed for special occasions since all of temple life was not static. There was history to be read and interpreted and the dress and phylacteries of priests to be scrutinized. Forms and precedents were no haphazard matter. A detailed prescribed way to do everything!

Critic

Really to attend the message of this short book—four chapters, fifty-five verses—is to see into the life of Israel and also into the limitations of this prophet who is both the product of his times and a critic of them. As critic he sees himself set above the erring ones. As prophet he lacks the grace to say: *we* fall short; but always *you*.

His treatise opens with a preamble in which he quotes the Lord as proving his love by reminding the Israelites, descendants of Jacob, how much better off they are than their neighbors, the Edomites, descendants of Jacob's brother Esau. God had proved his preference by sending Edom more hardship than Israel. But even Israel did not deserve too many blessings because the people were cheating on the temple, guardian of the covenant.

Blind Leaders of the Blind

The priests were the first to bear the brunt of Malachi's ire:

"A son honors his father, and a servant his master. If then I am a
father, where is my honor? And if I am a master, where is my fear?
says the Lord of hosts to you, O Priests, who despise my name. You
say 'How have we despised thy name?' By offering polluted food
upon my altar. And you say, 'How have we polluted it?' By thinking
that the Lord's table may be despised. When you offer blind animals
in sacrifice, is that no evil? . . . Present that to your governor;
will he be pleased with you or show you favor? says the Lord of
hosts." 1:6–8

Speaking for the Lord, Malachi reminded the priests that the
fame of their God had gone abroad, "For from the rising of the
sun to its setting my name is great among the nations," and yet
the priests "sniff at me, says the Lord of hosts," as if it made no
difference that the offerings which represented their devotion were
blemished. ". . . if you will not lay it to heart to give glory to my
name, says the Lord of hosts, then I will send the curse upon
you. . . . Behold, I will rebuke your offspring, and spread dung
upon your faces, the dung of your offerings, and I will put you out
of my presence." Rough talk from a tough God to a backsliding
generation.

Family Commitment

But Malachi had one tremendous insight. "Have we not all
one father? Has not one God created us? Why then are we faithless to one another, profaning the covenant of our fathers?" He
was speaking to Jews about their true relationship to their own
people, the family of Israel, and he bore down on moral conduct
within the family as the essence of obligation to the Lord. Judah's
own people were marrying foreign women; what sort of purity of
race and worship would *that* produce? One thing it evidently
produced was currently satisfactory marriages for the Jewish men,
because foreign wives were popular and divorce from Jewish
wives was on the increase.

You cover the Lord's altar with tears, with weeping and groaning
because he no longer regards the offering or accepts it with favor at

your hand. You ask, "Why does he not?" Because the Lord was witness to the covenant between you and the wife of your youth, to whom you have been faithless, though she is your companion and your wife by covenant. 2:13–14

Covenant! Malachi's great word. Husbands had promised themselves to their wives in marriage just as they pledged themselves to God. "For I hate divorce, says the Lord the God of Israel. . . ." There was no message for the divorced wives, because according to the customs of their times they had no recourse except to be returned to their former homes.

Some of the people complained of economic favoritism:

"You have said, 'It is vain to serve God. What is the good of our keeping his charge . . . ? Henceforth we deem the arrogant blessed; evildoers not only prosper but when they put God to the test they escape.' " 3:14–15

Malachi's answer was that if a man did what was right the Lord would note it in his "book of remembrance. . . . and I will spare them as a man spares his son who serves him."

A Final Day of Reckoning

Malachi's second great insight was that a day of reckoning was inevitable. He visioned the Lord's coming suddenly to his temple: ". . . the messenger of the covenant in whom you delight, behold, he is coming, says the Lord of hosts. But who can endure the day of his coming, and who can stand when he appears?" He will be "like a refiner's fire . . . till they present right offerings to the Lord." But before he came he would send his messenger.

It is probably this emphasis on the coming of a messenger who would precede the coming of the Lord that caused the church fathers who defined the order of the books of the Christian Bible to put Malachi at the end of the Old Testament. They took his reference to a messenger as a glimpsing of the place of John the Baptist, who later claimed to be the forerunner of Jesus.

In a final appendix to Malachi's book, possibly added by a later editor, the Lord was quoted as following his reminder to keep the law of his servant Moses with a promise:

"Behold, I will send you Elijah the prophet before the great and terrible day of the Lord comes. And he will turn the hearts of fathers

to their children and the hearts of children to their fathers, lest I
come and smite the land with a curse." 4:5

His bearers knew that Elijah had never died, but instead "a
chariot of fire" had taken him up "by a whirlwind into heaven."
What more natural than that he should return as a forerunner of
the Messiah on the final day? Indeed, later, when Jesus asked who
people said he really was, his disciples answered that some said
he was Elijah. Malachi thus became a prophet in the sense of one
who discerns the shape of things to come, as well as one devoted to
the restoration of righteousness on the part of a covenanted people.

After Malachi

And so, with the end of the book of Malachi, the library of
scripture called the Tanak or Torah by the Jews and the Old
Testament by Christians comes to a close. But the history of the
Jews as a people of their book goes on. In fact, for centuries they
were called "the people of the Book."

Theologically, authoritative history of the Jewish people leaves
off with the background disclosed by Malachi. Antiochus IV,
Epiphanes, returning from an invasion of Egypt, quelled a revolt
of the Jews in Jerusalem and in 167 B.C. forbade Jewish religious
practices. Then came the great Maccabean revolt, instigated by
Judas Maccabeus and his guerrilla forces and continued under
his sons, certainly one of the most stirring chapters of Jewish history. The struggle for Jewish freedom and identity continued, both
military and ideological. In 63 B.C. Pompey captured Jerusalem
and brought Palestine under Roman rule. In 48 B.C. Julius Caesar
defeated Pompey but was assassinated by Brutus and Cassius; in
42 B.C. Mark Antony took control of Palestine from Cassius; in
31 B.C. Octavius defeated Antony and became master of the
Roman world, including Palestine.

In 7 B.C. Jesus was born, a practicing Jew who took exception
to Jewish legalism and stressed the oneness of all humankind before a universal God. Not a few Jews joined the schism and the
sect was augmented by increasing numbers of gentiles. In A.D. 6
Augustus Caesar put Judea under a Roman prefect. In A.D. 30

Jesus was crucified by the Roman prefect Pilate. Thereafter for the followers of Jesus, Jewish history became in part Christian history.

The emigration of Jews from Jerusalem and Palestine continued, both because of persecution and because of the economic advantages of trade in the wider Mediterranean area. With the Jews went the solidarity of the Jewish community and the strength of the Jewish faith upheld by continuing devotion to Jewish scripture. But it was never the primary facts of Jewish history which sustained and empowered the Jewish people. It was their interpretation of the facts, which is, of course, what the Old Testament is all about. They had discovered God. Not predicated him, or set him up as an hypothesis, but found him. This basic fact is the capstone of their experience. The terms set up between their God and themselves were hard but possible; knowing the hand which led them gave them the courage to covenant, also the honesty to assemble their early history and open it for the rest of the world to read. And to continue making Jewish history.

Not only Jewish history, however, but the Jewish scripture itself continued to develop; not in the sense of accretion but through deepened understanding. Later scholars were quite as dedicated as the priestly redactors of the original books, and today's scholars continue to clarify and authenticate the text as they uncover early manuscripts, collate non-biblical documents, make archaeological exposures, decipher ancient languages, and utilize the dating techniques of modern science.

New books have not been added to the canon; that is, to the thirty-nine declared authoritative by a council of rabbis in A.D. 90 at the little town of Jamnia, near the Judean coast. Official Judaism has held that books written later may be ethically and morally useful but cannot be considered divinely inspired as these thoroughly scrutinized scrolls were said to be. As soon as the canon was closed, the reverence with which the temple in Jerusalem had been regarded was transferred to the holy writings.

Even at Jamnia there was never unanimity as to what books should become scripture. Many Jews, as well as Christians, in the prosperous cities around the Mediterranean insisted upon including fifteen other books, which came to be called the Apocrypha (meaning "hidden away"). The Greek Church included the apocryphal books in their complete Bible and the Roman Catholic Church followed the Greek text, i.e. the Septuagint. Protestants in general have followed the Jewish decision, limiting the canon to the thirty-nine books. But increasingly the Apocrypha is included in modern translations.

The history of English translations alone is a saga of heroic determination and detective-story fascination. Jewish and Christian scholars may emphasize differing theological concepts but they stand on common ground in their devotion to furthering the authenticity of the text of the scripture they share.

For Christians, of course, the story of God's revelation of himself continues through the record of the life and works of Jesus, a record with commentary incorporated in a compilation of books known as the New Testament. For both Christians and Jews the history of the involvement of God in the affairs of man, and of the interrelationship of man and God, is a continuing record.

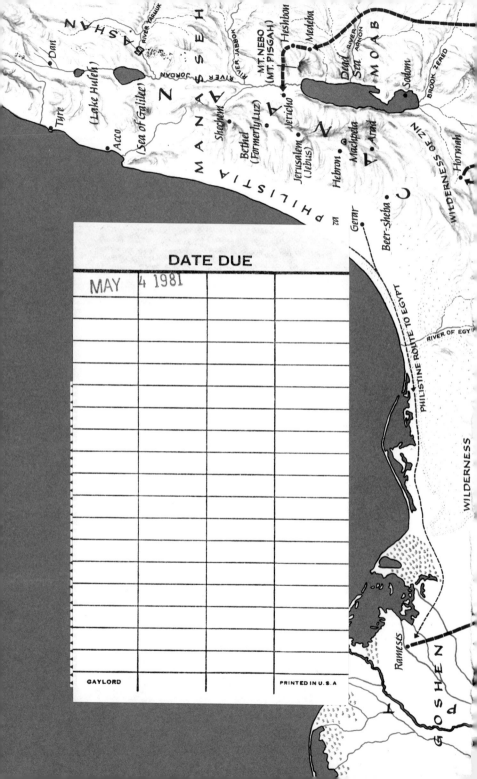

DATE DUE